Warriors into Traders

CLASSICS AND CONTEMPORARY THOUGHT,
edited by THOMAS HABINEK

Warriors into Traders

The Power of the Market in Early Greece

David W. Tandy

UNIVERSITY OF CALIFORNIA PRESS

Berkeley   Los Angeles   London

*The publisher gratefully acknowledges the contribution
provided by the General Endowment Fund,
which is supported by generous gifts from the
members of the Associates of the University of California Press.*

University of California Press
Berkeley and Los Angeles, California

University of California Press, Ltd.
London, England

Library of Congress Cataloging-in-Publication Data
Tandy, David W.
    Warriors into traders : the power of the market in early Greece / David W. Tandy.
        p.   cm.—(Classics and contemporary thought ; 5)
    Includes bibliographical references and index
    ISBN 0-520-20269-4 (alk. paper)
        1. Greece—History—Geometric period, ca. 900–700 B.C.   2. Greece—Commerce—
History.   3. Greece—Economic conditions—To 146 B.C.   4. Homer—Political and social
views.   5. Hesiod—Political and social views.   6. Literature and society—Greece.   I. Title.
II. Series.
DF221.5.T36   1997
938—dc20   96–23278
                                                                                                                    CIP

Printed in the United States of America
9 8 7 6 5 4 3 2 1

For Corinne and Peter

*Hear this, O ye that swallow up the needy, even to make the poor
of the land to fail,
Saying, When will the new moon be gone, that we may sell corn?
and the sabbath, that we may set forth wheat, making the ephah
small, and the shekel great, and falsifying the balances by deceit?
That we may buy the poor for silver, and the needy for a pair of
shoes; yea, and sell the refuse of the wheat?*

—AMOS 8:4–6

*Princes! Écoutez la voix de Dieu, qui vous parle par ma bouche,
redevenez bons chrétiens, cessez de considérer les armées soldées,
les nobles, les clergés hérétiques et les juges pervers comme vos
soutiens principaux; unis au nom de christianisme, sachez
accomplir tous les devoirs qu'il impose aux puissants; rappelez-
vous qu'il leur commande d'employer toutes leurs forces à
accroître le plus rapidement possible le bonheur social du pauvre!*

—CLAUDE-HENRI DE SAINT-SIMON,

NOUVEAU CHRISTIANISME (1825)

CONTENTS

LIST OF ILLUSTRATIONS

TABLES

FIGURES

MAPS

PREFACE

This contribution to a flourishing field—the study of the emergence of the Aegean world in the eighth century B.C.—is concerned with the roles of the economy and poetry, especially the part each played in the first stages in the development of the polis, the Greek city-state. In this work I hope to show that a drastic adjustment in the distribution of status and wealth within Greek communities was a decisive factor in the evolution of this peculiarly Western political institution. I also am interested in and examine the roles of Homer(s) and Hesiod(s) in this process.

Several aspects of this study may set it off from others that have recently appeared. First, I have tried to restrict the inquiry to the eighth century. Second, I have employed theoretical and comparative materials to a greater extent, I believe, than any of my predecessors. Third, I have chosen an economic focus for the analysis of the changes that occurred during the period, not because of any materialist predilections on my part, but because I came to see the change within the local Greek economies as the most highly visible and separable of the broader social changes that led up to, accompanied, and even characterized the beginnings of the polis.

Because this book has been written both for ancient historians and classicists and for economic anthropologists and economic historians, I have translated passages from the Greek sources and have transliterated Greek terms that resist effective translation. For the Old Testament, I have used the King James Version. The frequent commentary in the notes is an intentional response to the nature of much of the previous work on eighth-century Greece. Entering into this project as a philologist, I frequently found varying assumptions underlying each of the disciplines that I encountered: archaeology, anthropology, demography, economics, history, political science, psychology, and sociology. I also encountered experts on early

Greece who appealed to other disciplines and worked from assumptions that I could not easily follow. In the notes I respond to this cross-disciplinary obfuscation, to clarify the basis for the statements, assumptions, and conclusions in the text. I also supply a running commentary, as it were, on the process by which I have sorted through the evidence and reached my conclusions. Too often, I have found in my own reading and study, words mask incomplete understanding or inadequate argument; too often, it is difficult to see why a particular mode of inquiry is being undertaken or how it is being pursued. Too often, the line from argument to conclusions is not at all clear. The method of presentation I have chosen is designed as much to offer a step-by-step explanation of my line of reasoning as to support my argument. If nothing else, I hope to present an argument devoid of jargon.

In the course of writing, I have received support for research and travel from the University of Tennessee, the American Council of Learned Societies, and the National Endowment for the Humanities. I am grateful to each organization. There are also many people to be thanked. Early and later versions of ideas and chapters included in this work benefited from the criticisms and encouragement of Walter Donlan, Robert Drews, Page duBois, Moses Finley, Michael Gagarin, Anne Mayhew, Ian Morris, Walter Neale, and Peter Rose. It is safe to say that none of these people agrees with (or in some cases is even aware of) my conclusions, and each would be angry if I implied otherwise. My thanks to Nancy Demand, who shared her work on Cyprus with me before it was published, and Luigi Spina, a stranger from distant Pisa who generously sent me materials that I had trouble locating. The Interlibrary Loan staff at Hodges Library at the University of Tennessee also helped locate materials essential to this study and were relentlessly helpful.

I would also like to thank the following individuals and institutions for permission to reproduce illustrations: the Royal Geographical Society (fig. 8), Alexander Cambitoglou and the Archaeological Society at Athens (fig. 11), John Boardman and the British School at Athens (fig. 12), and Demetrius U. Schilardi and the Swedish Institutes at Rome and Athens (fig. 13). Thanks also to Seth Watson for his drawings. Marian Rogers of Bibliogenesis copyedited the manuscript with consummate professionalism; the improvements she brought to the text and the errors she caught seemed countless. Mary Lamprech, editor at the University of California Press, oversaw the book through production. There is no aspect of this book that was not improved by their efforts.

To my colleagues at the University of Tennessee, especially those in the Department of Classics who put up with me while I finished this project, I express deep gratitude; others showed less patience with me, among them Robert Gorman, Thomas Heffernan, Bob Leggett, Ilona Leki, Michael Logan, Fred Moffatt, and John Zomchick. Not to spread blame, I couldn't have done this without them.

Finally, I dedicate this book with love to my daughter, Corinne, and my son, Peter. The struggle will be theirs next.

ONE

Introduction

This is a study of the economic upheaval that shook mainland Greece and the Aegean in the eighth century B.C. and of the role that poetry played in the upheaval. The appearance, before the end of the century, of the polis, the Greek city-state, marks the triumph of the constraints of legal and political institutions over those of kinship—the oft-remarked and variously coded shift from status to contract (Maine), from Gemeinschaft to Gesellschaft (Toennies). Another explanation for this transformation in eighth-century Greece may be found, however, in a sudden change in dominant economic institutions.

When the great administrative centers of the Mycenaean world began to collapse around 1200 B.C., repercussions of their fall were felt throughout the Greek peninsula and the Aegean. Agamemnon's Mycenae, Menelaus's Sparta, Nestor's Pylos, Oedipus's Thebes, Theseus's Athens—all great centers of material prosperity for hundreds of years—suffered precipitous and radical decline. A variety of theories, ranging from invasion by the Dorians (the descendants of Heracles in later Greek myth) to a climatic change of catastrophic proportions, have been put forth to explain the abrupt end of these magnificent economic centers. While there is no agreement on the cause of the collapse of the Mycenaean world—Robert Drews has called it, simply, "the Catastrophe"[1]—there is little doubt as to what followed. The abandonment of settlements and a sharp reduction in population in settlements that continued to be inhabited clearly indicate that the Greek Dark

---

1. Drews 1993, 4. Drews thoroughly discusses the many theories for the collapse (1993, chaps. 3–8). More detailed regional studies of the twelfth century are collected in Ward and Joukowsky 1992. The collapse may not have been as rapid as once thought (see Rutter 1992), but its precipitousness is still certain, and by 1050 the Aegean world had hit rock bottom.

Age had begun. Linear B, the writing system employed at the Mycenaean administrative centers to keep track of the movements of goods and of obligations of various kinds, ceased to be used. Contact with the outside world came to a halt. As a distinguished Oxonian has pointed out, even the use of oil lamps appears to have ceased: a dark age indeed. With the exception of the settlement now called Lefkandi, on the large island of Euboea off the east coast of Greece, there is little evidence of prosperity in the archaeological record, in stark contrast to the preceding age.[2]

THE ARGUMENT

The eighth century dawned in Greece on a world that had remained substantially unchanged for several centuries. I will argue that between about 800 and 700, the dominant economic institutions in Greece were radically transformed: the redistributive and reciprocal system in which all people were assured of livelihoods (graded by people's position in society) was replaced by a system in which markets were important to survival, perhaps even crucial. This economic transformation can be seen as the catalyst for all the various phenomena that collectively mark the end of the Dark Age. Indeed, for many Greeks the end of the Dark Age was as catastrophic as its beginning. By the end of the eighth century, and inseparable from this transformation and this second catastrophe, the Greek polis had begun to coalesce.

Two structural aspects of the transformation appear especially significant. The first is the great increase in population, which has figured prominently in scholarly literature in recent years (chapter 2). Settlements on the Greek peninsula and the islands of the Aegean increased in number and in size. Recent calculations have suggested an astonishingly huge increase in the number of burials in Attica and the Argolid, an increase perhaps as large as six- or sevenfold between 780 and 720. Although, as I show, the increase is much smaller than this, perhaps only about threefold, it is sufficient to generate profound changes in social and economic organization. Put another way, the increase in population is not as great as once thought, but the impact of the smaller increase is much greater than might be thought. Accompanying this increase, large or small, are shifts in people's behaviors, a clear sign that pressure is being brought to bear on social organization.

---

2. Apart from the mainland, there is also Kommos in central Crete, which appears, like Lefkandi, to have been in continuous use during the Dark Age. It is necessarily the case that with the passage of time archaeologists have been finding more and more material from the Dark Age; for some reason these finds have generated some talk about whether there was a Dark Age at all. Of course, the Dark Age *must* become less dark; it cannot become darker.

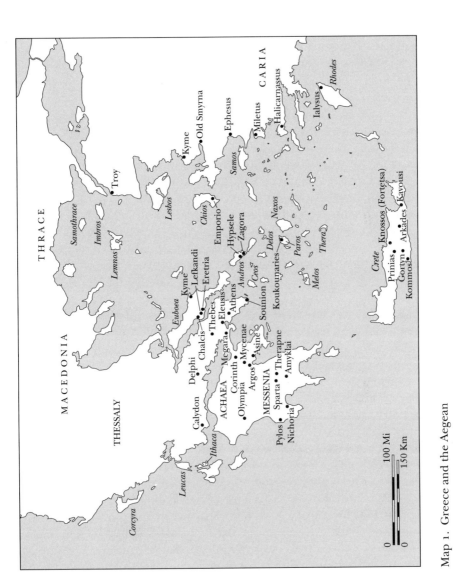

Map 1. Greece and the Aegean

The increase in population has long been associated with the establishment of the first Greek settlements in the west. In the course of the eighth century the Greeks "colonized" portions of southern Italy and Sicily, beginning with Euboean contacts with the Etruscans north of Rome before 800 and concluding with at least a dozen foundations of substantial proportions before 700. The traditional explanation is that overseas activity was undertaken in order to export the growing population from Old Greece. If this were the case, one would expect the overseas colonies to be situated in places that were particularly suitable for the agricultural and herding technology of the Greeks. The evidence seems to show, however, that the early settlements were situated in places that were highly suitable as trading posts or waystations on a circuit extending from Italy to the Levantine coast; that is to say, they were situated where agricultural resources were poor, or at least not good. One may therefore draw the conclusion that these were not agricultural settlements for a surplus population; rather they seem to have been trading centers and stopping places on new trade routes.

This new trade activity is the second important aspect of the transformation that took place (chapter 3). Stretching from Al Mina in northern Syria to Etruscan Italy and undertaken with the Phoenicians (who preceded the Greeks on these routes) as partners, trade was organized outside the older institution of the *oikos*. It appears that the gains from trade accrued to the traders in such ways that the traders, if not others, viewed the gains separately from their obligations to members of their communities at home. Furthermore, the traders were mostly *aristoi* ("best men"), and opportunities available to them were largely unavailable to the growing mass of Greek farmers and herders.

The polis originated in these changing circumstances and in the tensions and struggles that arose from these changing circumstances. The growing population forced changes in Greek life, but more important to the transformation was the new trade and the nature of the unobligated wealth that came from it. There were two important results of the appearance of this unobligated wealth. First, the collapse of redistributive formations completely reversed the manner in which status and wealth were handled. At the beginning of the eighth century, status attracted wealth; by the century's close, the obverse obtained, as wealth became the attractor of status. Second, there is evidence of private property—and the debt associated with it—in Greece at this time, part of the response of the *aristoi* (who made the rules) to their new opportunities in trade. The introduction of private property and the concomitant collapse of redistributive formations generated a new type of debt and resulted in the political exclusion of those who incurred such debt. (This pattern of exploitation finally led in Athens to Solon's sixth-century legislative reforms, which canceled debts and outlawed debt bondage.) The polis came into existence when a newly institutionalized political and economic center undertook to exclude the peripheral members of the community from the economic mainstream.

I will document the changes in economic conditions with archaeological evidence for the most part, but I will also present the theoretical basis of my analysis (chapters 4 and 5), including an extensive reworking of Karl Polanyi's important work on the substantive (vs. formal) economy in small- and other-scale societies. Polanyi has become influential in studies of ancient Greece and Italy primarily through the work of his young friend Moses Finley; his own identity and work are not well known. Some view Polanyi as a little-known but nevertheless pervasive influence on the interpretation of the ancient Near East and Mediterranean and welcome his influence; others, however, do not.[3] I welcome it and will try to show why others should as well. Polanyi's insistence on focusing on institutions and on *how* goods move within the community at large—as opposed to *why* individuals move goods—can help to illuminate the early Greek world.

In part 1 of this study I take up the changes in economic institutions, and the roles of population and trade in these changes, which benefited some people and harmed others. In part 2, I document and discuss responses from those who benefited and those who were harmed. Members of the elite employed special tactics to separate themselves as a class from the rest of the population (chapter 6). They attempted, for instance, to disguise the fact that the relationship between status and wealth had been reversed with the collapse of redistributive formations under the onslaught of ill-restrained market forces. The archaeological records yield rich evidence of their strategies of display, including gift giving, feasts, councils, and warrior burials—strategies they undertook to obfuscate, not ameliorate, the reversal and the profoundly detrimental effect it had on many people.

I call these strategies tools of exclusion, and of the many who had roles to play in them the most important may have been the poets. Homer and Hesiod, poets whose works have survived, can be studied with profit. Both are significant sources of information about preexisting and changing social and economic structures. The works of both can also be interpreted in the light of their positions in society as it was being transformed. Comparative evidence about singers in other cultures and the possible importance of "rememberers" in Greek and other societies support the argument

3. Mario Liverani, who is sympathetic to Polanyi, believes that an article could be written entitled "The impact of Polanyi's theory on scholars who did never read it" (sic; Liverani 1990, 20); Morris Silver believes that Polanyi's approach is the worst thing that ever happened to our understanding of antiquity (Silver 1983; 1985; 1986; 1995, xxii–xxiii, 97–177).

that Homer's *Iliad* and *Odyssey* and Hesiod's *Theogony* are the work of poets who are beholden to the *aristoi,* and thus serve to support these powerful leaders (chapter 7).

Hesiod's *Works and Days,* by contrast, offers a different response to the newly emergent system and was composed by Hesiod under conditions that had changed since the *Theogony.* Hesiod's voice in *Works and Days* is one of explicit protest on behalf of those who are being harmed. *Works and Days* is also valuable as a lens through which to observe the productive methods and economic life generally of an *oikos* located far away both geographically and politically from the center of power in the emerging polis. Hesiod's poem provides important evidence for the economic upheaval from this other perspective. His advice on survival can be read as a cultural defense against the new economic realities. Comparative evidence from primitive communities beset by changes brought by colonial rule indicates that Hesiod's call for economic autarky through traditional techniques of production—doing X at this time of year and Y at that—may be perceived as a reification of culture (chapter 8).

Thus I will begin with broad strokes and move to fine, dealing at first with the emergence, in general, of the Greek communities from the stagnant Dark Age, and then focusing on the plight of a specific community, Ascra in Boeotia, on whose behalf Hesiod sang his *Works and Days.* In conclusion I will recapitulate the economic and social processes through which the world in which Hesiod found himself took shape, and then refocus the argument away from Hesiod's fields to the town, drawing lessons from the preceding discussion to wrap up and close my analysis.

ASSUMPTIONS AND METHODS

Before beginning I want to lay out some of the assumptions from which I start and also some responses to anticipated questions about my treatment of evidence. Other assumptions will be addressed in their place.

Chronology

A few words about the reliability of the chronologies. When one first approaches early Greece one thing one notices right away is that the chronology of the archaeological materials is not fully settled—that is, we are not certain *exactly* when certain archaeological contexts should be dated. (There are those who would argue, for instance, that the Dark Age is a fiction created by an inaccurate chronology of the period, that the several hundred years that comprise the Dark Age may be only a single hundred.)[4] In chapter 2 I count corpses, and, like just about everything in this period, they are dated by the pottery buried with them. To determine annual rates of population growth, it is important to date the pots correctly; unfortunately we cannot always be certain about their dating. We are saved by the incontrovertible observation that relative dates are in their way more helpful than absolute dates, for relative dates indicate an order of events In the exercise of perceiving and explaining change, the absolute chronology "established" by archaeologists becomes unimportant; it is far more important that the evidence for any broad period be internally consistent. If pots or burials that I assume date from 750 would be better dated to 725, the differential is not particularly relevant to the *processes of change* that affected how society was organized. The appendices to chapter 2 show the statistical problems that arise from chronological disagreements. Estimates of the duration of each period have a great impact on the estimated annual rate of population increase; but probably more important than fixing a precise period is realizing that *any* increase in population density will create problems. In the Greek case, a large increase led to large problems.

Comparative Evidence

There is little question that comparative evidence can help us achieve a better understanding of the eighth century. If we restrict ourselves to the information (however important) articulated in the archaeological record and in the Homeric and Hesiodic poems, the picture is obscure. I do not think I need to defend my heavy use of comparative materials in both the text and the notes; I may, however, have to defend the great amount of comparative evidence I cite from "primitive" cultures.

When I first took up this project and read Chester Starr's latest work on the early Greeks, it struck me that perhaps my defense would not have to be as elaborate as I had first thought, for Starr had remarked that "the Greeks in the Dark Age were as primitive as any people studied by the anthropologists."[5] Although I cannot agree with Starr on a number of critical points concerning the eighth century, I will attempt to defend his sweeping statement by citing Burton Benedict's criteria, which anthropologists usually have in mind when they use the term "primitive" to describe a society: (1) the society is relatively small in scale, (2) it has a simple technology, (3) it is

---

4. James et al. 1991.

5. Starr 1986, 32. But he does not explain himself, beyond quoting Ronald Willetts (1982, 235): "Greek cities in their highest prosperity still retained many of the usages peculiar to the tribal communities from which they had sprung," a statement made regarding the retention of custom over law after writing began to be used on Crete.

homogeneous in that there is little necessary division of labor according to gender, and (4) the society lacks (or lacked until recently) a written language.[6] Some have called Dark Age Greece a small-scale society—this seems to me as good a term as any. When appropriate, the term "preindustrial" can be accurate, as certain activities of the eighth-century population are open to fruitful comparison with much later, even very recent, activities and institutions in Europe.[7] Both "small-scale" and "preindustrial" are also euphemisms for "primitive," employed in order to avoid offending those who find comparisons between archaic Greeks and the !Kung San offensive. Regardless of the terminology, the fact remains that the closest analogies to eighth-century Greek society are non-Western, primitive communities: the early Greeks were, until the organization of the polis, primitive and not what we call Western.[8]

Homer: Iliad *and* Odyssey

Accusations of circularity fly fast and furious whenever one takes up the argument that Homer's world accurately describes the society of a specific period. My views on the subject are in essential agreement with those of Ian Morris, to whose treatment, much fuller than what follows, I refer the reader.[9]

The *Iliad* and the *Odyssey* are narrative poems that describe more or less clear and consistent social institutions and values. Not all, however, would agree with this statement. Anthony Snodgrass, for example, observes that the world of the Homeric heroes is so inconsistent as to be altogether nonhistorical. He concludes that Homeric society reflects "a mixture of practices, derived from a diversity of historical sources."[10] But perhaps Snodgrass demands too much from Homer; as A. G. Geddes remarks, "Not all [Snodgrass's] readers . . . will be convinced that, for example, the use of the plough is incompatible with the transmission of property among the kin of one sex."[11] In an important article on social diversity in Dark Age Greece, James Whitley argues that the perceived inconsistencies are in fact merely a reflection of the diversity that one would expect among the small-scale com-

---

6. Benedict 1970, 165.

7. By "preindustrial" I mean of course "nonindustrial"; compare the essentially synonymous "preliterate," "nonliterate," and perhaps even "illiterate." I do not ordinarily use the term "premodern," because I think it has too many associations; "precapitalist" resonates too fully.

8. See further the beginning of chapter 4.

9. Morris 1986b.

10. Snodgrass 1974, 118; earlier he suggested that epic society was an "artificial amalgam of widely separated historical stages" (Snodgrass 1971a, 39).

11. Geddes 1984, 19, in reference to Snodgrass 1974.

munities that filled the landscape, a reflection of the diversity that is now emerging from the archaeological record.[12]

In favor of a coherent Homeric world, Arthur Adkins long ago argued—again not to applause from every corner—that the Homeric world makes good sense in general: "There is a degree of coherence and consistency in the values themselves, and an appropriateness to the society, that seems beyond the inventive ability—or indeed the likely inventive desire—of an oral bardic tradition."[13] Walter Donlan has argued that the world of Homer is consistent in many ways with observations made by economic and political anthropologists,[14] a correlation I take up in earnest in chapter 4. This relative clarity and consistency indicate that the poems reflect or recall *some* world at *some* time.

But *what* world? The decipherment of the Linear B tablets has demonstrated clearly that the poems are of no historic value for the late Mycenaean Age, and few scholars indeed cling to this notion. Antony Andrewes concludes that the society of the epics belongs to the twelfth and eleventh centuries.[15] Moses Finley maintains that Homer's world "is a picture of the early Dark Age, the tenth and ninth centuries BC, distorted here and there by misunderstandings and by anachronisms."[16] Bjørn Qviller is convinced that the Homeric world is located "at the end of the ninth or the beginning of the eighth century,"[17] the period Kurt Raaflaub also proposes, adding that this dating thus reflects the collective memory of the audience, "at the very most three generations or one century before the poet's own time."[18] Morris has made a strong argument that the Homeric poems reflect eighth-century society for the most part.[19]

Morris's argument for an eighth-century date for the society described in the Homeric poems builds on the work of Ruth Finnegan, who in her broad

12. Whitley 1991a.

13. Adkins 1972a, 10; cf. Adkins 1960b, chaps. 1–3; 1963; 1971; 1972b; *contra:* A. A. Long finds no "consistent pattern of society" (Long 1970, 137 n. 58). Cedric Whitman's argument (1958, 87–101) that there are aesthetic similarities between Homeric epic and eighth-century (Geometric) vase decoration and R. B. Onians's attempt (1951, esp. chap. 1) to show that the physiognomy of the Homeric heroes is Geometric have met much criticism over the years.

14. Donlan 1982a, 1982b, 1985. Cf. Morris 1986b; Rihill 1986; Tandy 1989.

15. Andrewes 1967, 45. Generally, Homeric military organization is "neither the army of the Mycenaean kingdoms, nor the army of that aristocratic society whose decline is for us the beginning of known Greek history: it falls in between, in the period of the migrations" (Andrewes 1961, 138).

16. Finley 1978, 153. Adkins (1971, 2) embraces this conclusion.

17. Qviller 1981, 113.

18. Raaflaub 1999, 45.

19. Morris 1986b. Cf. Diamant 1982, esp. 44.

study of oral traditions has depended heavily on the proposition that oral poetry has no existence independent of its performance and so is "more dependent [than written literature] on its social context."[20] Marilyn Gerriets's observations about the saga literature of pre-Viking Ireland support Finnegan's ideas: "The relevant sagas purport to tell the history of particular peoples. These 'histories' are placed in the distant past, but critical examination indicates that they reflect the political circumstances of the time of their compilation, not of the time when the events they relate supposedly occurred."[21] There are other parallels. It has often been pointed out, for instance, that the *Song of Roland* tells us much more about the twelfth-century world of its composer than about the world in 778, when the battle at Rancevaux occurred.[22]

It is clear that the essential institutions of a heroic world must be recognizable to the audience, or the oral recitation will not succeed; for recognition to be possible, those institutions must be contemporary or nearly so.[23] This is why many modern critics are able to perceive broad consistency in the Homeric world; the inconsistencies and incongruities that other scholars perceive are problems that belong to us, not to Homer's audience. This conclusion, in keeping with current anthropological research,[24] allows us to answer James Redfield's question, To whom does the Homeric world make sense?[25] The answer must be, To most of the audience who listened to Homer.

Of course, this raises an additional question, When did they listen to the poems? To date Homer means to date the world that he presents, and I follow Morris in placing Homer in the latter half of the eighth century.[26] Seventh- and sixth-century dates are too late for a host of reasons, and the contents of the Homeric poems are "fully consistent with the evidence available"[27] for the eighth century. If archaisms (see below) reach back two or three generations, then it is fair to say that some parts of Homer's poems recall a world of about 800, a world that is fully recognizable but no longer, in fact, in existence.

---

20. Finnegan 1977, 29.
21. Gerriets 1987, 43.
22. See Morris 1986b, 86, 96; Finley 1978, 47.
23. See Morris 1986b, 86ff., and the references there to the ethnographical literature.
24. E.g., Goody and Watt 1968, 31–33; see further below, chapter 7.
25. Redfield 1975, 23: "Since [Homer] is telling his story to an audience, the meaning he conveys must be a meaning *to them*" (italics original). And Peter Rose: the epics contain "a picture of social, political, and economic relationships familiar to the poet and his audience" (Rose 1975, 131).
26. Morris 1986b, 93, 94ff.
27. Morris 1986b, 94.

reflect the ideological premises of the incipient polis. These three poems, I contend, were part of an array of ploys adopted by the new elite to disguise the fundamental change in the manner in which wealth and status were distributed. *Works and Days,* by contrast, takes a position that is critical of the new system. The sentiments revealed in *Works and Days* might have been expressed earlier had Hesiod's problems arisen earlier (or, if in fact they had arisen earlier, had his circumstances allowed him to address them).

There are large obstacles to using the epics to conjure a portrait of eighth-century life. Nevertheless, I think that, as presented, the world of Homer and both worlds of Hesiod made sense to their audiences. The analysis I will offer of Greek orality and society should clarify what the poems reflect and refract: a world firmly set in the last part of the eighth century, with elements, besides those embedded in the oral tradition, intentionally drawn from the *recent* past, from perhaps as recently as the first half of the eighth century. This is not terribly distant and is perhaps best conceptualized as a throwback to the experiences of the grandparents of Hesiod's neighbors. Why a throwback? The answer is ideology, an ideology that partly steered many of the social and economic changes of the eighth century and partly was a result of them. Though it may be imprecise to assert that the epics (and the *Theogony*) are at times *pre*scriptive rather than *de*scriptive, it is nevertheless my hope that after reading this book, many will agree with me that a new understanding of the economy and society of the eighth-century Aegean leads to a different appreciation of all aspects of the material and literary records.

PART ONE

The Economic Transformation

TWO

More Greeks

Elevated as man is above all other animals by his intellectual faculties, it is not to be supposed that the physical laws to which he is subjected should be essentially different from those which are observed in other parts of animated nature. He may increase slower than most animals; but food is equally necessary to his support; and if his natural capacity of increase be greater than can be permanently supplied with food from a limited territory, his increase must be constantly retarded by the difficulty of procuring the means of subsistence.

THOMAS ROBERT MALTHUS, *AN ESSAY ON POPULATION*

On mainland Greece and the Aegean islands, the human condition and the number of persons experiencing it had not changed very much for several hundred years when, in the latter part of the ninth century, the population began rather suddenly to grow. This sudden growth had a devastating effect on the way(s) people lived and produced their livelihoods.

The increase in population density in Attica and the Argolid during the eighth century was dramatic. Although not necessarily easily isolated, the growth in the population of Attica and the Argolid may be profitably viewed as a kind of fulcrum upon which the lever of economic development rested. Put simply, the increase in population appears to have been caused primarily by an improvement in nutrition, supplemented by greater opportunities abroad (trade); a larger population in turn led to improved food production and supplied more Greeks to go abroad. Thus food and trade caused and resulted from the population phenomenon. Of course, circumstances had to be to some extent fortuitous for the population to begin to grow; less fortuitous and certainly less fortunate were the economic and political results of this eighth-century development, by which I mean the wholesale change in economic formations that accompanied or led to the ideological principles and institutional foundations of the polis.

Clues hinting at the magnitude of the increase in population began to be picked up almost twenty years ago, when Anthony Snodgrass calculated an enormous increase in burials during the eighth century. On their own, however, the numbers do not prove anything. And there are at least three reasons for this. First, we cannot know whether we have found all or even most of the cemeteries used by a community under scrutiny. This remains a problem in estimating settlement size in Dark Age Lefkandi in Euboea. It would not be by itself justifiable to say that the data are somehow sufficiently representative and consistently representative over time as to provide patterns in burial volume that reflect, more or less, densities of population in the community that used the burial sites. But the data acquire greater validity if the statistical conclusions based narrowly on corpse counts (and less narrowly on cemetery size) line up straight with other, broader evidence, such as number and size of settlements, number of wells within them, and number and type of offerings to the gods. Admittedly, even these supporting phenomena are subject to other explanations than demographic fluctuations: the number of wells and offerings may represent a response to climatic change, the number and type of offerings may be explained by changes in community taste in religious activities.

Second, we cannot be certain whether the community being examined had chosen, in the course of the time studied, to change its criteria for whom it would inter and whom it would not. This objection focuses on a indeterminable change in community taste (not necessarily religious) that can skew the results. In the case of the Greek evidence, one must respond with a careful scrutiny of the evidence as regards gender and age and hope to observe changes in pattern, if not to account for the motives for the changes, at least to account for the changes themselves. In fact, a pattern of selectivity, of deciding who would receive burial and who would not, is spelled out clearly in the archaeological record.

A third objection, related to the first and one I quickly learned *any* statistician would bring up at the outset, that the data collected are neither arbitrary nor sufficient, is fatal, and for this reason I have relegated most statistical analysis to the brief appendices to this chapter.

DARK AGE POPULATION

Following the collapse of the Mycenaean economic centers, which began about 1200, the population of Greece appears to have been reduced by perhaps as much as 75 percent over the course of the next 200 years. The size of settlements was much smaller than before, and the actual number of settlements was reduced by perhaps seven-eighths (from about 320 in the late thirteenth century to about 130 in the twelfth to about 40 in the eleventh).[1]

---

1. Snodgrass 1971a, 364; 1980a, 20. V. R. d'A. Desborough (1972, 19–20) places a greater portion of the decline in the first 100 years, estimating for large areas of Greece the number of settlements dropping from 294 in the thirteenth century to 55 in the twelfth, a decline of more than 80 percent; Snodgrass's estimate of the drop is more gradual from the thirteenth to the twelfth century (320 to 130 is less than 60 percent). Desborough supplies the following figures for the thirteenth and twelfth centuries respectively for settlements in sever-

I know of no important disagreement among the experts on this point. Recent excavation and survey work does not contradict this pattern. In the twelfth and eleventh centuries, "fertile and well-watered" Messenia, for example, "was occupied by scarcely more than 10 percent of the people who had lived there in the thirteenth century."[2] In the southern Argolid, there are at least 27 settlements in the Late Bronze Age, and only 1 in the Dark Age.[3] In Boeotia, there are "virtually no sites on the landscape" between 1000 and 800;[4] Hesiod's village of Ascra in Boeotia, for example, which enjoys exceptionally fertile soil, shows no sign of habitation before the ninth century.[5] The number of settlements dropped very quickly, and except for a modest and temporary increase in the tenth century for a limited number of settlements, population density remained consistent and very sparse throughout the Aegean world until the latter half of the ninth century, after almost four centuries of decrease and subsequent stagnation.[6]

How large were the largest Dark Age settlements that experienced a meteoric increase in population in the eighth century? Many agree with Snodgrass, who surmised that a prominent Dark Age site may have had a population as small as 100 or 200.[7] Settlements varied in size, sustaining populations that probably rarely exceeded 400 or 500.[8] Most agree that Lefkandi, the leading settlement in Euboea during the Dark Age and a focal point in the changes that arose as the Dark Age dissipated, was one of the larger settlements in Greece during the Dark Age. Snodgrass argued that we

---

al broad geographical areas: southwestern Peloponnesus, 150 to 14; Laconia, 30 to 7; Argolid and Corinthia, 44 to 14; Attica, 24 to 12; Boeotia, 27 to 3; and Phocis and Locris, 19 to 5.

Snodgrass has noted more recently that "we have to base our interpretation of Early Iron Age society, for the foreseeable future, on the datum of a tiny population, based in small, widely-separated settlements, with broad tracts of country having no permanent habitation" (Snodgrass 1993, 37). On the breadth of destruction, see Drews 1993, chap. 2, esp. 21–29.

2. McDonald and Hope Simpson 1972, 143.

3. Jameson, Runnels, and van Andel 1994, 229, fig. 4.4. The desolation of the southern Argolid is dramatically presented by figures 4.17 and 4.18, maps of sites of the Protogeometric and Early Geometric periods: the maps are virtually blank. Before this latest publication the site counts were 18 for LH III, o for the following period (van Andel and Runnels 1987, 162, table 2; Runnels and van Andel 1987, 325).

4. Bintliff 1985, 215.

5. Bintliff and Snodgrass 1988, 61.

6. As I already mentioned in chapter 1, it is necessary to point out, to those who eagerly declare that the Dark Age is becoming less dark, that it is impossible for the obverse to obtain. The Dark Age cannot get darker; it will always be progressively less dark, and so there is no possible rejoinder to criticisms such as Nicholas Purcell's: "The dwindling numbers of, and material wealth in, recoverable sites in peninsular [Dark Age] Greece is overemphasized" (Purcell 1990, 34).

7. Snodgrass 1983c, 171.

8. This upper limit is based on a probable sustainability of under 200 persons per hectare (80 per acre) (Renfrew 1972, 251; Snodgrass 1983c, 169; 1989, 26).

have found four cemeteries there and know of a fifth, but in order to justify a population of 500 persons, we would need to find over thirty additional cemeteries of the same dates and magnitude of the ones we know of. "Which is more likely: that there were [these further cemeteries] or that the population of Lefkandi did not even approach 500?"[9] By contrast, there are those who conjecture that the larger settlements, including Athens and Corinth, must have had populations running into four digits;[10] a high-end estimate would place Lefkandi's population above 1,900 throughout the Dark Age.[11] I think this is much too high.

Snodgrass's corpse counts at Lefkandi dovetail with other, nonfunereal evidence. In the tenth century Lefkandi appears to have had contact "with Cyprus, the Levant, and Egypt to the east, and with Thessaly and Macedonia in the north";[12] the Toumba cemetery, which was in use about 950–825, is "rich in gold objects and in Near Eastern imports as well as having close connections with Attica";[13] a newly excavated tomb in Toumba from about 900 contains no surprises: "The woman interred in it had been provided with gilt hair coils, crystal-headed iron pins and six bronze fibulae. At her midriff had been placed a bronze situla . . . and an engraved Near Eastern bronze bowl which retained slight but certain signs of its original gilding. . . . Her hands, with their nine gold rings, had been placed over the bowl."[14] This is all very impressive, compared to the rest of the Greek world. However, the idea that the Lefkandians themselves brought these goods from abroad is not supportable,[15] for, although probably the largest of Dark Age settle-

---

9. Snodgrass 1983c, 169. J. N. Coldstream (discussion in Hägg 1983c, 211) thinks that those thirty cemeteries may be there; the discovery that the Toumba cemetery at Lefkandi (in which the Heroon is located; see below, chapter 6) was larger than previously thought (French 1991/92, 34) proved first to be mistaken (French 1992/93, 40), and later accurate: there are definitely more graves in Toumba (M. R. Popham in French 1993/94, 37–38).

10. Morris (1987, chap. 1) takes this high-end position.

11. This estimate is calculated by plugging Snodgrass's counts (Snodgrass 1983c, 168) into Morris's observation that recovered burials represent 1.7 percent of the total population (Morris 1987, 100–101).

12. Sackett 1986.

13. M. Popham in Catling 1986/87, 14.

14. French 1992/93, 40, figs. 33, 34.

15. This is L. H. Sackett's doubtful conclusion (Sackett 1986); for some new evidence see below, chapter 3, note 1. The same uncertainty surrounds any explanation for the presence of Eastern architectural patterns and pottery at Kommos in southern Crete, where there has emerged a tenth-century temple (called A) built on top of what appears to be a Phoenician "tripillar shrine" (Shaw 1980, 246; 1981, 236, 248; Shaw in Catling 1980/81, 45–46). Temple A was replaced by Temple B beginning about 825, when Eastern materials (pottery) are found (Shaw 1982, 185; Shaw in Catling 1981/82, 56). This continuity from the tenth century onward suggests that Kommos was, like Lefkandi, a regional center of some prosperity (Snodgrass 1983a, 83).

ments on the mainland, Lefkandi was no more than a regional center; the few foreign goods that arrived in the tenth and ninth centuries indicate contact with the outside world, but there is no indication that Greeks brought these items into Lefkandi; it is not clear who brought them in, although the Phoenicians are necessarily likely candidates.

To return to the topic of population density, none of this evidence contradicts the conclusion that before the tenth century and after about 825 the population at Lefkandi was depressed. Those who argue higher settlement density appear to base their conclusions on expectations of a particular level of social organization that is unlikely on a theoretical level (the only level we have). As anthropological analogies and models from political anthropology suggest, the probable regression in agricultural production and techniques during the Dark Age and the continuity of these regressive techniques point both to a sharp reduction in density and to a long-term, continuing inability to increase population.[16] Those who seek a more elaborate social organization for the communities of the Greek Dark Age of course must argue for larger communities, but the evidence indicates smaller communities, not larger. In sum: population density in Dark Age communities remained low until the middle or even the end of the ninth century; if one must suggest a maximum, one might estimate 400 or 500 people at an uncrowded Lefkandi in the tenth century.

EIGHTH-CENTURY DATA: CALCULATION AND DEFENSE

If there is some disagreement on community size in the Dark Age, there is little question that in the course of the eighth century there occurred a remarkable increase in the number of population centers and the number of people within them. We might begin again with the most dramatic and controversial evidence: corpses. The figures that Snodgrass collated and published in 1977 for Athens and Attica and in 1980 for the Argolid are at first glance astonishing.[17] His conclusions may be recast to indicate an annual population increase for Athens between about 780 and 720 of 2.3 percent; for Attica outside Athens, 4.4 percent; and for Attica including Athens, 3.1 percent. Most of the growth occurred before 750. A similar pattern is perceptible in the Argolid. In historical terms the rate of increase is huge. (See appendix A.)

---

16. On social, economic, and technological regression in the wake of general "system collapse," see Renfrew 1979b, 482–84.

17. Robert Sallares (1991, 90) argues that there is nothing astonishing about Snodgrass's numbers per se, which is also my position. It is the case, however, that adjustments are necessary given the distribution of ages, and adjustment produces less, though still impressive, growth.

Snodgrass observed that "there is no sign . . . of mass infant mortality,"[18] but a related pattern of burial escaped his notice. Ian Morris has demonstrated a change in burial exclusivity in Athens and Attica at just this time. Morris was able to show that until LG II (735–700), only a very small percentage of those buried are infants and children, between 5 and 10 percent.[19] Suddenly, in LG II, 50 to 60 percent are infant or child burials, in the range of what palaeodemographers expect to encounter.[20] This increase is to be explained only by a change in the treatment of infants and children. Application of Morris's observation to Snodgrass's calculations reduces the 60-year per annum growth from 3.1 percent to 1.9 percent and confines virtually all the growth to before 750. (See appendix B.)

Camp's Drought

While I agree with Snodgrass[21] that the specific numbers I have generated in the appendices are of little use by themselves, save as monuments to the quantification of the unquantifiable, it is not unreasonable to speak of *relative* density in a given settlement based on datable graves, provided that we keep in mind that the number of corpses in the studied period, here basically the eighth century, must be coordinated with the number of burials *after* this period, here the seventh century.[22] If the later number decreases radically, much (though not all) of the increase in burials must be attributed to catastrophe rather than growth. Snodgrass maintains that the burial numbers in Attica level off at the close of LG II and remain constant on into the seventh century.[23] In actuality we have very little evidence for seventh-century burials, which, although largely unpublished, appear to be but a fraction of those in the last half of the eighth. This apparent drop-off, according to John Camp, "points to a substantial drop in population in the

18. Snodgrass 1977, 12.

19. Morris (1987, chap. 6 and app. 1) drew this conclusion from the analysis of the ages of those buried.

20. For example, Gy. Acsádi and J. Nemeskéri (1970, 242, 244, 254, tables 86, 87, 94) have meticulously gathered data for tenth- and eleventh-century Hungary and for other places at other times that indicate that infant burials are 35 to 55 percent of all burials.

21. Snodgrass 1977, 10–11.

22. One needs to heed the important caveat of David O'Connor, who, arguing against the general opinion of historical demographers that cemeteries are "most unreliable" data (Hollingsworth 1969, 43; cf. 289ff.) upon which to base conclusions, reminds us that the reliability of a grave count depends on the grave count chronologically subsequent to the end of the span of time in question. That is, "an increase in the number of burials . . . may indicate a numerically increasing population *or* a rise in mortality rate and thus an actually decreasing population. Which of the two possibilities is more likely at any given point depends on the subsequent behavior of the graph that could be plotted from these data and on the known historical evidence" (O'Connor 1972, 86).

23. Snodgrass 1977, 12.

last half of the 8th century."[24] Camp's ingenious theory that a long-term drought caused a dramatic increase in mortality has found little support[25] but is worth looking into because it illustrates the range of other materials that help us to recognize (if not to measure precisely) the growth of the eighth century. To support his analysis of the burial figures, Camp adduces other sources of evidence: wells and dedications.

Camp gives the following figures for wells in the Athenian agora: for the period 900–760, fourteen; for 760–700, twenty (of which four were still in use from the earlier period);[26] compare Evelyn Lord Smithson's earlier count of wells near the agora: 900–850, three; 850–800, four; 800–750, seven; 750–700, thirteen.[27] For Camp the increase in wells indicates a desperate search for water. The strongest evidence for drought seems to be that all of the wells in use near the agora were filled in around 700,[28] although this date in fact falls long after the increase in burials. Snodgrass dismisses the well closings on the ground that they "may have had no more than a local significance."[29] (In general, wells can be difficult evidence to analyze.)[30]

Potentially superior evidence is the substantial increase in offerings to Zeus Ombrios, the Rain God, on Mt. Hymettus, east of Athens. A large increase in the period after 750, from three to eight vessels per annum, can be explained by drought (farmers desperately in need of rain), by the simple fact of a shift to grain production (grains require much more rain than the hearty olive and fig) and an increase in population (there are more farmers to make offerings, and more rain is needed to increase per field production in response to the increase in the number of mouths to feed), by a substantial increase in community wealth, or—and we must keep in mind the sudden change in burial exclusivity at this exact time—by a shift in social attitudes. What Camp overlooks is a change in the *type* of vessel at this same time (see appendix C). Because this change, presumably voluntary, in relative preponderance of "open" and "closed" vessels, coincides precisely with the increase in the number of offerings, as well as with the change in burial exclusivity, we must not discount the change so easily. For example, the closed vessels may be harder to make, and so may be dearer to own and less likely to be dedicated. The change in vessel shape then may

24. Camp 1979, 400.
25. Anne Foley is inclined to see possible evidence for drought at this time in the Argolid (Foley 1988, 36–37).
26. Camp 1979, 397, 400–401 n. 12.
27. In Coldstream 1968, 360 n. 1.
28. Camp 1979, 397.
29. Snodgrass 1983c, 170.
30. Gallant 1982, 115 n. 36.

reflect more persons concerned about drought, or it may reflect fewer offerings on behalf of the community and more by individuals.

There are often many possible explanations for changes in archaeological patterns. It is clear not only that Camp's evidence may be interpreted in a variety of ways but also that the population increase indicated by the burial data clearly preceded the very end of the eighth century, when the drought is supposed to have occurred.

The timing is wrong: Camp's wells and offerings are not chronologically coincident with the burial data. He himself admits that there probably was an increase prior to the catastrophe, but because the LG I burials are so numerous, one can conclude only that even if a catastrophe did occur, the increase that must have preceded it was probably more catastrophic. Camp's drought, if it can be demonstrated to have occurred, only decreases the magnitude of the LG II death rate, affecting not at all the earlier growth. Camp has found few supporters.[31]

Other Interpretations of the Evidence

I mentioned above that the growth is not nearly so great as first appears because of the change in burial selectivity with the start of LG II in about 735. I have shown that the effect of this selectivity is to confine almost all of the growth in Athens and Attica to the period before 750. Almost precisely one generation before certain Athenians changed the way in which they chose whom to bury, whom not to bury, another enormous change in the interment process occurred, actually two changes. In about 760, after 300 years of more than 90 percent inhumations,[32] certain Athenians chose to cremate their dead and at the same time to mark the place of burial with above-ground pots of enormous and unprecedented proportions, the great wares of the Dipylon master and his workshop.[33] I would suggest at this point that these changes around 760 and around 735 are both responses to powerful social forces being whipped together by the increasing density of people. To characterize the nature of the metamorphosis of affairs at Athens, let us make a single comparison. Throughout the eighth century, the people of Kavousi in eastern Crete cremated their dead and interred the ashes in cist tombs; special tests developed by Walter Klippel, a zooarchaeologist, indicate that the bones of the interred range from fetus to

---

31. I have found only Thompson 1981, 343, and Themelis 1982, 167; there is, I suppose, no harm in following Jeffrey Hurwit (1984, 603): "Why not a boom and *then* a drought?" Morris (1987, 160–61) uses further arguments against Camp.

32. Morris 1987, 60–61, 120–25; Whitley 1991b, 101–2.

33. Morris 1987, 58–59, 81–82, 125–28; 1993a, 30–31. Whitley 1991b, 137–38.

adult.[34] The point here is the profound continuity at Kavousi of the burial of members of all age groups; by contrast, the pattern of interment in Attica shifted abruptly in about 760, followed one generation later by another shift, this time involving who received burial. Athenian behavior is demonstrably unstable.

Other Evidence for Growth

Corpses, whose change in number indicates relative, not absolute, increase, are not the only evidence of undisrupted population growth in the eighth century. The form of burial remains consistent throughout the period. The number of burying groups increases, and the population of these groups also increases.[35] In Attica, grave goods remain unchanged; they increase in worth in the Argolid, where stratification has clearly arisen in the eighth century.[36] At the Amyklaion near Sparta there are in the beginning of the second half of the century sudden abundances of metal and of pottery; these indicate a change in the use of the site, a change that indicates vigorous tendance.[37] These patterns argue further against any disruption that may have suddenly claimed many lives. As mentioned already for a different reason, the number of new wells increases substantially in the eighth century, as do offerings to Zeus on Mt. Hymettus; and both, we have just seen, are ambiguous pieces of evidence. (Wells increase in number around Perachora in the Corinthia from the mid-eighth century; dedications at the Heraeum there increase "in quantity and quality in the years before 735.")[38] Finally, one may seek to explain the increase in burials by the movement of people from without into these communities, but no such evidence is to be found in Attica or the Argolid.

There does, however, appear to have been significant movement *away* from these and other "urban centers." Table 1 in appendix A reflects the net movement away from Athens with coincident supporting numbers at Argos. To these we may add the change, beginning with LG I, in the burial

34. W. Coulsen in French 1991/92, 64.

35. Morris 1987, app. 1.

36. Athens and Attica: Snodgrass 1977, 12; Argolid: Tomlinson 1972, 72. Perhaps even more pertinent is the fact that the goods in late eighth-century Argive graves show that the increase in wealth coincided with clear signs of stratification. There are "have" graves and "have-not" graves (Hägg 1983a, 27). Although an admirer of Camp's drought thesis, as applied to the Argolid, Foley grants that "the general richness of the Late Geometric cists . . . casts some doubt on this theory" (Foley 1988, 52).

37. Calligas 1992, 42, 46–47.

38. Wells: Salmon 1984, 77; dedications: Salmon 1984, 94. The dedications actually cease abruptly about 735, but a replacement Heraeum appears to have been built nearby, where the dedications resume (Salmon 1972, 163).

pattern at Corinth, from family-group burials in the center of the settlement to use of a "common cemetery outside the urban area."[39] Burials also begin to occur outside instead of inside settlement areas at both Argos[40] and Athens.[41] In fact, the eighth century witnesses an increase in the *number* of communities, reversing the process perceived at the start of the Dark Age. Let us look at some of these new settlements, before taking up some of their specific characteristics in detail in chapter 6.

New Settlements

Zagora was a settlement on Andros, the northernmost of the Cycladic islands, that was apparently dependent on Lefkandi and then Eretria, both communities on Euboea, a mere 10 kilometers to the west. Its beginnings in the ninth century are unclear,[42] but it appears to have functioned as a staging point for Euboeans (as Koukounaries on Paros must have been for Greeks generally)[43] sailing eastward,[44] and we can tell that it grew in the course of the eighth century sufficiently, so that by the end of the century fortification walls had been thrown up around the 15-acre (6-hectare) community.[45] Theories about these walls are wideranging; the walls have been seen as protection against pirates and as a sign of the beginning of the polis; for now, we will observe only that there was a sufficient buildup of goods or persons to justify the construction of fortifications. Just up the coast a couple of kilometers at Hypsele a new eighth-century settlement has been excavated.[46] It was fortified but reveals a layer of destruction at some point between 750 and 700. The excavation is not yet published. (Both Zagora and Hypsele were abandoned not long after 700, although both continued to serve as religious sites into the archaic period.)

Emporio on Chios was a settlement about the same size as Zagora, though only its acropolis (about 6 acres [2.5 hectares]) was walled.[47] We will return to Emporio later on for a different reason; for now, it is worth

39. Williams 1982, 11.
40. Hägg 1982.
41. Morris 1987, 62–69.
42. Apart from a single sub-Protogeometric Cycladic *kotyle*, there is no ceramic material older than about 850 (Cambitoglou et al. 1988, 253–68).
43. Schilardi 1975, 88–89.
44. Descoeudres 1973. Jean-Paul Descoeudres argues that in fact Zagora was under the specific control of Eretria until the mid-seventh century, when, with the decline of Eretrian influence, it became independent.
45. Cambitoglou 1970, 304; Cambitoglou et al. 1988, 53–67.
46. French 1990/91, 63; see further Telebantou 1989.
47. Boardman 1967, 4–5.

pointing out that there were new persons on Chios beginning in the eighth century. They must have come from somewhere.

Similarly, on the island of Melos, depopulation gave way to gradual resettlement beginning in the tenth century, with an enormous increase, to judge from the number of datable pots, in population there in the second half of the eighth century.[48] On Thera, burial numbers increase beginning about 770, and eighth-century growth can be seen at Old Smyrna and Miletus on the Asian mainland as well.[49]

The great city of Eretria was itself probably an establishment of Lefkandi, which was virtually abandoned shortly after Eretria was founded. Eretria was near Lefkandi, its site chosen for two reasons: to accommodate more people and to have better access to the sea. The growth of Eretria began in earnest shortly after 800, and expansion continued until the end of the eighth century.[50] A goldsmith's workshop from the latter half of the century[51] and a locally worked gold diadem found in a context of the first half[52] point to both increased ranking and increased specialization of labor, both signs of increased population density.

Let us turn from these specific sites to another generality. A parallel to the net movement away from urban centers in the course of the eighth century is the surge in hero-cult sites. As the population grew land became more scarce, and people were forced to make claims on territory, which they did by building shrines to their ancestors.[53] (Similarly, François de Polignac has argued that it was at just this time that extraurban sanctuaries were generally on the rise.)[54] Thus we can observe simply that the new emphasis on hero cults in the eighth century may be interpreted as evidence of increased demand on the physical landscape—that is, there were more people inhabiting it.

Of course, the best place to look for evidence of the increase in population in Greece is the *apoikiai,* the "colonies" of the latter part of the eighth century. Believed by most scholars to have been motivated by overpopulation at home, the colonies probably came into being at least in part for other reasons (see chapter 3). Without question, however, the colonies are evidence of more Greeks, and it should come as no surprise that many of these Greeks came from Eretria, one of the leaders in the colonizing "movement."

---

48. Wagstaff and Cherry 1982, 142–43.

49. Thera: Morris 1987, 161; Old Smyrna: Akurgal 1983, 27–29; Miletus: Kleiner 1968, 24; Cook 1975, 799; Mitchell 1989/90, 104.

50. Mazarakis Ainian 1987.

51. Themelis 1983b.

52. A. Andreiomenou in Themelis 1983b, 165.

53. Snodgrass 1980a, 34–37; 1982.

54. de Polignac 1984, esp. 31ff.; 1995, esp. 21ff.

Returning to Attica and the Argolid, let me conclude by repeating that there had been a modest increase in population since about 825 (about 25 percent in Attica), but one can hardly call this any sort of predictor of what was to follow: according to Snodgrass's unadjusted numbers, between about 780 and 720 the number of burials in Attica increased almost sevenfold, between 790/780 and 710 those in the Argolid more than fivefold. When we adjust the numbers, the Attic increase is reduced to more than a three-fold increase—still impressive—and the increase from 780 to about 750 remains astronomical. What we have before us, then, is several centuries of stabilized density followed by seemingly unexplained explosions of population. (Appendix D offers comparative statistics for similar growth patterns in other places at other times.) Any change in population density is likely to usher in important social changes—the focus of this study.

WHY POPULATIONS INCREASE

Populations increase and decrease for reasons. Let's consider some straight-forward ways to approach population change.

Malthus

To employ the still useful terms introduced by Robert Malthus in 1798, the presence and absence of positive and preventive checks are responsible for fluctuations in population levels. Positive checks serve to increase the death rate, preventive checks to decrease the birth rate. The "ultimate check," as Malthus called it, "appears . . . to be the want of food."[55] The removal of these positive and preventive checks, and especially the diminution of the ultimate check, will produce profound increases of population. It should prove fruitful, therefore, to inquire into the forms these checks may have taken, and then to see which may have been operational in Greece prior to the start of the population increase—that is, which checks were beginning to be eliminated or neutralized shortly before the increase occurred.

There appear to be at least four positive checks (to encourage the death rate) in primitive societies: frequent warfare, famine and epidemic, inferi-or diet, and infanticide and other conscious efforts.

The effects of frequent warfare and famine on mortality rates are obvi-ous. Warfare produces many early deaths, while famine and disease claim especially the frail—the very young and the very old. Also limiting the size of settlements is inferiority of diet, both in quality and in quantity. Inferior

---

55. Malthus 1798, 12. Compare Adam Smith (1776, 182) twenty-two years earlier: "Countries are populous, not in proportion to the number of people whom their produce can cloath and lodge, but in proportion to that of those whom it can feed."

nutrition generates and exacerbates frailty. To maintain a population at the level of subsistence, conscious checks such as infanticide (especially of deformed and female offspring) and often fatal ill-treatment of newborns (apparently designed to allow only those of the strongest constitution to survive) are often practiced.[56]

There are three preventive checks (to inhibit the birth rate) that correlate with these positive checks: frequent warfare, inferior diet, and conscious checks, such as abortion. War-related absenteeism may not be an important preventive check in small-scale societies, but because a woman can be deprived of her husband before the end of her childbearing period, warfare may decrease the number of births. Furthermore, warfare also causes physical and mental stress, which can lead to a decrease in fertility resulting from an increase in the incidence of amenorrhea.[57] Inferior diet can also have a profound effect on human procreation. First, poorly nourished members of both genders have a reduced capacity to procreate;[58] second, in some primitive societies, it has been demonstrated that if an infant's diet of mother's milk is supplemented by easily digested, cultivated grains, the child is weaned sooner, the period of lactation is thus shortened, and correspondingly the period of amenorrhea and anovulation is shortened. The result is the reduction of birth spacing; that is, conception and delivery of the next child occur much sooner than before. In cultures where breastfeeding is extended until the arrival of the next child, birth spacing can reach an average as great as 44.1 months.[59] Conscious checks include abortion (if the society allows it), avoidance of sexual intercourse, coitus interruptus, and delay of marriage. Avoidance of sexual relations is often prac-

56. Female offspring are not always the primary target of population control, as the pharaoh's decree that precedes the narrative of the birth of Moses attests (Exod. 1:15–22). For infanticide in general see Wrigley 1969, 42–43, and Birdsell 1972, 354–63; also Boserup 1970, 48–50 (Japan and China); Lee 1972, 337; Marshall 1976, 165–66; Howell 1979, 120 (!Kung San); Mauss 1950, 98n. 75; Balikci 1970, 147–52 (Eskimos); and Blainey 1976, 97 (aboriginal Australians). An interesting but curiously unannotated survey of infanticide in "pre-Christian" cultures, with an emphasis on the conscious response of communities to "economic" concerns is Panizo 1965, esp. 602–3, 606–7. For ill-treatment of newborns see Carr-Saunders 1922, 160–61 (Eskimo); Boserup 1970, 48–50 (Indian); Stott 1962, 365–66 (Australian). According to Strabo (10.5.6), Ceans over sixty years of age drank hemlock to guarantee sufficient food for others. The context does not imply that this practice was undertaken only in times of shortage, rather that this practice ensured the settlement's prosperity. Such a practice is a parallel of infanticide operating at the other end of the human life span. (Unfortunately, both the date of the law and its reliability [Menander may in fact be the source] are suspect.)

57. Stott 1962, 368–69; Rakoff 1963, esp. 501, 505; Katz 1972, 360.

58. The gonadal function, "not necessary for maintenance of the life of the individual" but indispensable for reproduction, is reduced in both genders by undernutrition (Katz 1972, 358).

59. Konner and Worthman 1980, 788–89.

ticed within those societies that encourage or require a mother to carry her baby on her hip for as long as four years while performing her required chores; an additional hanger-on would be burdensome. Delay of marriage, which decreases the number of childbearing years, is often not so much a conscious decision as a matter of custom, but a custom often born of social need. Delay of marriage for males reduces very little the number of child-bearing years of a marriage; but given that the "proper" age for a woman's nuptials may range from sixteen to twenty-five years, it is certainly the case that a society subscribing to the former figure has a much better chance of (or interest in) growing rapidly.

Of all these checks on population growth, those directly related to the quality and quantity of diet would appear the most important. If this is so, it is clear that the *maintenance* of a population depends on the community's ability to acquire sufficient amounts of food and the nourishment from it. The Malthusian approach, however, argues a close relationship between population and agricultural production, even a dependence of the former on the latter, but does not attempt to explain whether it is population that forces increased production or increased production that actuates in-creased population. If we take an emphatically non-Malthusian approach, there may be a useful answer waiting.

Anti-Malthus

Ester Boserup has offered a proposition different from the Malthusians'. She argues that population is not a variable dependent upon the food sup-ply (the Malthusian assumption); rather, it is "the independent variable which in its turn is a major factor determining agricultural develop-ments"[60]—that is, food production increases or decreases only as required by an increasing or decreasing population. Boserup's argument is based mostly on observations of communities developing in the twentieth centu-ry, and therefore one is often observing a community's acceptance or rejec-tion of an available technology or tool. This is very different from a com-munity *developing* the technology or tool on its own. In the case of *ancient* primitive societies, a technology or tool is "put on the shelf" only after a decrease in the population has generated a less intensive production pat-tern. This is precisely the case in Dark Age Greece. Technology was available but not utilized.

The adoption of an advanced cropping pattern rarely occurs unless increased numbers demand it, for agricultural intensification always demands more work.[61] Production of more than is needed contradicts the

60. Boserup 1965, 11.
61. Boserup 1965, 35–42.

observation that primitive farmers "work to get the maximum return for the minimum effort."[62] This "Law of Least Effort," introduced by George Zipf,[63] is similar to the ideas of the Russian economist A. Y. Chayanov, whose peasant model articulated the "trade off between the drudgery or irksomeness of farm work (disutility of work) and the income required to meet the consumption needs of the household (utility of income)."[64] Individuals in a primitive community do not produce as much food as possible and thus do not create a "relative" surplus, which can be exchanged for nonagricultural goods, become a catalyst for larger families, or allow for the maintenance of specialists who can be freed from the subsistence production pattern and thus devote themselves to cultural pursuits for the benefit of the community. To the contrary, a primitive community produces only as much as it needs, leery to a person about expending valued leisure time just to produce more food. As Philip Smith and Cuyler Young observed, "The conclusion seems to be that what brings about changes in the cropping systems of independent cultivators is not a voluntary decision to produce more food above the needs of domestic consumption but population pressure, where there are more mouths to feed pushing against a naturally or artificially restricted amount of available land."[65] Hence when a population increases, the cropping or production pattern is intensified; conversely, when density is reduced, the production pattern often regresses.

Accordingly, only when an increase in population density demands increased production will the initial labor sacrifice be undertaken, and it is often the case that kinship ties make it easier to make the commitment to invest that labor.[66] The arduous practice of breaking new land involves more labor, but, after this commitment, an increase in output per worker-hour may soon result.[67]

---

62. Nye and Greenland 1960, 129.

63. Zipf's (1949, 5–8) primary interest was not individuals in primitive communities, but individuals in office management.

64. Ellis 1988, 106. Frank Ellis (1988, chap. 6) offers a full discussion of the "drudgery-averse peasant" (with elaborate mathematical models).

65. Smith and Young 1972, 16. Cf. Renfrew 1979a, 187: "Most preindustrial societies are in many ways conservative. They function successfully by carrying out traditional procedures whose effectiveness has been tried and proved over many generations. . . . In order to survive, the [pre-industrial] society must to some extent function as a system which resists change, and all innovations, even potentially useful ones, tend to be viewed with suspicion." For more on the "stagnationist view," see Persson 1988, 3–7.

66. For an interesting account of this phenomenon in sixteenth-, seventeenth-, and eighteenth-century Scotland, see Dodgshon 1988.

67. Boserup 1965, 33–34. This observation is generally applicable also to Neolithic communities: "Food production is a question of techniques; agriculture a question of commitment" (Bender 1978/79, 204).

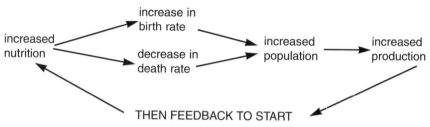

Figure 1. Renfrew's growth model

On the basis of the comparative evidence, Boserup's proposition goes farther than that of the Malthusians. But the Malthusians must also be reckoned with, for it is unavoidably true, based on the same comparative evidence, that improved nutrition is at least a sufficient, if not a necessary, prerequisite for growth. Colin Renfrew[68] proposed a model that seems to take both theories into account (fig. 1). The feedback from increased productivity to increased nutrition is the most important contribution here. Increased nutrition leads to population increase (a Malthusian notion); population increase leads to increased production (Boserup's proposition). The increase in production then feeds back to the model's start, and the cycle of growth and development continues, and the rate of population growth will accelerate.[69]

Not dissimilar is Young's general observation concerning "the reciprocal relationship between population growth and economic productivity": "As more labour becomes available through natural population growth, agricultural systems are intensified. This intensification eventually demands a still larger labour supply, and the birth rate, to choose one possibility, increases accordingly."[70]

CHECKS ON POPULATION IN DARK AGE GREECE

Whether one subscribes to the Malthusian or Boserupian approach, one is still faced with asking what population checks were in place during the Dark

68. Renfrew 1972, 27–30.

69. Cf. Persson 1988, 31: "Technological progress stimulated population growth in pre-industrial economies *and* was stimulated by population growth insofar as it increased the aggregate demand, which generated division of labour, regional specialization, and liberated the economy from some of the constraints imposed by indivisibilities in equipment and learning."

70. Young 1972, 838.

Age that may have been reduced near the beginning of the population explosion.

The positive check of warfare appears to have been absent: the Dark Age is notably lacking in evidence of significant violence.[71] The absence of warfare is indicative of a reduced population, limited resources, and a small amount of personal and community wealth, all in keeping with the archaeological record. Famines and epidemics are also absent from the physical record: there is no surge of burials that would suggest catastrophe of any sort. The absence of famine suggests that food production was highly varied, for with varied production, the failure of any single component does not spell disaster.[72] Since varied production usually indicates limited production, this method may guard against disaster in the short term but restrict growth (by Malthusian rules) in the long term.

The fall of the Mycenaean centers meant the collapse of the palace economies characterized by the elaborate agricultural delivery networks revealed in the Linear B tablets.[73] Reduced food production coincided with the collapse of the centralized economies and a decrease in population density (the result of emigration or death). The extensive and intensive farming of the Mycenaean Age folded back on itself: fewer people required less food. Pollen counts in Messenia—one of the few places in Greece where such counts appear possible—show that grain production was reduced to well below the population's historical consumption (that is, the percentage by which grain production was reduced was far greater than the percentage by which the population was reduced) and was practically absent by about 1100; the grain count returns to a higher level about 700.[74] The pollen

71. Snodgrass 1980a, 23. Occasional evidence of violent death (Popham and Sackett 1968, 14, fig. 24, and 35) indicates homicide rather than warfare.

72. Halstead and O'Shea 1982, 93.

73. Evenhanded treatments of the Mycenaean economy still of value are Finley 1957a and b; Sarkady 1975, 108–13. More recent are the sound surveys by J. T. Killen (1988) and Paul Halstead (1988, 1992). Palace (or temple) economies will be discussed in chapter 4. There is some debate about components of the Mycenaean diet, which I will report but not enter. Thalia Howe (1958) argues that the Mycenaeans and their Dark Age successors ate little grain, many vegetables, and much meat. Merle Langdon (1976, 88), against Howe, maintains that large amounts of grain were consumed in the Mycenaean and Dark ages. What is important here is that there was an elaborately organized agricultural system in place during the Mycenaean Age—diet for now not important—and that in the following period production was down dramatically, and grains virtually absent.

74. Wright 1972, 195–96, 199; cf. Lukermann and Moody 1978, 94, where evidence of an increase in the use of olive wood for burning is adduced. The date of the olive pollen sample is put back to "the later Mycenaean context" by William McDonald and William Coulson (1983, 325), though they admit that olive and olive oil consumption was probably very high in the Dark Age. See note 75.

record indicates that the versatile and less labor-intensive olive became the staple of the population of Messenia.[75] Moving eastward, we find that storage bins in use at Lefkandi early in LH IIIC (about 1200) contain carbonized remains of both spelt and barley, and of olives and figs.[76] By the end of LH IIIC (about 1100), the grain bins in this most prosperous of Dark Age settlements are empty and remain so until the eighth century, when there may be evidence of grain storage.[77]

In addition to harvesting the olive, the populations of the Dark Age began to herd animals on a large scale, especially bovines; although it is not clear that we have enough bone data to make a conclusive argument, this large-scale bovine herding appears to be reflected in Robert Sloan and Mary Ann Duncan's study of animal bones at Nichoria in Messenia. The proportion of bovine meat in the diet at Nichoria rose from 26 percent during LH IIIB2 (1250–1200) to more than 60 percent in the Dark Age. Correspondingly, goat consumption was cut in half between LH IIIB2 (27 percent) and the Dark Age (as low as 12 percent).[78] Sloan and Duncan also state that "the Dark Age residents of Nichoria had changed from a milk and cheese economy to a meat ranching economy specializing in beef,"[79] but this observation obscures the probable truth, that goats remained an important segment of the diet, while grains and dairy products were replaced by beef on the hoof. The change in butchering techniques, from a method that paid careful attention to the cow's lactation period to a method that disregarded it,[80] is certainly an indication of a shift from dairying to ranching. Goats are also butchered at a much younger

75. There are no lamps or other paraphernalia in the Dark Age archaeological record that would suggest nonsubsistence uses for the olive (Boardman 1977, 190), a lack of evidence that supports the notion that olives were being cultivated as a primary source of nourishment. (An alternative explanation of the increase in pollen should be mentioned: the olives were abandoned and allowed to go wild.) According to George Rapp, S. E. Aschenbrenner, and John Kraft (1978, 17), apparently in response to the change in the radiocarbon dating of the pollen samples (see note 74 above), there is "an increase in olive and grass pollen in the Late Bronze Age, the peak in olive pollen occurring in the Early Iron Age."

76. Popham and Sackett 1968, 13.

77. An argument could be brought forward that no new architecture has yet been found at Lefkandi between the end of LH IIIC and the start of MG. However, if the relatively constant burial figures (Snodgrass 1983c, 168–69) are to be interpreted as indicating consistent site use, why is there no carbonized grain in the burial pots? It would appear that grains were not consumed in large quantities during this period. For the evidence concerning later storage, see below, note 91.

78. Sloan and Duncan 1978, 76.

79. Sloan and Duncan 1978, 74. There is a problem with the small number of bones, but the pattern is exactly what we expect.

80. Sloan and Duncan 1978, 65.

age in the Dark Age (the average age at slaughter shifts from 12.7 years to 3.9).[81] Curiously, sheep, never particularly important to the Nichorian diet, represent no portion of the meat diet at all in the Dark Age; apparently, sheep were exploited for their wool, not their flesh. Swine remain an important part of the diet, which suggests that forests were being lost neither to an increase in goats nor to the cultivation of grains.[82] That ovine, bovine, and porcine distribution is in keeping with the testimony of the Homeric poems, where shepherds enjoy little status, while swineherding and cowherding are occupations of status, may indicate that this pattern persisted into the eighth century.[83] (Chicken eggs and fish are excellent sources of protein, but it is uncertain when the domesticated chicken made its first appearance, and it would appear that the Greeks at no time consumed fish in any significant quantity.)[84]

A diet of red meat,[85] olives, figs, and some grains—they were present but were not in any sense a primary source of nourishment—is clearly not the most beneficial one. Vegetable nutrients are best acquired firsthand, not secondhand (through the consumption of herbivorous animals) or third-

---

81. Sloan and Duncan 1978, 66.

82. On the connection between forests and ancient swine production see Harris 1985, chap. 4, esp. 86–87.

83. As I mentioned in chapter 1, I am assuming that the world of the epics is recognizable to the contemporary audience. The description of Eumaeus's relationship to Odysseus seems to have suffered from elite refraction, though perhaps it was still possible as late as 700. The swineherd Eumaeus and the cowherd Philoetius are given prominent roles in the *Odyssey* and enjoy high status. Each is designated *orchamos andron*, a line-end epithet attached otherwise only to the most prominent leaders in the *Iliad*, and in the *Odyssey* to Nestor's son Peisistratus, Odysseus's noble companion Polites, and Menelaus. Though patently base in his behavior, the goatherd Melanthius has sufficient status to mingle with the suitors in the *Odyssey;* there are no other important goatherds. Shepherds, on the other hand, are of virtually no account in either poem, arising in the *Iliad* only in eight similes and in the controversial iron-prize passage (23.835), where a shepherd appears to be a routine possession of a *basileus*. In the *Odyssey,* the only named shepherds are the horrible Laestrygonians, the exotic Libyans, and Polyphemus and his fellow Cyclopes.

84. The earliest evidence of the domesticated chicken is the two toy roosters buried with a male child at Athens about 740 (Coldstream 1977, 313). Lawrence Angel connects the chicken egg with the broadly observable population increase in the Aegean in the archaic and classical periods (Angel 1972/73, 99). On fish, see Gallant 1985, esp. 31–40, against the usual assumption that fish were an important component of the ancient Greek diet (e.g., Radcliffe 1921).

85. Not only from cattle but also from animals taken in the hunt; an increase in the number of domesticated dogs (Sloan and Duncan 1978, 69) not only supports the other evidence for herding but may also indicate that hunting was undertaken on an increased scale, which in turn is evidence of reduced settlement density, since a much greater area is required to support a population by hunting than by herding or cultivation. Increased hunting and herding are a result of or a response to the depressed population.

hand (through the consumption of carnivorous animals).[86] Life expectancy during the Dark Age was probably very short.

Finally, alongside these other positive checks, infanticide may have been practiced. On the basis of the analogies discussed above, there is reason to believe that infanticide was practiced in order to maintain the size of the settlements within the perceived limits of production. Infanticide in the classical, Hellenistic, and Roman worlds is currently the subject of some debate,[87] but the fact that it is practiced with such regularity in myth without any sense of reprobation attached to it, while of limited value by itself, is in keeping with the comparative material, which suggests that it may have been practiced during the Dark Age.[88]

Preventive checks on Dark Age population density can be handled rapidly. There was no warfare about which we can be certain. Poor nutrition reduced reproductivity, and I would adduce the Dark Age diet as an important cause of the depressed population. Finally, one may safely assume on the basis of the comparative evidence that conscientious efforts were undertaken to restrict settlement size. Had a situation arisen that led to the perception that an increase in family size was beneficial, conscious preventive checks would have been reduced.

GROWTH

We should look first for change in diet. The shift in production is a gradual one, but certainly under way as early as about 850. The spectacular evidence, found in the tomb of the "Rich Athenian Lady,"[89] is a model

86. This is succinctly explained by David Grigg: "All living matter derives its energy from the solar radiation received at the earth's surface. Green plants which contain chlorophyll can convert sunlight into carbohydrates by photosynthesis, thus fixing the sun's energy. Some of the carbohydrates are used simply to maintain the plant—respiration—but some are available for herbivores to eat; but *there is a great loss of energy between these two trophic levels as there is later when carnivores prey upon herbivores*" (Grigg 1982, 68–69; italics added).

87. Some have found no compelling evidence that exposure of infants was commonly practiced in the classical period (Van Hook 1920; Bolkestein 1922). Donald Engels (1980, 1984) has added arguments based on demographical probabilities to support the notion that there was little female infanticide in the Greek and Roman worlds. Others (Golden 1981; 1990, 87; Harris 1982) point out that the comparative and literary evidence suggests that exposure of infants, perhaps especially females, was practiced rather routinely. Robert Garland (1985, 80–82) is uncertain. See Patterson 1985 on limitations in the measurement of infanticide.

88. A. Cameron (1932, 108) may go too far when he says (without appealing to comparative materials) that the frequent presence of infant exposure in myth "implies the practice of exposure at the time when the myths arose," but it is tempting to find significance in the fact that in myth "there is no trace of any moral reprobation of exposure in itself" (p. 107).

89. Smithson 1968, 92–97.

granary 28 centimeters tall and a small chest upon whose lid are five model granaries, each about 10 centimeters tall. These models indicate that grain was stored, but it is not possible to determine how important a place in the broad pattern of production and consumption grains held at this time.[90] That is to say, the granaries tell us only that grains were consumed and stored to some extent and that some members of the community were thus getting support in their efforts, thwarted in previous centuries, to grow.[91]

It should be emphasized, however, that the models from the tomb of the "Rich Athenian Lady" do not necessarily indicate that grain storage was standard practice;[92] in fact, this find, along with a single other model,[93] is the only material evidence in the ninth century of grain production. Other models do not emerge for another hundred years.[94] I would argue that while the models are evidence of grain production and storage, the evidence from Messenia, together with that of the Homeric epics and Hesiod, indicates that this is not a long-standing practice: these granaries are new.[95]

90. No pollen counts are available for Attica, and there are no relevant seed remains.

91. If one takes what may be foundations of granaries at Lefkandi (Popham and Sackett 1968, 30–31, figs. 69–70; Popham, Sackett, and Themelis 1980, pls. 5–7, 8b) and reconstructs the structures that they supported in accordance with the scale of the models found in Athens, the reconstituted "granaries" vary in capacity from 64 to 450 bushels. That is, each in a year would feed anywhere from eight to sixty people (see chapter 8, note 92). (The single free-standing model from Athens appears to have about two and a half times the relative volume of the smallest from the lid of the chest. [Relative volume was determined by calculating the dimensions of each model in relation to the diameter of the base, which is all we have left from Lefkandi.] M. R. Popham and L. H. Sackett state that the bases of the "granaries" are 1.5 to 2.0 meters across; my measurements, however, indicate that they range from 2.0 to 2.4 meters. [Popham and Sackett (1968, 31) first conjectured that the foundations belonged to wine or olive presses and later conceded that "on present evidence, we may accept them as the foundations of granaries" (Popham, Sackett, and Themelis 1980, 25).]) Furthermore, the Lefkandi evidence is very difficult to date much before about 710 (the end of the settlement, which was a casualty, probably, of the Lelantine War [Popham and Sackett 1968, 35; Sackett and Popham 1972, 18, 19; Popham, Sackett, and Themelis 1980, 369]), at which point one can be quite confident that grains were a major source of nourishment, as Homer and Hesiod tell us.

Less uncertain is the Late Geometric building J at Old Smyrna, which looks very much like a large storage building (Akurgal 1983, 28, figs. 14, 15, and 18a [a reconstruction reproduced also in Coldstream 1977, 305, fig. 96b], pl. 17), though not necessarily for grain.

92. There is danger in attributing too much weight to the presence of these granaries; Langdon (1976, 89) asserts, for example, that they "*must* be copies of actual *large* granaries which were situated *about the countryside* for the storage of grain" (italics added).

93. Smithson 1968, 92 n. 41, no. 1 (now lost).

94. Smithson 1968, 92 n. 41, nos. 2–10, the earliest of which are Late Geometric.

95. Langdon (1976, 88) argues that the Athenian granaries are evidence that grain cultivation was practiced continuously from Mycenaean times, which is illogical and in contradiction to the evidence.

Grains were being cultivated at this time, but there had been a time, recently, when that was not the case. Furthermore, it is probable that the segment of the population that benefited was at this time small, for there is no evidence yet of any increase in population. From what we know about the interdependence of grain production and population, both grain and a larger population should be present now. We have only granaries, which may be judged the *starting* point for Renfrew's cyclical or feedback model (see fig. 1).

As the eighth century draws to a close, grains are being consumed at greatly increased levels. The increase in offerings to Zeus Ombrios on Mt. Hymettus near Athens may be explained by an increase in the number of grain growers.[96] The higher number of entombed granary models indicates increased interest in production and probably also a more complex form of social organization within which the grain is being stored.[97] In the Homeric poems, the plowed field (*aroura*) is formulaically *zeidoros*, "grain-giving";[98] mortals are regularly characterized as those who eat the fruit of the *aroura*, bread (*sitos*).[99] In the *Odyssey* and in Hesiod, people are characteristically *alphestai*, which may mean "bread eaters."[100] References to working fields with a plow appear in similes.[101] On the Shield, workers plow a rich and wide field; in the *temenos* of a *basileus*, grain reapers are at work.[102] Hesiod and his fellow land users employ the plow; but Hesiod's belabored

96. See tables 5 and 6 in appendix C.

97. To judge from the increase in granary models in the latter half of the eighth century (Smithson 1968, 92 n. 41, nos. 2–4, 8–10). Also see note 91 above.

98. *Il.* 2.548, 8.486, 20.226; *Od.* 3.3, 4.229, 5.463, 7.332, 9.357, 11.309, 12.306, 13.354, 19.593. Curiously, on two occasions in the *Iliad zeidoros* is replaced by another word (18.541: *pieira;* 21.232: *eribolos*); in the *Odyssey,* such substitution also occurs twice (2.328, 23.311: both *pieira*), a much lower frequency given the greater number of instances of *zeidoros*. This would be in keeping with the *Odyssey*'s later date, when more fields are under cultivation for the purpose of grain production, but interestingly there is no such substitution in Hesiod (*WD* 117, 173, 237).

99. *Il.* 6.142, 21.465; *Od.* 8.222, 10.101. Cf. *Il.* 5.341, where gods are differentiated from mortals: they do not eat *sitos*.

100. *Od.* 1.349, 6.8, 13.261; *Hymn. Hom. Ap.* 458; Hes. frags. . 73.5. 211.12, *Shield* 29, *Th.* 512, *WD* 82. Hjalmar Frisk (1973, 81, s.v. *alphano*) and Pierre Chantraine (1968, 67, s.v. *alphestes*) agree that it is unclear whether the word is derived from *alphano*, "to earn, acquire," hence "achiever," "industrious one," or from *alphi*, "barley," hence "bread eater." Not until the fifth century do we find it used to mean "bread eater," although Stephanie West (in Heubeck, West, and Hainsworth 1988, ad *Od.* 3.349) believes "grain-eating" is extremely likely at Hes. frag. 211.12. Even if the word means "bread eater" in the *Odyssey,* it reflects less the world of Eumaeus than the world of the *Odyssey*'s audience.

101. *Il.* 10.353, 13.703; *Od.* 13.32. At *Od.* 18.371–75, Odysseus challenges Eurymachus to a plowing contest.

102. *Il.* 18.541–47, 550–60.

instructions on how to construct a plow suggest that not all farmers were yet expert at their craft.[103]

To make parcels already in use more productive and to break new, perhaps heavier, ones, the plow was reintroduced, at least on a limited basis, in the ninth century (it had fallen into disuse when population density decreased following the collapse of the Mycenaean central organization). The plow's more broadly based reimplementation in the following century is in keeping with Boserup's theory concerning changes in the production pattern and with Renfrew's model. The initial, small-scale grain production, which required the use of this shelved technology, led to a modest increase in population, which in turn created pressure to implement large-scale grain production. Just as the spread of agriculture and settled village life coincided with an increase in population in the Neolithic period,[104] and the introduction of the heavy plow, the nailed horseshoe, and the horse collar coincided precisely with a fourfold increase in per annum growth as the first millennium A.D. drew to a close,[105] so the increased use of the plow and

103. *WD* 42off. Howe (1958) argues from the text of Hesiod that "the practice of intensive and relatively large-scale agriculture in Greece was a new experience for a large proportion of the population at the time" (Howe 1958, 45). I would suggest also that the plow passage may be part of Hesiod's commitment to the reification of peasant culture (see chapter 8).

104. Population density in the Palaeolithic period was about one person per 10 square kilometers; with the introduction of agriculture in the Neolithic the average density of settlements that had acquired the new technology leaped to one per square kilometer, while the total population of Europe expanded from about a quarter of a million persons in the sixth millennium to more than a million in the fifth. There is no question that the advent of agriculture in southern and western Europe in about 3000 B.C. had much to do with the increase in population to well over two million (McEvedy and Jones 1978, 19).

105. Shortly before A.D. 1000, the populations of northern and central Europe experienced a leap in annual growth from 0.1 percent to 0.4 percent (Russell 1958, 105; 1972, 39). More important than the magnitude of the growth rate per se (0.4 percent is not a high rate) is the fact that the growth rate *quadrupled*. Coincident with the quadrupling of the growth rate was the adoption of the heavy plow (White 1962, 41–44; 1972, 147; Wailes 1972, 168–70) and, a short time later, the introduction of the horse collar and the nailed horseshoe (White 1962, 57–62; Le Goff 1972, 81), which allowed the farming of heavy soils for the first time. There followed a third stage of agricultural development, the introduction of the three-field system, which produced 50 percent more food and a more balanced diet (White 1962, 69–71). The growth rate of 0.3 percent to 0.4 percent was maintained until the latter part of the eighteenth century. (Over the centuries there were two dips in the curve, one representing the plague of 1347–1353, the other reflecting the Thirty Years' War, 1618–1648. In both cases, the population fell off dramatically but rebounded equally quickly, with the growth rate resuming at 0.3 percent after reaching the predisaster level.) The steady growth pattern was broken with the introduction of inanimate labor in about 1750, at which point the per annum rate leaped to 0.5 percent, reaching 0.8 percent by 1800.

The two great long-term increases are without question connected to improvement in

the reappearance of grains coincided with an increase in population in the eighth century.

It would appear at first disconcerting that Hesiod's plow does not have an iron plowshare, for this would be evidence of an intensification of technique, to take advantage of unbroken parcels of heavy soil. But it may well be that Hesiod's instructions for the construction of a plow focus, because of his audience's incomplete understanding of the relatively new device, on the appropriate woods for the discrete parts of the plow, and on their joints and joinings.[106] Iron plowshares from ancient Greece have not been uncovered, no doubt because the iron was always recycled into a new share.[107] The *Iliad* provides good evidence for both the iron plowshare and the recycling of its material. When Achilles offers a prize of rough-cast iron at the funeral games of Patroclus, he says of its winner:

> He will have it for five full years to use, for not for lack of iron will the shepherd or the plowman go into the polis, but this will provide it.[108]

Note that the passage not only implies the use of an iron plowshare; it also suggests that iron was not so easy to come by, or at least that there were those who wanted others to think that was the case.

The people of Greece acquired a superior diet before the bulk of the population growth in the eighth century. By the ninth century, the people of Attica, at least, had access to a superior diet, in terms of both quality and quantity. They became healthier and more fertile; with critical nutritional checks removed, the population took off, albeit slowly at first. The improvement in nutrition meant that more children were being born, more would

---

agricultural techniques, which increased production (see generally Slicher van Bath 1963, chap. 3).

106. A. S. F. Gow's observation (1914, 266 n. 49) that Hesiod makes no mention of the share because "he is considering only the wooden parts of the implement" is not particularly satisfying. Most recently on the plow, see Richardson and Piggott 1982.

107. Schiering 1968, 151.

108. *Il.* 23.833–35. The utility of iron to someone plowing is clear; I admit that it is difficult to imagine how a shepherd might use iron, though knives and axes are made of iron in Homer. A bronze shepherd's crook has been found on Cyprus (Gray 1954, 11). Of course, a reference to a plower or a shepherd may simply be a reference to a minor figure in the *oikos* who would find himself ordered to go to town on an errand.

survive, and they would live longer.[109] Soon, as opportunities in overseas trade expanded, encouraging an increase in family size, the increase became very rapid indeed, reaching almost 2 percent per annum between 780 and 720. This increase, although much smaller than previously argued, effected profound changes in the quality of life for a broad spectrum of Greeks.

109. The increase in the quality of mothers' diets will mean fewer stillborn infants, hence more children who might subsequently die as youngsters; thus we see another (partial) explanation for the change in Athenian burial selectivity.

More Greeks:
Appendices

First, a few remarks concerning numbers. Theoretically, populations grow exponentially, in accordance with the differential equation

$$dx/dt = rx$$

where x is the population at any given time and r is the rate of growth (expressed as a percentage) of that population. The solution is

$$x = x_o e^{rt}$$

where x_o is the population at $t = 0$ (Maynard Smith 1974, 16–17). This is precisely what one finds in the case of populations both in newly settled areas, such as colonial America (McEvedy and Jones 1978, 286; Malthus 1798, 7 n.1) and Pitcairn Island (Birdsell 1957, 49–50), and in the apparent analogues of continuously settled areas that have for a long time been characterized by depressed populations. The Greek settlements of the Dark Age fall into this latter category. Exponential growth is found under very narrow conditions, that is, under the circumstance of virtually inexhaustible resources. According to theory, the limit of growth is eventually reached and then surpassed, leading to a Malthusian catastrophe, a possible explanation for the end of the Mycenaean Age. This theoretical catastrophe is documented on occasion in animal populations (Dumond 1972, 287).

In actuality, however, populations, especially human ones, grow logistically, in accordance with the logistic equation

$$dx/dt = rx(1 - x/k)$$

where the growth rate r is limited by k, the carrying capacity of the environment, that is, the maximum stable density of the population. The solution is

$$x = 1/(1/k + [1/x_0 - 1/k]e^{-rt})$$

The model for this type of growth is that of yeast bacteria with a limited supply of nourishment. The population begins its growth exponentially, but shortly before the midway point toward the limit of its support, the growth rate slows dramatically, and instead of outreaching the supportable maximum (leading to Malthusian catastrophe), it slowly approaches it. This is the growth pattern for many populations in nature (Allee et al. 1949, chap. 21, figs. 97–107).

Appendix A.
Snodgrass's Burial Counts

Snodgrass's specific conclusions (1977, 11–12; 1980a, 22–23; 1983c), anticipated by Coldstream (1968, 360–61), have been generally accepted (see Kelly 1976, 51–53; Murray 1980, 65–66; Sparkes 1982, 47; Starr 1982, 420; Wagstaff and Cherry 1982, 143; Sourvinou-Inwood 1983, 34 and n. 5; Whitehead 1986, 6–7; discussion in Hägg 1983c, 210–12).

Snodgrass extrapolated his raw data into burials per thirty-year generation; I present the raw data and work with them as annual burials in table 1. The generated annual increases (or decreases; see table 2) will allow us to compare the data with other demographic changes in history.

The numbers in table 1 are taken directly or extrapolated from Snodgrass (1977, 12; 1980a, 22–23). EG (Early Geometric), MG (Middle), and LG (Late) are labels that refer to types of pottery; these labels in turn are assigned specific dates.

Snodgrass used Coldstream's (1968, 330) chronology for Athens and Attica, but Courbin's (1966, 177) for the Argolid, because he was depending on the burial collation of Hägg (1974), who followed Courbin, the chief excavator at Argos. But one can easily see that Courbin's chronology generates far more growth for the region for the simple reason that it is twenty years shorter than Coldstream's. I give both because while Coldstream's Argive chronology generates fewer annual burials, it provides a pattern of growth that is very similar to the Attic situation, which is especially interesting, since the Argive burials are from urban cemeteries. The specific pattern in Athens and Attica is a net movement of people into the countryside; at this point I offer no explanation for this deurbanization process (I will take it up in chapter 8) and merely point out that the similarity of the "urban" Argive data to the Athenian suggests that there may be more recoverable data in the Argive countryside that would reflect even greater

TABLE 1. Datable Burials in Athens, Attica, and the Argolid, 900–700 B.C.

	EG (900–850 B.C.)		MG I (850–800 B.C.)		MG II (800–760 B.C.)		LG I (760–735 B.C.)		LG II (735–700 B.C.)	
	Total	Annual	Total	Annual	Total	Annual	Total	Annual	Total	Annual
Athens	36	0.72	31	0.62	36	0.90	59	2.36	133	3.80
Attica	7	0.14	15	0.30	11	0.28	66	2.64	150	4.29
Both	43	0.86	46	0.92	47	1.18	125	5.00	283	8.09
				MG						
			Total	Annual						
Argolid	37	0.46[a]	45	0.56[a]			33	1.65[a]	67	3.35[a]
		0.53[b]		0.56[b]				1.65[b]		1.68[b]

SOURCE: Raw data from Snodgrass 1977, 12; 1980a, 22–23.

NOTE: Snodgrass used Coldstream's chronology for Athens and Attica, and Courbin's for the Argolid.
[a]Courbin, whose chronology for the Argolid is EG 900–820; MG 820–740; LGI 740–720; LGII 720–700.
[b]Coldstream, whose chronology for the Argolid is EG 900–830; MG 830–750; LGI 750–730; LGII 730–690.

TABLE 2. Annual Increase in Burials in Athens, Attica, and the Argolid, 875–710 B.C. (from the Midpoint of One Measuring Period to the Midpoint of the Next)

Period	Athens N	Athens %	Attica N	Attica %	Both N	Both %	Argolid period	Argolid N	Argolid %
EG–MG I (875–825 B.C.)	0.72–0.62	–0.30	0.14–0.30	1.52	0.86–0.92	0.13	EG–MG (860–780 B.C.)[a]	0.46–0.56	0.25
							(865–790 B.C.)[b]	0.53–0.56	0.07
MG–MG II (825–780 B.C.)	0.62–0.90	0.83	0.30–0.28	–0.15	0.92–1.18	0.55	MG–LG I (780–730 B.C.)[a]	0.56–1.65	2.16
MG II–LG I (780–748 B.C.)	0.90–2.36	3.01	0.28–2.64	7.01	1.18–5.00	4.53	(790–740 B.C.)[b]	0.56–1.65	2.16
LG I–LG II (748–718 B.C.)	2.36–3.80	1.59	2.64–4.29	1.62	5.00–8.09	1.60	LG I–LG II (730–710 B.C.)[a]	1.65–3.35	3.54
							(740–710 B.C.)[b]	1.65–1.68	0.06
MG–LG II (780–718 B.C.)	0.90–3.80	2.32	0.28–4.29	4.40	1.18–8.09	3.11	MG–LG II (780–710 B.C.)[a]	0.56–3.35	2.55
							(790–710 B.C.)[b]	0.56–1.68	1.37

[a]Courbin's chronology for the Argolid: see table 1, note a.
[b]Coldstream's chronology for the Argolid: see table 1, note b.

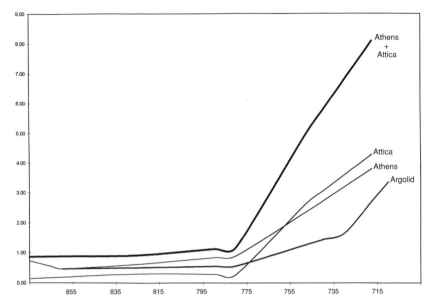

Figure 2. Burials per annum in Athens, Attica, and the Argolid (using Courbin for the Argolid)

increase there. It is easy to see that the most impressive part of the growth in the eighth century belongs to its first half. Figure 2 makes this easy to see.

More recently, Anne Foley has collected numbers for Argos only (see tables 3 and 4). They are not out of line with Snodgrass's counts. (Again, both Courbin's and Coldstream's chronologies are provided; Foley prefers Courbin's.) Foley also documents a large increase in population at neighboring Tiryns in the Argolid (Foley 1988, 266, table 7). The number of sites increases dramatically after 780 in Achaea and continues to increase into the Archaic Period (Morgan 1991, 138, 140). We might also cite the settlement numbers from the Southern Argolid survey (the first number indicates the number of definite sites, the second the number of uncertain sites; from Jameson, Runnels, and van Andel 1994, 229, fig. 4.4):

Late Helladic	27	11
Protogeometric	1	0
Early Geometric	0	1
Middle Geometric	3	3
Late Geometric	16	5
Archaic	27	13

TABLE 3.   Datable Burials in the Argolid, 900–700 B.C.

EG		MG		LG	
Total	Annual	Total	Annual	Total	Annual
28	0.35[a]	34–38	0.45[a]	57+	1.43[a]
	0.40[b]		0.45[b]		0.95[b]

SOURCE: Data from Foley 1988, 35–36.
[a]Courbin
[b]Coldstream

TABLE 4.   Annual Increase in Burials in the Argolid, 860–720 B.C.
(from the Midpoint of One Measuring Period
to the Midpoint of the Next)

	N	%	
EG–MG			
860–780 B.C.	0.35–0.45	0.31	[Courbin]
865–790 B.C.	0.40–0.45	0.16	[Coldstream]
MG–LG			
780–720 B.C.	0.45–1.43	1.92	[Courbin]
790–720 B.C.	0.45–0.95	1.07	[Coldstream]

SOURCE: Data from Foley 1988, 35–36.

Appendix B.
Adjustments to Snodgrass's Counts

Morris (1987, chap. 6 and app. 1) was able to determine the number of adult burials (table 5), and by doubling this figure we may approximate the total number of deceased, buried or not (table 6).

When Morris's percentages are applied to Snodgrass's figures, the result is the most accurate measurement so far of the population increase in eighth-century Athens and Attica (I apply Morris's percentages to Snodgrass's numbers because Morris does not break down the data for EG and

TABLE 5. Burials in Athens and Attica, by Age, 900–700 B.C.

	Adult/Youth		Child/Infant		Total
	N	% of Burials	N	% of Burials	N
EG & MG 900–760					
Athens	110	91.7	10	8.3	120
Attica	47	94.0	3	6.0	50
Both	157	92.4	13	7.6	170
LG I 760–735					
Athens	65	95.6	3	4.4	68
Attica	35	87.5	5	12.5	40
Both	100	92.6	8	7.4	108
LG II 735–700					
Athens	53	47.3	59	52.7	112
Attica	68	40.5	100	59.5	168
Both	121	43.2	159	56.8	280

SOURCE: Raw data from Morris 1987, app. I.
NOTE: Uncertain burials are distributed proportionally.

TABLE 6.   Deaths in Athens and Attica, 900–700 B.C.

	EG (900–850 B.C.)		MG I (850–800 B.C.)		MG II (800–760 B.C.)		LG I (760–735 B.C.)		LG II (735–700 B.C.)	
	Total	Annual	Total	Annual	Total	Annual	Total	Annual	Total	Annual
Athens	66	1.32	57	1.14	66	1.65	113	4.52	126	3.60
Attica	13	0.26	28	0.56	21	0.54	116	4.64	122	3.49
Both	79	1.50	85	1.70	87	2.18	229	9.16	248	7.09

NOTE: Data represent Morris's (1987, app. 1) percentages applied to table 1.

TABLE 7.   Annual Increase in Deaths in Athens and Attica,
875–718 B.C. (from the Midpoint of One Measuring Period
to the Midpoint of the Next)

	Athens		Attica		Both	
	N	%	N	%	N	%
EG–MG I (875–825 B.C.)	1.32–1.14	–0.32	0.26–0.56	1.53	1.58–1.70	0.15
MG I–MG II (825–780 B.C.)	1.14–1.65	0.82	0.56–0.54	–0.08	1.70–2.18	0.55
MG II–LG I (780–748 B.C.)	1.65–4.52	3.10	0.54–4.64	6.62	2.18–9.16	4.42
LG I–LG II (748–718 B.C.)	4.52–3.60	–0.76	4.64–3.49	–0.94	9.16–7.09	–0.85
MG II–LG II (780–718 B.C.)	1.65–3.60	1.25	0.54–3.49	2.99	2.18–7.09	1.89

MG). What this adjustment adjusts is the growth in LG II, which was modest before and is now virtually zero, even negative. Snodgrass's numbers,
before this adjustment, suggest an increase of between six and seven times
in the course of sixty years; adjusted as in table 6, the increase is less than
three and a half times. In annual terms, the growth for the longer period of
780 to 718 is reduced from 3.1 percent to 1.9 percent (table 7). Snodgrass
(1991, 16; 1993, 31) has acknowledged that Morris's observation that more
people were participating in the burial process beginning in the eighth century would explain much of the increase that he had measured (as visual-
ized in figure 3).

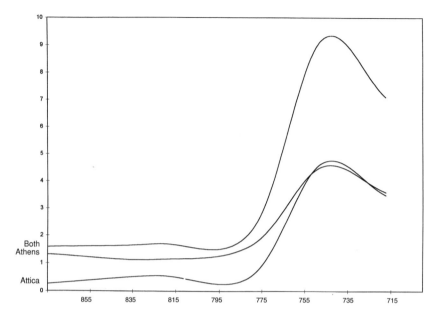

Figure 3. Burials in Athens

Appendix C.
Dedication Patterns
on Mt. Hymettus

Camp (1979, 398; adapted from Langdon 1976, 75, table 1) offers the figures provided in table 8 (I have added the per annum numbers). In table 9 the vessels are broken down by type, as discussed in chapter 2.

TABLE 8. Offerings to Zeus Ombrios on Mt. Hymettus, 875–600 B.C.

	Total	Annual	% Increase
875–800 B.C.	25	0.33	—
800–760 B.C.	91	2.28	3.36
760–735 B.C.	82	3.28	1.11
735–700 B.C.	294	8.40	3.13
700–600 B.C.	589	5.89	—

SOURCE: Raw data from Camp 1979, 398.

TABLE 9. Offerings to Zeus Ombrios, by Vessel Type, 875–600 B.C.

	Closed (Storage or Serving)		Open (Drinking)			
	N	% of Offerings	N	% of Offerings	Total	Annual
875–800 B.C.	11	44.0	14	56.0	25	0.33
800–760 B.C.	13	14.3	78	85.7	91	2.28
760–735 B.C.	32	39.0	50	61.0	82	3.28
735–700 B.C.	35	11.9	259	88.1	294	8.40
700–600 B.C.	12	2.0	577	98.0	589	5.89

SOURCE: Raw data from Langdon 1976, 75, table 1.

Appendix D.
Historical Patterns of Growth
and the Greek Numbers

So that later we may better understand the social impact of the population increase, let us see how the growth in eighth-century Greece stacks up against similar population spasms in history.

Wrigley has stated that a long-term growth rate (births minus deaths) as high as 5 percent per annum is highly unlikely: "Four percent has very rarely been attained and then only briefly; three is a rapid rate of growth; and, except in recent years in the developing countries few populations have shown rates of growth as high as two percent per annum" (Wrigley 1969, 54). We saw that the modest increase in the forty-five years between about 825 and 780 represents annual growth of less than 0.5 percent, very slight in a community with such low population density at the start of the measuring period. But the annual growth is significant because it demonstrates a reversal in density pattern: the previous pattern was one of stagnation. The sudden sevenfold increase in the next sixty years in Attica works out to just over 3.1 percent per annum; the increase in the Argolid is 2.6 percent; our downward adjustments reduce the Attic rate to just less than 1.9 percent.

But even Snodgrass's inflated growth rates are well within Wrigley's guidelines and compare favorably with the 3 percent natural increase in North America in the eighteenth century (Malthus 1798, 7; McEvedy and Jones 1978, 286). Potter's figures, adjusted for slave importations, show this clearly (table 10). The growth from 1700 to 1790, ninety years, is 2.9 percent; from 1720 to 1790, seventy years, it is 3.0 percent. The population of Pitcairn Island, immediately after settlement in 1790 by six mutineers of the *Bounty* and eight or nine Polynesian women, doubled its size a little more often than every twenty years (>3.5 percent) for almost seventy years; beginning in about 1820 the settlement of the Bass Strait Islands doubled every

TABLE 10.   Population Growth in North America, 1700–1790

	N (in Thousands)	% Increase
1700–10	275–348	2.4
1710–20	348–444	2.4
1720–30	444–600	3.0
1730–40	600–809	3.0
1740–50	809–1,102	3.1
1750–60	1,102–1,470	2.9
1760–70	1,470–1,990	3.0
1770–80	1,990–2,546	2.5
1780–90	2,546–3,639	3.6

SOURCE: Raw data from Potter 1965, 638–39, 642.

twenty-five years (2.8 percent) for almost a hundred years. (Add to these dependable accounts the amazing tale of Nonnia, an Australian aborigine who fled civilization around 1860: beginning a settlement with two female aborigines as his consorts, after thirty years he was the proud leader of a closed population of twenty-eight. The annual increase here is an astonishing 6.5 percent. [For the figures see Birdsell 1957, 49–52.])

Compare, too, the growth rates of many more recent populations (table 11). Albania's growth rate in the 1970s was 3 percent (McEvedy and Jones 1978, 112); from 1960 to 1991 it was 2.3 percent (UNDP 1993, 207).

Among countries categorized as "low-income economies" we find these weighted averages of per annum growth for the years 1973–1984: Zaire 3.0 percent; Niger 3.0 percent; Tanzania 3.4 percent; Kenya 4.0 percent. All such sub-Saharan countries grew at a rate of 2.9 percent for the period. "Middle-income economies" with impressive per annum growth for 1973–1984 are Honduras, with 3.5 percent; El Salvador, 3.0 percent; Cameroon, 3.1 percent (all data from World Bank 1986, 228, table 25). Similar data can be found in almost any United Nations publication (e.g., UNDP 1993).

Cipolla attributes growth rates of more than 3.0 percent per annum from 1965 to 1975 to large areas of the world, including all of South Asia and most of Africa. In fact, the "less-developed regions" of the world had a growth rate during this period of 2.7 percent (Cipolla 1978, 94–95). Bairoch estimates the per annum growth in less-developed, non-Communist nations throughout the entire world to have been 2.3 percent in the 1950s and 2.6 percent in the 1960s (Bairoch 1975, 6, table 1); in 1975, he estimated annual growth to be 2.9 percent in South America, 2.7 percent in Asia, and 2.5 percent in Africa (Bairoch 1975, 8).

TABLE 11. Population Growth in Select Regions of the World in the Twentieth Century

	1925–1975		1950–1975		1960–1991		1991–2000 (estimated)	
	N (in Millions)	% Increase	N (in Millions)	% Increase	N (in Millions)	% Increase	N (in Millions)	% Increase
Central America			9.25–18.5	2.8				
Colombia			11.5–22	2.6	15.9–32.9	2.3		
Ghana	2.5–9.8	2.7			6.8–15.5	2.7	15.5–20.2	2.9
Greenland Eskimos	0.01–0.05	3.2						
Libya			1–2.5	3.7	1.3–4.7	4.0	4.7–6.4	3.4
Mexico			27–60	3.2	37–86	2.8		
Sub-Saharan Africa					210–520	2.9	520–680	2.8
Taiwan (post-refugee)			7–16	3.3				

SOURCES: McEvedy and Jones 1978, 119 (with chart), 174–75, 224–25, 245, 291–96, 302–4; UNDP 1993, 181, 207, tables 23 and 45.

There are many more persons involved in all of these modern examples; thus the eighth-century rates of growth seem quite reasonable. External help (in the form of improved health care and sanitary conditions) has supported such growth, and intensified agriculture has also contributed to it to an important degree.

I offer these figures to illustrate that the population increase in Greece, even if it was as great as some would suggest, is not without historical analogues. But even when greatly reduced, the increase was the harbinger of a great transformation.

Many interested in population growth and decline in the Third World concentrate on the mortality rate, assuming that there is a more or less constant live birth rate always hovering near its upper limit. On that assumption, which I will demonstrate is just not true, a decrease in the mortality rate is what generates growth. What results is a numbers game. Wrigley again: "Except where the age structure of the population is very unusual the maximum rate of [births] is about 50 per 1,000 per annum. Birth rates above this level are very exceptional and rates above 45 are uncommon. . . . In large pre-industrial populations minima would rarely be less than 15 per 1,000" (Wrigley 1969, 62). If a reasonable constant birth rate is 40 per 1,000, then we might say that during the Dark Age, the mortality rate was also 40 per 1,000. (Or we can say that both rates were 45 or 30 or 20 per 1,000.) This approach shows that even when we have no truly reliable numbers, the growth in the eighth century was very difficult and rare, but plausible. Snodgrass's per annum increase of 4.53 percent for Athens and Attica from MG II to LG I means the birth rate exceeded the death rate by 45 per 1,000 for over thirty years! This is mathematically possible, again, like the increase itself, in line with Wrigley's limits: 50 births and 5 deaths per 1,000. But the longer-term growth, from MG II to LG II, better than sixty years, is "only" 3.1 percent, easily achieved by a proportion of 41–10 per 1,000. It is achieved even more easily and explained very easily if Sundt's Law can be perceived in operation. Sundt's Law states that more often than not it is not contemporary economic or moral conditions that generate a baby boom; rather, a baby boom is usually caused by a preceding boom of babies, now grown up (see Sundt 1855, 20–23; Michael Drake in Sundt 1855, xvii).

My adjusted figures make the same demands in the shorter term (MG II-LG I) but substantially less in the longer term (MG II-LG II), for 1.9 percent over sixty plus years is impressive but hardly all that unusual.

THREE

Early Movements of Goods and of Greeks

For I do not liken you to a man skilled in contests, such as are common among men, but to someone who, traveling here and there with his many-benched ship, is a captain of sailors who are traders, is mindful of his cargo, and watching over his merchandise and his precious gains.

EURYALUS TO ODYSSEUS, *ODYSSEY* 8

Strangers, who are you? From where do you sail the damp sea lanes? Is it on account of some trade or do you wander at random, like pirates over the sea, who wander risking their lives and bringing trouble to people of other places?

NESTOR TO TELEMACHUS, *ODYSSEY* 3,
AND POLYPHEMUS TO ODYSSEUS, *ODYSSEY* 9

During the Dark Age, the Greeks had little archaeologically measurable contact with the outside world. Excavations at Lefkandi on Euboea have produced evidence of tenth-century contact with Cyprus, the Levant, and Egypt, and a tenth-century shrine at Kommos in southern Crete appears to have been built under Phoenician direction or influence,[1] but, in the main, the Greeks of the Dark Age appear to have kept to themselves and to have attracted little attention. The little trade that did go on was apparently passive, performed by outsiders entering the Greek communities. Not until the eve of the population increase do we perceive Greeks engaged in active trade abroad in any significant way.[2]

---

1. For Lefkandi, see Sackett 1986; Popham in Catling 1986/87, 14; Popham 1995. L. H. Sackett believes that "the Euboeans themselves took part in sea ventures"; this is not at all certain, although we now have an early ninth-century burial of what appears to be a Lefkandian "trader," buried with his weights (Popham and Lemos 1995). The earliest evidence of a Lefkandi-Cyprus connection is now Euboean wares found in tenth-century contexts on Cyprus (Lemos and Hatcher 1991). The "Hero of Lefkandi," whom we will consider in chapter 6, was buried in a bronze amphora that either was manufactured on Cyprus or had a Cypriot connection of some sort (Catling 1993, 86). For Kommos, see Shaw 1982, esp. 185ff.; Shaw in Catling 1981/82, 45–46, 56.

2. "Passive" trade is Marx's (1973, 256) term. Weber's thesis was that "the shift from passive to active trade was the first step leading to the gulf between the western and the eastern city" (Finley 1976/77, 322 [= 1983, 18]); cf. Weber 1921, 1212–34. On Weber's clear debt to Marx on this specific matter (and other matters, as well as the better-known fundamental disagreement in general), see Mommsen 1974, 47–71; on Weber's ideal *Stadt* and its influence on Marxists, see Weiss 1986, 94–98.

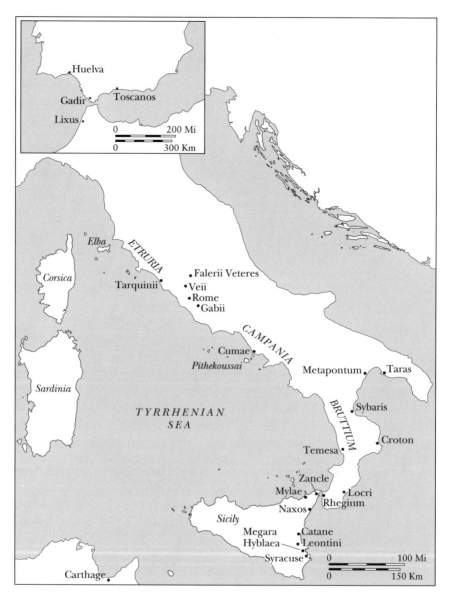

Map 2. The Greeks in the west

Inset labels:
Huelva
Gadir Toscanos
Lixus

0   200 Mi
0   300 Km

Main map labels:
Elba
ETRURIA
Corsica
Falerii Veteres
Tarquinii
Veii
Rome
Gabii
CAMPANIA
Cumae
Pithekoussai
Metapontum
Taras
Sardinia
Sybaris
TYRRHENIAN SEA
BRUTTIUM
Croton
Temesa
Zancle
Mylae
Locri
Naxos
Rhegium
Sicily
Megara
Hyblaea
Catane
Leontini
Syracuse
Carthage

0   100 Mi
0   150 Km

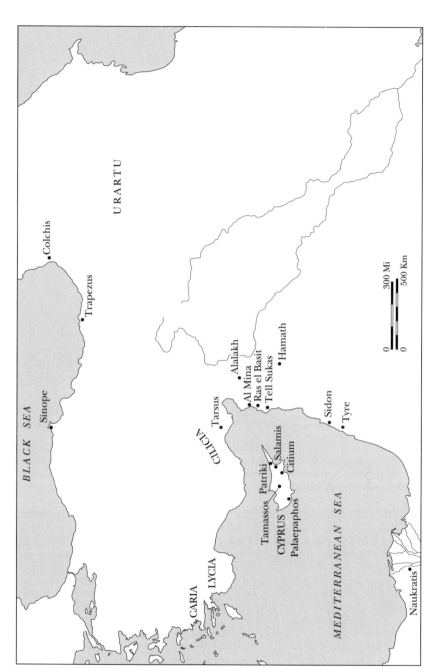

Map 3. The eastern Mediterranean

EARLY TRADE

This first active trade was undertaken at great distances, as the Greeks pursued opportunities far to the west and east. Since we will see that the Greeks learned their lessons from the Phoenicians, it makes sense to look first to the east.

Al Mina

Greek involvement at Al Mina ("The Port"), on the Orontes Delta in northern Syria, began before 750, perhaps before 800.[3] Al Mina was an emporium (port of trade), a controlled market where goods were in some manner exchanged.[4] The settlement did not resemble at all the Greek communities at home, because it was devoted exclusively to the movement and transfer of goods.[5] Abandoned since 1194, when Alalakh, the city a few miles upriver that the port had served, was destroyed, the site was developed initially probably by Phoenicians—the Greeks probably became involved after the foundation—as a port of trade that was designed to connect the Aegean to the great civilizations at Urartu, Assur, Babylon, and elsewhere in the Asian interior.[6] The presence at Al Mina of the distinctively Euboean pottery ves-

---

3. Rosalinde Kearsley (1989, 145) argues that on the basis of the *skyphoi* alone, it is difficult to place the Euboeans at Al Mina before 750; Mervyn Popham and Irene Lemos (1992, 154–55) do not find Kearsley's chronological assumptions compelling and criticize her late dating; Popham would put the Euboeans at Al Mina by 800, "if not earlier" (Popham 1994, 26); David Ridgway would put them there as early as 825, although he emphasizes that Al Mina is essentially a Syrian town with a few Euboean traders in it (Ridgway 1992, 24–26). Joan du Plat Taylor (1959, 91) long ago argued for a date before 800, to which John Boardman still subscribes ("by about 800" [Boardman 1990, 186]). Anthony Snodgrass, more sympathetic to Kearsley, emphasizes that while there may be Euboean *skyphoi* at Al Mina before 750, there aren't very many and the enormous preponderance of Euboean pottery falls in the period following 750 (Snodgrass 1994b, 4–5). The pottery was first published in Robertson 1940. Furthermore, there has been some sharp debate about just how "Euboean" the earliest pottery is. J. N. Coldstream has rejected the earliest Euboean evidence as insignificant (1977, 93–94), a volte-face from his earlier stand (1968, 357). Chemical analysis of the clay has proven inconclusive (Popham, Hatcher, and Pollard 1980). Paul Courbin (1977) suggests that a *pyxis* found in Lebanon may have been manufactured in Argos in about 825, which would suggest a Greek presence a bit earlier, though a solitary *pyxis* does not necessarily demonstrate that a Greek, much less an Argive, brought it there. Putting aside for now the uncertainty over its precise provenance, the pottery indicates a presence at Al Mina perhaps as early as the late ninth century or early eighth century (Coldstream 1968, 312–13; Popham, Hatcher, and Pollard 1980, 151; Boardman 1980, 43).

4. On ports of trade, see Revere 1957; Polanyi 1963. On controlled markets, see below, chapter 4.

5. Woolley 1938, 14; 1953, 169.

6. Woolley 1948, 148. Indeed, Leonard Woolley surmised that such a halfway point had to exist somewhere and that the mouth of the Orontes River was the logical site, and thus

sels that we call pendent-semicircle *skyphoi* is clear evidence of Euboean leadership of the Greeks. It is probably more than coincidence that on the Greek mainland the earliest (850–825 B.C.) pictorial depiction of a ship has been found at Lefkandi on Euboea.[7] And thus it is no surprise that in the oral tradition only Euboea was known as *nausikleite*, "famous for ships."[8]

What were the Greeks moving into and out of Al Mina? Although examples of the telltale Euboean ware are found at a number of other sites in Syria, and also in Palestine,[9] it seems doubtful that the Greeks were trading primarily pottery, since Greek pottery was not significantly superior to eastern products.[10] While there is general agreement that the Greeks were moving iron and copper to Greece, especially to Eretria and Chalcis, the "city of bronze," in Euboea,[11] it is not at all certain that this was the case. The physical evidence suggests that iron sufficient for Greek (Euboean) needs was moved via Pithekoussai in the west (see below) and later from the Black Sea. This does not rule out the possibility that *in the beginning* the Euboeans went to Al Mina to get iron and other metals; but, after coming into contact with the Etruscans, the Greeks must have been moving other goods besides iron out of Al Mina. In the *Odyssey*, Mentes the Taphian stops in Ithaca as he carries iron to Temese, to exchange for copper.[12] Homer tells us nothing about where the iron has come from, but if Temese is correctly identified as Tamassos on Cyprus,[13] Mentes is taking the ore eastward from Ithaca.[14] It then seems much more likely that the ore has come to Ithaca from the west

found Al Mina. A. J. Graham (1986) has made clear how uncertain the evidence is for a Greek hand in the foundation of Al Mina, although Boardman is less uncertain of an early Greek presence (1990, 175–77).

7. Popham 1987, 354–55, with figs. 1 and 2. There are earlier ships on pots from Crete (950–900 B.C.: Brock 1957, 12, no. 45, pl. 135) and the Halicarnassus peninsula in Caria (950–900: van Doorninck 1982, 278, fig. 1).

8. In both of the Homeric Hymns to Apollo, at *Hymn. Hom. Ap.* 31 and 219.

9. Boardman 1957, 6; 1980, 45 n. 30. The charted distribution of the *skyphoi* in the Levant and Cyprus can be found in Coldstream 1977, fig. 29.

10. T. F. R. G. Braun (1982, 9) believes that the presence of the *skyphoi* at Hamath on the Orontes indicates a preference for them over local wares.

11. Boardman 1980, 42.

12. *Od.* 1.184.

13. Temese has been identified as either Tamassos on Cyprus, the most outstanding source of copper in the Mediterranean, or Temesa (also called Tempsa), in the heart of Bruttium, the only significant copper-mining area in southern Italy. The former identification may be preferred because of both the greater antiquity of Cypriot Tamassos and the uncertain dating of the earliest exploitation of Italian copper. See further West in Heubeck, West, and Hainsworth 1988, ad 1.184.

14. Snodgrass (1989, 30) refers in passing to this scene as an example of "exchanging native iron for foreign copper"; I don't see it this way at all.

than from the east. The eastward movement of the iron suggests that Greeks were eventually carrying iron *into* Al Mina rather than out of it.

One other question that needs to be addressed is whether there were sufficient or adequate sources of iron at home in Euboea. The answer to this question appears to be yes. In the territory controlled by Chalcis, there were enormous deposits of iron and other metals, some still unexhausted today. The Eretrians seemed not to have any deposits in their territory, but there were quite ample and presumably accessible sources in northeastern Boeotia, just across the Euripus.[15] So the answer to the simple question seems to be yes.

Why then did Euboeans go abroad seeking iron? This question is not so simple. It appears that iron obtained in one's home territory or at least from nearby sources was not as desirable as iron obtained at a distance (see chapters 4 and 5). Iron (or any other commodity) generated at or near home was perceived as obligated in some way to the community in which it was generated; iron (or any other commodity) obtained at a distance was not so obligated and could be used by individuals (and groups) without concern for the community at home (see chapter 4).

The Euboeans at Al Mina seem to have been participating in a successful cooperative venture with Cypriots and Phoenicians. In the early eighth century, northern Syria—including Al Mina, Ras el Basit, and Tell Sukas, the smaller ports of trade that also attracted Greeks to their heterogeneous populations and have yielded much Euboean pottery[16]—was under the domination, or at least the protection, of the inland kingdom of Urartu.[17] The special status of Al Mina as a port of trade for the long-distance movement of nonsubsistence goods allowed it to survive the unrest that affected the rest of the area in the eighth century. In 720, Sargon, king in Assur, conquered Cilicia and Syria; there is no sign of disruption at Al Mina, however. In 696, Sennacherib, Sargon's successor, put down a rebellion centered in

15. On the deposits see Bakhuizen 1976, 45–52.

16. On Ras el Basit and Tell Sukas, see Boardman 1980, 45, 52, references, on p. 269 n. 29, and map on p. 34.

17. Robert Drews's (1976, 30–31) suggestion that Corinthians learned about iron deposits on the north coast of Anatolia from Urartians, who also controlled the eastern Euxine (Urartian Qulha is probably Colchis), is ingenious. That Greeks were present at Sinope and Trapezus in the eighth century, however, is far from certain. Drews's (1976, 29) argument that Corinthians founded Sinope and Trapezus (as Sinope's port of trade) is compelling, but the date he suggests—as early as 750—is difficult to embrace; Stanley Burstein (1976) would also put the Greeks in the Black Sea before 700. For a new summary of all the arguments see Tsetkhladze 1994. For difficulties encountered by ships entering the Black Sea, see Carpenter 1948, answered, though not fully, by Labaree 1957. A. J. Graham (1958) argues for a date perhaps before 700. If the Greeks *were* present this early, it is clear from Drews's argument that iron was the reason.

Cilicia. Tarsus, home to many Greeks, few of whom, however, were Euboeans,[18] was destroyed; Al Mina shows minor architectural disruption only, perhaps unrelated to Sennacherib's activities. By about 695, buildings of Level VII had fallen into decay and were replaced by new buildings in Level VI.[19] This break not only coincides with Sennacherib's action; it also corresponds to a shift in Greek leadership from Euboea to Corinth. Before the break there are a few Corinthian shards; after the break there is almost exclusively only Corinthian ware; Euboean ware is absent.[20] This Corinthian coup was perhaps made possible by the Lelantine War, which annihilated the power of both Chalcis and Eretria. This change in Greek leadership aside, Al Mina's good fortune in the context of Sennacherib's crackdown can be explained by its special position as a port of trade without political aspirations—without, in fact, much of a permanent population. Al Mina was thus relatively buffered from outside disruption. Tarsus, by contrast, although a major station for moving goods, was also a city of permanence and prominence. Sennacherib destroyed Tarsus because it was a political threat, and that threat far outweighed any economic contribution it may have been making.

Although it is not clear what specific items the Greeks were bringing into and taking out of Al Mina, we can be confident, on the basis of what we know about other ports of trade in the ancient Near East (e.g., Tilmun [modern Bahrain]),[21] that, in general, luxury goods, not subsistence goods, were being moved in both directions. Among these luxury goods were metals, exotic and utilitarian (often both).[22] Such goods also included textiles (the famed work of the Babylonian weavers, for instance),[23] slaves,[24] and other commodities that have left no physical trace.[25] It is unlikely that subsistence goods were involved in great quantities because there is little evi-

---

18. As is indicated by the distribution of predestruction pottery; see Boardman 1965.

19. Woolley (1938, 18) placed the break, wrongly, at about 650; we owe the revision to Joan du Plat Taylor (1959, 91).

20. Robertson 1940, 18f.; Hanfmann 1956, 173–74; Boardman 1980, 48.

21. The millennia-long history of Bahrain as a port of trade is clearly articulated in the fine collection of essays in al-Khalifa and Rice 1986.

22. Gold and silver plate are mentioned at *Il.* 23.740–45; *Od.* 4.128–29, 4.612–19, 14.122–23.

23. Silver 1983, 810–11 and n. 38; Crawford 1973, 74.

24. Acquired through piracy. See Braun 1982, 14, for a contemporary Assyrian account of raids undertaken by Ionians.

25. Pace Braun (1982, 13), the fine robes of the Trojan women in the *Iliad* (6.288–92), which may at first suggest that the Greeks imported cloth or finished goods from the East, more likely indicate merely a knowledge of an affluent East. The references to gold and silver plate (above, note 22), which are in the hands of Greeks, may be more conclusive, unless in fact the knowledge of an affluent East has simply been transferred to the heroic "past."

dence anywhere in the Near East, the Aegean, or the western Mediterranean that subsistence goods regularly moved through ports of trade.[26]

Although we cannot be sure about the nature of trade at Al Mina, we are able to speak with some certainty about trade in the far west.

Pithekoussai

The first Greek colony in the west was on the island of Pithekoussai (modern Ischia), facing the later site of Cumae in Campania. It seems quite clear that Pithekoussai ("Ape Island") was settled with an eye toward trade with the Etruscans to the north. The earliest pottery remains at Pithekoussai are chevron *skyphoi,* a post-pendent-semicircle type of Euboeo-Cycladic style that dates from around 770.[27] There is, however, evidence of Euboean contact with Etruscans at Veii as early as 800,[28] and the pottery found there now includes the pendent-semicircle *skyphoi* that point to a Euboean presence also at Al Mina.[29] Thus contact with the primitive but materially affluent Etruscans clearly precedes any permanent settlement at Monte di Vico on the naturally well-fortified north coast of Pithekoussai. This, together with the discovery of iron-smelting works, clearly indicates that the settlement at Pithekoussai existed as a base of operations for the acquisition of iron from the Etruscans, and probably also copper and tin from other sources with access to central Europe. Etruscans controlled the metalliferous areas in Etruria and on the island of Elba, which was rich in iron-ore deposits.[30]

26. Mayhew, Neale, and Tandy 1985. The exception is the port of trade at Tyre, into which Israelite merchants brought wheat (Ezek. 27:17); none of the other goods described in Ezekiel (27:12–24) are subsistence items.

27. Boardman 1980, 165; others date the earliest sign of settlement to "about 775" (Buchner 1966, 12; cf. Drews 1976, 19; Bonfante 1986b, 6; Torelli 1986, 51); "not later than c. 760" (Coldstream 1968, 354); "770" (Vallet 1958, 56, followed by Roebuck 1962, 100 n. 3); "around 770" (Hurwit 1985, 79); "770–760" (Frederiksen 1984, 64); "around 750–760" (Collis 1984, 46). David Ridgway (1973, 23) perceives "the presence of a substantial population by c. 750." Martin Frederiksen is sympathetic to the notion that the "highly developed trade and social organization which can be inferred on Pithecusae by 760 B.C. may suggest that it had originated a generation earlier, in about 800 B.C. The question remains open" (Frederiksen 1984, 64–65). Yes, the question remains open, but it is certainly begged by the materials from Al Mina and Etruria.

28. Coldstream 1968, 335.

29. Boardman 1980, 165; Jean-Paul Descoeudres and Rosalinde Kearsley (1983, 52) would date the Euboean *skyphoi* to after 750.

30. See Buchner 1966, 12. Some (Buchner 1969, 97–98; Snodgrass 1971b, 43 and n. 36; 1980b, 339; Ridgway 1973, 18; 1992, 91) believe that a sample of slag from the acropolis at Pithekoussai was mined at Elba. The entirety of the proof can be found in a letter to Buchner from Professor Giorgio Marinelli of Pisa, who determined that the sample is hematite from Elba (see Buchner 1969, 97–98). This testimony has been accepted uncritically by most of the

The following reconstruction of the birth of this settlement would appear as good as any. Strabo states that Pithekoussai was founded by Eretrians and Chalcidians,[31] and the archaeological record agrees. Before the settlement was founded, adventurous Euboeans, perhaps in search of iron ore, encountered the Etruscans in central Italy. The Etruscans were, like the more mobile Greeks, socially organized in an ill-defined hierarchy and economically organized reciprocally, perhaps redistributively (see chapter 4). The leaders of the Greeks made gifts to their counterparts in the Etruscan communities, who in turn not only offered access to their communities' iron-ore deposits, for which the communities had little or no use, but also perhaps provided a portion of each participating community's population as labor.[32] Both sides were pleased to participate in this arrangement. In fact, between 800 and 760, the local ironworking skills of the Etruscans improved as the number of chevron *skyphoi* brought in by the Euboeans increased— "a clear case of cause and effect."[33] In addition to the Euboean ware, there are many scarabs, seals, and other luxury goods of eastern provenance.[34] There is even an Etruscan warrior's burial at Cumae that is remarkably similar to the hero's tomb at the West Gate at Eretria (see chapter 6).[35] Trade in goods that are archaeologically invisible may have been

---

experts, many without citation (e.g., Rathje 1979, 179; Grant 1980, 44). Although it is not clear why this attribution is so certain—Fe_2O_3 is, after all, only one of the several principal ores of iron (Wertime 1980, 11–12)—the "certainty" of the Elba evidence is not important, because the fact remains that unless the Greeks brought the iron with them (see below, note 37), they must have gotten it from Etruscan-controlled mines.

31. Strabo 5.4.9.

32. Those who might consider such an arrangement preposterous might well compare the Dutch purchase of Manhattan Island for twenty-four dollars' worth of baubles; the arrangement that I propose finds a strong parallel in the trapping-post system in North America in the eighteenth and nineteenth centuries, whereby the Native Americans traded animal hides, taken on "their own" land and by their own labor, for worthless trinkets.

33. Ridgway 1973, 26; see further Ridgway 1992, 137–38; Snodgrass 1980b, 361–62. Alan Blakeway (1933, 1935) first pointed out that trade preceded settlement in the west, which supports the conjecture that the Greeks' purpose in being there was to move goods.

34. Buchner 1966, 12. Michael Grant (1980, 45) believes that "what tempted the Etruscan leaders to supply these Euboean visitors with iron or copper was, above all else, the prospect of gold in return." Fibulae found in the Warrior's Tomb at Tarquinii, which dates to before 700, are virtually identical to those found on Pithekoussai and dating to the mid-eighth century (Strøm 1971, 144).

35. First published by Giuseppe Pellegrini (1903). J. N. Coldstream surmises that the similarities may be attributed to the fact that the warrior was of mixed Euboean and Etruscan parentage (Coldstream 1994a, 54–55; see further Coldstream 1993 on some of the interesting consequences of mixed marriages on the frontier, among them facilitation of the spread of writing); Ingrid Strøm (1971, 147) concluded that he was an Etruscan leader, Giorgio Buchner (1979, 133) a Cumaean Greek. Coldstream's thesis is supported by the social mobility that

equally or more important. Wine, for example, transported in skins and so leaving no trace, was used later by Greeks to gain access to metalliferous areas in central Europe and may well have been an important factor in Euboean contact with the Etruscans.[36]

The Euboeans must have been substantially outnumbered; otherwise, it would seem, they would have seized access to the iron ore. But perhaps seeing the opportunity for cheap labor, they maintained the arrangement. The settlement, where at least some of the ore was processed,[37] was set up on Pithekoussai, at a distance for reasons of security: it was pointlessly dangerous to take up residence in a strange and potentially perilous place. Pithekoussai thrived until about 700, when it became overshadowed by Cumae on the mainland, which had been settled earlier[38] by the same Euboeans, who apparently came to feel more secure than they had initially. Tradition held that the founders of Cumae named their new settlement after Kyme, a

---

Jean-Paul Morel identifies in the Etruscan and Euboean settlements (Morel 1984, 144–50). Of course, this is not surprising when one considers the side-by-side work of Euboeans and Phoenicians both at Al Mina and at Pithekoussai; recall also the story of the political rise at Tarquinii in Etruria of the Corinthian Demaratus, who emigrated there in 657 and whose son Lucumo by the Etruscan Tanaquil became Lucius Tarquinius Priscus, fifth king at Rome (Livy 1.34–35.6; Polybius [6.11a.7] seems to be the earliest person to mention Demaratus).

36. Peter Wells (1980, 63–66, 95–97) argues that much evidence in central Europe reflects the acquisition from the Greeks of both wine and its context—drinking hall, goblets, etc. Emiline Richardson (1964, 38) had already suggested this for the Etruscan-Greek contact. Perhaps more important, but certainly more invisible, than the wine itself would have been the technology of viticulture that the Euboeans might have shared with the Etruscans. (Werner Keller [1974, 55–56] misinterprets the evidence of grape seeds in burials as meaning the Etruscans "introduced the grape to Italy and established it there.")

37. Snodgrass (1983b) argues sensibly that little of the iron moved by ship was already processed. But the remains from the workshops on Pithekoussai indicate activity too great to have been only for local use. Graham (1971, 44) incredibly suggests not only that the iron was worked on Pithekoussai for local consumption only; he further asserts that the Euboeans had plenty at home and, like other Greeks, had no need to travel to fetch it. This simply does not agree with the facts. There was iron across the Euripus (above, note 15), but not "at home." (Graham does not recognize the difference between local iron and iron from a distance.) S. C. Bakhuizen (1977/78) argues that at the center of the settlement at Pithekoussai were Chalcidian ironworkers who brought their expertise and their own Euboean iron ore to the island in order to create fine finished products for the Etruscans to the north. The question then arises, What did the ironworkers receive in return from the Etruscans?

38. "About 725" (Buchner 1966, 12); "a little before 725" (Boardman 1980, 168); "740" (Vallet 1958, 56); "within the bracket 760–730 B.C." (Coldstream 1977, 230); "by 760" (Richardson 1986, 215); "about the middle of the eighth century at the latest" (Bengtson 1988, 53); "between 750 and 725 BC" (Grant 1980, 45); "around 750" (Hurwit 1985, 80); "a date c. 740 B.C. is about the best conclusion that can be offered" (Frederiksen 1984, 62), with which Coldstream has recently concurred, adding "about a generation, that is, after the beginning of Pithekoussai" (Coldstream 1994a, 54).

town on the home island of Euboea.[39] Pithekoussai remained a player in the trade in the west well into the seventh century but was no longer a leader.[40]

Euboeans were present in Pithekoussai to acquire and refine iron ore. They were not there to grow food[41]—the volcanic land is good only for vines—nor were they there because the Lelantine Plain at home was already too small. The reason for the Euboean presence was economic,[42] and this is remarkable, for the settlement on Pithekoussai, the first *apoikia* (home away from home), with its partner Cumae, is an obvious paradigm for the colonization "movement" that followed (see below).

But what did the Euboeans do with the iron ore and iron? At the time of its foundation Pithekoussai was (and remained) the westernmost outpost in the Euboean, and later Corinthian, and more generally Greek, trading network, the eastern terminus being Al Mina. Identical Euboean *skyphoi* from the second half of the eighth century have been found at Pithekoussai and Al Mina.[43] Pithekoussai was not a port of trade; in spite of its mixed population of Greeks and non-Greeks, it was not a place to which goods were brought for transfer by different groups. It produced goods for transfer eastward and for consumption there. Much of the iron certainly went to Greece, where there may not have been much iron, and what iron there was, was already spoken for. A good deal may have reached Al Mina, not only both refined and unrefined iron[44] but also iron already worked into artistic items and articles of military equipment by the famed artisans of Chalcis and elsewhere.

39. The founders of Cumae were Hippocles of Kyme in Euboea and Megasthenes of Chalcis (Strabo 5.4.4). Bakhuizen (1985, 123) seriously questions whether Kyme on Euboea even has a claim to have ever existed. I am sympathetic, but what would people from Kyme in Aeolis be doing in Campania? It is possible that this very question generated a belief in the existence of Euboean Kyme.

40. Ridgway 1992, 40.

41. Cook 1962; Woodhead 1962, 33; Graham 1983, 219. Buchner (1979, 135–36) once and for all rejects the passage in Strabo (5.4.9) as evidence for agriculture as the raison d'être of the settlement at Pithekoussai. See further Ridgway 1973, 23. Evidence of farming recently uncovered in southwestern Pithekoussai—a farmstead found in 1992 (Fratta 1994)—does not contradict the obvious fact that a group of persons would not have settled on Pithekoussai with any expectation of agricultural self-sufficiency.

42. Pithekoussai and Cumae "were not, geographically speaking, either the nearest or the most obvious places to choose, unless access to Italian metal deposits was one aim, if not the only one" (Finley 1979a, 17).

43. Braun 1982, 9.

44. Snodgrass (1983b, 23) suggests (see above, note 37) that in fact a large portion of this Etruscan iron traveled from Pithekoussai in its unrefined state. That may be so, but the presence of iron ingots in the hulls of archaic ships suggests the refining of iron into "blooms" and the trading of them.

We can surmise that the luxury goods found in Etruria, Pithekoussai, and Cumae were products of the places to which the iron was moved. There were bronze cauldrons from northern Syria in Cumae[45] and Etruria[46] and numerous Rhodian globular *aryballoi,* made from about 725 on, in Pithekoussai and Etruria.[47] Similar cauldrons and the Rhodian ware are found also in mainland Greece and northern Syria and on Crete.[48] As of 1968, eighty-seven seals of northern Syrian provenance had been found on Pithekoussai, and five in Etruria;[49] one from Pithekoussai and one from Falerii Veteres in Etruria are virtually identical.[50] The initial growth of the trade network is well attested by the presence of oriental trinkets in Euboea and at Athens in the ninth century[51] and then on Pithekoussai in the eighth.[52] Pots made in northern Syria in the late eighth century have been found on Pithekoussai; pots found at Al Mina may have been manufactured on Pithekoussai.[53] Very similar flasks have been found in a Phoenician context on Rhodes and Pithekoussai.[54]

Pithekoussai and Cumae clearly focused primarily on acquiring iron ore and probably other minerals, but it appears that, in addition, by the middle of the eighth century there was an elaborate and large-scale system for the

45. Amandry 1956, 242–43.

46. Herrmann 1966, 145.

47. Ridgway 1973, 15.

48. Cauldrons: Boardman 1980, 65–66; ubiquity of Rhodian ware: Coldstream 1968, 276. The presence of Rhodian ware in northern Syria (Saltz 1978, 51; Ahlström 1993, 692 n. 5) is likely the result of Phoenician rather than Euboean activity (Coldstream 1977, 299).

49. Ridgway 1973, 15–16.

50. Buchner and Boardman 1966. Compare no. 43 from Falerii Veteres (fig. 30, p. 24) and no. 5 from Pithekoussai (fig. 1, p. 2). They are set side by side in Ridgway 1973, fig. 3, p. 15; 1992, fig. 38, p. 136.

51. Coldstream 1977, 41–42, 64–65; 1982, 264–65; for Athens see faïence beads described by Evelyn Lord Smithson (1968, 114–15) as "from Syria"; for Lefkandi see R. A. Higgins in Popham, Sackett, and Themelis 1980, 222–23, pl. 234d, e, f (beads similar to Smithson's); 224, pl. 233d, e (necklaces and pendants). It may well be that these finds are less indicative of a network coming into shape than of the presence of Phoenicians in the Aegean (Coldstream 1969, 1982), but of course it adds up to the same thing, for soon the Greeks and the Phoenicians would be partners in the network. Hans Georg Niemeyer offers a convenient distribution map of "orientalische Funde" in the Aegean between 1000 and 600 (Niemeyer 1984, 63, fig. 57).

52. Coldstream 1977, 228–30.

53. Buchner 1982.

54. Grave 56 at Ialysus on Rhodes contains two flasks nearly identical to one found in a burial at Pithekoussai. Just how sophisticated the Phoenician economic arrangements with the local Greeks on Rhodes were is the subject of a study by Donald Jones, who ingeniously argues that the flasks, which held perfumes, were made locally, while the perfume was made in Tyre and shipped in bulk to the "bottler" (Jones 1993).

movement of goods from Pithekoussai to Al Mina and back again, with numerous stops along the way. One of the stops on the way was Emporio on the Aegean island of Chios. Chios, which had enjoyed continuous settlement from Mycenaean times, underwent significant growth in the eighth century.[55] The earliest pottery found at Emporio is a pendent-semicircle *skyphos*,[56] which agrees exactly with Ion's ancient tale of Chios's settlement by Euboeans.[57] It is rather obvious that Emporio developed as part of the network. Compare also the pattern of evidence on the island of Samos, Chios's great rival: before the second half of the eighth century Samos's contact with the outside world was restricted to its Ionian neighbors; but, with the development of the trade network, we find on Samos for the first time numerous items from the Argolid, Attica, and Euboea.[58]

With every archaeological report, it is becoming clearer that none of this activity on the part of the Greeks was undertaken without the help of the Phoenicians, who had been working almost the same routes for 200 years before the Greeks got involved.[59] Still, if the Greeks had not been involved, this trading activity would not have had the enormous impact on community organization in Old Greece that it did (see chapter 5).

For now let us consider how Pithekoussai and Al Mina compare with each other. The two had much in common, but Pithekoussai differed in that it was a colony, according to René Maunier's definition: emigration with government—that is, occupation with legislation.[60] The Greeks at Pithekoussai, numbering probably in the thousands,[61] organized themselves in ways rem-

---

55. Boardman 1967, 250.

56. Boardman 1967, 117, no. 157, pl. 30.

57. Paus. 7.4.9–10; see further Wade-Gery 1952, 6–8, 66–67.

58. Shipley 1987, 42.

59. Sherratt and Sherratt 1992/93, 364–66, figs. 1a, b, c, and d on pp. 372–73 (maps of trade routes from the tenth to the sixth century). See also Niemeyer 1990; Negbi 1992. The subtlety of the Phoenician interaction with the Greeks is discussed by Günter Kopcke (1992).

60. Maunier 1949, 7. His categories of "skeleton" and "habitable" colonies are not particularly useful for the Greek activity.

61. Six thousand is my own high-end estimate. If the percentage of eighth-century burials remains consistent (only 5 percent of the cemetery has been excavated), there may be as many as 17,000 burials for the period 750–700 (Coldstream 1994a, 51–52), which would imply an even larger population. Ian Morris suggests a population between 4,000 and 5,000 at Pithekoussai about 700 (Morris 1987, 166). Ridgway is more wary and seems to suggest (without actually doing so) a population for the latter half of the eighth century of about 1,500 (1992b, 103). It is extremely difficult to estimate the population, more difficult even than making an estimate for Old Greece, because the simple application of a formula such as Morris's (1987, 74; see chapter 2 above and appendices there) must be modified by the concession that literally countless participants in the venture at Pithekoussai went home to Old Greece and Phoenicia before they died. In fact, the bodies that weren't buried in Pithekoussai may be inflating our notion of population pressure in various places in Old Greece.

iniscent of communities in Old Greece; the Greeks at Al Mina, far fewer, did not. Phoenicians made up perhaps 15 percent of the population at Pithekoussai[62] and were busy especially in the last third of the eighth century,[63] but also earlier, establishing and maintaining ports of trade and processing centers in Iberia (e.g., Toscanos) and northwest Africa (Lixus), but not colonies (Carthage excepted).[64] At these western ports of trade and processing centers the Phoenicians were working alone, without partners.[65] Generally speaking, the Greeks never went farther west than the Tyrrhenian Sea (until the Phocaeans settled at Massilia [Marseilles] in about 600); the MG II Attic krater (800–760 B.C.) found at Huelva in Iberia must have been taken there by Phoenicians, who also must be responsible for bringing other Greek goods and Cypriot goods to Iberia beyond the Pillars of Heracles in the eighth and early seventh centuries.[66] It is perfectly likely that Phoenician activity in the western Mediterranean intersected with and even to some extent depended on Pithekoussai on a regular basis.[67] In conclusion, we can observe that, beginning with Pithekoussai, the Greeks colonized; they strove to establish communities designed to process and add value to goods and to serve the interests of certain persons in both colony and mother-city.

What, Who, and How: The Evidence in Homer

Nothing in the Homeric poems contradicts the archaeological record. In fact, some of the evidence in Homer is instructive about what goods were being moved, by whom, and how.

There is just one description of a market in the epics, one that I will categorize below as a one-time market. During a break in the siege of Troy, the Greeks turn their attention from the battle to the sea:

> Many ships from Lemnos were at hand carrying wine, ships that Jason's son Euneos had sent out; Hypsipyle had borne Euneos to Jason, shepherd of the

62. This is the estimate of Ridgway (1992b, 120).

63. On the dating of the Phoenician colonies, see Niemeyer 1990, 480. Often the Phoenician activity is pushed back farther than the evidence would suggest.

64. See Whittaker 1974; Aubet 1993. By almost any definition of "colony," Carthage qualifies. It was organized very much like a Greek colony. The traditional foundation date (814) is proving difficult to support archaeologically.

65. Niemeyer 1990, 485–86.

66. Shefton 1982, 338–43, including the distribution map on page 340; Karageorghis 1995, 95.

67. Eighth-century Euboean and Corinthian pottery found at Carthage may have been manufactured on Pithekoussai, according to Maria Aubet (1993, 196), who also surmises that the gold and silver that Phoenicians were moving from Huelva and Gadir in southern Spain to Tyre and Old Greece were being processed by specialists at Pithekoussai on their way east (Aubet 1993, 240).

people. And only to the Atreidai, Agamemnon and Menelaus, had Jason's son given wine to carry off, one thousand measures. From this source the flowing-haired Achaeans *got wine, some by* [exchanging] *bronze, some by shining iron, some by hides, some by whole oxen, some by slaves.* And they had themselves a festive feast (*dais*).[68]

Here wine is exchanged for metals, hides, livestock, and slaves. Mentes the Taphian, we noted above, moves copper (bronze) and iron.[69] Other Taphians deal in slaves.[70] Phoenicians move jewelry as well as cattle and sheep, wine, grain, and slaves.[71] Some of the goods moved to one-time markets are clearly staples and slaves. The important role that these "invisible" goods play in the epics helps us to visualize the Euboean-Etruscan relationship. There is nothing in the epics that contradicts the archaeological evidence for the movements of metals.

Who among the Greeks moved these goods has recently been debated. The *Odyssey* implies that the nobility looked down on such activity, leaving it to "foreigners"—hence the taunting remark of the Phaeacian Euryalus to Odysseus that he resembles less a noble athlete than the "captain of sailors who are traders."[72] I do not think this tells us very much, for two reasons. First, the strategy of epic distancing may be in play here.[73] Second, there is the important matter of appearances: if it is the case, as I shall argue later, that goods from abroad contributed to the development of private property and of debt-driven land transfers and that the epics are part of a concerted effort to distract the *demos* from perceiving this, it is not surprising to see this apparent separation of agent from action.

To judge from the activities of Odysseus and his men (not to mention the Taphians), it would appear that people went to sea in their eikosors (twenty-oared ships, with a single bank of oars) and pentekontors (fifty-oared ships, perhaps double-banked) to acquire goods by several methods. There may have been special-purpose ships in the eighth century—Homer calls one a *phortis*, which modern commentators usually translate as "broad-beamed merchantman"[74]—but all were oar-driven variations on these two types, and

---

68. *Il.* 7.473–75. There is a subtle reference to a market also at *Il.* 23.743–45, where the Phoenicians give Thoas (Euneos's grandfather) a gift, apparently in order to have access to trade with the Lemnian population. See chapter 5.

69. *Od.* 1.182–84.

70. *Od.* 14.452, 15.427.

71. The Phoenicians took away *biotos* (*Od.* 15.446, 456) from Eumaeus's island home of Syria, known for its cattle, sheep, wine, and grain. They left jewelry (*Od.* 15.460) but took with them the young Eumaeus, who was stolen by Taphians and sold to Laertes, Odysseus's father.

72. *Od.* 8.162.

73. See chapter 1.

74. There are two references to a *phortis* in Homer (*Od.* 5.249, 9.322), rowed by twenty men; the eikosor appears in apposition to the *phortis* in *Odyssey* 9.

it appears that the pentekontors probably did most of the moving.[75] Piracy was in fact the primary intention of such forays from home. This is clear from Odysseus's activities and from the several references to piracy in the *Odyssey*.[76] In addition to his general ravaging of the area around Troy, Achilles also went to sea to practice piracy.[77] In situations of relatively equal strength, parties exchanged goods in a one-time scenario. Parties known to one another maintained their relations by exchange of gifts; payment might be made for safe mooring. There must have been a fine line between piracy and the acquisition of goods by other means.[78] Of course, Phoenicians were present in the Aegean in the ninth and eighth centuries; so it would be easy for Homer to attribute (practically) all trading—and much piracy as well—to the Phoenicians.[79]

Finally, ports of trade are not absent in the epics. Evidently there are specific places where slaves were brought and then sold (ransomed), Euneos's Lemnos among them.[80] Homeric references to weights, such as the talent (*talanton*) and the half-talent (*hemitalanton*), and the bundled spits in eighth- and seventh-century burials, also suggest the kind of equivalencies one would expect to be in use in an emporium.[81] More on these later.

75. For the full range of ships available for use in the eighth century, see Casson 1971, 43–60; Wallinga 1993, 33–64: all are variations on the two types, single- and double-banked, although there is no certainty that the double-banked version goes back as far as the eighth century. H. T. Wallinga (1993, chap. 3, esp. 64–65) argues aggressively in favor of there being two-banked (*dikrotos*) galleys; but he is in the minority (see, for example, Morrison 1994, 206–7). Regardless of where one stands on the *dikrotos*, necessarily most of the carrying must have been done by pentekontor, a ship rowed by fifty men. Here is some unintentional reportage by Homer: Odysseus's ship that went to visit the Cyclops appears to have had a crew of fifty plus two officers, for when subsequently Odysseus splits his crew in half to investigate Circe's domain, twenty-two men accompany Eurylochus (10.203–8); the Cyclops, Homer tells us, ate six of his men (9.289, 311, 344). QED: Odysseus's ship had a crew of fifty.

76. Strangers are asked whether they are pirates as a matter of course at *Od.* 3.73, 9.254. Among other references to piracy: 1.398, 14.86, 23.357.

77. *Od.* 3.106.

78. "Little but an ideological hairline divided the noble who voyaged in order to come home loaded with valuable gifts (*Odyssey* 3.301–302, 4.80–92, 19.282 ff.) or to exchange iron for copper (*ibid.*, 1.182 ff.) from the 'commander of sailors out for gain (*nautai prekteres*), always thinking about his cargo' (*ibid.*, 8.159 ff.)" (Humphreys 1978, 167). Morris (1986a, 6) insists that "after 700 B.C., in spite of the increasing volume of commodity trade which was probably taking place, the *ideal* still remained personalised gift exchange" (italics original).

79. On the depiction of Phoenicians in Homer see Winter 1995.

80. Lemnos: *Il.* 21.40, 23.747. Also Samothrace and Imbros: *Il.* 24.753.

81. Terms like *tessaraboios*, "worth 4 oxen," *enneaboios*, "worth 9 oxen," and so on (12, 20, 100: see references in Knorringa 1926, 4) indicate that cattle were a measurement of worth or a standard of value, not to be confused with a medium of exchange. (Nor is there any reason to believe they were a unit of account.) See further Donlan 1981, esp. 104–5.

There does not seem to be a lot of use in trying to determine, with Benedetto Bravo, for example, whether *aristoi* actually undertook or only underwrote such expeditions; in the latter scenario the activity would be carried out by agents who were or were not dispossessed *aristoi.*[82] As S. C. Humphreys has remarked, "It was the aristocracy, in the first place, who wanted gold and ivory from Egypt, bronze from Etruria, Phoenician textiles, and slaves from Sicily and the Black Sea."[83] We are concerned here not with agents but with beneficiaries.

The distinction drawn by Alfonso Mele between *prexis* commerce and *ergon* commerce is worth mentioning here. *Prexis* commerce as practiced by the nobility was a full-time process of moving (mostly) luxury goods in the fashion discussed above. *Ergon* commerce involved the movement of (mostly) subsistence goods that were the product of one's own *erga* ("labor"). *Ergon* commerce was only one activity among many in which an *ergon* trader engaged.[84] We shall see that Hesiod practiced this type of trade.

The "movement" to colonize appears to be a combination of *prexis* and *ergon* commerces. Set up to exploit the mineral wealth of the west, the colonies, in the process, generated agricultural products for export to Old Greece and other points on the trade routes that stretched from Pithe-koussai to Al Mina. Thus the colonies, in addition to performing the primary and original functions suggested below, are self-sufficient cogs in a larger machine. Begun as exploitative outposts for *prexis* commerce, they became important players in *ergon* commerce.

EARLY COLONIZATION

"Colony" is the term I will employ in discussing Greek activity in the west. There are at least two reasons, however, why "expansion" may be a better term. First, increasing population density generated more people, so that colonization, if not caused by increasing population, at least accommodated it. Second, colonizing activities were, in some cases, expansions of labor bases and capital bases. "Colony," however, is the word students of these western settlements use, and it is too late to change the terminology.[85]

We are interested here in the origins of the eighth-century colonies, not their later development, and we will begin by examining two tidy theories of the cause of the colonizing "movement."[86] The first argues that the

82. Bravo 1974, 1977.
83. Humphreys 1978, 167.
84. Mele 1979.
85. As Moses Finley (1976) makes very clear.
86. This is not to imply that all scholars subscribe to one or the other position. Often, discussion of the motivation of the colonizing "movement" is simply avoided. Here are two good

Greeks on the mainland ran short of land and turned to emigration as a solution.[87] Land-poor individuals and families were forced to the west to seek new lives. Each participant received by lot a holding, or *kleros,* without encumbrances in the new settlement and was thus self-sufficient and an active member in a new social organization. This theory, in its various articulations, emphasizes that the choice of site was based on the quality and quantity of the new land and not on the quality of the harbor there or the quantity of mineral or other nonagricultural resources.

The second theory argues that all western colonies were founded with an eye toward either trading with the local populations and participating in the newly created Euboean trade network or establishing markets for their goods.[88] This theory, then, would define the colonists who received and then worked their *kleroi* as essentially entrepreneurial. Something between these two positions is probably the case. A list of the eighth-century western colonies with their traditional dates of settlement and their founders is provided in table 12 (see also map 2).

The Euboean Settlements

I have already discussed Pithekoussai and Cumae, but I should note here that some believe that agriculture was the main interest on Pithekoussai[89] and therefore also at Cumae,[90] and others argue that Pithekoussai's focus was the movement of iron, while Cumae's was agricultural.[91] As I have already observed above, the Euboeans on Pithekoussai may have become less anxious about their relations with the Etruscans and Campanians, and so moved to the mainland to take advantage of better agricultural land. Consider what the later settlements can tell us. Naxos is located on the east coast of Sicily, at the first landfall after passing the toe of Italy. There is no agreement about why the Chalcidians chose the site. Naxos has a decent harbor but little land, and that good only for viticulture, although presumably the native population already there thought it was all right to live

---

examples of avoidance: "The primary purpose of this colonization is clear—to get away from Greece" (Hopper 1979, 27); "Just as mixed were the motives for going; compulsion, desperation, ambition; to farm, to trade, to take a chance" (Forrest 1986, 23). These advance our understanding not at all.

87. Gwynn 1918.

88. So Dunbabin 1948, 8–18, following Blakeway 1933, 1935. A. G. Woodhead (1962, 33) very strongly disagrees, but Carl Roebuck (1962, 101) is clear on this: "The security offered by Ischia would have been advantageous both to an agricultural settlement and to a trading post, but it scarcely seems necessary to sail from Chalkis to the Bay of Naples to find a safe and reasonably fertile island for a small colony of farmers, who would not have known the route."

89. Cook 1962, 114.

90. Woodhead 1962, 33.

91. Vallet 1958, 57–58.

TABLE 12   Greek Colonies in the West

Settlement	Date	Founder
Pithekoussai		Chalcis and Eretria
Cumae		Chalcis and Eretria (and Pithekoussai)
Naxos	734	Chalcis
Leontini	729	Chalcidians from Naxos
Catane	729	Chalcidians from Naxos
Zancle	bef. 716[a]	Cumae and Chalcis
Mylae	716[b]	Chalcidians from Zancle
Rhegium	not before 716	Chalcidians from Zancle and Messenians
Syracuse	733	Corinth
Megara Hyblaea	728	Megara
Taras (Tarentum)	706	Sparta
Sybaris	c.720	Achaea
Croton	709	Achaea
Metapontum	773[c]	Achaea

SOURCE: Dates are the traditional dates presented in Graham 1982, 160–62. For a discussion of the validity of the dates, see Compernolle 1960, 410–19; also Gomme, Andrewes, and Dover 1970, 204. Graham provides what must be a controversial list of dates of the earliest evidence of settlement of each colony (pp. 160–62).

[a]Dates for Zancle and Rhegium, not attested in antiquity, have been determined relative to the foundation of Mylae.

[b]"Difficilmente potrebbero scendere all'ultimo quindicennio dell' VIII sec. a.C." (Bernabò-Brea and Cavalier 1959, 117); Whitehouse and Wilkins acknowledge eighth-century materials there, but "the city on the sea shore was not established before about 650 BC" (Whitehouse and Wilkins 1989, 106).

[c]This is Eusebius's impossibly early date; about 700 is more like it.

there.[92] Leontini, about 65 kilometers south and inland on a rich plain of bottomland, appears to have been founded by Naxians as an agricultural community (natives were displaced here too).[93] Catane, midway between Naxos and Leontini, sits on the northern edge of the Laestrygonian Plain. Thus perhaps Catane was also set up for agriculture,[94] but Catane has an excellent harbor and could as well have been founded by Naxians who sought additional, and even easier, access to the sea. These settlements may seem a mysterious trio, but it may be surmised that Naxos, located at that first landfall, was founded specifically for the purpose of founding the other two sites, as soon as they could be located. Then it would follow that Leontini developed as a breadbasket and Catane as a regional clearinghouse for

92. Boardman 1980, 169 with n. 29.
93. Thuc. 6.3.3; Boardman 1980, 169–70; Malkin 1987, 176 with n. 175.
94. So Dunbabin 1948, 10.

local goods and agricultural production. The problem with this explanation is that the distance from Naxos to Leontini is about 65 kilometers, and oxen—no horses were used for hauling—travel at best just over 3 kilometers per hour. All we may be sure of is that Leontini and Catane are definitely secondary settlements and that Naxos is without question situated on the route connecting Etruria with Greece and points east.

Zancle (later called Messene) was clearly founded as early as the 720s[95] in order to protect the Straits of Messina, the passage between Sicily and Italy that provided access to and from Pithekoussai and Cumae. Mylae is located on the north coast of the island and may have been founded to help feed Zancle.[96] More likely it was settled to keep an eye out for unwelcome parties who had sailed around Sicily the long way, or to offer refuge to southbound Euboean vessels when the straits were too choppy to navigate. Rhegium on the facing Italian coast was founded for the same reason as Zancle: defense of the straits.

We see, then, a pattern. Pithekoussai, a settlement dedicated to acquiring (and later processing) metals, expands to Cumae. Naxos, a foothold on the nearest point of Sicily, expands to Leontini and Catane. The foundation of Zancle marks the beginning of control of the Straits of Messina, Rhegium its completion, and Mylae is a supplement or an expansion of Zancle. Thus between 750 (probably the earliest date for Cumae) and about 715 (the founding of Rhegium)—a single (long) human generation, a mere thirty-five years—we witness a concerted Euboean effort to control the routes to the west and to safeguard their enterprise at the Bay of Naples.[97] Finally, it is clear that the beginnings of Euboean activity in the west are based on the movement of goods rather than on the production of food for local consumption.

The Dorian Settlements

The evidence in the Dorian settlements is less conclusive. Syracuse was founded by Corinth in the same period that Corinth began to participate in Mediterranean trade. Corinthian materials begin appearing at Al Mina in the late eighth century, and the high quality of the harbor at Syracuse certainly suggests an interest in bringing goods in and shipping goods out. In

95. Coldstream 1977, 231; Thucydides gives the unlikely story of an initial foundation by pirates from Cumae (6.4.5).

96. Dunbabin 1948, 12.

97. Molly Miller argues for an organizational scheme involving all these Euboean settlements, within which Pithekoussai and Cumae focused on the acquisition of metals, Zancle and Rhegium on communications, and the other Sicilian settlements on agriculture (Miller 1970, 239–40). This very attractive scheme is probably too elaborate in its specifics to be sustained by the evidence.

fact, trade with the native population, the Sicels, preceded the foundation of Syracuse,[98] and the first Greeks who lived there displaced a native population.[99] The good agricultural land may be coincidental or just wise: it was intended that Syracuse be a permanent settlement. Two facts argue against agricultural motives for the foundation. First, on the way to found Syracuse, the Corinthians stopped at Corcyra and evicted the resident Euboeans, who had settled the island and had been using it as a stopping place on their journeys from east to west since perhaps 760.[100] The Corinthians' stopover at Corcyra seems to indicate their concern about Euboean activity between Old Greece and Italy and their desire to get control of the seaways used by the Euboeans.[101] Given this special stop-and-evict operation, it would appear probable that Corinth sent colonists to Syracuse with trade in mind. Second, although some have interpreted the Corinthian move as a response to an increase in population at home, the archaeological record indicates that though there had been some changes in burial behaviors (as we saw in chapter 2), there was no significant population problem at home.[102]

Megara Hyblaea is quite a mystery. Founded by Megarians, the settlement sits on a small area of flatland about 20 kilometers north of Syracuse. There is decent anchorage nearby, and there was no need to displace a native community, but the site is clearly inferior to that of Syracuse.[103] The archaeological record suggests earlier settlement,[104] but a date after the foundation of Syracuse would explain the inferior site. In addition, the proximity of the excellent harbor at Syracuse and reports of difficulties surrounding the foundation—Thucydides tells us that Megara Hyblaea was the settling group's third stop[105]—support the later date. But whatever the date, nothing at the site suggests that agriculture, rather than trade, was the reason for its choice. The settlement appears carefully planned from the start: a large enclosed precinct, with perhaps a cult shrine within it, opens onto

98. Dunbabin 1948, 13 n. 5.

99. Holloway 1984, 269.

100. For the Euboean presence before eviction see Calligas 1982.

101. Strabo (6.2.4; cf. Plut. *Quaest. Graec.* 11, 293a-b) is our witness. Whether one places the takeover of Corcyra in 733, on the way to Syracuse, or in 706, which is the date given by Eusebius, in either case the takeover smacks of eagerness to control the sea lanes.

102. Roebuck considers the settlement at Syracuse to have been undertaken "to ease overpopulation in the Corinthia" (Roebuck 1972, 112; cf. Will 1955, 319–21). Dunbabin (1948, 15) concedes that "population pressure at home may have been one purpose. But the main object of the rulers of Corinth can hardly have been other than to form a trading colony."

103. But it seems unlikely that therefore we can conclude that "the Greeks occupied vacant land (offered them by a local chief)" (Holloway 1984, 269).

104. Coldstream 1968, 324–25. Georges Vallet and François Villard (1952, 322–25) would push the date of Megara back to 750, Naxos as far back as 757. Cf. Vallet 1958, 56.

105. Thuc. 6.4.1.

the agora,[106] and different sections of the city are devoted to different activities.[107] We might suspect from this that the settlement was nonagricultural. I am not willing to make a certain conclusion, however, for the flatland is too small for much agriculture,[108] and the anchorage too small for much trade.[109]

Spartan Taras, situated on the best harbor in southern Italy and abutting fine agricultural land, is a similar case. It looks to be a likely inroad on the fading Euboean monopoly. Strabo's tale that Taras was founded by the Partheniai, bastards born during the long campaign of the First Messenian War and later denied rights of citizenship by the returning warriors,[110] explains only that an explanation was deemed necessary, and the name of the disenfranchised group—Partheniai means "men born of virgins"— would seem to have begged the specific explanation that Strabo offers. There are several reasons why Sparta would *not* be expected to participate in the colonizing "movement." (In fact, this was Sparta's only attempt.) First, after the First Messenian War, Sparta controlled both Laconia and Messenia, thus having access to some of the finest agricultural land in the Peloponnesus. There was no shortage of food or land (or labor). Second, the Spartans historically eschewed foreign trade, preferring their unique brand of self-sufficiency. It is worth mentioning here the detail in Strabo that the departing Partheniai were promised land in Messenia if the colony failed. This, and the fact that the settlers brought with them the worship of Apollo Hyakinthios, suggests that the Partheniai were in fact disenfranchised "nobles" from Amyklai, near Sparta.[111] As we will see, the disenfranchisement (through involuntary land transfer?) would support the general proposition that many of the colonies were led by land-poor entrepreneurs.

---

106. The cult building (house 23.5) is divided into three rooms and measures 9.8 by 7 meters; see Vallet, Villard, and Auberson 1976, 272–74, with drawing on p. 274.

107. Owens 1991, 38; for the layout of the settlement see Vallet 1973, 85, fig. 2; Malkin 1987, 165, fig. 2; Holloway 1991, 49–51 with fig. 60. The layout dates from the original settlement (Vallet, Villard, and Auberson 1976, 407).

108. "Environmental conditions necessary for agricultural success were not lacking in Megara Hyblaia's territory" (De Angelis 1994, 95), but that success was unlikely to produce a great quantity.

109. Roebuck (1972, 108) and Ronald P. Legon (1981, 70) suggest that the shrinking of Megarian territory along with the arrival of refugees expelled from the Perachora by the Corinthians would be explanation enough for Megara Hyblaea. But this does not help us perceive the settlers' intentions.

110. Strabo 6.3.2. Strabo also mentions that Taras was the second attempt to settle the area, the first being Satyrion (now located: see in general Whitehouse and Wilkins 1989, 105).

111. G. L. Huxley (1962, 37) and Paul Cartledge (1979, 124) connect the Partheniai with Amyklai; A. H. M. Jones (1967, 12) and Cartledge (1979, 123) connect the foundation at Taras with social or economic discontent or unrest at home.

The Achaean Settlements

The Achaean foundations in the instep of Italy complete the picture of eighth-century activity in this part of the west. Sybaris is characterized by a rich plain but also by convenient access to overland routes to the Italian west coast; Croton has decent farmland but is more clearly situated where it is because of the fine double harbor; Metapontum, essentially harborless, was connected to Posidonia on the west coast by an overland route. Posidonia represents an early challenge by Sybaris to Euboean control of the area and to the Euboean monopoly on exchange with the Etruscans.[112]

Homer on Colonization

Homer reveals no specific knowledge of the colonization movement; this omission may be explained by the poet's strategy of distancing his epic material. But Homer seems to betray familiarity with the phenomenon when he describes the settling of the island of Scheria. The Phaeacians emigrated from the land of the Cyclopes, and their leader settled them in Scheria, "far from bread-eating men":

> He drew up a wall around the polis and had houses built, and he constructed temples of the gods, and he divided up the plowlands,[113]

presumably into *kleroi*. It is perhaps similarly revealing that in the opinion of Alcinous, the *basileus* of the Phaeacians, the land farthest from Scheria is Euboea.[114]

Snodgrass recently observed a fundamental and important difference between the nature and pattern of eighth-century, western settlements and the nature and pattern of seventh-century, northern settlements (which may in fact go back to the ninth century). The latter were closer to home, of course. But more important for our inquiry, they were crowded up against one another, one after the other; furthermore, there are indications of greater care in the laying out of settlements in the north, greater care than in the west.[115] These two differences, I would suggest, can be explained at least partly as follows: the northern settlements were designed from the

112.   Boardman 1980, 178–80; Graham 1982, 109–10.
113.   *Od.* 6.9–10.
114.   *Od.* 7.321–22.
115.   Snodgrass 1994a, 92–93; 1994b, 6–9.

start to be poleis, not outposts, and there was no reason for strategic spacing of settlements in the north (except perhaps that being close together, the northern settlements might better fend off the local populations, which were more aggressive than in the west). So the differences between western and northern settlement patterns seem to support my assertion that the western settlements were in their foundations commercial first, and residential ("political") second.

Certainly, the distance of the western settlements from Old Greece suggests a trade interest rather than an interest in land use.[116] There is, however, a possible land-related explanation that is closely related to the presence of the Euboean trading enterprise; it has to do with the divisions of holdings through inheritance (see chapter 5). If population increased in Corinthia and Laconia in the eighth century, land would have become less abundant, and through their division the larger parcels would have been available to a smaller percentage of the population. This has little if anything to do with production sufficient to feed the community; rather, it is a matter of dividing up land and making reasonably sized parcels available to all. An evicted individual or group has only two options: remain evicted and move from the center to an inferior parcel or leave.

Since their activities precede any observed population increase, the leaders of the Euboean settlements may be presumed to have been unevicted entrepreneurs engaging in risky ventures. In the Dorian settlements, which began much later, the leadership was either similarly constituted or was held by evicted nobles in search of a livelihood. The persons who followed the leaders were evicted free persons in search of a new start, eager only "to reproduce . . . pre-existing [economic] conditions."[117] (In fact, migrants in general can expect to have their social and economic roles reduced when participating in a new settlement,[118] and, to judge from Herodotus, there were times when migrants were unwilling participants.)[119] The *oikist* of Syracuse, Archias the Bacchiad, would fit either leadership category. In both cases, the absence of a livelihood or the possibility for its increase was the *cause* of the colony.

---

116. So Andrewes in Burn 1960, 127; this is further supported by Karl Polanyi's paradigm for long-distance trade; see Polanyi 1975; Renfrew 1975; Dalton 1975.

117. Whittaker 1974, 75.

118. Eisenstadt 1954, 5–6.

119. According to Herodotus (4.153), certain emigrants from Thera in the seventh century were not necessarily willing settlers of Cyrene, for the colonizers were chosen by lot from each of the seven villages on Thera. In support of the authenticity of a fourth-century inscription (Meiggs and Lewis 1988, no. 5.23–51 [pp. 5–9]; translated in Graham 1983, 225–26) that backs up Herodotus's story, see Graham 1960 and Jeffery 1961b. Of course, supporting Herodotus's story is not the same as supporting its accuracy (Dougherty 1993).

This situation can come about when markets become overly obtrusive, when market forces interfere with everyday life; what results is the designation of certain goods as no longer obligated to the community. The social parallel is the beginning of differential access to basic resources.[120] The obtrusion of markets in Old Greece and the havoc the newly dominant economic institution wreaked will be taken up next.

120. This term is borrowed from Morton Fried (1967, 235) and discussed fully in the next chapter.

FOUR

Structure and Change in Dark Age Greece from the Fall of Mycenae through the Homeric Epics

Il y a fonctions mentales, comme celles du droit et de l'économie, dont pour un peu on oublierait qu'elles en sont: c'est qu'elles s'accomplissent dans nos sociétés suivant un mécanisme dont l'homme lui-même paraîtrait absent.
LOUIS GERNET, "LA NOTION MYTHIQUE DE LA VALEUR EN GRÈCE"

Increases in population density at home and in entrepreneurial activities abroad contributed to monumental change in the Greek communities. Dominant economic institutions were transformed as the polis came into existence. To chart the evolution of economic and social institutions, I shall draw heavily from the rich comparative materials that are available in the ethnographical records of recent societies, to flesh out the archaeological and poetic testimony of eighth-century Greece.

WAYS OF VIEWING THE ANCIENT ECONOMY

Before proceeding, let us consider different ways of approaching the ancient economy. Two extreme approaches are encapsulated in the late nineteenth-century brouhaha known today as the Bücher-Meyer controversy, named for its principals, Karl Bücher and Edouard Meyer.[1] Bücher and the followers of his *oikos*-theory were among the first "primitivists"; Meyer was the leading "modernizer," who observed, for example, that the seventh and sixth centuries B.C. in Greece correspond very closely to the fourteenth and fifteenth centuries A.D. in Europe, which ushered in the modern world of the fifteenth and sixteenth centuries, just as the seventh and sixth centuries brought in the classical period.[2] Although I should point out that Moses Finley himself warned against too great a dependence on anthropological

---

1. The most important published pieces by the principals have been collected by Moses Finley (1979b), who himself has discussed the controversy often (see esp. 1976/77; 1980, 42–49).

2. Meyer 1895, 118–19. This general statement of course grows out of certain misconceptions or misassumptions about preindustrial and especially ancient economies.

parallels, I and many other students of early Greece subscribe to Bücher's position. We do so because of the heuristic value of the anthropological literature that has appeared in the twentieth century and continues to appear. Paul Cartledge's restatement of the two positions is welcome because he shows clearly that the burden resides squarely on the shoulders of the "modernizers" to show that Greek society was *not* primitive.[3]

It is also the case that this axis of inquiry, the debate between primitivism and modernism, is arguably of limited usefulness, for the divergence between the two sides may in fact be better recognized as the divergence between economistic approaches to antiquity and sociological ones.[4] I am prone, as will soon be clear, to the sociological approach. What may appear to some as a sharp focus on production and distribution, on economic motives and actions, is in fact a broad view of society at large, as I hope to demonstrate.

The economist Karl Polanyi argued that economies are almost always "embedded" in noneconomic social institutions and are thereby inextricably bound up in tightly woven fabrics of socially prescribed activities.[5] He warned us against attributing to premodern societies the market mentality of the nineteenth century, emphasizing that we must rid ourselves of Adam Smith's proposition that man has an innate "propensity to truck, barter and exchange one thing for another."[6] Furthermore, an economy's "embeddedness" requires that we avoid attempts to separate economy from society,[7] especially when we are addressing societies that had no concept of "economy" separate from their other, "noneconomic" activities.[8] Thus, as Michel

3. Cartledge 1983. Max Weber's solution, as it were, to this conflict was to focus on institutions. For a fuller discussion of the debate concerning the ancient Greek economy, including the Bücher-Meyer controversy, see Will 1954; Pearson 1957b; Austin and Vidal-Naquet 1977, 3–8, and notes on pp. 28–30.

4. Tandy and Neale 1994, 24.

5. Polanyi 1944, 43–55; 1947; 1953; 1957a, 67–78; 1977, 47–56. Polanyi originally used the term "submerged" in chapter 4 of *The Great Transformation* (1944), though he did use "embedded" in his notes (p. 272), and it is the term "embedded" that has become associated with him. One possible modification of Polanyi's strict observation about the embeddedness of the economy is that an economic system can be defined as a subsystem of the social system (Wheatley 1972, 617; on contemporary society see Parsons and Smelser 1956, 1–100, 306–8).

6. Smith 1776, II.ii.1, p. 25. "To start with, we must discard some nineteenth century prejudices that underlay Adam Smith's hypothesis about primitive man's alleged predilection for gainful occupations" (Polanyi 1944, 44).

7. In this, of course, Polanyi agrees with Marx but criticizes him for making the common mistake of attributing nineteenth-century social and economic motives to preindustrial societies. (Marx follows Ricardo [Polanyi 1944, 126].) See further Humphreys 1969, 202–4.

8. Aristotle was able to discover the "economy" as it became gradually "disembedded" (Polanyi 1957a). More and more, Aristotle noticed, there were those whose motive in trade was not self-sufficiency, but "maximization."

Austin and Pierre Vidal-Naquet put it with regard to ancient Greece, "It follows that to study the place occupied by the economy in a society of this kind one cannot apply the concepts and terminology of modern economies, for these apply only to the world for which they have been created."[9]

Polanyi's approach has generated a great deal of (sometimes) bitter debate among scholars of several disciplines, primarily economics, sociology, and anthropology.[10] Unfortunately, most ancient historians have in the main ignored the debate as well as Polanyi's work. The notable exception is Finley, who worked with Polanyi in the Interdisciplinary Seminar at Columbia University in the 1950s (though he declined to contribute to the collection of papers that grew from the seminar, *Trade and Market in the Early Empires*) and much of whose work, especially his study of reciprocity in *The World of Odysseus*, reflects Polanyi's influence.[11] The treatments of Polanyi's career and economic approach by Helen Codere, Sally Humphreys, Yvon Garlan, and Lucette Valensi have not kindled the enthusiasm they ought to have, especially among Anglo-American scholars.[12] There are exceptions to this generalization. Maria Aubet, Walter Donlan, Ian Morris, and James Redfield have all utilized Polanyi's approach in studying early Greece.[13] Leslie Kurke's work on Pindar and Herodotus applies with great profit Polanyi's notion of the embeddedness of the economy in antiquity.[14] Polanyi's critics may be correct in their argument that his influence is enormous but not well recognized (see chapter 1). Be that as it may, in this and the next chapter, I wish to make plain Polanyi's position and approach, for I consider it indispensable to the topic before us.

An important proposition from which Polanyi was working and from which I am working here is that small-scale communities are not aware that their economic activities are different from their noneconomic activities for the simple reason that there *is* no difference. It is rather unfortunate that, though forewarned, most of Polanyi's critics fall into what Polanyi termed the "economic solipsism," the belief that the way *we* do things is the *natural*

9. Austin and Vidal-Naquet 1977, 8.

10. Many, among them Clifford Geertz ("a debate in which, I confess, I find it difficult to take much interest" [1980a, 198]) and Philip Curtin ("The controversy has not been especially enlightening" [1984, 14]), have expressed bemused amazement at the brouhaha.

11. Finley 1978, 51–78; see Vidal-Naquet 1965; Tandy and Neale 1994.

12. Codere 1968; Humphreys 1969; Garlan 1973; Valensi 1974. For a more recent assessment, see Tandy and Neale 1994.

13. For example, Aubet 1993, esp. 79–83; Donlan 1982b, 1989c, 1993, 1994; Morris 1994d; Redfield 1983b; 1986. Sitta von Reden's recent book (1995) came to my attention too late to integrate into this study. She is not unaware of Polanyi, and his ideas play an important part in her analysis of Homeric exchange (chap. 1) and early market exchange (chap. 5).

14. Kurke 1991, 166–67, 227, 249; 1995.

way to do things.[15] Finley, in one of his earliest publications,[16] and Johannes Hasebroek[17] in a sense anticipated Polanyi's important point, but as A. W. Gomme testily put it, Hasebroek made "the error of assuming that because a thing was not done in earlier times in the same way we do it now, it was not done at all, of supposing that before the age of steamships, railways and motor-cars no-one travelled, before the age of printing hardly anyone read a book, that because in antiquity men had not our elaborate facilities both of transport and of international banking, therefore they did, practically, no trade—only a little, of the simplest kind of barter."[18] Hasebroek, however, was forced to overstate his case (as Polanyi also often did), since the majority of classical scholars tended to follow Meyer. In fact, for example, the great Rostovtzeff had genuinely no idea that he was trapped in the economic solipsism.[19]

Also, it is assumed here that people in small-scale societies do not ordinarily attempt to "maximize" their specifically economic or material returns from transactions because they consistently seek to acquire only what is appropriate; and, in fact, they engage in transactions primarily to meet social expectations and thus win social "points" or avoid opprobrium. This does not mean, however, that there are no "sharp" persons in primitive communities, nor that the "savages" of past or present are so "noble" that their generosity knows no bounds. It is rather that generosity is the only stance or strategy that the society allows. Polanyi put it bluntly when he wrote of "tribal" societies in general: "The premium set on generosity is so great when measured in terms of social prestige as to make any other behavior than that of self-forgetfulness simply not pay."[20]

By laying out models of the social systems into which economic systems are submerged we will be in a better position to interpret the evidence from the early Greek world. It will be obvious that we are of course dealing with the same anthropological phenomena, from a different angle.

Elman Service[21] and Morton Fried[22] have each articulated schemes for the evolution of social organization. Service's quite specific evolutionary

---

15. Polanyi 1977, 14–17.
16. Finkelstein 1935, 320.
17. Hasebroek 1933.
18. Gomme 1937, 43.
19. Reinhold 1946; Finley 1980, 53.

20. Polanyi 1944, 46. A misunderstanding of this point has prevented many from understanding Polanyi in general; see, for example, Silver 1983, esp. 825–26, and 1986, 138, 141, where Finley is also taken to task.

21. Service 1971.

22. Fried 1967, with whom I concur that there is no "theoretical need for a tribal stage in the evolution of political organization" (Fried 1966, 539).

categories are band, tribe, chiefdom, and state. My long-held conviction that social organization in the early Greek polis did not derive its structure or structural nomenclature from tribal organization has been vindicated by the work of Denis Roussel and Felix Bourriot, which has been synthesized and clearly reported by Walter Donlan:[23] the *phylai* ("tribes") of the early polis reflect an attempt by newly constituted leadership to disguise a change in rules. Hence I will eschew the use of the term "tribe" and will for the same reason employ Fried's tripartite typology, which more or less corresponds to Service's: there are egalitarian (= Service's band and tribe), rank (= chiefdom), and stratified societies, which follow one upon the other until the arrival of the state, a "complex of institutions by means of which the power of the society is organized on a basis other than kinship."[24]

DARK AGE SOCIETY: FORMS OF SOCIAL ORGANIZATION

From the start of the Dark Age, depressed population was the rule throughout Greece, and social organization became decentralized as a consequence. The diet of at least the inhabitants of Nichoria in the southwest Peloponnesus shifted from a grain to a meat-and-olives base and the exploitation of livestock shifted from milk and cheese to meat on the hoof. The archaeological record shows a reduction in the number of settlements after the collapse of the Mycenaean centralized organizations and in the number of people in each settlement.[25]

Egalitarian Society

The smallest of these settlements would each fit Fried's description of an egalitarian society, which is characterized by the community's awareness that there are "as many positions of valued status as there [are] persons capable of filling them."[26] All adults of the same age and gender perform

23. Roussel 1976, esp. 193–263; Bourriot 1976; Donlan 1985. Antony Andrewes (1961, 132) remarked long ago of Homer: "It may be fairly said that tribes are wholly foreign to the poems." Longer ago Max Weber (1921, 389) characterized tribal divisions in the Greek polis as "ethnic fictions."

24. Fried 1967, 229. Eli Sagan, in his controversial *At the Dawn of Tyranny*, criticizes Elman Service, who recognized within his model that forms of social organization can degenerate, for not recognizing the possibility of the regression of organization (Sagan 1985, 235), which I believe must be recognized as what happened in Dark Age Greece. (This was already taken up by Renfrew 1979b, 482–84.) Otherwise, so far as I can tell, Sagan (1985, 225–51) is in general agreement with both Fried and Service on the points treated in my text, although his approach to state formation has not found much support (see Runciman 1986; Sagan 1987; Runciman 1987).

25. See above, chapter 2. The largest sites were in all likelihood supporting well under 500 people.

26. Fried 1967, 52.

the same tasks. Egalitarian societies are usually hunting, fishing, and gathering communities that do not recognize property as privately held. For example, the Keewatin Eskimos, like other egalitarian societies, do not claim exclusive rights to the best hunting and fishing grounds. !Kung bands restrict themselves to broadly articulated territories but do not recognize ownership of game within them: "The animals belong to no one until shot."[27] Prestige is acquired most often through prowess in production, usually hunting, but this prestige is not, apparently, convertible into political power.[28] This is not to imply that egalitarian societies are without leadership. In fact, the opposite is true: "An egalitarian society does not have any means of fixing or limiting the number of persons capable of exerting power. As many persons as can wield power—whether through personal strength, influence, authority, or whatever means—can do so, and there is no necessity to draw them together to establish an order of dominance and paramountcy."[29] Leadership is ambiguous in such a social system insofar as the leaders change with great frequency and "orders" are not always heeded by "subordinates." Hence Fried invests leaders in egalitarian societies with "authority" but not "power."[30] In Weberian terms, leadership here is usually "charismatic."[31]

Rank Society

Rank societies have more "qualified" persons than positions of status; that is, in rank societies the number of status-laden positions is limited.[32] It is not difficult to see how an increase in population density can create such a situation. It is also clear that increased density will also increase the amount of goods controlled by the holder of each status-laden position, for, although per capita wealth remains the same, the total wealth of the community has increased more than has the number of leadership positions. Property is ordinarily assigned for usufruct by a chief, who acts on behalf of the community. This is the way things work among the Trobrianders of Papua New Guinea[33] and also among the Amerindians of the North Pacific coast, where each high-ranking member of the community controls his group's house or houses and, though only the administrator of these possessions, is spoken

27. Fried 1967, 58–59.
28. Fried 1967, 66.
29. Fried 1967, 33
30. Fried 1967, 83.
31. Weber's useful typology (1921, 215–16) is "charismatic," "traditional," and "legal." Service (1966, 52–54 [~ 1979, 51–52]; 1975, 50–53) gives a number of examples of charismatic leadership in egalitarian societies.
32. Fried 1967, 109.
33. Malinowski 1921, 4.

of as "owner."[34] Generally speaking, the division of labor is the same as in an egalitarian society, with the modification that the holder of rank may have to do *more* work than the others in order to distribute more and maintain his rank.[35] If an individual should expend energy in a specialization, the production from it will bring only an ephemeral prestige that does not lead to political power. Political power resides at the center of a redistributive system, where, we will see, persons are perceived as "rich" as much on the basis of how much they give away as on the basis of how much they hoard. It follows that "rank has no *necessary* connection with economic status in any of its forms, though it frequently does acquire economic significance."[36] Furthermore, the strength of a leader resembles power rather than authority in that although commands (as in an egalitarian society) may not be obeyed, the strength of social pressure is very great. As a result, commands are usually obeyed, but not so much because the commander has the power but because the society has it. We see, then, that social pressure, dependent on kinship, is more influential in rank societies than in egalitarian societies and, in the absence of any legal system, serves to dictate appropriate behavior. In Weberian terms, leadership is often "traditional."[37]

After the shift in many—though not all—communities from egalitarian to rank society, life in general is of the same quality as before: there is still equality in access to necessary things, and the main framework of economic relations persists. The main difference is the institutionalization and reduction (per capita) of positions of rank. The two most significant factors behind this are "ecological demography," by which Fried means an increase in population with a shift in production to agriculture, and the emergence of redistribution,[38] about which I will have much to say below.

We can postulate the existence of rank societies in the Dark Age, though it is certainly possible that egalitarian organization was still the norm in many communities. I would suggest that prior to the later population increase and the development of overseas trade, most of the communities in the Greek world were at the lower end of rank society (so Donlan, who characterizes Homeric society, using Service's typology, as a set of "low-level" or "immature" chiefdoms).[39]

---

34. Drucker 1965, 50.

35. Fried 1967, 114–15.

36. Fried 1967, 52.

37. How kinship relations firm up in support of "traditional" leadership is well illustrated among the Tikopia by Raymond Firth (1936, 328–29) and generally by Service (1975, 79–80).

38. Fried 1967, 182–84.

39. Donlan 1982a; Bjørn Qviller is inclined this same way, emphasizing the similarity in the weakness of the *basileus* and the big men of the ethnographies (Qviller 1981, 117–20); on the terminology see Earle 1991b, 3, who prefers "simple" and "complex" chiefdoms. Ian Mor-

The Evolution of the Basileus

The Dark Age evidence for hunting and meat-herding fits Fried's paradigm for egalitarian society. But in the more populous Dark Age communities there must certainly have been ranking. The institutionalized position of paramountcy located in the semblance of a political center was called the *basileus,* a vestige of the Mycenaean Age, when the *qa-si-re-u* was a relatively unimportant intermediary situated somewhere between the outermost political periphery and the *wanax* in the center of an elaborate redistributive system.[40] After the Mycenaean collapse, power was decentralized, and *basileus* became the rubric of power.[41] This "decapitation" theory has been so named and also challenged recently by John Lenz, who cannot agree with it because, like Michel Lejeune (see below), he does not believe that the Mycenaean position was so highly situated.[42] Robert Drews subscribes to this continuity theory and emphasizes that a plurality of *basilees* in many locations works against the thesis that during the Dark Age a single *basileus* ruled at a given location in the manner of a king or solitary chief.[43] Ellen Wood argues that the enormous gap in Homer between the *basilees* and other *aristoi,* on the one hand, and the ocean of faceless peasants, on the other, is a vestige of the Mycenaean Age, when the *basilees* were minor political figures but nevertheless allied with the state, not with the fields.[44] Lejeune maintains that the *basileus* had been a kind of master of the guild of smiths,[45] Stefan Hiller that the *qa-si-re-u* headed a production corporation of at least five craftsmen at Pylos.[46] Pierre Carlier believes that the role of the *basileus* must have evolved during the second millennium at Knossos, Pylos, and Thebes and seems also to have varied epichorically.[47]

---

ris (1987), by contrast, sees much greater ranking in the Dark Age. He is followed by Yale Ferguson (1991, 178), who appears to concede that the larger settlements would nevertheless be chiefdoms, albeit "complex."

40. Hooker 1976, 184–90, esp. 189; also Ventris and Chadwick 1973, 119–25, esp. 121–22; Killen 1988.

41. Andreev 1979; Thomas 1978, 191; Fine 1983, 25; Donlan and Thomas 1993, 65.

42. Lenz 1993a, 113–21. For more adherents to the theory see references collected in Lenz 1993a, 108 n. 204.

43. Drews 1983, 112–14.

44. Wood 1988, 89–93.

45. Lejeune 1971, 169–85, followed by Burkert 1985, 50, and Baumbach 1988, 138; Pierre Carlier (1984, 108 n. 624) adds other scholars who support Lejeune to some extent or another.

46. Hiller 1988, 55–56; he was to a certain extent anticipated by Margareta Lindgren (1973, 127), who would have him be a state comptroller who distributes metals to specialist craftworkers at and near Pylos.

47. Carlier 1984, 108–11.

He concludes that we will not be far off if we define the *basileus* as a mayor or petty king ("roitelet") who in the wake of the collapse of the Mycenaean world became in the course of the Dark Age a king "au sens plein du terme."[48] The word resists etymology,[49] but it is clear that the destruction of the Mycenaean centers thus brought power to these leaders of newly independent communities, antidecapitation theory notwithstanding.[50] Without appealing to but clearly in line with Weber's characterization of such leadership as charismatic, Carol Thomas observes that the "Dark Age *basilees* seem to have been leaders whose position is rested on personal characteristics."[51]

Stratified Society

To complete our survey of categories of social organization, let us turn to Fried's third category, the stratified society. "A stratified society is one in which members of the same sex and equivalent age status do not have access to the basic resources that sustain life."[52] A stratified society is the incipient pristine state, a social system anthropologically without documentation (and without correspondence in Service's typology); it is the prelude to the state. Population density may often be a factor behind stratification and state formation,[53] although it does not appear to be a necessary one. Two noteworthy aspects of stratified society are the exclusion of a segment of the population, and the concomitant tendency of the ranking individuals to socialize only with one another and to arrange to have their ranks accompanied by economic advantage. (In fact, among the Lowland Classic Maya, wealth became a "prerequisite for achieving office.")[54] In its efforts to estab-

48. Carlier 1984, 115–16.

49. The many attempts at an etymology can be found in Frisk 1973, s.v, and Chantraine 1968, s.v, both of whom conclude that *basileus* is a loanword. The most recent attempt I could find argues for a derivation from a PIE compound noun meaning "battle leader" (Georgiev 1984, 127–28), which would be astonishing given what broad consensus exists on the position of the *basileus* in the Mycenaean world.

50. Donlan (1985, 297) suggests that the *basilees* each oversaw several "phratries," each of which was comprised of several *phyla*. If Donlan's solution to these enigmatic Homeric terms is right, he has freed us from being concerned with how the phratries fit into the earliest history of the polis.

51. Thomas 1983, 1251.

52. Fried 1967, 156.

53. Robert Stevenson (1965, 331–32) has perceived in Africa "a pronounced general conjunction between state formation and higher population density." Don Dumond (1965, 314) also concludes that "population increase may be expected to result in some tightening of social organization." See further Dumond 1972. Generally speaking, grave goods from prehistoric communities show greater evidence for ranking as the communities increase in size.

54. Rathje 1969/70, 359.

lish institutions and agencies as maintainers of an order of stratification, the state—pristine or secondary—concentrates on four basic foci of organization: hierarchy, differential degrees of access to basic resources, obedience to officials, and defense of the area.[55] Note especially the second of these, for "the central question is one of the alienation of rights of access from portions of the social community, and one aspect of such alienation is the private transacting of critical economic activities."[56] Law, generated and enforced by the state, replaces social pressure as the guide for appropriate behavior. Commands must be obeyed, because a commander has power by virtue of the institutionalized position he occupies. In Weberian terms, leadership has become "legal."

The evidence for stratification in the Greek world is essentially archaeological. In the course of the eighth century, ranking increases with the population. Goods buried in certain graves in the Argolid and in Athens increase in value; in the Argolid, there are haves and have-nots. Burial patterns at Corinth and elsewhere suggest an emerging elite. None of this can prove institutionalized positions of power, but the special treatment of many of the elite, to which we will soon turn, suggests that there is an attempt under way on the part of the elite to separate themselves from the rest of the community in order to maintain economic advantage over others. When Greek communities reached this extent of organization, poleis appeared.

In discussing these rubrics of organization, I have tried to convey one general and two specific points. The general point is that, in the main, both the mode of food production and population density, interdependent phenomena, contribute to the loosening and tightening of social organization. The specific points are that with the appearance of stratification, social polarization manifests itself in the locking out of a portion of the population from "access to basic resources," as Fried would put it, or from the mainstream of the flow of goods (that is to say, holders of rank have an economic advantage); further, kinship constructs lose their broad efficacy in controlling individual behavior and are replaced by legal institutions designed to maintain the newly stratified hierarchy.

DARK AGE ECONOMY: FORMS OF ECONOMIC INTEGRATION

It is time to turn from society to economy. In the discussion that follows, the term *integration* is used to refer to the integration in society of the production of divided labor. This division of labor "springs from differences

---

55. Fried 1967, 235.
56. Fried 1978, 41. By "private" I presume Fried means "apart from the society at large."

inherent in the facts of sex, geography and individual endowment."[57] The three discrete forms of economic integration that can be identified in societies are reciprocity, redistribution, and exchange.[58] One is not found to the exclusion of any other; often two or all three are found simultaneously. In addition, these systems do not necessarily follow one upon another in an evolutionary manner.[59] But in any given single movement of a good, one of the forms can be perceived as the system that organizes the movement, and it is possible also to identify the form of economic integration—which can be called the dominant form of integration[60]—upon which most members of a community or society depend for their livelihood (food, clothing, and shelter).

We saw that in both egalitarian and rank societies, kinship relations ordinarily dictate the movement of goods. The two economic institutions within which these goods move are called reciprocity and redistribution.

Reciprocity

The institution of reciprocity,[61] which has often been called "gift exchange" or "gift/counter-gift," is a system whereby goods within a society move along the lines of a grid of kinship or other relationships. The outstanding characteristic of this system is its symmetry,[62] though goods need not move between the same two parties; rather, the system is symmetrical in that when one party gives something to another, it is understood that the giver will receive something, perhaps from the very recipient, but often from some *other* party located somewhere within the social grid (see fig. 4). Gifts can-

57. Polanyi 1944, 44.

58. Polanyi originally (1944, 47–67) identified four forms of integration: reciprocity, redistribution, householding, and exchange. Later he dropped householding (1953, 224–27; 1957b, 250–56), admitting that it "is actually redistribution on a small scale" (1960, 308). This tripartite arrangement probably remained unchanged until his death in 1964, although it was resurrected in his name in *Dahomey and the Slave Trade* (1966). Both Neil Smelser (below, note 102) and Marshall Sahlins (below, note 61) suggested modifications to Polanyi's typology.

59. Although, as with forms of social organization, there is often a correlation between population density and the appearance of markets (e.g., among the Yoruba: Hodder 1965, 103), the potentially nonsequential order of appearance of these economic forms is illustrated well by Philip Curtin (1984, chap. 4, esp. 87–89).

60. "By dominant is meant that [form of integration] which provides the bulk of material livelihood" (Dalton 1962, 62).

61. The best broad discussion of this system is Mauss 1925. Sahlins (1965b, 147–49 [= 1972, 193–96]; also 1968, 82–86; cf. Service 1966, 14–21 [= 1979, 16–22]) broke reciprocity into three categories: "generalized," "balanced," and "negative." Donlan (1982b) successfully tested these categories on the "Homeric" world.

62. As we shall see, reciprocity may also be characterized as circular; Agnew 1979, 100: "Reciprocity, however unbalanced or exploitative, is an intrinsically circular relation."

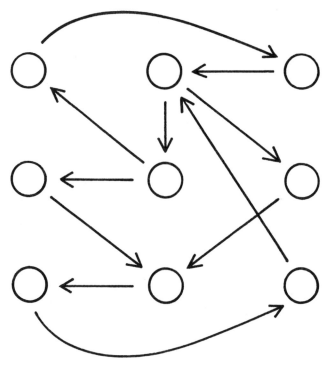

Figure 4. The symmetry of reciprocity. Everyone gives and everyone receives.

not be refused and are required by social norms: they create a social bond or respond to an existing social requirement.

The classic example of an internal reciprocal economy is that of the inhabitants of the Trobriand Islands off the northeast coast of Papua New Guinea. As a result of Bronislav Malinowski's researches during World War I, we know that Trobrianders were assigned garden plots by the *guya'u* ("chief"), and each member of the tribe with his family dutifully grew his crops, primarily yams. There were various times of cropping, and the distribution of the production at these times is an excellent example of a reciprocal internal economy. The production of a garden was not consumed by its tiller and his family; rather, "the man is obligated to distribute almost all his garden produce among his sisters; in fact, to maintain his sisters and their families."[63] Our toiling tiller then depended for his own and his family's nourishment on the production of his wife's (or wives') brother(s). It

63. Malinowski 1921, 8.

was a proud Trobriander who was able to leave many yams on his sisters' doorsteps. This system is a clear example of what Polanyi means by an economy's "embeddedness": the Trobriand economy was in fact no different from the kinship system itself.

Other movements of goods can be extremely complex, moving as they do between parties according to a set of rules called *mapula*, which Malinowski defined as "repayment," "equivalent," "the general term for return gifts, retributions, economic as well as otherwise,"[64] but which has proven to be more complex than this, as an informant explained to Annette Weiner:

> If my father gives me [*mapula*] a coconut palm and several years later a strong wind comes and knocks down the palm, my father will give me another one. If I go to the trade store and buy a kerosene lamp and later the lamp breaks do you think Mr. Holland will give me back my money? *Mapula* is not the same as *gimwali* [to buy and sell]. If anything ever happens to that coconut palm my father will always replace it [*mapula*]. When my father dies, his brothers will come and give me money and take the palm back. If they do not do this, I continue to use the palm until I die. Then someone from my father's matrilineage must come and make a payment for the palm tree. If no one comes, the palm is lost to them and my own matrilineal relatives will get the palm.[65]

This may be hard to follow, but, again, what is this if not an economy embedded in the kinship grid?

There was another type of gift giving among the Trobrianders, which, instead of operating within a grid of existing obligations, actually generated new obligations. When the *guya'u* wanted something done by a member of his tribe, he gave that person a gift that could not be refused and that obligated the recipient to service.[66] This type of reciprocity is often found in external economic systems (see fig. 5). Here the leaders of ethnic groups or even "nations" exchange gifts to promote goodwill between them. The gifts must be accepted and reciprocated by either a countergift or service.

---

64. Malinowski 1922, 208.

65. Weiner 1992, 25–26. For *gimwali*, see chapter 5 below.

66. Malinowski 1921, 11. A close (if trivial) analogy in our own modern, Western Christian culture is the exchange of gifts at Christmas. Members of a family ordinarily perceive no obligation to give presents but have the desire to do so, thus fulfilling the expectations of the recipients. Similarly, when Mr. Jones from across the street knocks unexpectedly on Mr. Smith's back door and gives Smith a holiday bottle of whiskey, the recipient feels strongly obligated to make a counterprestation, even if such an act had never previously crossed Smith's mind. Thus that bottle of whiskey creates an obligation that the recipient will meet if at all possible, even if it requires his remembering until next year. The North American practice of keeping track of dinners "owed" is another example of gift giving in action, embedded in society (cf. Nash 1966, 31).

Figure 5. External reciprocity between "nations"

In the Trobriand *kula* ring of aristocratic external reciprocity, luxury goods were thus exchanged, and these luxury goods were designated for this purpose and traveled around a very large area, in principle always returning eventually to the original giver or his heir.[67] Typically, external reciprocity features the exchange of luxury items, while internal reciprocity involves subsistence goods.[68]

The most commonly attested reciprocal economies in antiquity are external, between two (or more) closed societies. The most accessible example is the tenth-century relationship between Hiram and Solomon,[69] where the obligation is handed back and forth, with Hiram sending Solomon supplies of cedar and fir trees, gold, and even laborers, and Solomon reciprocating with thousands of measures of wheat each year and other gifts. When the Temple was completed, Solomon gave Hiram, king of Tyre, twenty "cities" in Galilee:

> And Hiram came out from Tyre to see the cities which Solomon had given him; and they pleased him not. And he said, What cities are these which thou hast given me, my brother? And he called them the land of Cabul [garbage] unto this day. And Hiram sent to the king six score talents of gold.[70]

How are we to make sense of Hiram's generous response to Solomon's action unless the sense resides in an understanding that Hiram was required to reciprocate for a gift that Solomon perhaps hoped that his "brother" would never see? If the quality of one participant's gifts proved consistently inferior in the other's opinion (or perhaps in the opinion of the other's subjects), presumably the relationship would be terminated, or

---

67. Malinowski 1920, 178f. For a good synopsis of the complexities of the *kula* see Belshaw 1965, 12–20.

68. For a nuanced reading of the cultural and historical baggage carried by *kula* objects and by other categories of goods among both the Trobrianders and the Maoris see Annette Weiner's outstanding *Inalienable Possessions* (1992).

69. 1 Kings 5:1–9:14.

70. 1 Kings 9:12–14.

violence might ensue. In this case Hiram attempted to embarrass Solomon by outgiving him.

There are many other first-millennium examples of such external arrangements within and outside the Levant and the Near East, some indistinguishable from the Hiram-Solomon relationship, including the consistent and sometimes problematic use of "brotherhood."[71] On the one hand, the consistency of language underlines the institutionality of external reciprocity; on the other hand, the use of kinship terminology in these transactions emphasizes the essential parallelism of the two spheres of nation and family.

Each and every example of reciprocity is open-ended: a balance is never reached whereby no further obligations exist. Something is always owed, in one or another direction. This is why a negative prestation, theft, predictably creates a relationship (enmity) between two parties. Just as people can be exchanged by reciprocity by means of marriage exchange, so the negative of such an exchange, the vendetta, is also characteristic of reciprocal societies.

One final point about reciprocity: individuals act in response to pressure from peers, without any motive save that of maintaining their positions. Not meeting one's obligations leads to embarrassment and social opprobrium; more than merely meeting one's obligations enhances one's status. This is perhaps nowhere more clear than among the Kwakiutl Indians of the Pacific Northwest of North America. Participants in the Kwakiutl potlatch are obliged to give goods to others, to receive goods from others, and to repay them also, with "interest" ranging from 30 to 100 percent. Every "economic" activity found in the potlatch fulfills a social obligation and nothing else.[72]

Greek examples of reciprocal activities can be found in Homer. One example illustrates how a gift can firm up status and generate obligation. In the funeral games of Patroclus, Antilochus cheats Menelaus in the chariot race. Menelaus calls on Antilochus to swear that he did not cheat, and Antilochus responds by apologizing and giving Menelaus the mare awarded him for first place. Menelaus then gives the mare back to Antilochus.[73] Don-

71. See Liverani 1990, 197–202. Cf. Zaccagnini 1987, 62: "Thus a whole state formation is metaphorically represented as a family (micro-) structure and interactions between state formations are shaped and formalized according to the pattern of inter-family relations"; Liverani 1990, 199: "The family terminology, and in particular the brotherhood metaphor, is an appropriate metaphor for the political world, because it does not deter 'brothers' from quarreling." It was stunning to hear King Hussein of Jordan refer to Yitzhak Rabin as "brother" at the slain Israeli's funeral in November 1995.

72. See further Mauss 1925, 31–41; Codere 1950; Drucker 1965, 55–66.

73. *Il.* 23.570–611.

lan explains: "So Menelaus appears magnanimous and generous, as befits his superior status; the gift-*receiving* Antilochus is even more firmly indebted to [Menelaus and Agamemnon]."[74] The system is not simple.

The Greek practice of *xenie,* usually translated as "guest friendship," is clearly an example of reciprocity embedded in society. Odysseus receives gifts throughout his travels homeward. His guest-friend Mentes uses Ithaca as a resting place on his journeys through the Mediterranean, a perquisite inherited from his father: in Mentes' words, "We claim to be guest-friends of each other through our fathers from long ago."[75] Telemachus has great difficulty refusing a gift from Menelaus at the conclusion of his visit to Sparta.[76]

In the Greek system (the Menelaus-Antilochus case above notwithstanding), the rules of *xenie* ordinarily call for the inferior party to acknowledge his lesser position by outgiving the superior party. This is well illustrated by the famous "gold-for-bronze" exchange in the *Iliad.* When Diomedes and Glaucus meet on the battlefield, they exchange personal histories; in the process they (and the audience) learn that the two warriors are guest-friends to each other by inheritance (compare the Trobriander *mapula* above) and that Diomedes holds a superior position to Glaucus. Then they exchange gifts.

> And thus did both [Diomedes and Glaucus] speak and jumped down from their chariots; they took each other's hand and exchanged trust. And then in turn did Zeus the son of Cronus take Glaucus's wits away, for he exchanged armor with Diomedes son of Tydeus, giving gold for bronze, armor worth 100 oxen for armor worth 9 oxen.[77]

Within the rules of *xenie,* Glaucus should give the more valuable gift, but in his nervousness he miscalculates and gives too much. The poet criticizes Glaucus for this miscalculation.[78] Presumably, this narrative is entertaining for the poet's audience, who understood the institution of *xenie* better than we do.

As late as the beginning of the seventh century, reciprocity is still in use in the local arrangements near Thespiae in Boeotia:

> Give to him who gives, and do not give to him who does not give. One gives to a giver, but one does not give to a nongiver. Give is good, but Snatch is evil, a giver of death.[79]

74. Donlan 1989c, 5.
75. *Od.* 1.187–88.
76. *Od.* 4.589–619.
77. *Il.* 6.232–36.
78. Donlan (1989c) has recently set the record straight. For a thorough review of the treatment of this formerly vexing passage both in antiquity and in modern scholarship, see Calder 1984.
79. *WD* 354–56.

Thus Hesiod advises his audience. One can see that "generosity" is shown with circumspection; it is the only tactic that pays, and Hesiod advises that it be used only when it pays—a realistically reasonable response and consistent understanding of the system. Another passage from Hesiod illustrates the open-endedness of reciprocal arrangements and provides an example of how generosity is often grounded in small-scale societies. Hesiod encourages his brother to take good measure from a neighbor, and pay it back well, in the same measure, even better if you can, so that you may later find him reliable should you need him.[80]

Elsewhere in the Greek world, the initial contacts between Euboeans and Etruscans (see chapter 3) may have been facilitated by gift exchange. Stops along the eighth-century trade network provide evidence of reciprocity among members of local nobilities. On Cyprus, for example, excavators found an Athenian pedestaled mixing bowl from the first half of the eighth century,[81] as well as quite a bit of Euboeo-Cycladic ware of the same period and later.[82] Other finds pointing to a gift-giving network throughout the course of the eighth century have been found at Knossos[83] and across the Levant and Etruria (see chapter 3). It is difficult to imagine an explanation for this distribution other than gift exchange. Gifts were not necessarily exchanged one for another; they were given, an obligation was created, and the recipient responded in some way. Prestations were made by traders to get access to metals,[84] by traders to gain protection at an anchorage or harbor, and by elites to demonstrate a solidarity of their class (an important reason to which we shall return). The earliest example of writing on Ithaca, on a shattered wine decanter, appears to read *[x]enFos te philos kai p[isto]s [h]etairos,* "dear guest-friend and reliable companion."[85] The inscription dates from about 700 and may reflect precisely the situation found throughout *Odyssey* 4, when Telemachus and Nestor's son Peisistratus are entertained by Menelaus, and later when they leave in book 15. Both young men are clearly *xeinoi* and are treated equally by the Spartan *basileus;* as they prepare to leave Menelaus says to them: "It is right to treat a present *xeinos* as a *philos.*"[86]

---

80. *WD* 349–51.

81. Dikaios 1963, 198, no. 222; Karageorghis 1969, pl. 5. J. N. Coldstream (1983, 201 n. 1) identifies it as Attic. V. R. d'A. Desborough (1979, 122) first suggested gift exchange as the reason it is present; Coldstream (1983; 1989, 93) concurs. Einar Gjerstad (1979) probably goes too far by suggesting a marriage between an Attic woman and a Cypriot man.

82. Karageorghis 1969, 26; Coldstream 1983, 205–6, figs. 6–7.

83. Coldstream 1983, 204, figs. 1–5.

84. Certainly the case at Veii (see chapter 3); probably also at Hamath on the Orontes, whether brought there by Greeks or not (Coldstream 1983, 203, 207).

85. In Jeffery 1961a, 230, pl. 45a, b.

86. *Od.* 15.74. This was first proposed by Eric Havelock (1982, 195–96).

To conclude, we can observe that reciprocity must have been the dominant form of integration in most localities in the Dark Age but must also have been found commonly at all levels of society during the eighth century and subsequently. Thus we are not using Homer and Hesiod to demonstrate sociological truths about the Dark Age but rather to reveal contemporary integrative institutions., I think that much of the *xenie* in Homer, as in the case of Hiram and Solomon, is for display purposes. As for the reciprocal arrangements urged by Hesiod in *Works and Days*, these appear to be defensive ploys, as we will see in chapter 8. On a theoretical level, we must remember that reciprocal relations and actions are always open-ended: there is always an obligation left unmet. A reciprocal arrangement abhors closure.

Redistribution

The system of redistribution is characterized by centricity (see fig. 6). Goods travel from the social periphery via a social/economic hierarchy to an appropriative center.[87] The goods are then distributed back to the periphery, with the intention of maintaining or increasing the status of the center that attracted the goods to begin with. This is the *form* that characterizes the *rules* that regulate the movements of goods. Part of the *substance* is that the periphery sends goods to the center because the center "deserves" to receive those goods, and the periphery receives those goods back from the center because the social structure demands that return. Another way of speaking of this substance is to speak of *folk views* or *myths* that combine with the rules to constitute the economic formation.

To use (in this case without reluctance) the disciplinary language of the ethnographers (more on this later), the big man in the center is obligated by his community to redistribute what he receives, whether he receives it internally or externally (an important distinction also to be taken up later), and his status, even when already firmly established, is reinforced by his generosity toward his people. A particular good has a different meaning depending on whether it is traveling toward the center or away from it. For example, when a member of the peripheral population sends a goat to the chief at the center, it is perceived by all as an act of deference. When the chief invests that goat in status in the form of a feast for the periphery,

---

87. I use the adjective "appropriative" carefully here, to distinguish between appropriation and exploitation. Appropriation is acquisition from a community property; it marks an exchange between two parties who bear the same relationship to the means of production. Exploitation is an action that is marked by an exchange between unequals. In the case of agricultural production, the difference is between production from community-held land (and labor) and production from privately held land (and labor). See further Wright 1982, 83.

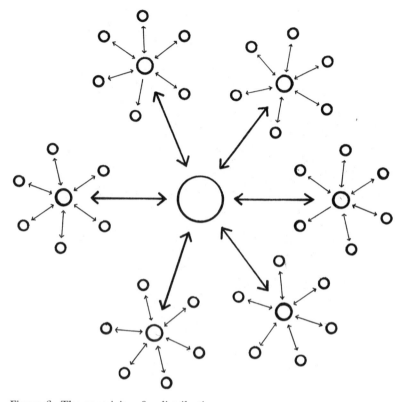

Figure 6. The centricity of redistribution

the goat on the spit serves as a manifestation of the chief's benevolence. Rules dictate that the goat moves back and forth; folk views supply connotative baggage (sometimes called symbolic meaning) for the movement.

Redistribution, like reciprocity, inhibits the increase of the community's wealth, for it requires the investment of wealth in the maintenance of status instead of in its own increase. This wealth can be comprised of subsistence goods or of luxury goods.[88] Its increase is quite *in potente,* for it cannot exist until it is named; as Harry Pearson argued, the economy has no surplus until it is perceived and named.[89]

---

88.   Since there is a limit to how many plows or looms a person can use, extra wealth must be comprised of luxury goods (and perhaps herds and orchards).

89.   See Pearson 1957a, esp. 326. Cf. Dalton 1960 and 1963 against Harris 1959.

There are many examples of redistribution. Redistributive systems have been found in the societies of Java,[90] Dahomey,[91] the highlands of Papua New Guinea,[92] and many other primitive societies that are sufficiently sophisticated to have a political or "economic" center. Let us return to the Trobrianders, who practice redistribution alongside reciprocity. Our tiller gives the majority of his production to his sister(s), but by a variety of avenues, including dues and tribute, and polygamy, as much as 30 percent of the total production winds up in the possession of the *guya'u*, who does one of several things with it. He may exchange the yams externally, getting in return consumable goods that he may then distribute among his people; he may share his yams by throwing a feast, a ceremony that unifies the community's support for him—this is a vegetative version of the goat; he may redistribute the yams to members of the community who, for any of a variety of reasons, cannot in any other acceptable manner be provided with nourishment; or—and this is the most common action—he may pile up his yams for the purpose of display. The yams inevitably rot in their specially designed, open-for-viewing yam house, but not before they have served to underscore the high status of the *guya'u:* he has more yams than anyone else.[93]

Ancient examples of redistribution are just as instructive. While Solomon maintained a reciprocal relationship with Hiram, the internal system was redistributive: "And Solomon had twelve officers over all Israel, which provided victuals for the king and his household: each man his month in a year made provision."[94] These twelve chiefs collected goods from their peoples and presented the goods to Solomon, who in turn guaranteed the status of the twelve. An even better biblical example is found in the tale of Joseph in Egypt. Joseph advanced within the pharaoh's bureaucracy by successful dream interpretations, including one that proposed that 20 percent of all production be delivered to the pharaoh by the people to protect against bad years.[95] When a bad crop came, the contents of the great storehouses were made available to the people.[96] The system functioned to benefit them in lean years, and, whatever we may think about it, the people accepted, willingly or unwillingly, that the system was beneficial. When, through an apparent scam, the pharaoh, represented by Joseph, managed to acquire all the

90. Geertz 1960, 11–15; 1980a, 249.
91. Arnold 1957; Polanyi 1966, 33–59.
92. Feil 1987, chap. 5.
93. Malinowski 1921, 8–10.
94. 1 Kings 4:7.
95. Gen. 41:34–36.
96. Gen. 41:56.

land in the kingdom while also continuing to expropriate 20 percent of all production, the people said to Joseph: "Thou hast saved our lives: let us find grace in the sight of my lord, and we shall be Pharaoh's servants."[97] The Egyptian bureaucracy operated smoothly for a very long time.[98]

The palace economies of Mesopotamia[99] and Mycenaean Greece[100] were quite complicated, so that the center acted as a clearinghouse for many types of goods, a response to these societies' greater specialization of labor and production. Careful record keeping was necessary to monitor such an elaborate system.[101] To the rules that regulate this form of integration may be added this folk view: the participants believed that by delivering from the periphery the items demanded by the center they would then receive what was a "fair return," as one can see in the response of the Egyptians to Joseph's land alienations just mentioned above. The system's embeddedness, as well as its substance, is found in the society's rationalization of the movement of goods, including land and labor. The myth of the people, their folk view, is that the center (as a place) is good and that it is in the best interest of the community to send goods to the center and to receive in return something deemed appropriate.

Neil Smelser argued that the economic systems of Egypt and Mesopotamia are not redistributive but "mobilizative, i.e. subordinated to collective social goals, especially wars." He explained that "mobilization differs from redistribution insofar as it does not solidify and maintain a system of stratification (as the redistributive system does) but collects goods and services into the hands of those responsible for pursuing the broad political aims of society."[102] This is, however, a difference of *substance*, not *form*. Mobilization

97. Gen. 47:25.

98. For a general introduction to the Egyptian redistributive system, see Frankfort 1956, 100–115; Lévy 1967, 7–8. On the taxation system in effect during the reign of Ramesses II (1520–1484), see Montet 1958, 113, 257–58.

99. Frankfort 1956, 64–73; Oppenheim 1977, 89, 95–97.

100. Finley 1957a and b; Renfrew 1972, 296–97, 462–65; Hooker 1976, 184–90; Fine 1983, 24–25; Killen 1988, 1994; Halstead 1988, 1992. Polanyi is surprisingly good on Mycenae: "The authentic core of the Mycenaean economy was the palace household (*oikos*) with its storage rooms and its household accounts which listed personnel, land-ownings and small cattle, assessed deliveries in wheat or barley, oil, olives, figs, and a number of other staples (largely unidentified) and handed out rations" (1960, 342). It would appear now that incoming revenues were converted also into the provisioning of public banquets (at Pylos and Thebes: Piteros, Olivier, and Melena 1990, 171–84; at Knossos: Killen 1994, 73–78). This of course cannot come as a surprise: this is our goat again.

101. Ventris and Chadwick 1973, 195–231, 313–50.

102. Smelser 1958/59, 179–81. He was followed by S. N. Eisenstadt (1963, esp. 45–46), Manning Nash (1964; 1966, 31–33) and T. F. Carney (1973, 20–23, 59–84). To Egypt and Mesopotamia, Nash (1966, 33) would add Mesoamerica, rightly implying that *any* culture that had monumental works at its center would be so classified.

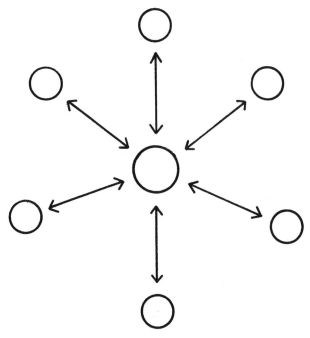

Figure 7. The centricity and simplicity of householding

is a *type* of redistribution: in both mobilization and redistribution goods travel to the center. With redistribution goods travel back to the periphery; with mobilization goods do not return, but consequences are provided in lieu of goods. In exchange for a part of his production, an individual on the periphery of the formation enjoys a monument that ensures divine protection or celebrates the society's greatness, or a war chest that protects the society's way of life or destroys an unacceptable neighboring culture. In mobilization, as in all redistributive systems, the justifying myth or folk view is the same: the center is good. This is neither an irrelevant nor a simplistic characteristic of a redistributive system, for it appears that *the prestige enjoyed by the center is the glue that keeps the system intact.* The goat's connotation may depend on the direction in which it is traveling, but the fact that it moves at all depends on the prestige of the center.

There are other types of redistribution. Polanyi originally proposed "householding" as a discrete form of economic integration, but householding is nothing other than redistribution on a small scale, as he himself admitted (see fig. 7).[103] This is an appropriate subclass of redistributive systems describing not only the ancient peasant household and the large

103. See above, note 58.

estates of classical Greece and especially of Rome, which spawned the mano-
rial or seignorial systems of the European Middle Ages,[104] but also the elaborate structures of dependency that developed in pre-Viking Ireland.[105]
Although householding is a kind of redistribution, it is nonetheless instructive to a better understanding of larger systems of redistribution, for householding's single goal of autarky illustrates an important limitation of redistribution: redistributive formations, especially on a small scale, tend not to
expand.

The only wealth that might possibly be called personal is stolen goods,
but these seem to be no different than goods acquired through external
reciprocal exchange[106] and are most often distributed among the community. As in the case of reciprocity, there is an absence of closure in the movement of goods: all transactions are open-ended. Even goods newly arrived
in the local economy are ordinarily obligated to others, because they have
been acquired on behalf of the whole community.

The Evidence in Homer: Wealth Follows Status

Although, but also partly because, the epics are focused on the elite at the
center, the Homeric poems offer a number of examples of the movement
of goods within redistributive formations. It is useful to recall the reciprocal
arrangement between Solomon and Hiram within which Solomon gave to
Hiram twenty cities in Galilee and to compare Agamemnon's offer to
Achilles:

> seven well-inhabited citadels (*ptoliethra*), Kardamyle and Enope and grassy
> Hire, and holy Pherai and deep-meadowed Antheia, and pretty Aipeia and
> viny Pedasos. All are near the briny, on the far side of sandy Pylos; in them
> men dwell rich in lambs and rich in cows, and these men will honor him with
> gifts as they would a god, and beneath his scepter they will meet his luxurious
> demands.[107]

This incident of an offer and the offer's language show at least three things:
(1) Agamemnon, like Solomon, controlled a tribute-producing network,
any portion of which might at any time be reassigned (that is, the commu-

104. For the best short treatments of medieval householding see Pirenne 1933, 57–66;
Bloch 1961, 163–75; Bloch 1966, 238–46.

105. Gerriets 1987.

106. On brief reflection it is clear that external reciprocal relationships can exist only if the
parties are of roughly equal strength. If one party is stronger, it will simply *take* what it wants,
and this negative prestation will create an obligation on the part of the suffering party to seek
restitution (or to live with it).

107. *Il.* 9.149–56 (~ 291–98). "Meet his luxurious demands" requires some explanation.
Literally the Greek says: "They will fulfill his shining pronouncements"; his pronouncements,
in this context, would certainly be for tribute. See Hainsworth 1993, 78–79.

nities involved in such reassignments do not appear to have any choice about who provides their protection), (2) as the Solomon parallel shows us, we should perhaps be less impressed by these seven epic *ptoliethra:* after all, Solomon's twenty Galileean cities turned out to be *Cabul,*[108] (3) it doesn't matter *who* occupies the center, only that there *is* a center. Another glimpse of a redistributive system can be had at Scheria, where we are told by the island's leader, Alcinous, that "twelve distinguished *basilees* rule throughout the people (*demos*) as rulers, and I am the thirteenth."[109] Of course, the very existence of this strong central group of thirteen *basilees* implies redistribution; one is reminded of Solomon and his twelve tributaries. When Odysseus is about to leave, Alcinous publicly announces, presumably addressing the twelve *pares* among whom he is *primus:*

> But come now, let us give him a great tripod and a cauldron, each man of us; in turn we will get requital by taking a collection throughout the people (*demos*): it is a hard thing for one man to make a proper gift from his own gift store.[110]

Thus Alcinous and each of the other *basilees* are able to recoup their "loss" by taxing the people and will be able to continue to do so as long as it does not appear unfair, or at least avoidable.

Primus inter pares may be an inaccurate description of arrangements at Scheria. All thirteen *basilees* can exact gifts from the *demos,* but Alcinous is clearly more powerful than the others, since they meet at his house and he appears to declare policy on behalf of the community. Lenz argues[111] very convincingly that in the eighth century there coexisted, as he puts it, "kings and councils of kings,"[112] a very good way to account for arrangements at Scheria. I will return to these councils in chapter 6.

The status of Glaucus and Sarpedon, Lycian allies of the Trojans, clearly attracts land and goods from the periphery, but also obligations, as Sarpedon makes clear:

> Glaucus, why is it that in Lycia the two of us are especially honored by seat, cuts of meat, and full cups, and that all look at us as if we are gods, and that we possess a great precinct (*temenos*)[113] on the banks of the Xanthos, a good

---

108. It is not particularly useful here to open the question of the probability of Agamemnon controlling settlements in Pylian territory; we are not looking for historical plausibility, just verisimilitude in systems. See the attempts at exact identification of the seven *ptoliethra* in Hope Simpson 1957 and 1966.

109. *Od.* 8.390–91.

110. *Od.* 13.13–15.

111. Lenz 1993a, 218–32.

112. Lenz 1993a, 218.

113. On the meaning of *temenos,* see below, p. 130.

piece of land for a vineyard and for grain-bearing land? Thus now we must, seeing that we are [counted] among the leading Lycians, take a stand and participate in fiery battle, so that one of the close-armored Lycians may so speak: "Ha! No fameless men are our *basilees*, who rule all Lycia and consume fat thighs and choice, sweet wine. Indeed, noble is their strength, since they fight among the leading Lycians."[114]

In an exhortation to the leaders of the Greeks, Menelaus reminds them that at meetings they drink *demia*, the drink of the people (*demos*), that is, the product of the people's labor, and so they ought to go out and distinguish themselves in the field.[115]

The situation in which Eumaeus the swineherd finds himself on Ithaca is excellent testimony regarding redistribution from the peripheral perspective. Eumaeus's responsibility is to supply the *oikos* of Odysseus with swine; his ability to do this has allowed him to maintain his livelihood both before Odysseus left for the war and during the subsequent occupation of the *oikos* by the suitors of Penelope. Eumaeus himself tells us: "I myself keep and tend these swine and choose the best of the boars and send it to the suitors."[116] He keeps his swine according to age and gender, but there are fewer boars than one would expect, "because the godlike suitors are reducing their number by eating them, for the swineherd was constantly sending them the best of all the fatted hogs."[117] We see that whoever occupies the center matters little to Eumaeus, at least in terms of his day-to-day activities in relation to it,[118] for what holds this and perhaps many other redistributive formations together is the myth, the folk view, of the institution that governs the movement of goods. Perhaps it would be an overstatement to say that "the center is good," whoever runs it, but it is clear that the notion of obligation to the center is the glue without which the institution falls apart. Compare the center-occupier of Agamemnon's seven cities.

Those in the center are good because they have *arete*, usually translated as "excellence" and defined succinctly by Arthur Adkins: "*Arete* in Homer is courage and physical prowess and success and social position and posses-

---

114. *Il.* 12.310–21. "We possess" probably really means "we enjoy the fruits of our appropriation of." This underlines the ruthlessness that exists alongside precariousness. Without going into the connotations of specific words, one can see that the passage is saturated with status-laden terms.

115. *Il.* 17.248–55.

116. *Od.* 14.107–8.

117. *Od.* 14.17–20.

118. This is not to say Eumaeus does not have opinions. He would prefer to work for Odysseus (14.61ff.), and he does not like the suitors (14.81ff.), but his livelihood is the same under both.

sions and fame."[119] Glaucus and Sarpedon have received land and possessions because they have *arete*. They state this explicitly. If they fail to maintain that goodness, they risk losing their possessions. We are forced by the
evidence in Homer to conclude that *wealth follows status.*

Thus far we have seen examples of the redistributive structure within
which goods move and obligations are acquired and met. There are also
instances of specific divisions that reflect the importance of redistribution
in Homeric society. These illustrate how, in practice, divisions are made in
various ways and with some degree of uncertainty.

In the *Iliad,* the *dais* ("feast") is a regular and important institution of
power. It is a meeting of leaders designed to reinforce or reorder the hierarchy. On the home turf of Agamemnon, the primus inter pares before the
walls of Troy, leaders gather regularly. Food is prepared, and shares of it are
distributed. These shares are frequently called equal and may have been
equal most of the time; but, on one occasion, a recently prominent warrior's
equal share far exceeds the share of the others: after Ajax fought Hector to
a draw in single combat, the two sides withdrew, and the Greek leaders
returned to the camp:

> When they were at the huts of the son of Atreus, Agamemnon lord of men sac-
> rificed a bull for them. . . . They flayed it . . . , they cut it all into joints . . . ,
> and ran them through on spits (*obeloi*); they roasted them with care and drew
> them all off. In turn, when they . . . had completed the *dais,* they feasted (*dain-
> unto*), and a spirit lacked nothing of the equal feast (*dais*). The hero son of
> Atreus, broad-ruling Agamemnon, *honored Ajax with the long backbone.*[120]

In this context, "equal" probably means something more like "commensurate to one's status."

But there are other examples where "equal" does mean "equal." Take as
an example the division of the spoils from the ambiguously successful visit
to the cave of Polyphemus the Cyclops:

> Now when we reached the island where the other well-benched ships lay
> moored together, our companions (*hetairoi*), ever expecting us, sat around
> weeping; then we got there and dragged our ship onto the sand, and from it
> we ourselves debarked onto the shore of the sea. We took the lambs of the
> Cyclops from the hollow ship and divided them up so that no one on my
> account might go away cheated of an equal share. The ram my well-greaved
> *hetairoi* gave separately to me alone when the sheep were divided up.[121]

119. Adkins 1960a, 28; cf. 1960b, chap. 3.
120. *Il.* 7.313–22.
121. *Od.* 9.548–51.

Odysseus then sacrifices the ram, and all the *hetairoi* share it. At least two aspects of this story are instructive. First, even after much loss of life and some very risky activities, the survivors of the raid on the Cyclopes are willing to share their booty with the entire fleet. That is, people receive a share, even when they do not participate directly, the assumption being that they have in the past or will on another occasion (perhaps we may assume that "equal" shares will cease for those who habitually fail to contribute). This is a function or by-product of the open-endedness of reciprocity and redistribution. It is Odysseus's responsibility (*moi:* "on my account") to make sure shares are equal.[122] Second, not only is the difference between an ordinary share and the leader's share not very great, but the leader appears obligated (at least on this occasion, because he does it) to return the extra ram in the form of a feast. He receives it as an act of deference and returns it as an act of benevolence. One easily perceives that it becomes quite a juggling act to acquire many possessions and to maintain power within these rules.

The Basileus *in the Eighth Century*

I discussed the evolution of the institution of *basileus* in the Dark Age only in part above. Clearly the role of the *basileus* in a polity that is at least a rank society practicing redistribution is more complex than in smaller-scale arrangements. We see this complexity on Scheria and on Ithaca in Odysseus's absence. It is this institutionalized position that I would like to address.

In addition to the various arguments concerning how *basileus* may have evolved as a rubric of power, there is disagreement about just what the *basileus* in fact became. There are those who argue that there were no Dark Age "kings";[123] others have come around to assert kingship during the Dark Age and in Homer based on evidence of hereditable power.[124] I have no trouble with either position, provided we understand that while it is possible to conceive of hereditable power or leadership, what(ever) is inherited is no more secure than when held by its previous holder. I simply don't like the term "king," because it makes this fact *less* clear, not *more*. As Lenz himself, who sees the *basilees* as "kings,"[125] points out, "If what I identify as kings better fit anthropological chiefs, then my arguments for individual leader-

---

122. The same concern and responsibility for "equity" is expressed verbatim by Odysseus after he sacks the city of the Cicones (*Od.* 9.42) and by Nestor about his father's distribution of livestock taken from Augeas of Elis (*Il.* 11.704).

123. Andreev 1979; Qviller 1981; Drews 1983; Halverson 1985, 1986; Rihll 1992.

124. Van Wees 1992, 32–36, 281–98; Lenz 1993a, 233–37.

125. "'King' is a convenient translation of '*basileus*'" (Lenz 1993a, 176). Van Wees laments: "No-one used to have any hesitation in calling the ruling prince of a Homeric community a *king*" (van Wees 1992, 281).

ship are still valid."[126] He then pools together "chiefs, big-men, and kings," acknowledging that "big-men" are different, being supplantable in life, a fact he apparently considers unlikely in the Homeric world.

To sum up, in the Greek communities of the Dark Age (with the exceptions of the largest centers), reciprocity was the norm for the movement of most goods.[127] Until at least about 850—that is, until population density began to increase—redistribution was probably very limited, restricted to instances of the divisions of the production from a hunt, or following the slaughter of livestock.

The redistributive formations as we find them in the *Iliad* and *Odyssey* are fairly new and in many localities probably still functioning in the time of the epics; if not still functioning, then they are being remembered. That is, in Homer the arrangements of power in fact obtain either in the audience's world or in their collective memory. By Hesiod's time, they have become defunct. Their demise is the topic of the next chapter.

126. Lenz 1993a, 129.
127. And remained the norm in Thrace into the classical period (Mauss 1921).

FIVE

A Great Transformation

All for ourselves, and nothing for other people, seems, in every age of the world,
to have been the vile maxim of the masters of mankind.

ADAM SMITH, *WEALTH OF NATIONS*

The earliest evidence for Dark Age redistribution of subsistence goods are the model granaries of about 850 in the tomb of the "Rich Athenian Lady" (above, chapter 2), although the redistribution indicated there is not necessarily large-scale. What can we say with confidence? We can be fairly certain that the buried woman's family probably had a hand in a redistributive process, that the woman was a member of a rich family, and that a source of the family's wealth was probably land and the production from it. But the extent of the redistributive system, whether it served a large community or only a closed autarkic household, we cannot know. We must also be careful to resist thinking that the redistributor had autocratic control over the contents of the granaries. To succumb to such thinking is to impute to this system a characteristic without analogy in the ancient and modern worlds. The kinds of societies with which we are dealing did not, do not, operate that way. Some people were certainly participating in a redistributive system; perhaps many were. Soon many would, since the granaries seem to indicate a general change in diet. The increased incidence of granary models (see chapter 2) in eighth-century burials[1] and occasional foundations (such as the theta structures at Lefkandi)[2] certainly support the notion of both increased grain production and centralized responsibility for its storage. Knowing, as we do, about the later stage in this evolution, we may assume that the leaders of the communities soon had the responsibility and power to collect, safeguard, and redistribute subsistence goods on behalf of their communities. As the communities grew, ranking became more strict and

---

1. Smithson 1968, 92 n. 41.

2. Popham and Sackett 1968, 30–31, figs. 69–70; Popham, Sackett, and Themelis 1980, pls. 5–7; see discussion above, chapter 2, note 91.

qualified persons began to outnumber even more than before the leader-ship positions available. As ranking became more strict, the increased density began to swell the communities' reserves.

To illustrate: if the population multiplied by four times, and positions of paramountcy increased by only two times, at the end of the period of increase each paramount leader regularly collected twice as much as when the period of increase began. While this does *not* constitute a per capita increase in community wealth, simple arithmetic indicates that it *does* constitute a fourfold increase in centralized goods and a twofold increase in centralized goods per leader and could provide a greatly increased centralized source of goods that might be used for ventures abroad. The centralized materials were still obligated to the community, but it appears that gains (*kerdea,* sing. *kerdos*) generated by the movements of the materials at some point became unobligated.

Unobligated *kerdos,* with or without the impetus of increased centralized goods, would generate the shift in the ownership of goods and in land tenures, accompanied by the change in the way status and wealth were distributed.

EXCHANGE

The driving force in the transformation that shook the Aegean was the introduction of markets into the economic realities of the Greek communities. These markets constituted the third form of economic integration, which Polanyi called exchange.

Exchange[3] is a system in which goods move between two parties. This system has two distinctive characteristics that allow us to identify it as a separate form of integration. First, a market exchange is *negotiated* (quid pro quo) between individuals or groups inside or outside the community and therefore is *voluntary* (at least in form). Second, a transaction in this system neither responds to nor creates a social bond: the relationship is terminable at the end of the transaction. Some networks are established, an apparent grid of relationships that resemble social ones, but these are strictly temporary "business" relationships, for the individual goods involved have specific values independent of the social constraints that in other systems inform the transaction itself; that is, each good or batch of goods is valued separately.

This third form of economic integration operates side by side with reciprocity and redistribution. In many societies some goods will move within reciprocal networks, other goods within a redistributive system, and still

3. I will use "market exchange" and simply "markets" as synonyms. Polanyi (1957b, 266) defined exchange as "the mutual appropriative movement of goods between hands."

others within markets, which often exist in order to allow for the transfer of goods unavailable within the other two forms. Goods exchanged in markets are usually not subsistence or "necessary" goods; thus markets are peripheral to the social mainstream of a community.[4]

It is always important to keep separate what is economic and what is social or cultural.[5] Among the Tiv, for example, it is important to perceive that social functions are performed *at* markets, not *by* markets, which is something altogether different.[6] The Afikpo markets in Nigeria provide a *place* for exchanging news and gossip and for performing certain rituals.[7] The Mossi of Upper Volta use their smaller market centers as places of entertainment and relaxation, and for affairs of the heart not approved by relatives.[8] Rituals are also commonly performed there.[9]

Since markets usually make available external items that do not move via intra- or even intercommunity reciprocity, they tend to be geographically peripheral also. To take one typical example: among the Yoruba of Nigeria there is "a remarkable lack of correspondence between location of traditional markets on the one hand and the location and hierarchy of settlements on the other."[10]

Polanyi's paradigm for long-distance trade might be briefly and fruitfully introduced here, for it clarifies two important aspects of market activity: the introduction of markets from without and their placement on the geographical and social periphery. B. W. Hodder has articulated Polanyi's position concisely: "Markets are not the starting point but rather the result of long-distance trading, itself the result of division of labour and the variable geographical location of goods. The true sequence of events, it is argued, is thus: (i) trade route; (ii) market established on this trade route; and (iii) 'local' markets developing around the original 'parent' market as a network of tracks or roads develops."[11] Hence a market depends on external factors for both its existence and its location; historically, a market did not depend on the activities of communities near it (see fig. 8). In this essentially alien institution of the market we see the economy "disembedded." A communi-

4. See Bohannan and Dalton 1962b, 3, 7–10.

5. This may not be very different from the etic/emic (outside/inside) distinction employed by anthropologists. See the introduction to Duncan and Tandy 1994.

6. The latter scenario is what Paul Bohannan and Laura Bohannan (1968, 191–92) believe they were witnessing; cf. Bohannan and Dalton 1962b, 9 n. 6.

7. Ottenberg and Ottenberg 1962, 126–27, 134.

8. Skinner 1962, 249–50, 271.

9. Skinner 1962, 274–76.

10. Hodder 1965, 99.

11. Hodder 1965, 97–98 with fig. 1. See Polanyi 1975 (= 1977, chap. 12); Dalton 1975; Zaccagnini 1987.

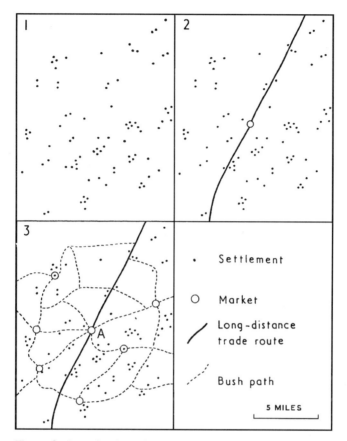

Figure 8. Introduction of markets (Hodder 1965, fig. 1, by kind permission of the Royal Geographical Society)

ty that participates in this system must acknowledge the social independence of the system and the conflicts that arise from the goods being stripped of their social and ethical values.[12] Market goods, however few, move separately from the rest of a society's organization, for transactions can be and are undertaken on the basis of only the denotation of a good, with no consideration for the connotation either of the good or of its transfer. In noting the similarity in thinking between Louis Gernet and Polanyi, James Redfield remarks that "both contrast market-exchange with

12. The "neutrality" of the market vis-à-vis kinship restraints is clear among the Tiv (Bohannan and Bohannan 1968, 191).

gift-exchange." Redfield goes on to explain that both market exchange and gift exchange "are forms of social relation, but in market-exchange the relationship is entered into for the sake of the commodity, while in gift-exchange the commodity is exchanged for the sake of the relationship."[13] Hence the myth or folk view is different from that found underpinning a reciprocal system, for the myth says that reciprocity is by nature noble and market exchange is by nature base. The former is seen as truth, the legacy of the community; the latter is seen as a lie, a threatening force to be treated with keen wariness. Many cultures consider market activity genuinely weird. Market exchanges are transacted "at arm's length." Morally speaking, there is no contact: market exchange is often "silent exchange."[14]

Sometimes the process of external trade is *literally* silent. Hamilton Grierson was the pioneer in this area;[15] Richard Thurnwald was more succinct:

> [Silent trade] is known to us from ancient times, and consists in objects being laid down at a central spot by a person who then withdraws, whereupon, in accordance with traditional agreements or notified by certain signals, the other parties to the transaction appear, carry off goods, and, after a certain time, lay down at the place agreed upon the counter gifts, which they have in readiness for the purpose, and of which the nature has been fixed by tradition, and in their turn withdraw. If the first donors consider the counter gifts insufficient, they leave them lying in order to be changed or added to, as required; otherwise they take them away. Such conventional forms obviously presuppose a certain mutual understanding and are found to be necessary with timid peoples who feel themselves inferior.[16]

Herodotus tells us that the Carthaginians undertook exchanges in this manner with the natives on the Atlantic coast of Africa.[17]

The presence of markets will not cause reciprocal and redistributive networks to break down, but the greater the role markets play in the movement of goods, the greater the disruption those markets will create. That is, the more that market exchange insinuates itself into a community's social constitution and the less peripheral that markets become, the more disruptive they prove to be. This is not to say that market exchange is somehow economically "worse" for the general well-being of the community or the individual, for up to this point no independent "economy" has been perceived

---

13. Redfield 1983b, 401.

14. See further, generally, Herskovits 1940, 159–62, and Price 1980; specifically (Japan), Kurimoto 1980.

15. Grierson 1903.

16. Thurnwald 1932, 149.

17. Hdt. 4.196.

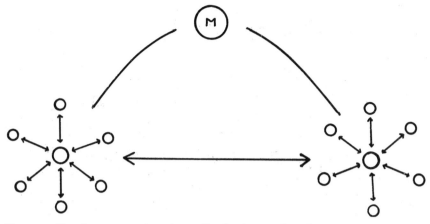

Figure 9. Simultaneous reciprocity, redistribution, and markets

by the community; but as markets become *dominant*,[18] they are viewed—by some, though not by all—as disruptive and ignoble.

Market systems can obtrude upon societies to varying degrees and take many different forms. Among the several types of market systems that we can identify are what we might call the peripheral, controlled, dominant, and limited market systems.[19]

PERIPHERAL MARKETS

Market systems can obtrude upon societies to varying degrees and take many different forms. Most markets in history have been peripheral; very few subsistence goods moved through them. Rather, goods not available through the reciprocal and redistributive systems are available in peripheral markets. Few individuals depend on these markets for their livelihoods.

The Trobriand market (*gimwali*) exists comfortably beside the internal (subsistence and *mapula*) and external (*kula*) reciprocal systems and the internal redistributive system; in fact, *gimwali* exchanges are transacted in the very shadow of the aristocratic *kula* exchanges.[20] (Figure 9 schematizes this simultaneity.) I say "comfortably" because the *gimwali*, though perceived as very different from other forms of exchange and deprecated by

18. See chapter 4, note 60.
19. These categories are certainly not Polanyian in origin, and not necessarily mine either. They probably owe their existence to discussions with the people I thank in the preface.
20. Malinowski 1920, 182–83.

the Trobrianders, is so peripheral that it is not seen as disruptive in any significant way. Here is a good encapsulation: "When scornfully criticizing bad conduct in Kula, or an improper manner of giving gifts, a native will say that 'it was done like a *gimwali.*'"[21] Again, market exchanges, so long as they are peripheral, are perceived but not discouraged, present but not obtrusive, perhaps irritating but not disruptive.

In the *Iliad*, Greek warriors appear to acquire their means of nourishment mostly from regular ravagings of districts neighboring Troy, whence they abscond with livestock.[22] On a single occasion, however, we witness a peripheral market in action (already discussed in a different context in chapter 3):

> Many ships from Lemnos were at hand carrying wine, ships that Jason's son Euneos had sent out; Hypsipyle had borne Euneos to Jason, shepherd of the people. And only to the Atreidae, Agamemnon and Menelaus, had Jason's son given wine to carry off, one thousand measures. From this source the flowing-haired Achaeans got wine,[23] some by [exchanging] bronze, some by shining iron, some by hides, some by whole oxen, some by slaves. And they had themselves a festive feast (*dais*).[24]

Note that there are clearly no fixed rates of exchange after Euneos pays the thousand measures of wine to the sons of Atreus in order to enter this "one-time" market. His ships have come from nearby Lemnos to exchange their large number of wine containers for whatever may be offered within a framework at the opposite end of the market spectrum from a self-regulating market (see below). Like the Trobriander *gimwali*, this is not a *dominant* market but one that is emphatically peripheral to the quotidian lives of Homer's Achaeans. This single instance of a one-time market is treated within the narrative as a special event on which the Achaeans depended for their livelihoods not at all.

A detail from the funeral games of Patroclus in the *Iliad* may offer a glimpse at another such one-time market:

> Straightway the son of Peleus set up other prizes for swiftness, a silver mixing bowl, well worked: it held six measures, and it was by far the most beautiful one over all the earth, since Sidonians in their great skill had worked it carefully, and Phoenician men carried it across the dark-faced sea, and they set it

21. Malinowski 1922, 219.

22. E.g., Achilles' sacking of Thebe, Eetion's city (*Il.* 1.366–69).

23. *Oinizonto* means "got wine"; it is usually mistranslated as "purchased wine" or "bought wine." It is clearly a verb that has more to do with wine than with buying it; "got wine" or "acquired wine" is better.

24. *Il.* 7.467–75.

in the harbor and gave it as a gift to Thoas; as a ransom for Lycaon the son of Priam Euneos the son of Jason gave it to the hero Patroclus.[25]

Thoas is Jason's father-in-law and Euneos's grandfather. This (Phoenician?) technique of paying off the local leadership (here Thoas, king of Lemnos) in order to establish a one-time local market appears to have been well learnt by Thoas's grandson! If nothing else, the Thoas episode betrays Homer as someone who knows about markets (or at least how one-time markets are set up) but has chosen not to make overt references to them.

CONTROLLED MARKETS

Under this rubric may be placed a great number of markets in history, many of which have been misidentified by economic historians as self-regulating markets.[26] Examples of controlled markets include the medieval European urban food markets,[27] on which only about 10 percent of the total population depended for their livelihoods, and the European ports of trade from the late thirteenth to the fifteenth century,[28] where prices were affected by nonmarket factors such as import tariffs and where luxury goods and mostly exotic foodstuffs were moved. Also under this rubric may be placed the markets of ancient Babylonia and Assyria, where prices were fixed and on which, in fact, few depended for their livelihoods.[29] Mostly luxury or prestige goods were transferred in the ancient emporia, such as Tilmun (Bahrain) and Al Mina.[30] The prophet Ezekiel gives a vivid image of the port of trade at Tyre, cataloging for us the fine goods from faraway places that were exchanged through the use of equivalencies.[31] Polanyi argued that such "submonetary systems," as he called them, could process enormous amounts of materials without money or even calculation. Once a rate of exchange is determined, goods, while they last, are moved continuously between the two parties at the agreed rate. "There is no need for any knowledge of how many units of goods either of them possesses, nor—if the rate happens not to be 1:1—of how many units of the other's goods each of

---

25. *Od.* 23.740–46. Philip Stanley (1986, 9) first noticed this passage for what it was.

26. Most recently Silver 1983 and 1986. Walter Neale's corrective article (1957a) has been ignored by the "modernizers."

27. In feudal Europe, "the society . . . was certainly not unacquainted with either buying or selling. But it did not, like our own, live by buying and selling" (Bloch 1961, 67); cf. Pirenne 1933, 167–76.

28. Pirenne 1933, 140–59, 206–19.

29. "[The] institution of markets . . . was in Mesopotamia clearly of limited and marginal importance" (Oppenheim 1977, 385 n. 13); cf. Polanyi 1957c.

30. For Tilmun see, for example, Oppenheim 1954; for Al Mina see chapter 3 above.

31. Ezek. 27.

them is supposed to receive, nor even of how many each actually receives, as long as the rate at which the operation progresses is the agreed one, since both necessarily have received the right amount at whatever moment the transaction is discontinued."[32]

Among the actors at Tyre, Ezekiel names the Greeks (Javan), who traded slaves and metals: "Javan, Tubal, and Meshech, they were thy merchants: they traded the persons of men and vessels of brass in thy market."[33] Draco's law on homicide, which dates from about 620, makes reference to an *agora ephoria,* a "border market," presumably along the shared boundaries of city-states—between Athens and Eleusis, for instance, or perhaps between larger political units, such as Attica and Theban-dominated Boeotia.[34] Ancient food markets were mostly one-time markets that spontaneously arose during times of natural disaster. An excellent example comes from thirteenth-century Egypt: a tomb was looted, and a woman was accused of holding the gold in her house. When asked where she had acquired the gold, she replied: "I got it selling barley in the year of the hyenas, when everyone was short of food."[35] In most controlled markets, subsistence goods were not moved; but large amounts of other goods *did* change hands.[36]

In the *Odyssey,* Mentes tells Telemachus that he is carrying iron to Cyprus to acquire copper. This may be an example of participation in a controlled market there.[37] It is difficult to determine whether the special exchange arrangements that entail the ransoming of prisoners involved ports of trade, at Lemnos and at Samothrace and Imbros.[38] When Euneos

---

32. Polanyi 1960, 345; see further Tandy and Neale 1994, 15.

33. Ezek. 27:13. Ezekiel himself was active in the first third of the sixth century. It has been argued, however, that the description of the port of trade of Tyre reflects a reality of the first half of the eighth century or even of the early ninth century (see Bernal 1993, 247 n. 17 and bibliography there).

34. IG²1 15.27; lucidly discussed in both Bonner and Smith 1930, 112–24, and Meiggs and Lewis 1988, no. 86.27 (pp. 264–67). I should mention that the inscription of Draco's law on homicide was only executed in 409/8, but since it is the only part of Draco's legislation to survive the annulments undertaken by Solon, it seems likely that the inscription bears a reasonable resemblance to the original, especially in details such as a reference to the border market. In his discussion of Draco's law, Demosthenes (23.39.7) indicates that by border market Draco was making reference to the boundaries of a person's own country. Appian (*BCiv.* 5.1.9) uses the adjective to describe those who live in the space between the Romans and the Parthians: their very location prompts a conclusion that they are traders (*emporoi*).

35. Montet 1958, 71, 267. Her response is a clear example of a one-time market, not (pace Silver [1983, 798; 1986, 78]) evidence of quotidian self-regulating markets.

36. On ports of trade generally see Polanyi 1963; also Arnold 1957; Revere 1957. On Babylonian and Dahomeyan ports of trade see Belshaw 1965, 85–94; on medieval Norway, see Hodges 1978.

37. *Od.* 1.184.

38. *Il.* 21.40, 23.747 (Lemnos); 24.753 (Samothrace and Imbros).

brought his wine to Troy, some Achaeans exchanged slaves for it;[39] according to Ezekiel, the Greeks moved slaves at Tyre.[40] Hesiod's claim that the greater the load one takes on a communal venture ship, the greater will one's *kerdos* compound an existing *kerdos*[41] suggests a guaranteed return on one's safe delivery of goods (such a guaranteed return is possible, however, only if prices are fixed or are very, very high,or if costs are trivial [see below], which occurs most often, if not exclusively, within controlled markets):

> You yourself wait for sailing time, until it comes; then drag your swift ship[42] to the sea and furnish on board a fitting cargo, in order to gain a *kerdos* [and bring it] to the *oikos*. Just so my father and yours, Perses, you utter fool, used to sail in ships, because he was in need of a good livelihood (*bios*). Once he came here in his black ship, after making it across much open sea, having left behind Aeolian Kyme. He was not fleeing riches, wealth, and prosperity, but the evil poverty (*penie*) that Zeus gives to men. . . . Praise a little ship, but put your cargo in a big one; the greater the cargo, the greater will be the *kerdos* on top of *kerdos*, if the winds hold back the heavy blasts. Whenever you turn your witless spirit to *emporie* and wish to evade debts and delightless hunger, I will indeed point out to you the rules of the much-roaring sea.[43]

Hesiod does not articulate what the freight includes. Perses is not encouraged to undertake *emporie* for the same reason their father did (because of *penie* and insufficient *bios*),[44] but to get out from under the debt (*chrea*) that stripped Perses of his *oikos*, and the hunger (*limos*) that hounds a landless man. The only other motive for *emporie*—a word apparently derived from *emporos*, "passenger on a ship"—would be to unload extra goods at certain times of the year, which may be implicit in what Hesiod is talking about here. For whatever motive, it seems likely that there were irregular trips by landlubbers either to one-time markets as they may have arisen (compare Euneos above) or to controlled markets. It is very difficult to guess which; but, in either case, the single important implication of Hesiod's advice to his brother is that the only risk being undertaken is in the transporting of the

39. *Il.* 7.475.

40. Ezek. 27:13.

41. *WD* 644–45, quoted below.

42. M. L. West (1978, ad 631 [p. 316]) suggests that this epithet "suits a warship better than a merchant-ship." Of course, this supports the position that there were not many Greek merchant ships until the sixth century (above, chapter 3, notes 74–75; below, chapter 6, note 128).

43. *WD* 630–38, 643–48.

44. The fundamental difference between Hesiod's father's and Perses' predicaments is the difference between a subjectively observed inadequate yield from a holding and no holding at all, easily objectified.

goods ("if the winds hold back the heavy blasts"),[45] and that the greater the cargo, "the greater will be the *kerdos* on top of *kerdos*." The latter means either that there are fixed rates of exchange ("prices") at the goods' destination or that the costs of the goods are so trivial (in Hesiod's case they are fully absorbed by his *oikos*) as to guarantee an excellent "profit."[46] It is rather likely that in the latter case, as I said above, prices will be very high, but more important, Hesiod's costs are practically nil. In either case one's *kerdos* will be proportionate to the number of goods.

Many markets, especially the ancient ones, have been both controlled and peripheral. Controlled markets become dominant only when much of a community's wealth becomes tied up in them, and the subsistence (in Greece, the *bios*) of many persons becomes dependent on them.

DOMINANT MARKETS

In a market-dominant economy, individuals in a community depend on the existence of markets for their livelihoods. A sudden dependence on markets frequently leads to social disruption, brought on by the subordination of the "substance of society" to the "laws of the market."[47] Communities beset by the arrival of dominant markets often suffer social disjunction and cultural recommitment or reformation. Before the German administration of the area, the Bulu of southeast Cameroon, for example, had distributed their goods within reciprocal and redistributive networks. After the Europeans arrived and brought with them markets and money, the individuals in the society did not change their goals, which were to achieve both wealth and prestige; rather, they made adjustments to the *means* by which these traditional goals were met, the market-dominant economy bringing with it a more rapid avenue to attaining these goals.[48] The Bulu were forced to relocate their villages along new roads, becoming sedentary as they abandoned seminomadism, their traditional way of life. Their response was to embrace their kinship relations and the culture, even inventing "la race Bulu."[49]

---

45. Pausanias (9.32.1) describes the winds between the Peloponnesus and the Boeotian port of Kreusis, where Hesiod would have brought his goods, as especially violent (*biaioi*).

46. In fact, there are excellent examples of the latter arrangement in the anthropological record, including within exchange networks in New Guinea. For these last, see Sahlins 1972, 280ff.

47. Polanyi 1944, 71.

48. Horner 1962, 189.

49. So George Horner (1962, 186), who adds: "Such external change has reinforced the concept of Bulu society, even beyond that which was possible in the traditional [precolonial] period."

Thus the creation or emphasis of culture became a defensive posture. Among the Gusii in Kenya, the introduction of markets by the British produced a tension between "affluent" farmers and others less fortunate.[50] These African cases[51] are examples of a change in the economy brought from without, and it would appear that the shift in the local Greek economies was also externally generated. We will be able to compare the Greek response to economic change with these African cases generally and with the Bulu phenomenon specifically. Speaking in a different context and to a different point, David Trump observed that "the Greeks were coming into contact with culturally more advanced peoples to the east, and may have felt the need to stress the value of their own traditions."[52] This is an understatement.

The total disembedding of the economy is completely and utterly disruptive, for even subsistence goods move through higgling-haggling, and kinship and social relationships are strained, even shattered. Previously, movements of goods supported social ties, and those social ties maintained a predictable movement of goods; now, goods move without much regard for the complex grid of social expectations. One consequence of a shift to a market-dominant economy is the introduction of debt, with the debtor no longer able to fall back on the social constitution for relief.

No doubt many types of market-dominant systems can develop. Each evolves from the dominance of a system within which goods of specific denotation are exchanged "at arm's length," and within which each transaction is in principle voluntary, and any continuing transactions are terminable by either party equally.

One direction that a market system may take is the self-regulating market.[53] It is this system that economists, including Polanyi, mean by "market economy." In this market-dominant system, the livelihoods—food, shelter and clothing—of the majority of the members of the society depend on the presence of markets, and such a market system is characterized by a feedback or self-regulating mechanism such that the quantity of all goods

50. LeVine 1962, 536.

51. For the effect of newly arrived wealth on Ghanaian society see Hymer 1970. See also Mallon 1983, esp. chap. 8, for a New World example of disruption caused by market dominance; see Ruiz 1988 for the effect of capitalism on Mexico (especially Sonora) from 1882 to 1910.

52. Trump 1980, 257; a new emphasis on cultural values is also behind Marcel Detienne's (1963) reading of Hesiod and Hesiod's world, to which we will turn later.

53. An excellent brief description of the self-regulating market system is Neale 1957a, 358–60. Neale articulates the outstanding characteristics of what he calls the "price-making" market, in order to discourage economic historians from seeing *all* market systems as "price-making" ones.

supplied at a specific price will equal the demand at that price, and in which the supplier requires payment in money that can be earned only by selling one's inputs in the market. In the self-regulating market system, there are markets for goods, labor, land, and money. The markets for labor and land especially accentuate and exacerbate the disembedding of the economy. (Land and labor are in fact fictitious commodities, since the amount of land and labor do not respond to the market's demand but are products of nature.[54] Only the price may fluctuate, and only to that extent is there a "land market" or a "labor market.") This is precisely the system that was in place in nineteenth-century Europe and that dominated the economic thought of that century, and, until Polanyi's work appeared, this century also. It is also precisely this system that many economic historians think that they can pinpoint in the ancient Near East and Greece.[55]

Before one can argue that any such system existed in antiquity, however, the self-regulating feedback mechanism must be proved to be in place; that is, it must be demonstrated that goods were produced to be brought to market because (most) people depended for their livelihoods on the incomes so generated. For example, when a peasant producer sells goods in the market for a particular price, there may be an *appearance* of supply and demand being regulated by price, but, in reality, this peasant will bring his goods to market at virtually *any* price, since there is no advantage in keeping his surplus production at home. The peasant's self-sufficiency usually insulates him from any meaningful dependence on the market. Similarly, deliveries of goods may occasionally respond to demand, but in many situations—such as Euneos's one-time market—the goods have been produced probably without such intention, and a shortage has attracted existing goods to a specific spot. Unless production can be shown to be responding to demand and unless most people can be shown to depend on the market for their incomes, a self-regulating market system is not in operation.[56] Save for late fourth-century Athens, nowhere before the Roman Empire can it be said that the majority of people in any settlement derived their livelihoods from mar-

---

54. "Labor and land are no other than the human beings themselves of which every society consists and the natural surroundings in which it exists. To include them in the market mechanism means to subordinate the substance of society itself to the laws of the market" (Polanyi 1944, 71). Cf. Polanyi 1947, 61–62.

55. See Silver 1983, 1986; Figueira 1984.

56. If, occasionally, there can be perceived isolated movements of goods, apparently in response to demand, this alone is evidence only of the presence of a few "sharp" people. See Mayhew, Neale, and Tandy 1985, 128–29, 132–33. And compare Robert McC. Adams (1974, 239): "Entrepreneurial behavior, in particular, is characteristically nonhabitual and virtually impossible to aggregate."

kets.[57] Until the late fourth century B.C. there is no evidence for a supply-demand-price mechanism in international exchanges.[58]

LIMITED MARKETS

The limited market system is one in which goods move between two parties with limited consequences for other members of the community. The transactions take place along the "spokes" of a collapsed redistributive system. I propose that the emergence of this system can be seen in Greece in the second half of the eighth century.

Autarkic redistributive households, large and small, still operate as they did before, but the economic relationships among the households, and especially along the "spokes," have become disembedded. Goods, subsistence and prestige, no longer move between the center and the periphery according to social expectations. All goods that move between separate households, including the fictitious commodities of land and labor, do so without regard to the kinship grid.

The cause of a shift from redistribution to limited markets is the participation by the redistributive center in outside controlled markets. The rules of redistribution are not perceived to apply to the prestige goods acquired on the outside, and so the rules change. The new wealth also renders unnecessary the accumulation of wealth from within the existing redistributive economy, because the center is able to provide itself with its own status symbols and thus does not need to collect or redistribute those symbols from the periphery. The rules have changed, and the redistributive folk view no longer obtains; the prestige of the center, which is the glue that has kept the redistributive system intact, is threatened as the old economic formation breaks down.

One of the symptoms of this breakdown is the introduction of private ownership, the transfer of community wealth from public space to private space. Eventually, many goods end up in the private space of an elite ruling class. The wealth at the center, previously required to be redistributed to the periphery, is no longer so distributed. At the same time, the periphery is no longer required to contribute to the center, and thus its property is now socially unencumbered, hence "private." But, importantly, while the

57. Even those who lived and worked in the ancient emporia did not depend on a self-regulating market, for the emporia were not self-regulating. Prices, in essence, were fixed: again see Mayhew, Neale, and Tandy 1985, esp. 128–29.

58. So Polanyi 1957a, 87. There has been some spirited debate concerning the nature of the late fourth century grain trade that was cornered by Cleomenes in Egypt and wreaked havoc on the Athenian importers: see Polanyi 1977, 240–51; Figueira 1984, esp. 29–30; Tandy and Neale 1994, 22–23.

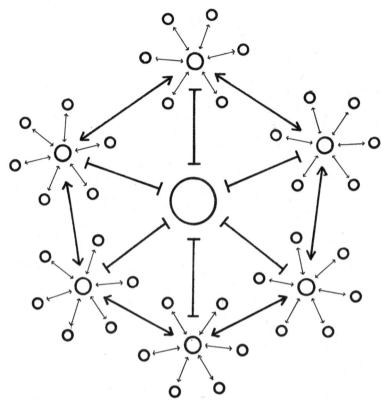

Figure 10. Limited market system. The independent households still move goods internally by redistribution. Transfers of goods on the "spokes" and many transfers along the "rim" are negotiated. All parties go to outside markets independently. The spokes now serve primarily to facilitate land alienations.

periphery is no longer required to contribute to the center, neither does the periphery receive anything from the center (see fig. 10).

What formerly belonged to the community at large now belongs to individual members of the community, and the movement of prestige gifts and land, and of some subsistence items, is controlled by a small group located at what appears to be the old redistributive center. Often the persons outside the center fail to realize that the activity of the center and their relationship to the center have changed, and this failure simply exacerbates the related problems of debt and involuntary land transfer.

Relationships among households and the movements of goods among them are now *negotiated* with little regard for the social grid. Previously, smaller households could depend on the "spokes" of the system to provide help in hard times; now the smaller households are forced to use the "spokes" to acquire all nonsubsistence and some subsistence goods. Since the center is able to control the negotiations, the peripheral person or household becomes indebted. In a redistributive system, thanks to the social "safety net," a person owes only so much as he has or can give; after the introduction of private ownership, in this system of limited markets, as in *any* disembedded system, a person can owe *more* than he has or can give.

The shift to limited markets occurs when the elite at the community's center, because of their involvement in outside markets and their accumulation of goods from outside markets and other sources, perceive that they have more and take advantage of the situation. There is now wealth available, unobligated at the center, and the wealth is capable of growth in the sense that it can be turned over with an eye toward its own increase instead of being consumed by the community through redistribution. The individuals outside the center must now toil to create and maintain their own reserves, since there is no longer any social protection against hard times apart from the solidarity with others located on the rim.

LAND TRANSFERS, SEPARATIONS, AND ALIENATIONS

In egalitarian and rank societies, and within reciprocal and redistributive economic formations, land transfers are infrequent, always the result of "social" and not "economic" forces, land use being dictated by the community at large and under temporary or more permanent leadership.[59] Transfers are possible in principle but rare in reality. In a self-regulating market system, land alienations occur regularly and, of course, for purely economic reasons. By the feedback mechanism built into the self-regulating market system, land is ideally alienated from the economically less efficient party to the economically more efficient. The party that takes over the land then becomes the proprietor of it and maintains ownership by overseeing the production from it more efficiently than his predecessor. Although the alienated party may continue to perform the actual tasks on the holding, he no longer "owns" it.

In a limited market system, transfers occur because of changes in the rules. One excellent example is that of land separations by the talukdars from the Oudh ryots in India of the nineteenth century. "When asked whether [the talukdar] formerly had the power to [evict], [the ryots] said,

---

59. In the following discussion of land use, "transfer" and its related forms refer to the handing over of land use or control from one party to another; "separation" refers to the experience of the party handing over the land to another in a transfer; "alienation" refers to the separation of a party from land through sale. Further qualifications will follow in their place.

'of course he had—the man in power could do anything,'"[60] but they were perplexed by the evictions from their traditional holdings because they could not perceive *why* the talukdar would evict them. This is a good example of the shift from redistribution to limited markets through the introduction of private ownership. Another comes from Bisipara, in eastern India, where parts of holdings were alienated not necessarily because of any inefficient use, but because of expensive social obligations, such as the underwritings of funerals and marriages.[61] "Each sale decreases the yield from his estate and makes him progressively more vulnerable to less expensive contingencies."[62] Eventually the holder loses all property; the new owner does not alter the use of the land. Land had always been transferable in principle (because the big man was able to reassign usufructs), but separations occurred rarely because there was no reason to do so, since all land belonged to the community at large; now, after the introduction of private ownership, lands belonged to individuals, and so separations of lands from individuals could occur.

To turn to Dark Age Greece, we may surmise that land was transferable but rarely transferred. Even after the small population had begun to expand, the size and quality of familial holdings were not squeezed. The only possible noncomparative evidence for alienability is of course literary, and there we find little. Moses Finley gives three examples of what he terms land alienability.[63] Although they are rather unclear, they bear repeating:

1. Diomedes says of his grandfather Oineus and of his father Tydeus:

[Oineus] remained there [at Calydon], but my father wandered and settled in Argos; for thus somehow did Zeus and the other gods wish it. He married one of the daughters of Adrastus and established a house rich in sustenance; his grain-bearing fields were sufficient, his numerous orchards of trees were all around, and he had many sheep: he excelled all Achaeans in the spear.[64]

2. Alcinous to Odysseus:

O, I pray to father Zeus and Athena and Apollo, seeing that you are such a man as you are, who thinks the very thoughts that I do, would that you might take my daughter and be called my son-in-law by remaining here. I would give you an *oikos* and possessions, if you should be willing to remain.[65]

60. Neale 1962, 71.
61. Bailey 1957, 73–75.
62. Bailey 1957, 75.
63. Finley 1968, 31 (= 1975, 158–59).
64. *Il.* 14.119–25.
65. *Od.* 7.311–15.

3. Eumaeus says that he was promised a *kleros* by Odysseus:

> For indeed have the gods kept a homecoming from the very man who would
> have loved me consistently and would have given me possession of the sorts of
> things that a good-hearted *wanax* gives to his *oikeus* (*oikos*-man); to wit, an *oikos*
> and a *kleros* and a much-wooed wife to an *oikeus* who toils much for him, and
> the god causes his work to prosper, just as my own work here prospers, to
> which I give my attention.[66]

What Eumaeus is hoping for here is offered later by Odysseus to him and
also to Melanthius:

> And if the god subdues the proud suitors under me, I will bring both of you
> wives, and I will bestow possessions and houses built near mine.[67]

To these may be added the gift of a *temenos* to Bellerophontes by the Lycians
(as part of a package from a *basileus*):

> When [the *basileus*] recognized that [Bellerophontes] was the fine offspring
> of a god, he kept him there, and he gave him his daughter, and he gave him
> half of his entire royal honor; and the Lycians cut out a *temenos* for him out-
> standing compared to others, a fine tract of orchardland and one of plowland,
> that he might have the enjoyment of it.[68]

Very similar language is employed by Achilles when he meets the Trojan
Aeneas on the battlefield and taunts him:

> Or did the Trojans cut out for you a *temenos* outstanding beyond others, a fine
> tract of orchardland and one of plowland, that you might have the enjoyment
> of it, if you will kill me.[69]

Finally, for the sake of completeness, there is the *temenos* offered to Meleager if he should fight the Kouretes:

> They promised him a great gift: wherever the plain of lovely Calydon is rich-
> est, there they bade him to choose a fair *temenos* of fifty fields, half of it
> vineland, the other half light plowland, to be cut out from the plain.[70]

Without question, these examples show that land was indeed transferable to
the extent that land and other possessions could be given by one party to
another. But not a single one of these examples is arguably anything more
than a transfer; just as important, in not a single case is the newly acquired
land *necessarily* already in use under some third party's usufructory rights,

66. *Od.* 14.61–64.
67. *Od.* 21.213–15.
68. *Il.* 6.191–95.
69. *Il.* 20.184–86.
70. *Il.* 9.574–80.

and so separated from that third party, for the depressed population suggests that there was at this time plenty of land that the leaders might give to worthy parties, be they from within the community or without. Walter Donlan has made a very clear argument that *temenea* in the epics are arable plots not yet under cultivation and so available for cultivation by a new party.[71] At best, Finley's (and the other) alienations are transfers.

But our observations should not stop here. In his words to Glaucus about their leadership of the Lycians, Sarpedon says that "we possess a *temenos* on the banks of the Xanthos."[72] The word *temenos* refers to something "cut out," that is, separated from a larger whole,[73] and the word translated by "possess" probably more properly means "enjoy the use of" or "appropriate for oneself." The very same verb (*nemesthai*) is used in the description of the gift of the *temenos* to Bellerophontes and the theoretical gift to Aeneas, and it emphasizes the contingent nature of landholding. The broader context of Sarpedon's statement emphasizes how important it is to perform up to the community's expectations if one wishes to continue to enjoy the fruits of leadership. This makes sense only if land could be taken even from leading members of a community. In fact, this passage is powerful evidence that land and other "possessions" were obligated to the community and were not "owned" outright without such obligational encumbrances. Similarly, Odysseus learns in the underworld from his mother that Telemachus is maintaining his father's holdings (*temenea*) because he throws the proper feasts (*daites*) and is just.[74] For both the Lycian warriors and Telemachus, the meeting of obligations ensures continued use of land. This is just what we expect.

A Homeric simile has provoked much speculation. In the *Iliad*, a battle that is being hotly contested and whose outcome is indeterminate is compared to two men out in the fields:

> Just as when two men wrangle over boundaries, holding measures in their hands, in a common plowland, and the two of them in a small space vie for an equal share; just so did the battlements separate the contestants who over [the

71. Donlan 1989a.
72. *Il.* 12.313.
73. In fact, Bellerophontes', Meleager's, and Aeneas's (theoretical) *temenea* are each described as "cut out" from the plain. There is great deal of literature on the *temenos*, especially as it pertains to the Mycenaean world, where the word *te-me-no* appears to be a category of land ownership or usufruct. See the sensible synoptic article by István Hahn (1977), who emphasizes Henri van Effenterre's (1967) point that "it is always the people itself who give the *temenos*" (Hahn 1977, 304), which in turn emphasizes the contingency of all of this. On the difference between allocating the possessions of the people (as Alcinous does at *Od.* 13.13–15) and the distribution of land already under the plow, see Donlan 1989a.
74. *Od.* 11.184–86. Contrary to appearances, Telemachus's position is probably no more fragile than that of Glaucus and Sarpedon.

battlements] assaulted each others' ox-hides round their breasts, both well-rounded shields and shaggy light hides.[75]

George Thomson holds that this passage indicates that lands were held in common, seeing in this description a characteristic of the English medieval fiefdoms to which he was accustomed to compare the Homeric world.[76] As Thomson points out, the word for "boundary" here probably means "a day's mule distance," but that does not mean we have feudal common lands, any more than the word *epixunos,* translated as "common," supports his model. Such philological arguments do not work for our understanding of the heroic world and will not work here.[77] Alison Burford Cooper interpreted the passage as a dispute between two brothers or relatives over the division of an inheritance.[78] But in the absence of other testimony, we must restrict our conclusion to the observation that this passage is about cheating over boundaries; the passage tells us nothing about land tenure. In keeping with the picture in the rest of the epics, the most specific we can make the argument is to say that it is over usufructory rights to land.

When we get to the end of the eighth century, to the world after Homer, land is certainly transferable, even alienable, in both principle and practice. It is true that we cannot be certain precisely how the land regimes of the western colonies were constituted. But the general picture that, in the new foundations, land was distributed by lot and was explicitly made inalienable supports the likelihood of alienation at home. That is, they would not have explicitly forbidden alienation if it were not fairly common—or newly more frequent—at home. A story in Athenaeus narrates how Aethiops the Corinthian, "as he was sailing with Archias to Sicily when Archias was about to found Syracuse, exchanged with his dinner mate a honey cake for the *kleros* that he was going to have at Syracuse, having drawn it by lot."[79] This tale is often treated as an exception to the strong prohibition against alienation, and thus as oblique evidence for that prohibition. Finley deals with the tale this way: "I hold no brief for this story, but to treat it as an 'exception,' as Asheri and others do, seems to me methodologically remarkable. If

75. *Il.* 12.421–26.

76. Thomson 1961, 299, 318–19; 1954, 840–46. Walter Leaf and M. A. Bayfield (1898, ad loc.) and many others had already made the same point, though not with the same philological grace and ideological fervor.

77. We can learn no more from this passage than we can from Linear B about the economic reality of the Mycenaean world based on the supposed meaning of words found there: all the tablets tell us is that there were different categories of land use. See Finley 1957b, 137–39 (= 1983, 208–10) against those (e.g., Palmer 1954; Brown 1956) who would interpret the various categories of land on a narrowly philological basis.

78. Cooper 1977/78, 163–64.

79. Ath. 4.167D, perhaps going back to Archilochus.

there are exceptions (and this particular story neither offers a reason nor permits one to be deduced), then the 'principle' of inalienability has simply disappeared. Besides, it is odd to dismiss this explicit text as an exception when we have not a single text stating the supposed rule."[80] But the fact is that there probably was no rule at all, for before alienations began there were no rules against them: alienations simply didn't happen. It must have been very simple: if you worked your land, it was yours.

We are not surprised that when the city of the Epizephyrian Locrians (in southernmost Italy, right around the toe from Rhegium) was founded in 673, the citizens, according to Aristotle, had a law that prevented the sale of one's estate (*ousia*), that a man may "not sell unless he might show that clear misfortune had befallen him."[81] At Leucas (in northwestern Greece), there was a law or laws to protect the old holdings (*palaioi kleroi*).[82]

Hesiod is clear about what was going on in Boeotia. When Hesiod's father came to Greece from Asia Minor, he "settled near Helicon in a pitiful village, Ascra, bad in winter, difficult in summer, never any good."[83] That he was able to acquire a holding does not mean that he acquired it from another party; but there is no question that Hesiod's brother Perses—be he real or not—had his land alienated, and thus, at least by the time of *Works and Days*, land was alienable. Hesiod urges his brother Perses to propitiate the gods in the proper manner "so that you may acquire the *kleros* of other men, and not another man yours."[84] Land is alienable now. Hesiod's injunction later to "first of all get yourself an *oikos*"[85] indicates that Perses no longer has control over a plot, that he lost rights to it to another party, and that this can apparently happen to anyone.

How did Perses lose his *oikos*? He lost it by accumulating *chrea* ("debts"; sing. *chreos* and *chreios*). He lost his land presumably (but not necessarily) to a member of the ruling elite that control the center, the public space of the agora. The evidence for the mechanism of the loss is the unambiguous statement that he needs to acquire an *oikos* in order to get out from under poverty:

I command you [Perses] to consider discharge of debts (*chrea*) and avoidance of hunger. First of all [get yourself] an *oikos* and a woman and a plower ox [a

---

80. Finley 1968a, 29 (= 1975, 157). Finley is referring specifically to Asheri 1966, 19.
81. Arist. *Pol.* 1266B, 20f.
82. Arist. *Pol.* 1266B, 21ff. Whether these examples involve the original *kleroi* is not clear, and furthermore we are in no position to be certain whether the arrangements at Locri and Leucas were identical or contradictory to that of their mother-cities, or something in between. See Finley 1968a (= 1975, 153–60).
83. *WD* 639–40.
84. *WD* 341.
85. *WD* 405.

bought woman, not a wife, one who could follow the oxen] and get all goods into their right place in the *oikos.*[86]

Later, Hesiod tells Perses that full-time *emporie* is one way "to evade *chrea* and delightless hunger."[87]

We should ask what this debt is and whence it came. Gernet observed that in the Greek language *chreos* "is applied to a global notion in which there appear . . . four related ideas: the idea of a constraint that weighs on the debtor; the idea of an obligation that is punishable in case of default; the idea of the very thing that, once received, 'obligates'; the ideas, in addition, of propriety, duty, and even religious observation."[88] The range of meaning for *chreos* can be seen in Homer. Odysseus's absence has brought about a *chreios* for Telemachus.[89] Ares acquires a *chreios* when he is caught in bed with Aphrodite.[90] The Trojans fear that the Achaeans will pay them back a *chreios* for the defeat the Trojans administered to them the day before;[91] similarly, *chreios* is used to describe the motivations of recurring raids by Pylians and Eleans against one another;[92] likewise, Odysseus's trip to Messene to collect a *chreos* after the Messenians took 300 head of sheep from Ithaca.[93] These last two examples illustrate the obligations created by negative prestations. Finally, there are two uses that appear to refer to debt pure and simple (to the extent that there is such a thing), and so mirror the uses in Hesiod: Eurymachus the suitor asks Telemachus whether Mentes the Taphian trader (Athena in disguise) was visiting Ithaca to see to a *chreios*;[94] Mentes/Athena says later that he/she is off to visit the Cauconians, "where a *chreios* is owed me."[95] It would appear that one man's *chreos* can become another man's *kerdos*.

Perses has piled up *chrea* as a result of a change in the rules. In Hesiod's father's lifetime, the political and economic center, whether at Thespiae or at Ascra, provided help in predictable fashion to those in need. With the advent of private property such provision was still made but now with strings attached. Perhaps, though hardly necessarily, because of inefficient

86. *WD* 403–7. The bracketed portion may be a later addition (West 1978, 259–60, ad loc.).

87. *WD* 647.

88. Gernet 1981, 147.

89. *Od.* 2.45.

90. *Od.* 8.353, 355.

91. *Il.* 13.746.

92. *Il.* 11.686, 688, 698.

93. *Od.* 21.17.

94. *Od.* 1.409.

95. *Od.* 3.367.

management of his holding, Perses was forced into taking on *chrea,* and he lost his holding. Within an economic formation that allows for private ownership of land, a man can have a *kleros* free and clear—or it may be encumbered, in which case he has a *kleros* and some *chrea.* Once a man loses his *kleros* in the discharge of his *chrea,* some *chrea* may still remain. This is what happened to Perses. The next stage, in some places, would be debt bondage of the sort that Solon's legislation addressed in early sixth-century Athens. Something like this may be behind the development of sharecropping in the production by the Messenians in Spartiate helotage.[96]

Before moving on, it is appropriate to mention the analysis of Edouard Will and Marcel Detienne, who argue from the premise that land was *not* alienable, that is, transferable through sale, and therefore the accumulation of debts led to the loss of control of production. The agrarian crisis, as Detienne called it, originates "in the practice of successive divisions, a practice that was the result of the breakdown of the primitive family."[97] Sons of a small holder have a choice whether to divide their inherited property or not, but because of the inferiority of the holding (because of population pressure), divided or not, they are on occasion forced to borrow from a neighbor, usually a wealthy one. This is why, according to Will and Detienne, Hesiod advises: "Take good measure from a neighbor, and pay it back well, in the same measure, or better if you can."[98] A series of bad harvests leads to the debtor being "sucked down little by little into even greater misery. From loan to loan, he will finally be forced to 'sell' his plot of land."[99] But, says Will, land is not alienable, and so all the wealthy *aristos* can accomplish is eventually to gain complete control over the small holder's *production.* Although title is not ceded to the *aristos,* in effect the land no longer belongs to the indebted small holder. Over time, the production on more and more holdings comes under the control of the wealthy families.[100]

However attractive their proposal (Engels's primitive family aside), I cannot see how one can avoid concluding that Perses' land was literally separated from him. Perses has no *oikos,* and so no *kleros.* We saw that a *kleros* can be "acquired."[101] The comparative materials and the implications of the

96. See further Halstead 1992.
97. Will 1957, 17.
98. *WD* 349–50.
99. Detienne 1963, 25–26.
100. Detienne 1963, 26.
101. Relying too much, unfortunately, on the Linear B documents, Edouard Will asserts (1957, 15) that the verb in *WD* 341 (*onei*) that I have translated as "you may acquire" must be translated as "tu pourras essayer d'acquérir" or "tu pourras proposer à ton voisin de te céder

"colonial" rules governing lots support the alienability of holdings in Old Greece. Perses lost his land.

THE TRANSFORMATION: STATUS FOLLOWS WEALTH

Probably by the time of the peak of the population boom, which encouraged the out-movements of goods and of people, private ownership of property and limited markets had come into play. *Status now followed wealth:* "Excellence (*arete*) and renown (*kudos*) attend upon wealth," says Hesiod.[102] This fundamental change from the previous situation, where the obverse obtained, is one of the most striking emblems of the arrival of the polis.

How did the transformation occur? First, population affected social processes. The increase in population density without question had an important effect on the nature of life in Old Greece. In the beginning there was little pressure on the land because population had been so sparse for so many years. But over the course of a couple of generations of growing population, a land shortage was bound to present itself. The population increase had an even greater impact, however. It affected the distribution of wealth. As we saw above, an increase in population predictably exceeds an increase in leadership positions. The result—which we must conclude was the case in eighth-century Greece—is a substantial increase in the amount of goods available per leader. These goods are of course still obligated to whence they came, and the leaders, now wealthier than before, are still required to be generous, now to a larger number of people; but the increase in goods is a sign that things have changed, and such a situation may make easier the task of perceiving and naming a surplus. *The economy can now have a surplus.*[103] Another inevitable result of population increase is conflict over land use. The nobility were using the rich bottomlands for grazing their herds, which served mostly a display function, at a time when the population had increased sufficiently to force people to seek out more land for growing grains. This tension over land use, according to Donlan, led to the rise of the hoplites and to the broader availability of individual freedom.[104]

Second, trade. We may surmise that by the end of the population boom, by the middle of the eighth century, there was sufficient pressure on the

---

son *klèros*." This is another example of reliance on Mycenaean materials to explain a very different world.

102. *WD* 313.
103. See Pearson 1957a; Dalton 1960, 1963.
104. Donlan 1986.

land in individual communities to encourage out-movements of people. Some of these people took to the sea to move goods abroad. Goods brought in from outside market activities augmented the already increased wealth per leader that was the result of the centripetalism inherent to redistributive formations. While it is unclear what role the initial, population-driven increased wealth per leader may have played in the origin of outside trading, it seems likely that the new wealth from abroad wreaked havoc within the communities. Because not received *from* the community, the wealth was *not* obligated *back* to it. There were no rules by which to handle these unobligated *kerdea,* acquired both by gift exchange and through markets. The result was a series of changes of the highest order, especially in the way property was handled.

The decrease in available land was due only partly to a population increase that meant more sons, and so smaller parcels. The issue of whether to use prime land for grazing or agriculture increased the tension between groups. Finally and most important, the change in economic organization generated by the arrival of unobligated wealth exacerbated the entire picture. With the advent of limited markets and the concomitant introduction of private property, land in Old Greece had become alienable. The population increase is *not* the most direct cause of alienations. It is the cause of displeasure, and with the reduction of parcel quality, some people wanted to migrate. Alienation has its roots elsewhere, as I tried to show above. Landholdings, previously secured by one's participation in the community's organizational processes, became unencumbered with the breakdown of the redistributive system, itself perhaps not long-standing. The holdings, now unencumbered, were paradoxically encumberable in a specific and quantified way for the first time. Before this situation arrived, a man owed only as much as he could give; now he could owe more than he had. This shift from unquantified to quantified obligation led to alienations of land to the former protectors of community wealth. Even members of that former protecting group were not immune to loss of property, if it is in fact the case that several of the earliest *oikists* were land-poor entrepreneurs.

Hesiod is upset with Perses because the division of their father's estate appears to have been handled poorly;[105] if the original holding had been larger or better, perhaps there would have been no problem (whatever it actually was). Or perhaps the problem was a direct result of population pressure in the countryside outside Thespiae. But Perses' loss of his inherited holding has a wholly different cause. His land was alienated from him

105. *WD* 37–39.

because he became indebted—he owed too many *chrea*.[106] The people in the newly defined center took his land away.[107]

The world of Hesiod and Perses is devoid of evidence of redistribution. The economic arrangements found in the epics are not present in the peasant's life at Ascra. We will see later that reciprocity has an important social function at Ascra, but it is essentially a strategy of defense against the new rules.

The economic shift caused great distress for many. A fuller stratification was achieved in that holders of land, but not of luxury-capital, were excluded from participation in the economic mainstream. Agricultural produce was no longer brought to a redistributive center, as presumably had been the case when Hesiod's father moved into Boeotia; the locked-out peasants whom Hesiod exhorts found themselves forced to move their goods into outside controlled markets.[108] At this moment, the polis was born, spiritually if not physically.

In the previous system, wealth followed status; in the new system, status followed wealth. That is simple enough, although a further qualification will illustrate how important the economic aspect was to the profundity of the distress. In the previous system, status and wealth were both basically zero-sum. With status, this is not a surprise: we saw that it is typical of rank societies and it is clearly present in the *Iliad*. With wealth, this is also clear on at least three counts. First, the archaeological record of goods and population indicates long-term stagnation; there has been no growth in community wealth. Second, without technological change and a perceived surplus in the center of an economic system, especially a nonmonetary one with few markets and little outside contact, a community's wealth will not increase. Third, even if a surplus exists, it has to be perceived in order to function as "capital," that is, in order to be invested. The economy had no surplus;[109] in fact (of course), there was no independent economy. Thus, in the former system, there may have been tension over who filled the status positions, but there was more or less enough wealth to follow that status. In the new system, tension was created by the reversal of the two factors.

---

106. *WD* 647.

107. This appears to be the implication of *WD* 403–5, where Hesiod bids Perses to rid himself of debt and be released from hunger. Then he may acquire an *oikos*, a woman, and an ox, which means he no longer has a plot.

108. *WD* 641–45.

109. Pearson 1957a.

Wealth, the newly independent factor, increased enormously and suddenly, thanks partly to the increase in population, but probably also to the perception of the surplus and the investment of it in trading ventures. Positions of status, the newly dependent factor, did not increase commensurately. Wealth tugged at the limited status with the result that there was no status remaining that might be acquired through non-wealth-related *arete*. This is precisely what Hesiod is complaining about.[110]

The shift to limited markets meant the beginning of differential access to basic resources. This is not to imply that before the shift everyone had access to good arable or lush meadows. Of course, also, there had always been slaves and laborers for hire (the *thetes* of the epics), whose standing could hardly have been much different than servile;[111] and, of course, land must have been occasionally transferred. But in the main all free people were able to acquire livelihoods through available land. With the advent of the polis, political centers were built not around redistributive centers, but around monuments honoring the participants' organization, and a portion of the population was locked out, physically and ethically, from this organization. The birth of this peasantry marks the birth of the spirit of the polis, a political organization that is barely recognizable without the civil commotion that was a symptom of the continuous class struggle, what later Greeks called *stasis*.[112]

The displays of animal wealth—now for the most part unobligated because not acquired through status—came into direct competition with the increasing need—a result of the increased population—to use the rich bottomlands for agriculture. Furthermore, these displays of wealth, probably never absent from the Greek world, were now being made in response to the new rules, that is, in order to prevent those outside the center from perceiving the new economic advantage the center now wielded. The center attempted a number of strategies to shore up the erosion of the folk view that supported a redistributive formation that no longer existed. I call these strategies tools of exclusion.

110. And, of course, Alcaeus, Theognis, and others later.

111. Consider the many categories of slavery, as if any slave is "more free" or "less free" than another: they are all slaves. Bondage and servitude are essentially identical (see Finley 1963/64, 248; 1983 [1965], 153; 1978, chap. 3; Beringer 1982).

112. See de Ste. Croix 1981, 78–80.

PART TWO

The Responses

SIX

Tools of Exclusion

The archaeological and literary evidence indicates that in the eighth century the emerging aristocracy sought to establish and maintain a separate position for themselves to the exclusion of others. The elite undertook to achieve this goal in a variety of ways, but three activities in particular suffice to illustrate their general goal and are clearly recorded: gift giving, councils and feasts, and hero cult and warrior burial.[1] (The blossoming of Panhellenic centers and the activities at them are also important evidence of the intent of the *aristoi;* see chapter 7.)

ELITE PRESTATION

I have already discussed gift giving and gift-giving networks. Such exchanges serve to establish extracommunity networks and encourage interest beyond the single settlement. In an incidental way, then, these prestations promote Hellenic unity. In terms of social strategy, these prestations separate participants from nonparticipants; in terms of economic strategy, they establish a special collective that can exchange goods that are unencumbered by community demands. Status is acquired through prestation; more important, already established status positions are maintained and strengthened. Thus these networks simultaneously bring coherence to the leading group and distinguish participants from nonparticipants. We saw in chapter 3 that the archaeological record attests to many examples of vases and other artifacts in contexts far separated from their provenances: Attic vases on Cyprus and

---

1. I use the term "warrior burial" (instead of "tomb cult") to emphasize the process of interment in public space rather than the subsequent tendance. I will elaborate below.

Crete, Euboean materials on Cyprus. Gift exchange almost certainly played a role in the opening of Etruria and Campania to Greek interests. Examples abound in the epics, the most prominent being the general behavior of Odysseus and others in the *Odyssey*[2] and the oft-misunderstood "gold-for-bronze" exchange between Glaucus and Diomedes in the *Iliad*.[3]

COUNCILS AND FEASTS

One must agree with Oswyn Murray that the *symposion* was a powerful force in the maintenance of aristocratic authority in the eighth century.[4] We have seen that throwing feasts is one of several avenues by which individuals acquire and maintain status positions in primitive redistributive systems. The *symposion*, as it came to be called in the early sixth century,[5] allowed a leader to firm up relations with his *hetairoi;* this was as true in the epics as in the time of Alexander the Great. The *symposion* may have developed later into public feasts (redistribution through redefinition of the goat), just as had been the case in the Mycenaean period.[6] Most of the evidence for the purpose and function of the *symposion* in eighth-century Greece is literary (Homer) and archaeological.[7]

The Testimony of Epic

The importance of such gatherings in the *Iliad* is clear. The leaders of the Achaeans regularly meet in two perhaps distinct but nevertheless similar settings. One is the *boule* (pl. *boulai*), or council, which meets to determine policy, usually to decide what specific issues will be brought before the collected host, which may have an interest in such affairs but no say in them. *Boulai* are held on several occasions in the *Iliad*. Agamemnon calls for a *boule* of the

2. For a brief review, see Finley 1978, 64–66.

3. *Il.* 6.232–36. See above, chapter 4.

4. Murray 1980, chaps. 3 and 12; 1983a, b, and c. Murray (1983c, esp. 196) perhaps goes too far in asserting that the *symposion* was *the* social control that enabled the elite to maintain their superior position. In addition to Murray, see the essays in Detienne and Vernant 1989 [1979] and the fine survey in Schmitt Pantel 1992.

5. First attested in Alcaeus (70.3, 368.2 L-P); the latter, if not both, from the feminine singular form *symposia*); Theognis (298, 496; both probably later additions) and early drinking songs (frag. ad. 1002, 1009.2) admit *symposion.*

6. See above, chapter 4, note 100.

7. Murray, who uses Homeric and comparative evidence with good result, insists also on "genetic" argument, that is, the use of evidence from the archaic period. But it seems more valuable to study earlier evidence to see how institutions may have evolved rather than the reverse. The earlier informs the later, not the other way around. The very term is not found in the epics (see note 5). As I hope to show, there is sufficient literary and archaeological evidence from the eighth century for us to avoid appealing to the sixth and fifth for pertinent information.

leaders of the Panachaeans, who are then listed (Nestor, Idomeneus, the two Ajaxes, Diomedes, Odysseus, and Menelaus).[8] Other *boulai* have broader attendance. One called by Agamemnon is attended by Nestor and other leaders;[9] another, called by Nestor, is attended by all the *basilees* of Greeks, including Diomedes, the two Ajaxes, Meriones, Menelaus, Odysseus, and Agamemnon: "And they followed with him, the *basilees* of the Argives, as many as were called to the *boule*."[10] A regular forum, a place where one could exhibit nonmilitary *arete* and acquire *time* ("honor"),[11] the *boule* clearly had restricted membership: only *basilees* attended.

The other type of meeting was the *dais* (pl. *daites*), or feast, which also had restricted participation. A meal was shared by approximately the same persons who ordinarily attended the *boule*. "Business" was not *necessarily* addressed at the *dais;* the *dais* was a display of solidarity through sharing. And although the *dais* is often called "equal" (*eise*), this does not always mean that participants received shares equal to one another's, but shares commensurate with the status of each individual, as the Ajax incident in the *Iliad* shows. After Ajax fought Hector to a draw in single combat the two sides withdrew, and the Greek leaders returned to the camp and shared a *dais*. Each received an "equal" share, but "the hero son of Atreus, broadruling Agamemnon, honored Ajax with the long backbone."[12] *Time* is distributed at the *dais,* and so it is relevant to bear in mind that *dais* in fact means "share from a division," and that the verb from which the noun is derived, *daiomai*, means "distribute."[13] In the *Iliad*, heroes are said to be good or not good at both *polemos* ("war") and *boule*.[14] In a fragment of Hesiod, we also find that the descendants of Aeacus "found delight in *polemos* as well as *dais*."[15] In fact, the same persons who attend *boulai* also volunteer as a group for military endeavors.[16]

The *dais* is a place for the distribution of honor and goods. The *dais* is

8. *Il.* 2.402–8. M. T. W. Arnheim (1977, 21) suggests that this particular *boule* is especially restricted to the seven leading *basilees* of the Achaeans.

9. *Il.* 2.53. Odysseus refers to it at 2.194, there implying that the *boule* had more than a small attendance.

10. *Il.* 10.194–95.

11. *Il.* 16.630; cf. 9.54, 12.213.

12. *Il.* 7.321–22. See above, chapter 4.

13. Frisk 1973, I.341, s.v. *daiomai:* "(ver)teilen." The poet seems quite aware of this, hence the *figura etymologica* at *Il.* 9.70: *dainu daita*, "divide the feast."

14. These two arenas of expertise for the hero are generally contrasted in the *Iliad* and specifically combined at 2.202, 9.53–54, 12.213–14, and 16.630. See further discussion in Schofield 1986, 9–10.

15. Hes. frag. 206.

16. For example, those who volunteer to fight Hector are Agamemnon, Diomedes, both Ajaxes, Idomeneus, Meriones, Eurypylus, Thoas, and Odysseus (*Il.* 7.162–68). When

not in formal terms different in economic function from the *boule*. These meetings, whether *boulai* or *daites*, are not only a strong source of power for the attenders as a special group, but also the context within which the pecking order is regularly sorted out within that group.[17] A couple of passages from epic will serve to demonstrate this.

"Business" in the form of Agamemnon's offer of restitution to Achilles is conducted at a *dais*.[18] In the *Odyssey*, the leaders of Phaeacia are summoned by Alcinous to greet Odysseus.[19] This gathering appears to be (though it is not called) a *boule*. At the *boule*, a *dais* is announced and prepared for these same leaders.[20] During the *dais*, Alcinous reveals the organization of the island: twelve *basilees* rule the *demos*, and Alcinous is the thirteenth.[21] The most appropriate time for Alcinous to articulate Phaeacia's political organization and his own paramountcy within it is during a *dais*, an institution upon which that paramountcy depends. The *dais*, of course, takes place at Alcinous's house, since he is currently the leading *basileus*. *Daites* are also contexts in which to exchange gifts; thus Odysseus was understandably pleased that the Phaeacians were busy arranging another one as he departed.[22]

Evidence of Halls

The archaeological record shows that a large number of halls were built, perhaps specifically for *daites*, throughout the Aegean area during the eighth century. Practically all communities of every time and location have meeting places, but in many eighth-century Greek communities such meetings, both *daites* and *boulai*, appear to have been institutionalized. Great halls have been found at Zagora on Andros, Emporio on Chios, and Koukounaries on Paros, among other eighth-century settlements. (The settlements of Zagora, Emporio, and Koukounaries were also mentioned in chapter 2 in connection with the general evidence for growth in the eighth century.)

The settlement of Zagora was founded around 800 and was abandoned about 700. In 1967, Alexander Cambitoglou excavated a series of connected buildings at Zagora, including one that was quite remarkable.[23] Room

---

Diomedes needed a companion for his intelligence gathering, the volunteers were the two Ajaxes, Meriones, Thrasymedes, Menelaus, and Odysseus (*Il.* 10.228–31).

17. For the general picture, see Donlan 1985, 304–5.

18. Called at *Il.* 19.179.

19. *Od.* 8.11ff. The "leaders" are *hegetores ede medontes*.

20. Announced at *Od.* 8.38, prepared at 8.61.

21. *Od.* 8.390–91.

22. *Od.* 13.23–26.

23. See Cambitoglou et al. 1971, plan IV; Cambitoglou 1972, 260, fig. 4 (= Coldstream 1977, 307, fig. 97); Cambitoglou et al. 1988, 79–88.

H19 (see fig. 11) measures 7.5 by 7 meters, has a great hearth in its center, and features a bench as high as 60 centimeters running along three of its walls. It is the largest room (51 square meters) and has the largest hearth and the longest bench. Cambitoglou is right to observe that it was "the centre of the residence of an important person of the settlement."[24] Other rooms have benches, and other rooms have hearths, but no other room at Zagora is so very likely a *dais* hall. It is in this room that the leadership of eighth-century Zagora met—fifteen leaders would be accommodated easily—just as Alcinous and his *pares* met in Scheria.

At Emporio, another settlement that underwent expansion in the eighth century, and that offers a basis of comparison for certain architectural details found elsewhere (at Zagora, for example), John Boardman found a great *megaron* hall within the walled acropolis (see fig. 12). This hall does not seem plausibly to have served any other purpose than what I am proposing. Built at least in the seventh century, perhaps in the eighth,[25] the structure measures about 18.5 meters by about 6.5 meters,[26] with a useful area in the main room of about 75 square meters. The building dominates the landscape and must have been the hall of the big man:

> The Hall stood in a commanding position on the saddle of the hill. From its door one looked straight down through the acropolis gateway. To the left stands the temple [of Athena] and its altars; immediately below, the main road to the summit passes down towards the north, and below the road the houses of the town cling to the steep slope. In such a position the occupant of the Hall could command the entrance to his citadel, the attention of his patron goddess, the respect and submission of his people.[27]

J. N. Coldstream volunteers that this is "the residence of the local chief."[28] It must be admitted that the *megaron* hall has no central hearth, but we can do nothing about this fact.

At Koukounaries on Paros, Demetrius Schilardi has excavated a large number of Late Geometric buildings, the most interesting of which for our

---

24. Cambitoglou et al. 1971, 30. Because he concluded that there are other impressive rooms in the settlement, he has discounted (Cambitoglou et al. 1988, 79) his earlier assessment of the importance of H19. But the fact remains that it is the largest of the excavated rooms and seems to be a focus of at least this sector of the settlement.

25. Boardman 1967, 34.

26. There is fuzziness here regarding the exact dimensions, reported by Boardman (1967, 31) as 18.25 meters in length, 6.4 meters in width at the north end, 6.85 at the south end. But Boardman's rendering of the foundations (p. 32, fig. 16) has the wrong scale attached to it J. N. Coldstream (1977, 308) gives the dimensions as 18.75 by 6.85. I base my internal area measurement on Boardman's measurements and his drawing, ignoring the scale.

27. Boardman 1967, 34.

28. Coldstream 1977, 308.

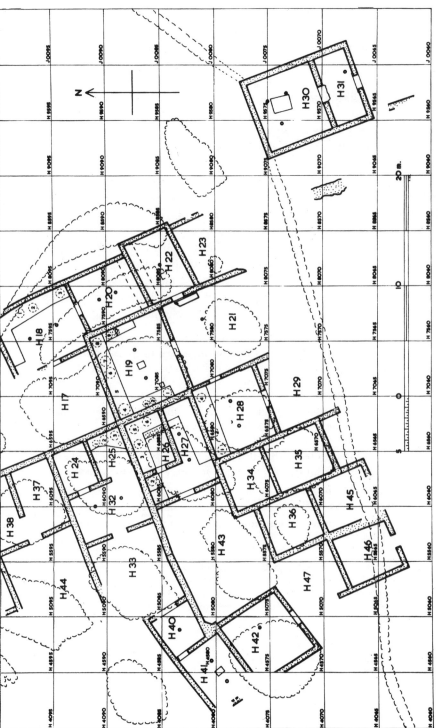

Figure 11. Zagora on Andros (Cambitoglou et al. 1988, plate 8, by kind permission of Alexander Cambitoglou and the Archaeological Society at Athens, Greece)

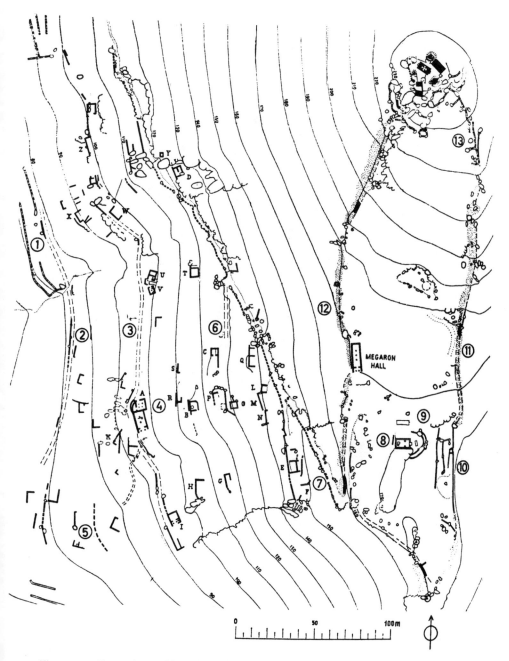

Figure 12. Emporio on Chios (Boardman 1967, 32, fig. 16, by kind permission of
John Boardman and the British School at Athens)

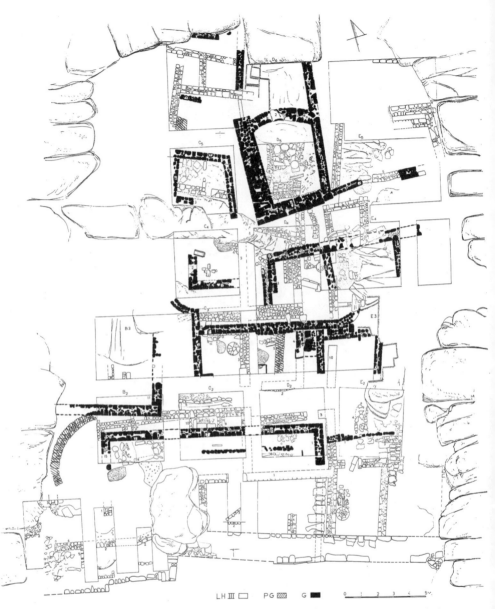

LH III ☐   PG ▨   G ▰   0 1 2 3 4 5 м.

Figure 13. Koukounaries on Paros (Schilardi 1983, 176, fig. 3, by kind permission of Demetrius U. Schilardi and the Swedish Institutes at Rome and Athens)

purposes is the building that stands over sectors B2, C2, and D2 (see fig. 13).[29] The Late Geometric settlement was rather crowded but apparently carefully planned; while most of the other structures run north-south to allow orderly traffic on the narrow streets that separate the houses, this structure, running east-west, is a single-roomed building 13.7 meters long but of unknown width (the south wall is absent).[30] Not much width is required, however, to generate square meterage in the same range of the structures at Zagora and Emporio.

Several funerary structures may well have included an element of hero tendance and also served as places for secular *daites*. The most prominent of these are the structure near the West Gate at Eretria, a *megaron* whose main room offers over 20 square meters of meeting space (on which see below);[31] the open-air eating place at Asine in the Argolid;[32] and the building that was raised around the "Hero of Lefkandi," whom we will soon meet. With the exception of the problematic Lefkandi building, all these structures were built during or very close to the eighth century and may be interpreted as part of the broad conscientious effort by local nobilities to establish a sort of elitist Panhellenism or Panhellenic elitism.

HERO CULTS AND WARRIOR BURIALS

Three types of hero cults are found in the Aegean area in the late eighth and early seventh centuries: long-standing hero cults, newly established cults devoted to mythic heroes, and newly established cults devoted to contemporary individuals.[33] The latter two types concern us but have little meaning if we do not look first at the long-standing cults.

Few long-standing cults have been unearthed to date, but they are significant for their very existence. The oldest yet found is the cult of Odysseus in a cave on Ithaca. Two votive tripod-cauldrons found in the cave date to at least as early as 800, and the several twelfth- and eleventh-century cups[34] also found may also be dedications to Odysseus, who is identified as the cult-

---

29. Schilardi 1983, 176, fig. 3.
30. Schilardi 1983, 177–78, figs. 4 and 7.
31. Bérard 1970, 65–70, plan III.
32. Hägg 1983b.
33. Much work was done on the hero cults in the 1970s and 1980s and continues. See James Whitley (1988) on the Argolid and Athens and Ian Morris (1988), who discusses the phenomenon broadly, concluding that the cults must have had different significances in different locations and social contexts. I would emphasize that my overview is not designed to be exhaustive; rather I am trying to make general points about the political use of these cults and their relationship to the economy and to epic. See Antonnacio 1993 and 1995 and Whitley 1994—more recent studies pertinent to my approach.
34. Cauldrons: Desborough 1952, 281; cups: Desborough 1972, 88, pl. 15A.

ed figure by a very late (after 300 B.C.) dedication on a mask.[35] The cult of Academus in Athens may date to as early as the late tenth century, as may that of Erechtheus.[36] Excavations on the island of Naxos have revealed one or more tenth-century burials, which appear to have been the focus of ten-dance into the sixth century.[37] As the cult of Odysseus (or his predecessor) appears likely to be at least as old as the ninth century, and the Athenian examples are uncertainly as old,[38] there seems little question that there was something important happening at Lefkandi beginning in the late eleventh or early tenth century.[39] There, in a structure at least 45 meters in length and 10 in width, has been found the burial of a cremated warrior with his wife and horses. Excavators believe that the great hall was constructed[40] *after* the interment of the deceased, perhaps as a place in which to gather and share a meal with the hero,[41] and that the hall was intentionally buried under a tumulus by about 950.[42] Only the excavators appear to be so certain, however; there really is no necessary reason to take this as a cult building.[43] If it is a big man's meeting hall, then it simply indicates that the largest settlement on the mainland had meetings of its leadership, nothing unexpected in a settlement with many people. If the building *is* a cult structure, it can instruct us negatively in two ways: the *heroon* at Lefkandi is *not* a sign of continuity with the Mycenaean world, and its discontinuation at so early a date means it had very little *direct* connection to later burials, cults, and attendant structures. It may well be an example of a very early (and unsuccessful) attempt to accomplish what would be attempted later. We can be confident about one aspect of this cult of the "Hero of Lefkandi": it was not inspired by the dissemination of the monumental epics, assumed by so

35. Benton 1934/35, 54. How early Odysseus became the culted figure is not clear, but it seems unlikely that this was originally a place of dedications to a major divinity whose place was taken by a traditional hero. Much more likely is the scenario that Odysseus, if not the culted figure from the start, replaced his predecessor at some point in time.

36. Coldstream 1976, 16.

37. Lambrinoudakis 1988.

38. In addition to the cults of Academus, Erechtheus, and Odysseus, there are seven others that Theodora Hadzisteliou Price would date to before the Geometric period at least, most notably the cult of Pelops at Olympia (Hadzisteliou Price 1979, esp. 223–24).

39. Popham, Touloupa, and Sackett 1982.

40. Popham, Touloupa, and Sackett 1982, 173; Coulton 1993, 49; Popham 1993. For a plan of the foundation see Touchais 1982, 590, fig. 110; also Calligas 1988, 231; Popham, Calligas, and Sackett 1993, pl. 5. Peter Calligas (1988, esp. 232) reasonably believes that the structure was the great hall of an important *oikos*, used as a burial site *after* its abandonment. This assessment effectively eliminates any pre-eighth-century evidence for hero cult.

41. On sharing a meal with the hero see Nock 1944, esp. 148–57. It should be added that there is no certainty that the hero partook in the feast; perhaps it was merely in his honor.

42. Popham, Touloupa, and Sackett 1982, 171, 174.

43. Whitley 1991a, 350 n. 65; 1991b, 185–86.

many to be the impetus of the eighth-century heroic burials we are about to consider. (Hector Catling's strong arguments for a connection of the "Hero" with Cyprus become especially interesting when we examine convergence of behaviors in Greece and Cyprus later in the eighth century, discussed below.)[44]

The best examples of newly established cults devoted to mythic heroes are the cult of Agamemnon at Mycenae, initiated near the end of the eighth century,[45] and the cult devoted to Menelaus (and Helen) at Therapne,[46] which was started up about the same time. Mycenaean chamber and tholos tombs that received votives beginning no earlier than the late eighth century may also be placed in this category.[47] Theodora Hadzisteliou Price believes that Homer's references to the tombs of Ilus and Aepytus are references to contemporary cults,[48] and the poet of the *Odyssey* may refer to an existing cult, of indeterminate vintage, dedicated to Phrontis at Sounion, the southernmost point in Attica.[49] Whether accidental discoveries of Mycenaean tombs[50] or new founder cults[51] abroad in the colonies (at Megara Hyblaea, for instance) have anything to do with the establishment of these cults is largely (for us) a moot question. It is probably the case that the cults came into being in a variety of ways and "[meant] different things to different people."[52] It is exceptionally difficult, as Lefkandi shows, to see the monumental epics as the primary impetus of the sudden appearance of the cults. The important question is, What purpose did these cults serve once they were established? The beginning of an answer may be found in the third type of burial.

44. Catling 1993, 85–92. See further Demand 1995. To the Lefkandi evidence may be juxtaposed the sub-Minoan tombs of the eleventh century that were part of the emergency excavations (to which reference will be made again below). Catling reports that three of the tombs, numbers 200–202, contain materials that are reminiscent of the Hero of Lefkandi and may be explicable in terms of the *Iliad* (Catling 1995).

45. Cook 1953, 33.

46. Wace, Thompson, and Droop 1909.

47. Coldstream 1976, 9 nn. 6 and 12.

48. Ilus at *Il.* 10.415; 11.166, 372; 24.379; Aepytus at *Il.* 2.604. See Hadzisteliou Price 1973, 140–42. We should add the tomb of old Aesyetes (*Il.* 2.793).

49. "But when we reached holy Sounion, the cape of Athens, there Phoebus Apollo, coming with his painless missiles, did kill the steersman of Menelaus, who held the steering oar of the swift ship with his hands, Phrontis son of Onetor, who outshone the *phyla* of men at steering a ship, whenever gales were blowing. . . . So [Menelaus], although eager for the trip, was kept there, in order to bury his *hetairos* and execute the proper rites" (*Od*.3.278–85). See further Abramson 1979.

50. This is J. M. Cook's proposal (1953) and Coldstream's main point (1976).

51. Irad Malkin (1987, esp. 261–66) argues that many of the cults in Old Greece are secondary to the founder cults in the west.

52. Morris 1988, 758.

A plausible analysis of the new cults is, I think, critical to an understanding of the new social mechanisms coming into play in the eighth century. As alluded to above, the general view (until recently practically a consensus) is that such heroic burials were a response to the dissemination of the *Iliad*.[53] The "Hero of Lefkandi" (if a hero at all) undermines this view, with which I am in complete disagreement. I *do* believe, however, that the monumental and not-so-monumental epics help us understand the new practice of hero tendance. When the epics became "Panhellenic" or were finally put to stone is not a particularly useful thing to know for our purposes; what is critically important is that we realize that the *Iliad* and the *Odyssey* were an important part of a contrived, broad effort to establish and support a self-conscious aristocratic class. The epics can be seen to be part of the broad effort discussed above to exclude a portion of the population from participation in the economic mainstream that had become the only available avenue to high status.

The newly established hero cults, as well as the contemporary warrior burials, may tell us the most about the workings of the *aristoi*. Heroic burials on Cyprus and Euboea, and fascinating parallels—articulated by scholars but not yet, I hope to demonstrate, fully understood—among burials in the Argolid and on Cyprus and Crete are spectacular pieces of evidence that should support my proposition that conscientious efforts were being undertaken to create and maintain an elite class.

Before turning to evidence from Cyprus, I should first point out that there is little certainty whether eighth-century Cyprus was beholden to any eastern power before Sargon II of Assur conquered it in 709.[54] Until the Assyrians came, however, there is good reason to believe that, apart from Citium, which was ruled by a king appointed by Phoenician Tyre, the island enjoyed independence.[55] The burials here surveyed are clearly either of Cypriots fully assimilated into Greek culture or of Cypriots emulating their linguistic cousins to the west; that is, it is reasonable to see them as offering evidence of "typical" Greek social mechanisms.[56]

---

53. L. R. Farnell (1921, 340, 342) was first to suggest that the hero cults spread under the spell of the *Iliad*. He was followed by Cook (1953, 33) and Coldstream (1976; 1977, 349–50). My response to Coldstream is the same as Steven Diamant's: "What seems to me a clear case of Homeric faith is Coldstream's extraordinary suggestion [1977, 349–50] that the magnificent 9th- and 8th-century cremation burials at Salamis in Cyprus show us burial custom modified by epic poetry, when surely it is the poetry which reflects the funerary customs" (Diamant 1982, 44 n. 39).

54. Karageorghis 1982b, 57.

55. Karageorghis 1982a, 532.

56. C. M. Bowra's (1934) brief survey of dictional points of convergence between the Homeric and Cypriot dialects is interesting. A. T. Reyes makes it clear that Greeks were well ensconced in Cyprus by this time (Reyes 1994, 11–13).

First, Salamis in Cyprus. Tomb 1, a chamber tomb, received the remains of a warrior in the mid-eighth century.[57] The technique of interment—cremation—may, significantly, be the result of Euboean influence, seeing that the Euboeans have already set up landfalls on Cyprus along their trade route. Within the chamber are large *amphorae*,[58] whose original contents cannot be determined. Outside the chamber in the *dromos* (the sloping entrance path) are the remains of horses and a chariot, which were interred when the *dromos* was filled and a tumulus piled up over the entire area.[59] The horses remind us of the Hero of Lefkandi and serve to emphasize the affinities between the Greek and Cypriot cultures instead of their differences.[60]

Tombs 2[61] and 47[62] resemble Tomb 1. Each has a long *dromos* leading to a chamber and containing the fossilized remains of horses.[63] Tomb 2 dates from the first half of the eighth century, and its *dromos* contains also the remains of a slave who was apparently sacrificed in the course of filling the *dromos*;[64] Tomb 47, which contains two burials, was first used in the second half of the eighth century.[65] As has been pointed out often, these burials resemble closely the rites accorded Patroclus in *Iliad* 23:

> Then, when Agamemnon the lord of men heard this, he straightaway dispersed the host (*laos*) throughout the balanced ships, but the funeral men stayed there and heaped up the wood and fashioned a pyre a hundred feet in this direction and that, and pained in their hearts they set the corpse on the top of the pyre. And they skinned and dressed many fine sheep and shining oxen of shambling gait in front of the pyre; and from all of them great-spirited Achilles collected the fat and hid the corpse in it from his head to his feet, and he heaped the skinned bodies all around. On it he set *amphorae* of honey and of oil, inclining them against the bier; energetically he threw four arch-necked horses on the pyre with a great groan. The lord had nine table dogs, and two of them he threw on the pyre after cutting their throats, as he slew with the

57. Karageorghis 1969, 25–28. The dating of all of the Cypriot materials has been moved back about a generation, a result of a recalibration of Einar Gjerstad's original absolute chronology. Thus where the pottery used for dating a find is Cypriot, I have pushed back the date fifty years. See Rupp 1988, 116–17.

58. Karageorghis 1969, 27, pl. 6.

59. Karageorghis 1969, 27, pl. 8.

60. The long-standing and widespread practice in Greece, Crete, and Cyprus, of burying horses with the dead is well illustrated by Elizabeth Kosmetatou's (1993) catalogue of horse sacrifices, even though she omits the voluminous evidence from Prinias on Crete (see below, with note 106).

61. Karageorghis 1969, 28–50.

62. Karageorghis 1969, 51–54.

63. Karageorghis 1969, 31–32, fig. 4, pls. 9–10 (Tomb 1); 53, figs. 5–6, pls. 16–18, 20 (Tomb 47).

64. Karageorghis 1969, 29, fig. 3.

65. There are a number of similar tombs at Salamis from the seventh century, but we restrict ourselves as much as possible to the eighth.

bronze twelve noble sons of the great-spirited Trojans—he contrived evil deeds in his heart—and he let fly the iron strength of fire, as it were to pasture.[66]

Patroclus was burnt on a pyre; containers of oil and honey were placed with the body; horses and young Trojans were sacrificed. These clear and striking similarities between Patroclus's rites and those of the nameless Cypriots tell us at least that there were Cypriots interested in burying certain of their dead in a manner that resembles how Achilles honored his late friend.

At Eretria, Claude Bérard uncovered a multiple warrior tomb adjacent to the West Gate.[67] There is no elaborate *dromos,* nor are there any horses, but the burial is clearly that of a hero, and an abutting *megaron* seems to have served as a meeting place where a ritual meal might be shared with the culted figure by his devotees,[68] or, as suggested above, routine *daites* may have occurred. Bérard dates the initial tendance of the site, which appears similar to the treatment accorded the early heroes at Lefkandi and Ithaca and, later, Agamemnon and Menelaus, to the last quarter of the eighth century;[69] additional bodies of both sexes, presumably relatives by blood or class,[70] were subsequently interred in the immediate vicinity (within a mysterious triangular formation) until about 680, and after reaching its peak in the last quarter of the seventh century, the tendance ceased in the sixth.[71] It seems likely that the hero protecting the West Gate died in a Lelantine conflict.

To the Eretrian hero cult may be compared the funeral games of Amphidamas, at which Hesiod won a tripod for his *hymnos:*

> At that time I went over to Chalcis for the contests of warlike Amphidamas; the greathearted one's sons had announced and set up many prizes. There, I boast, I won an eared tripod with a winning poem and carried it off. I dedicated it to the Muses of Helicon.[72]

Amphidamas, also probably a Lelantine casualty, was thus honored by games reminiscent of those that honored Patroclus. In an age when many members of the ruling class appear to have had such ordinary names as

---

66. *Il.* 23.161–78.

67. Bérard 1970, esp. plan III; see also Bérard 1972, where he further discusses some of the contents, especially the bronze spear point.

68. See above, note 41. The open-air eating place at Asine may similarly have served as a place for the sharing of a meal with the deceased, for dining in his honor, or for the routinized *dais* (Hägg 1983b, 189–91).

69. Bérard 1970, 22.

70. I suspect that Coldstream (1976, 15) goes too far when he suggests that what we have here is evidence of a powerful *genos*. Kinship is not necessarily a prerequisite for interment.

71. Bérard 1970, 65.

72. *WD* 654–58.

Thucles, Archias, and Lamis,[73] Amphidamas's name has a strong heroic ring.[74] H. T. Wade-Gery suggested that Hector of Chios gave his name to Hector of Troy, while the Agamemnon of the *Iliad* gave his to Agamemnon of Kyme.[75] Just what was the process that generated Amphidamas's name? Was it his given name?

The same question may be asked about Orsippus (Orrhipus) of Megara, who won the Olympic dash in 720.[76] He gained notoriety for being the first to run naked (he lost his girdle) and later was a successful general in campaigns against Corinth.[77] His name is as heroic as Orsilochus, of whom there are three in the *Iliad*[78] and one in the *Odyssey*,[79] and would appear to be a semantic variation on Hippodamus and Hippodamas.[80] Where did Amphidamas and Orsippus get their names?

Thus far a brief survey of newly established warrior burials and perhaps hero worship has shown that a certain element of the eighth-century population chose to give special attention to their dead and that this practice was shared by several communities. We have also seen that there appear to be eighth-century leaders with epic names and that there are points of convergence between several burials of self-styled warriors and the rites of Patroclus described in the *Iliad*. A last set of burials, I think, will make my proposition much clearer.

FIVE BURIALS WITH FIREDOGS

We saw above that Agamemnon initiates the preparation of a *dais* in *Iliad* 7. I have saved until now a better-known, similar incident from *Iliad* 9, when the embassy (Phoenix, Odysseus, and Ajax) come to Achilles' tent among his Myrmidons to attempt to persuade him to return to battle. Achilles interrupts his lyre playing and welcomes his friends. He then sits them down, bids Patroclus to pour some wine, and prepares a meal:

> So he spoke [to Patroclus], and Patroclus obeyed his dear *hetairos*. Achilles threw a great skillet on the light of the fire and on it set a sheep's back and a

73. The founders of Naxos, Syracuse, and Leontini (Thuc. 6.3.1–2, 6.4.1).

74. Names ending in -*damas* are quite common in the *Iliad* and the *Odyssey*, including an Amphidamas whose son Patroclus slew in his youth (*Il.* 23.87). Another Amphidamas was the father of the hero Meriones and a friend of Odysseus's grandfather Autolycus; he was a wearer of the notorious boar's tusk helmet (*Il.* 10.268).

75. Wade-Gery 1952, 7.

76. Förster 1891, 4.

77. It is unclear how old his history is (Fontenrose 1968, 92–93).

78. There are two from Pherae near Pylos at 5.540–49, one Trojan at 8.274.

79. A son of Idomeneus in a lie of Odysseus at 13.260.

80. *Il.* 11.335, 20.401.

fat goat's and the backbone of a big hog rich in fat. Automedon [Achilles'
charioteer] held it for him, and brilliant Achilles cut it. Then he carefully cut
the pieces smaller and ran them through on spits (*obeloi*), and the son of
Menoetius [Patroclus] kindled the great fire, a godlike man. But when the fire
had burned down and the flame became reduced, he scattered the embers
and laid out the *obeloi* over them, and he sprinkled them with holy salt after he
had set them on the firedogs (*krateutai*).[81]

After the guests have finished eating, Odysseus begins to speak by thanking
Achilles:

> Hail, Achilles, we aren't shortchanged in the equal *dais* either in the hut of
> Agamemnon the son of Atreus or even here now; there are many satisfying
> things here to feast on (*dainusthai*). But the deeds of the desirable *dais* are not
> our concern, but rather the great and utter disaster that we fear.[82]

With this epic incident in mind, let us turn to warrior burials from the late
eighth and early seventh centuries that together illustrate well the three
exclusionary tactics the aristocracy employed. There are five burials.

The earliest is Argos grave no. 45, excavated by Paul Courbin in 1953.[83]
Dated firmly to the last quarter of the eighth century by the pottery contained in it,[84] the grave yielded not only an intact and impressive bronze
breastplate and helmet,[85] but also iron objects: two double-axe heads,
twelve spits (*obeloi*), and two firedogs.[86] There are also remains of horses in
this burial. The double-axe heads have suffered greatly from oxidation but
are nonetheless recognizable. The *obeloi* are in deplorable condition. Only
one retains its shaft; the other eleven retain only what must be their handles: flat, nearly circular extensions about 6 centimeters in diameter. The
preserved length of the most intact *obelos* is 111 centimeters, its weight 1.24
kilograms, but it is impossible to determine how much has been lost from
the end of the shaft.

One of the two ship-shaped firedogs is 129 centimeters in length. The
other is missing more of the shaft but appears to have been almost the same
length. Both have supporting π-shaped legs (for clearing the embers that
they would straddle) 11 centimeters tall. The rears of the firedogs, which

---

81. *Il.* 9.205–14. *Krateutai* do not appear again in Greek literature, but it must be the case
that they are firedogs.

82. *Il.* 9.225–30.

83. Courbin 1957.

84. Courbin 1966, 174, 177; Coldstream (1977, 146) would date the burial about 710.

85. Courbin 1957, 340–67, figs. 19–22, 39–41.

86. Courbin 1957, 367–68, figs. 50–51 (axes); 368–70, figs. 52–53 (*obeloi*); 370–83, figs.
54–62 (firedogs).

represent the ships' sterns, are nearly identical, each taking the form of a swan's neck.[87] The fronts represent ship prows. The first firedog has a vertically rectangular prow with a prominent projecting line that reaches the same height as the uppermost portion of the swan's-neck stern. The second firedog lacks such a projection from the prow, though it may have been carried off by oxidation.

Another burial, at Kavousi in eastern Crete, discovered in 1895 but not fully reported until 1971,[88] contained a highly oxidized double-axe head[89] and fragments of a pair of firedogs.[90] Several bronze fibulae and a bronze pin date the tomb to the Late Geometric period,[91] and a bronze shield boss[92] indicates that the deceased was styled a warrior. Since the fragmentary firedogs are known only from Arthur Evans's photographs in the Ashmolean Museum, their dimensions are indeterminate, but they are clearly ship-shaped, though the single surviving prow is mostly only a projecting line.[93] The information from Kavousi shows that within a generation of Argos 45 someone was buried with a similar collection of goods on Crete.

The remaining three burials, all on Cyprus, will be discussed in the order of their discovery. We will find here even more evidence of similarity between Patroclus's burial and actual funerary practice: each of the tombs at Old Paphos and Salamis, like Argos 45, has horse remains in its *dromos*.

In 1960, Vassos Karageorghis found a warrior tomb at Old Paphos (Kouklia)[94] that he was able to date on the basis of the presence of a Cycladic bowl to the start of the seventh century.[95] A bronze shield boss identifies the deceased as a warrior.[96] We are especially interested, of course, in the firedogs and the *oboloi*. The pair of fully intact ship-shaped firedogs is 96.5 centimeters in length; the supports are 10.5 centimeters in height. The sterns on the rears are sharply and identically bent back to prevent spits from falling off, clearly less artistically shaped than the Argive pair. The triangular prows on the fronts, like those at Argos, are not alike. One has a projecting line (smaller than the one at Argos); the other lacks

87. Courbin's (1957, 372) description.
88. Boardman 1971.
89. Boardman 1971, pl. D', no. 10.
90. It is not possible to determine whether the *oboloi* that arrived at the Heraklion Museum in 1899 were from the same burial or even from Kavousi (Boardman 1971, 7).
91. Boardman 1971, 5, pl. A', nos. 1–4.
92. The boss (Boardman 1971, 5–6, pl. B', no. 6) "was found with some Geometric pots" (Droop 1905/6, 92).
93. Boardman 1971, pl. D', no. 12.
94. Karageorghis 1963.
95. Karageorghis 1963, 299, fig. 2.
96. Karageorghis 1963, 273, fig. 11.

it.[97] There are about twenty pieces of *obeloi*, without handles, and not a single one is whole. Six pieces are similar in having a notch that misled the excavator to identify all as "lances";[98] but these notches are identical to those on the Argive *obeloi*, which also feature "stops" to prevent the meat from sliding. Like those at Argos, the Kouklia spits have rectangular shafts for preventing slippage.[99]

At Salamis, a mid-eighth-century warrior burial (no. 79) yielded in 1966 another pair of ship-shaped firedogs, 110 centimeters in length.[100] The sterns are only suggested, there being a slight upward turn of the shaft at its end. The triangular prows both have small projection lines, perhaps originally identical, though one of the projections has been bent at some point out of its circular pattern. Also found were twelve whole *obeloi* of uniform size, 150 centimeters in length. Carefully bundled, the spits are held together by two rings, which themselves are connected by an iron loop, apparently for ease of transportation.[101]

In 1970, Karageorghis excavated a tomb at Patriki to study its limestone structure.[102] In addition to several pottery items, which date the tomb to around 750, two ship-shaped firedogs were found, as well as *obeloi*, both intact and in fragments, scattered both within the tomb and in the short *dromos*. The rectangularly shafted firedogs are about 98 centimeters in length, the π-supports 6 and 7 centimeters high. The sterns curve back in a manner resembling the sterns at Kouklia, and the prows are triangular with projecting, horizontal S-lines. The eighteen fully preserved *obeloi* are 61 centimeters long.[103]

Recent (though not fully published) emergency excavations of the University cemetery at Knossos have yielded numerous firedogs—none ship-shaped—and *obeloi* from the eighth century and even earlier.[104] At least one pair goes back to the tenth century, and this pair (if not an anomalous case), together with *obeloi* of rather substantial antiquity, has suggested two things: first, that whatever the significance of the ship shape—I consider the shape

97. Karageorgihis 1963, 277, figs. 17–19d.

98. Karageorghis later became convinced that they were *obeloi*; see Karageorghis 1970 and 1974, where he suggests that tenth- and ninth-century *obeloi* from Fortetsa near Knossos are of Cypriot origin.

99. Karageorghis 1963, 280–81, figs. 22–23.

100. Karageorghis 1967, 337–48; date: 346.

101. One firedog is shown in Karageorghis 1967, 343, fig. 148; for the firedogs and *obeloi* see also Karageorghis 1969, 91–92, pls. 51–53.

102. It was thought that because the tomb had been well looted, its architecture would be the only aspect of interest. See Karageorghis 1971, 401–3; 1972.

103. Karageorghis 1971, 402, fig. 112; 1972, 167, fig. 12.

104. Catling 1978/79, 47–49, figs. 13, 16; 1983, 37.

very important (see below)—we have at Knossos evidence of the combination of *obeloi* and firedogs well before the eight century; second, that there may be a Cypriot connection here, seeing that *obeloi* have long been found on Cyprus before the firedogs arise there in the eighth century. The firedogs (of any shape) are less clearly Cypriot. I do not think this anomalous material causes difficulty: if it is the same "kit" that we see later (a significant difference being the shape of the firedogs), then we have further evidence of the treatment of the elite by the elite that is independent of (because much earlier than) the Homeric tradition; if the kit is different, it is different. Until the emergency excavations, only *obeloi*, in bundles, had been found in the area, at nearby Fortetsa.[105]

Also reported from the University cemetery are several horse and dog burials, though these are separate from the warrior interments. Between 1972 and 1976, ten horse burials were excavated at Prinias in central Crete. These burials were connected by Giovanni Rizza to the epics, but I am less certain.[106]

Before turning to an analysis of the constituent parts of these burial remains, let me say that scholars have failed to distinguish properly the practical or symbolic use of these iron items in the world outside and prior to the grave, and the reason the items were placed in the earth. These are two separate questions. It is not clear, either, whether interred goods are to be read as more pertinent to the deceased or the giver, a matter that will prove largely irrelevant at the end of our analysis.

Spits

There was a tradition in antiquity, perhaps as old as Ephorus (fourth century), that Pheidon, tyrant of Argos, first introduced coinage on mainland Greece, perhaps in the seventh century. When he declared his coin of the realm, he buried the previous currency, iron spits.[107] Thus when Charles Waldstein found a bundle of 180 *obeloi* accompanied by an iron weight at the Argive Heraeum, he surmised that they were this old type of money associated with Pheidon.[108] Charles Seltman also came to this conclusion, carefully judging the total weight of the spits and the weight of the iron marker each to be equal to half a *mina;* hence six *obeloi* equaled a *drachme,* a "handful," and each *obelos* was an *obolos.*[109] Since Seltman, and in the wake of

105. Brock 1957, 202.
106. Rizza 1979, 294.
107. For the story, found in the late *Etymologicum Magnum,* see Cook 1958, 257.
108. Waldstein 1902–1905, 1: 61; Waldstein first called them "spears" (p. 77).
109. Seltman 1924, 118, table IV.

virtually countless finds of *obeloi* of various weights and lengths (though more often than not in multiples of six), scholars have stepped back a bit. Courbin became the leading proponent of the interpretation of the spits as "proto-money"[110] and argued rather convincingly that there seems to have been, in the area controlled by Argos in around 700, a standardized weight and length for *obeloi*;[111] the ubiquitous *obeloi* are not, however, of consistent weight beyond such narrow geographical limits.

In the end it is unclear what economic purpose the spits may have served before interment in a grave, though it seems reasonable to me that their consistent (within a find site) weight as well as regular number reflects their use by the "trading" nobility as a sort of value unit in an exchange, to take an example, of spits and fine cloths. As in the scenario that Polanyi proposed for exchanges in the ancient emporia, it would be agreed that X spits would be exchanged for Y lots of cloth. The goods would then be exchanged in accordance with this ratio until one of the parties ran out, marking the conclusion of the agreement.[112] The *obeloi* would provide flexibility to the submonetary exchanges at the great emporia that we can infer from Ezekiel's description of goods being brought into (and so out of) Tyre and from Aristotle's observation about how Greeks formerly, and barbarians still, exchanged goods.[113]

To the proto-money theory we may add the suggestion that the *obeloi* were merely practical: they were used to impale meat.[114] By this interpretation, the axes in the graves are for cutting firewood. Karageorghis, who allows for a later monetary use, suggests that the spits were practical, noting that the iron knife at Patriki was there "probably to complete the equipment."[115] Those who argue a culinary use for the *obeloi* also argue that they would be used for impaling prey in some form of afterlife. Those who argue for proto-money do not suggest any postmortem usage. But, clearly, the *obeloi* are present for *some* reason. Andreas Furtwängler's suggestion[116] that they are reli-

---

110. Courbin 1959b. Cf. the brief remark in Kurtz and Boardman 1971, 211: the spits are "pre-coinage currency."

111. Courbin 1983.

112. See Polanyi 1960, 345 (= Dalton 1968a, 326–27). Colin Kraay's (1964, 88–91) important conclusion that coinage, associated regularly with local political power, was not introduced to facilitate either internal or foreign trade has no bearing on our analysis of the spits, which do not indicate any such genesis for themselves.

113. Ezek. 27; Arist. *Pol.* 1257A, 23ff. Small lead weights that may have had a moneylike function were found recently at Vrychos on the northern Aegean island of Samothrace (Touchais 1988, 668).

114. Put forward most recently by Boardman (1971, 8).

115. Karageorghis 1972, 172.

116. Furtwängler 1980, esp. 83–84, 87.

gious symbols and Bruno d'Agostino's[117] that they are status symbols are important contributions here, for both scholars recognize the importance of the *process* of interment and the impact that the buried goods might have had on the community that witnessed the burial. This is why I use the term warrior burial instead of tomb cult, for the interment *event* is what is most important here, not the subsequent tendance. It becomes easier this way to see how similar burials can be to epic recitations. They are both public events.

Firedogs

Firedog interpretation has been less controversial. The usual analysis is that they were functional. Courbin[118] first brought attention to the *krateutai*, probably firedogs, on which Achilles prepares the meal for the embassy in the *Iliad*. We have seen that other heroes, without mention of *krateutai*, prepare their own and others' meals in the *Iliad*, often at a *dais*.[119] Courbin, Karageorghis, Waldemar Deonna, and Boardman are in agreement that their use in life and death was the same.[120] But there is no evidence that "Homeric" Greeks believed in the sort of afterlife that included meals at all, much less self-preparation of them.[121]

As for the common shape of the firedogs, only Deonna has offered an explanation: the ship "sometimes signifies the completed voyage of mundane existence and sometimes carries the soul of the deceased to the next world."[122] Karageorghis tends to agree with this explanation,[123] while Courbin does not, suggesting that they reflect (at Argos) an interest in maritime warfare.[124] Boardman also rejects it on the grounds that

> this symbolic use of a ship for the passage of the dead to the other world is not a feature of Greek burial beliefs nor is there any ship-symbolism in centuries of Greek funerary art and literature. Charon requires no more than a punt to

117. D'Agostino 1977.

118. Courbin 1957, 378.

119. E.g., Achilles (*Il.* 9.206–14), Agamemnon (7.314–18, 9.89ff.).

120. Courbin 1957, 378; Karageorghis 1963, 292–94; Deonna 1959; Boardman 1971, 8.

121. Stuart Piggott (1965) remarks that the Argos and Old Paphos pairs are reminiscent of later firedogs in Etruria and in La Tène Celtic graves. He concludes that "the concept throughout is the other-world feast" (p. 192). Greeks did not have other-world feasts (the Orphic activity described by Plato at *Rep.* 363D is its earliest attestation and an activity undertaken by a special minority) any more than they rode ships to the other world.

122. Deonna 1959, 252.

123. Karageorghis 1963, 292.

124. Courbin 1959a.

ferry souls across the Styx, not a warship, and for heroes the passage to the Isles of the Blest is taken by air.[125]

Boardman does not suggest any postmortem use for the firedogs, except to say that rich men might wish to have a fancy set of equipment for preparing food (he does not say when).[126] It is important before taking this any farther to recall that the "warship" of the eighth and seventh centuries was a multipurpose vessel, used for both war and the movement of goods.[127] Not until the sixth century do we find true "merchant ships," vessels powered exclusively by sail and designed specifically for heavy cargoes.[128] Thus if the shape of the firedogs points to an interest in a particular activity, it seems necessary not to discount the transferring of goods as the intended activity.

The firedogs, like the *obeloi* and the axes, may offer evidence of a belief in an active afterlife. But if the items and their contexts are to be connected in some way with heroic activities in the *epos*, where there is no such belief expressed (with plenty of opportunities for its expression), we must discard the possibility. Again (as with the *obeloi*), interpreters have failed to recognize the importance of the interment *process*.

It is quite simply the case that the "Homeric" Greek belief in an afterlife certainly did not include eating, and so the dead would not require such elaborate instruments of food preparation. When Homer's heroes die, their *psychai* leave their bodies, to flit away to the underworld, to the "next life." Evaluating the afterlife depicted in *Odyssey* 11, Walter Burkert remarks:

> No force, no vital energy emanates from the *psychai*. . . . As images crystallized in memory, *psychai* may persist in their activity of life or situation of death:

125. Boardman 1971, 8. Note that Boardman says "ship-symbolism." Occasionally we find a battle motif, with a ship in the background, on *prothesis* kraters and *amphorae*. An excellent example of this rare type is the eighth-century pedestaled krater in the Metropolitan Museum (34.11.2), which features below the *prothesis* two battle scenes on and in front of an unoared ship of the type the firedogs are emulating. It is reproduced in Ahlberg 1971b, fig. 1; details in Ahlberg 1971a, figs. 29–30.

126. Boardman 1971, 8. Cf. Kurtz and Boardman 1971, 208.

127. Anthony Snodgrass (1983b, 16–17) rightly concludes that it is likely that ships of twenty and fifty oars (pentekontors) were of this double purpose; see also Wallinga 1993, 33 n. 1. These "warships" are well illustrated in Casson 1971, figs. 62, 64, 65–66, 68–69; also in Morrison and Williams 1968, pls. 4d, 5, 6a, 6b; Kirk 1949, 98, fig. 2.

128. Snodgrass 1983b, 17; Humphreys 1978, 168; Casson 1971, figs. 81–82; Morrison and Williams 1968, pl. 19. There were broad-beamed ships in the eighth century that were capable of carrying more cargo than a pentekontor, but they were still driven by oar (in addition to wind). C. M. Reed (1984, esp. 38–40) argues that the special-purpose, wind-only ships appear very much earlier than the sixth century.

Orion the hunter hunts, Minos the king dispenses justice, and Agamemnon is surrounded by those who were slain with him.[129]

But, among other things, they do not eat (those who speak to Odysseus in *Odyssey* 11 drink blood, a special arrangement for communication purposes). Robert Garland describes the dead as follows:

> The Homeric dead are distinguished from their living counterparts in their lack of strength (*menos*), an attribute which they share with dreams. . . . The Homeric dead lack not only *menos*, but also the full command of their faculties. Achilles remarks that although there is soul (*psyche*) and image (*eidolon*) in Hades "the *phrenes* (wits) do not exist at all."[130]

Teiresias the prophet is a lone exception to this witlessness. The only other place dead persons may go is the Islands of the Blessed[131] or simply into the ground.[132] It must be allowed that those heroes who have gone to the Islands of the Blessed eat there.[133]

I would propose a simpler and I hope more satisfactory explanation for this elaborate paraphernalia. The axes that are found in two of the graves are not there to aid the deceased in gathering faggots. As symbols, axes are weapons of war first, culinary instruments second. If these are warriors' graves, the axes are warriors' weapons; only warriors—interreds and interrers—could afford iron armor and weapons.

The spits, I admit, would be handy for skewering a meal, but the fact that they come bundled in sixes and twelves suggests another interpretation, which is that they represent units of wealth. They are not a form of money, units of currency in daily use by a significant portion of the population; they may have been used in individual exchanges. It is certainly likely that they are, like armor and axes, part of a display of wealth; very few people could afford iron.

Finally, and most important, the firedogs are the outstanding symbol of

129. Burkert 1985, 196.

130. Garland 1985, 1.

131. Where the heroes who died at Thebes and Troy went, according to Hesiod (*WD* 161–73).

132. To be protecting spirits, as happened to the members of the Gold and Silver races (*WD* 121–26, 140–42).

133. *WD* 172–73.

the *dais,* the exclusive and exclusionary feast attended by the "best" men—
both dead and alive in the case of hero-tendance feasts.

The process of interment may be taken up again. To judge from their
descriptions in epic and on the monumental Athenian pots of the eighth
century, interments are public activities, displays for the benefit of the eyes
of all members, high or low, of the community. Thus when the deceased is
accompanied into the ground by powerful symbols of his class, the viewers
are reminded of the status of that class's membership. The collocation of
artifacts can be seen as a "status kit," items "possessed by individuals of
rather high status in the community, which were used by those persons to
assert and display that status, and hence to enhance it."[134] Burying firedogs
is a reinforcing action, underlining the exclusive might of the *dais.* Burying
armor and *oboloi* is an action that serves as a reminder of who has the wealth,
regardless of whether or not it was acquired properly (i.e., earned). Burying
horses and slaves seems to be an idiosyncratic action that finds responsive
iteration in the epics. If the general conception in the community is that
wealth follows status (there being no clear indication within the community that the obverse has come into play), a display of wealth along with status-
laden firedogs should only strengthen what has become a *mis*conception.

In a way, it is the firedogs that bring everything together, for they are
reflections of the three tools of exclusion. First, they are found in the graves
of good men, Homer's *aristoi,* men who had iron wealth and were therefore
"warriors." Second, they are a symbol of the *dais.* Third, their similarity to
one another provides additional evidence of a gift-giving network. Why are
the firedogs ship-shaped? I believe that it is reasonable to conclude that the
shape is testimony to the movements of goods by nautical means, testimony
even to how the firedogs reached their destinations. Thus the firedogs are
a reflection of not only how status is asserted but also how it is garnered and
maintained—through the acquisition of unencumbered wealth, wealth that
stands independent of the community. Some would connect the ships with
warfare, but I am wary of any assertion that those buried as warriors were in
fact warriors, for (as pointed out above) the same ships that may have carried "warlords" on piratical raids also carried goods for exchange through
trade or reciprocal activities, from one end of the Mediterranean to the
other. The fact is that there is more evidence in the eighth century for the
movement of goods than there is for warfare.

The social stratification reflected by the burial contents in general, and
the kit of ship-shaped firedogs with spits in particular, indicates a change in
ideology. It is clear that it has become possible and appropriate now to

---

134. Renfrew 1987, 89.

expend the resources within the community in a new way. The model I have constructed reflects this. The new wealth is new in two ways: it has come from outside, and it is under the unobligated control of the political center. It is a reflection of the new driving ideology of the Greek world: the center is separate.

But separate is not necessarily what the center wanted to be perceived to be, and the firedogs and their contexts together suggest that the leaders of the Greek communities addressed this problem of image by seeking to identify themselves with the leaders of the past. Bérard suggested that the eighth-century leadership sought to attract the attention of the nonnobility to the heroes of the past, from whom they claimed descent.[135] My model suggests a much closer linkage between contemporary and epic leadership.[136] The apparent motive behind the creation and exercise of the three tools of exclusion was to muddle the perception of the relative primacy of status and wealth, brought about in part by the introduction of wealth from the outside *by ship*.

These tools of exclusion were powerful forces in the transformation that was taking place in the eighth century. The oral tradition, the guardian and transmitter of the heroic "past," was intimately involved in the delivery of these deceptions to the peripheral elements of Greek communities; it was a fourth tool of exclusion and the most powerful. In this regard, the monumental epics may be perceived as pervasively influential. The oral tradition was a single tool but also the most powerful. The remainder of this study is devoted to the power of the oral tradition and to the difference between it and the new poetry that was perhaps first heard in Ascra and was perhaps effective in Thespiae.

135. Bérard 1982, esp. 97–102.
136. I draw the line far short of Wade-Gery's ingenious connection of the *Iliad* with a King Hector at Chios and Agamemnon at Kyme (Wade-Gery 1952, 7ff.), to which reference has already been made (above, note 75).

SEVEN

Epic and Other Memories

It was within the context of the several strategies of exclusion that the epic poems attributed to Homer and the *Theogony* of Hesiod were composed. To clarify the role of poetry in the response to the economic transformation, we must examine the place of the singer (*aoidos*) and his songs in early Greek society. The *Iliad* and *Odyssey* dominate our vision of eighth-century Greece, and these monumental songs are the works of one or more of the *aoidoi*, for convenience usually named Homer. By studying the *aoidoi* we may better understand both the context of these epic songs and—more important for our purposes here—the role of the *aoidoi* as historical agents. In the end, we should better understand how the *aoidoi* and similar role players were able to influence their audiences and thus helped the new economic elite that emerged in the great transformation maintain their power.

SINGING

First, a speedy debunking of the image that most students of antiquity hold of early Greek singers, and specifically of Homer—I refer, of course, to the old, blind singer who travels "from court to court," reciting to the accompaniment of his lyre (*phorminx* and *kitharis* are Homer's two words for this instrument) in exchange for room and board and perhaps more enduring payment. No singer in the epics is old; only one is blind; none travels. Ancient tradition tells us that Homer was blind,[1] and Hesiod says that he

---

1. He was believed in antiquity to be the singer of the *Homeric Hymn to Apollo*, who encourages his audience, if anyone should ask who the best *aoidos* is, to answer that "he is a blind man and lives on rugged Chios" (*Hymn.Hom.Ap.* 172). All cultures have singers, and often the singers are said to be blind. However, Albert B. Lord, who spent years studying the oral compositions of the Serbian *guslari*, relates that "our experience in those years seemed to indicate that blind singers were not usually good singers" (1960, 19).

traveled once to participate in a singing competition.[2] There is no other evidence that supports the traditional portrait of Homer.

Let us consider Homer's portrait of early Greek singers. Eumaeus the swineherd, in defense of his bringing the disguised Odysseus to the palace on Ithaca, asks:

> For who on his own goes out and summons another man, an outsider from another place, unless he be one of the *demioergoi*, a seer, or a healer of ills or a builder of wood or a divine singer (*theios aoidos*), who gives delight by singing? For these of mortals are renowned over the boundless earth.[3]

According to Max Weber the term *demioergos* "includes all those whose occupations served indeterminate large groups."[4] Weber did not address whether *demioergoi* were outsiders or not. Kenturô Murakawa argued that the term *demioergos* "was not limited to craftsmen alone, but that it comprised certain occupations which were indispensable in those days; and that demiurgoi who were especially skilled in such tasks were frequently invited 'from abroad,' most probably from beyond the boundary of the community (demos)."[5] Most other scholars who have taken up the problem of the definition of *demioergoi* have come to a similar conclusion, that Eumaeus's question is evidence that *demioergoi*—that is, seers, doctors, carpenters, and singers[6]—were characteristically outsiders and therefore itinerant.[7] But *demioergos* is a compound of *demos*, "people," and *ergos*, "worker." Moses Finley rightly opined that the availability of these craftsmen to the *demos* "would explain the word well enough." Finley continued: "Actually the logic of Eumaeus' question is that all invited strangers are craftsmen, not that all craftsmen are strangers. Probably some were and some were not, and of

---

2. *WD* 654–57, where Hesiod's mention of the competition at Chalcis on Euboea may be a reference to his *Theogony* (Wade-Gery 1949, 87; and above, chapter 1, note 43). Plato contributed to the misconception of singers as travelers. In a rather obvious example of modernizing, based on his observation of contemporary rhapsodes such as Ion, Plato relates that Homer and Hesiod "wandered about rhapsodizing" (*Rep.* 600D, 8–9).

3. *Od.* 17.382–86.

4. Weber 1909, 162–63.

5. Murakawa 1957, 387. Later (p. 407), however, he emphasizes that *demioergos* is a "term which stressed that they were part of the community."

6. To Eumaeus's list of *demioergoi* we may add heralds, whom Penelope calls *demioergoi* at 19.135. Murakawa (1957, 399–400, 410) and Cornelius van den Oudenrijn (1951, 96–97, 101–3) are primarily concerned with explaining why the term denotes high political rank among the western Greeks in the archaic and classical periods: in certain areas heralds were of "noble" status.

7. In the new Oxford commentary, Joseph Russo repeats what I presume remains the *communis opinio:* "These verses [*Od.* 17.382–86] are our earliest evidence for poets and other craftsmen as wandering professionals for hire in Greek society" (in Russo, Fernandez-Galiano, and Heubeck 1992, ad 17.385). To say the least, the situation is more complex than this.

those who were, none need have worked a circuit at all."[8] This assessment is consonant with George Thomson's simple observation that the *demioergoi* were "men who 'work for the community.'"[9] One last qualification: *demos,* "people," may include the entire community, but it often refers only to the peripheral members of the community, those away from the center.[10] It is probable that seers, doctors, and carpenters regularly and routinely provided services to the peripheral members of communities. Singers appear to be very different, so that *demioergos,* "worker for the people," in the restricted sense of the peripheral members of the community, is a wholly inappropriate category in which to place singers.

Turning to specific singers in the epics: there are no proper *aoidoi* in the *Iliad,* where the only singers are Achilles, who sings the famous deeds of men;[11] Paris, who plays a *kitharis,* presumably to accompany his own crooning;[12] the youth who sings the Linus song on the Shield to the accompaniment of his *phorminx;*[13] and the dirge leaders at Hector's funeral.[14] It is remarkable that Achilles sings, for thus he, like Odysseus in the *Odyssey,* resembles heroes in epics in other cultures who sing;[15] it is also remarkable that the poet equates himself with his source of support.[16] But Achilles' singing does not help us understand the stature of the individual *aoidos,* although Odysseus's might.

Apart from Odysseus, there are at least three singers in the *Odyssey.* Two have names and do not travel at all. Phemius, the singer at Ithaca who once sang for Odysseus but for the last twenty years has sung for the suitors of Penelope, apparently resides in the royal *oikos.* Demodocus, the blind singer at the court of Alcinous on Phaeacia, is fetched for performances and so probably lives outside but near the residence of that *basileus.*[17] Homer calls

8. Finley 1978, 56. Substantially with Finley on this are Carl Roebuck (1959, 36) and Bjørn Qviller (1980).

9. Thomson 1961, 355–56. Without explanation Thomson also adduces 3.432–35, where a smith (*chalkeus*) comes to Nestor's house to make, on the spot, gilt horns for a heifer that is to be sacrificed. I presume that Thomson assumed that the smith was not a member of Nestor's own *oikos.*

10. Donlan 1970, 383–85. Not until Hesiod (*WD* 256–62) does the differentiation between leadership and *demos* imply tension.

11. *Klea andron: Il.* 9.186–89.

12. *Il.* 3.54, though perhaps he is only playing music.

13. *Il.* 18.569–72.

14. *Il.* 24.720–22.

15. Certain Tamil and Celtic princes were known as great singers of epic strains (Kailasapathy 1968, 55–56). Compare also Solomon and David in the Judaic tradition.

16. There is little question that Hesiod uses very similar language in describing *aoidoi* and *basilees* in the *Theogony* (Duban 1980, 13–14). On Odysseus and Demodocus as each other's alter ego see Harrison 1971.

17. *Od.* 8.43–44.

each a "divine singer," the very pair of words Eumaeus used when he spoke of singers as *demioergoi*;[18] both are "far-famed"[19] and "trustworthy";[20] both sing "inspired songs"[21] and are "like unto the gods in voice."[22] Demodocus is "honored by the *laoi* (= *demos*)";[23] his name in fact means "received by the *demos*," but we will soon see that he has not done much for them lately. The third singer is Agamemnon's unnamed *aoidos*, to whom we will return. There is a fourth, unnamed "divine singer" (*theios aoidos*) in Menelaus's hall who provides instrumental accompaniment for some tumblers.[24] Presumably, however, at other occasions he recites epic verses, just as Demodocus and Phemius also play the lyre for dancers.[25] There are accompanied tumblers also in the *Iliad*.[26]

Audiences hold singers in high opinion for two simple reasons: audiences believe or enjoy the idea that singers are privy to special information and methods, and the singers encourage this belief or idea.[27] Phemius declares: "I am self-taught (*autodidaktos*), and god planted in my breast song ways of every kind."[28] In Homer's narrative Demodocus has received his song from the Muse[29] or from god;[30] Odysseus remarks that Demodocus's source must be the Muse or Apollo.[31] We learn from Eumaeus the swineherd that a good singer learns his songs from the gods.[32] Odysseus says that the Muse teaches singers the ways of song, that she loves the "family" (*phulon*) of singers.[33]

We can supplement the Homeric evidence by turning to Hesiod. The proem to the *Theogony* relates that Hesiod met with the Muses at the foot of Mt. Helicon:

18. *Theios aoidos:* Phemius four times (1.336, 16.252, 17.359, 24.439), Demodocus five (8.43, 47, 87, 539; 13.27).

19. *Periklutos:* Phemius once (1.325), Demodocus thrice (8.83, 367, 521).

20. *Erieros:* Phemius once (1.346), Demodocus twice (8.62, 471).

21. *Thespies aoidai:* 1.328, 8.498.

22. 1.370, 9.3.

23. *Laoisi tetimenos:* 8.472, 13.28. Charles Segal makes the excellent point that the idealized Phaeacians are a bard's ideal, attentive audience, who "accord him more honor than we see anywhere else in the poem" (Segal 1994, 141).

24. 4.17.

25. 8.261–64, 13.27 (= 4.17), 23.143.

26. 18.604, 606.

27. Penelope Murray emphasizes that invocations by the early Greek poets "spring from a real, religious belief in the Muses" (Murray 1981, 90).

28. 22.347–48.

29. 8.63, 73.

30. 8.44–45, 498.

31. 8.488.

32. 17.518–19.

33. 8.479–81.

[The Muses] once taught Hesiod fair song (*aoide*), when he was shepherding his sheep under holy Helicon. First the goddesses spoke this word to me: "Rustic shepherds, base reproaches, mere bellies, we know how to speak many falsehoods that are like truths, but we also know, when we wish, how to pronounce truths." So spoke the articulate daughters of great Zeus. And they gave me a scepter, a shoot of healthy laurel, a marvelous thing they had plucked. And they breathed into me divinely inspired song (*thespis aoide*) so that I might celebrate both the future and the past. And they bade me celebrate the generation of the blessed ones who are forever, and always to sing (*aeidein*) them themselves first and last.[34]

In *Works and Days,* Hesiod refers back to this vision: "I won an eared tripod with a poem (*hymnos*) and carried it off. I dedicated it to the Muses of Helicon, where they first sent me on the road of fine singing (*aoide*). . . . The Muses taught me to sing an incomparable poem (*hymnos*)."[35]

We see, then, that *aoidoi* enjoyed high esteem in the *Odyssey*, though we can see also from Phemius's captive position and from Demodocus's subservience (he sings or plays and stops when so bade) that they were in no way on equal footing with the *basilees* for whom they performed. We also see that while the basis of their esteem within the community may be their ability to sing pleasing songs, the *aoidoi* derive their legitimacy from their access to special information. *Aoidoi* regularly name the Muses or Apollo as their mentors and thus repeatedly and firmly establish their claim to be heard. The most elaborate of these assertions, of course, is the narrative of the genesis of the Muses that opens Hesiod's *Theogony*, while the most routinized form is found in the repeated invocations to the Muses for aid, most prominently perhaps in the passage introducing the Catalog of Ships in the *Iliad*:

Sing for me now, Muses who hold Olympian homes—for *you* are goddesses, and you are present, and you know all things, while *we* hear only a report and do not know anything—who were the leaders of the Danaans and who were their commanders? But the masses I could not tell or name, not even if I had ten tongues and ten mouths, and an unbreakable voice and a bronze heart within me, if the Olympian Muses, daughters of aegis-bearing Zeus, would not recite as many as came under Ilium. Now I will tell the leaders of the ships and all the ships together.[36]

Repetitions of these assertions before audience after audience accumulate to justify the poet's claim to be heard and believed.[37]

34. *Th.* 22–34.
35. *WD* 657–59, 662.
36. 2.484–93.
37. Penelope Murray (1981, 89) draws a distinction between two gifts of the Muses to a singer: "(a) they give him *permanent* poetic ability; (b) they provide him with *temporary* aid in

Limits and Controls

Of course, since the audience will not accept just anything from him, what an *aoidos* sings is limited in an important way by the audience's concept of what is "heroic" and by its memory of past performances. There is a dialectical relationship between audience and singer, a constant give-and-take, the audience limiting the singer by its social set of expectations, the singer attempting to expand those limits. But within this dialectic the singer in early Greece had the upper hand—for the audience, provided that the singer stayed within the limits of its expectations, would believe him because of his divine connection. This special relationship with god or his emissary was the foundation of the singer's credibility: it justified and, in a sense, licensed his claim to be heard and believed. Thus, as a supplement to his aesthetic merits as an entertainer, the singer empowered himself by appealing to the Muse, who then exercised an indirect control over the singer's audience. Schematically, the singer's "religious" control may be represented thus:

But there is little question that the control of the audience enjoyed by the singer is tempered by the control of the big man over the singer. A close inspection of singers' behavior reveals, in fact, that it is more than a little tempered. We need only turn to Agamemnon's *aoidos*, whose namelessness cannot undercut his high rank and whose predicament is extremely instructive. Resident in the royal household, Agamemnon's singer enjoyed sufficient status[38] to be the person assigned to protect Clytemnestra, with disastrous results for both singer and Agamemnon:

> Aegisthus kept trying to win over with words the wife of Agamemnon. At first the beautiful Clytemnestra kept putting off the unseemly deed, for she had a good heart. Now with her was a singer man, whom the son of Atreus, as he left for Troy, strongly did enjoin to guard his wife. But when the fate from the gods did bind her to be overcome, then [Aegisthus] took the singer to a deserted island and left him there to be the prey and spoil of birds.[39]

---

composition [italics original]," a distinction (she concedes) made little of by the singers themselves. See further on this Finkelberg 1990.

38. See Scully 1981 for a mostly sound survey of explanations of the status of this singer and of his role in this brief narrative.

39. *Od.* 3.264–71.

Perhaps Agamemnon's singer sang the wrong songs, songs Aegisthus did not want to hear. In his employer's absence, he invited his own undoing, according to Jesper Svenbro, by failing properly to acknowledge Aegisthus, his new big man.[40] He failed to praise the most proximate big man. Agamemnon's singer might have avoided his fate by adapting to the new set of circumstances, as several of his fictional contemporaries did.

There are many other examples in the epics of the big man's control over oral recitation, often wrongly thought to illustrate the agreement between singer and audience, an agreement or contract that is clearly secondary to the control of the big man. At Ithaca, Phemius has maintained his good health and livelihood by singing themes that his audience wanted to hear. He chose to adapt his themes with full knowledge of the consequences should Odysseus ever return. During his enforced singing in Odysseus's absence, he was asked on only one occasion to change his subject—by Penelope, who was immediately berated assertively by her son Telemachus.[41] Phemius presumably did not change his song and continued, as at other times, to sing the songs that the suitors wanted to hear. Homer tells us twice that he sang for them *anankei*, "under compulsion."[42] As if intended as corroborative testimony, Phemius himself, when begging for his life from the returned Odysseus, explains:

> neither willing nor eager did I come to your house to sing to the suitors at their feasts (*daites*), but they, being many more and stronger, led me here under compulsion (*anankei*).[43]

Odysseus responds to Phemius's plea and also to a similar one by Medon the herald with a smile of forgiveness.[44] Phemius was very lucky that Odysseus understood the rules of recitation.

On Phaeacia, Demodocus begins when he is told and stops when he is told; in a sense he is under the same compulsion in Phaeacia that controls Phemius on Ithaca:

> And whenever the divine singer stopped singing, Odysseus wiped away a tear, drew his cloak from his head, and taking up a two-handled cup poured offerings to the gods. But whenever he started again and the best of the Phaeacians forced him to sing, since they delighted in his verses, again Odysseus covered over his head and moaned.[45]

---

40. Svenbro 1977, 16–36, esp. 31; Stephen Scully (1981, 80–83) misunderstands.
41. 1.336–59.
42. 1.154, 22.331.
43. 22.351–53.
44. 22.371.
45. 8.87–92.

Demodocus stops when Alcinous, who has noticed Odysseus's discomfort, interrupts him;[46] that is why he receives, among other things at other occasions, a choice cut of meat from Odysseus,[47] who appreciates the change of subject matter from the Trojan War to the tale of Ares and Aphrodite. Demodocus chooses his themes as they are appropriate.

Those who find plausible H. T. Wade-Gery's proposition[48] that the *Theogony* was Hesiod's winning poem at the games of Amphidamas agree that the *Theogony* reflects its own context. The prominence of *basilees* in the invocation, where they are described in language almost identical to that used shortly thereafter of *aoidoi*,[49] would be appropriate under a variety of conditions, but especially if both *basilees* and *aoidoi* were present. And if the language used of these *basilees* is rather obviously echoed later in the poem in the description of Zeus's ascendancy after the Titanomachy,[50] it seems rather necessary for them to be present. It is certainly the case that if Hesiod's tripod-winning *hymnos* was not the *Theogony,* it was a poem with similar emphases, for who but *basilees* can afford to award tripods as prizes? We see from these examples that oral recitation is strongly influenced, perhaps even severely limited, by its context, and the most important part of the context is the individual who pays the bills: the big man. Hence it is no surprise at all that there is a fundamental similarity between the kingly advice that comes from Odysseus when taunted in public on Scheria and that offered by Hesiod near the beginning of the *Theogony*:[51] the *Odyssey* and the *Theogony* were generated under very similar conditions.

I want to repeat, however, what I said above about the audience not accepting just anything. Ultimately, the audience cannot be overlooked in any model, for Ruth Finnegan is correct in her conclusion that "an oral poem is an essentially ephemeral work of art, and has no existence or continuity apart from its performance. . . . Oral literature is more flexible and more dependent on its social context [than written poetry]."[52] W. R. Connor's analysis of the tyrant Peisistratus's return to Athens from exile in the 550s is perhaps instructive here.[53] Herodotus reports that Peisistratus entered Athens riding in a chariot, accompanied by a young woman dressed

46. 8.94–96.
47. 8.474–83.
48. Wade-Gery 1949, 87; see above, chapter 1, note 43.
49. *Th.* 80–103; for the specific parallels and a general discussion of this observation, see below and Duban 1980, esp. 13–14.
50. Duban, 1980, 18–19.
51. *Od.* 8.166–77; *Th.* 79–93: see Martin 1984.
52. Finnegan 1977, 28–29.
53. Connor 1987, esp. 42ff. Herodotus narrates the event at 1.60.

as Athena. Herodotus himself expressed incredulity at the Athenians' gulli-
bility, but Connor argues clearly that what may at first be perceived as political manipulation is in fact a two-way street: the ruled (the audience) are
apparently at least willing if not desiring to hear and witness certain behav-
ioral patterns on the part of the rulers. These witnessed and accepted patterns of behavior celebrate and thus cement the differences between the
displayers and the audience; an existing or even a new set of rules are
thus celebrated. (For an instructive parallel to Connor's analysis of the
Peisistratus-Athena procession, see Robert Darnton's discussion and
description of the routine *procession générale* in Old Regime Montpellier.[54]
The procession regularly rearticulated the three *états* of Old Regime
France.)[55]

To return to the topic at hand: we must not deny social control on the
part of the audience, who are not going to sit and listen to just anything.
Every successful oral recitation must contain material that appeals to all seg-
ments of the audience, including material that is in keeping with the folk
view that supports the manner in which the community is organized. A
recitation certainly must have virtues that transcend the mere pleasing of
the big man or big men.

We have seen that the success and safety enjoyed by Demodocus and
Phemius depended to no small extent on their ability to adapt to current
circumstances. The fate of Agamemnon's singer may be attributed to his
inability to adapt his songs to the new situation that had arisen at Mycenae.
It is perhaps useful in passing to compare the situation of Agamemnon's
singer to the misadventure of Thersites in the *Iliad*. Unhappy with the
behavior of Agamemnon and other *basilees*, Thersites, the ugliest man at
Troy, spoke out bitterly. Odysseus bludgeoned him soundly.[56] Thus Thersites paid for his criticism of the big men. Similarly, Agamemnon's singer
paid the wages of song to his big man; Phemius almost did.

Schematically, the control that the big man enjoys over the singer may be
presented thus:

---

54. Darnton 1984, chap. 3, esp. 116–20.
55. Darnton 1984, 124–28; cf. Dumont 1980, chap. 3, esp. 91. These phenomena in
Athens and Montpellier are both excellent examples of successful hegemony, to use Antonio
Gramsci's powerful term (Gramsci 1971).
56. *Il.* 2.212–77. On Thersites as antiaristocratic and blame poet, see chapter 8.

But we must keep in mind that the key to the respect that the singers enjoy in early Greek communities is their access to special, divine knowledge. The actual content of the songs of successful singers is clearly informed by the special interests of the *basilees,* the big men. A combination of schemata results in this one:

But there is also a dialectical relationship, a symbiosis of sorts, between singer and big man, for however much the big man may control what the singer sings, such control must be delicately and carefully maintained, and probably disguised by them both from the perception of the audience. That a singer has in a certain way a kind of upper hand at times is clear from what Phemius embeds within his elaborate plea for forgiveness: "There will be sorrow for you in the future, if you should kill me, a singer (*aoidos*) who sings (verb *aeidein*) for both gods and men."[57] The dialectic is clearly multiplex.

In oral recitations in the fictional contexts of the early epics, the song of an *aoidos* is heard and believed. One reason may be that an oral statement does not offer the hearer the opportunity to reflect on its content, but that is taking up a different subject. Without the religious control exercised by the singer over the audience, the song would be ineffective as a big man's tool.

Comparative Materials

An investigation of the position of oral poets in other traditional societies may help us understand Homer's (and Hesiod's) place in eighth-century Greece. Two very good examples of oral poets in societies are the nearly forgotten Kirghiz *akin* of Siberia, studied by W. Radloff in the 1870s,[58] and the Serbian *guslari,* discovered by Milman Parry and described by Albert Lord in his *Singer of Tales.*[59]

The *akin* was a powerful member of Kirghiz society, traveling from sultan to sultan, who regularly feasted large groups of subjects. Performing both heroic narrative and extemporaneous panegyric, the *akin* commanded preeminent esteem, for the art of poetry was highly prized in the culture. "Sultans consider it very necessary for their prestige to have one of these

57. 22.345–46.
58. Radloff 1885.
59. Lord 1960.

men attached to them, who will honour them by singing on all public occasions."[60] The hypnotic spell the *akin* weaves over the audience is described by Radloff:

> Deep silence embraces the reciter who knows how to arrest his listeners; they sit with upper bodies bent forward and with eyes shining, and they listen to the words of the reciter, and every well-turned word, every witty word-play calls forth spirited applauses of approval.[61]

The singer "every evening attracted round him a crowd of gaping admirers, who greedily listened to his stories and songs."[62] This response of the audience to well-turned heroic verse is startlingly similar to what we find in the *Odyssey*. Homer describes Phemius among the suitors as follows: "The famous *aoidos* sang to them, and they sat listening in silence."[63] Eumaeus uses a simile to articulate the impression the disguised Odysseus left on him:

> Just as when a man gazes at an *aoidos*, who with knowledge from the gods sings words of longing to mortals, and they are eager to listen to him without stopping, whenever he sings; just so did that man soothe me as he sat in my house.[64]

This power was limited, however, by the presence of the sultan or chief overseeing the feast, whom the singer seems bound to praise:

> When the chief of the expedition gave an entertainment to the Kirghizes . . . , this poet loudly and eloquently extolled the virtues of the giver of the feast—probably with a view to a noble largesse.[65]
>
> If there are rich and noble Kirghiz present, he knows how to interweave skillful, high praises of their families, the sort which he may expect to generate quite especially the approval of the nobles. If only poor persons are his listeners, he does not hesitate to insert venomous remarks about the presumptions of the nobles and the rich, and indeed to the greater extent, the more he acquires the applause of his listeners.[66]

The poet's "imagination was remarkably fertile in creating feats for his hero—the son of some Khan—and took most daring flights into the regions of marvel."[67] We see, then, the need on the part of the singer to conform to the demands of his context; he must treat the feast giver kindly or receive no reward for his trouble.

---

60. Chadwick and Chadwick 1940, 178.
61. Radloff 1885, iii.
62. Michell and Michell 1865, 290.
63. 1.325–26.
64. 17.518–21.
65. Michell and Michell 1865, 290.
66. Radloff 1885, xviii-xix.
67. Michell and Michell 1865, 290.

Although he appears dependent upon the big man during the recitation, the Serbian singer, by contrast, was able to acquire and maintain a reputation and its attendant status independently of that source of support. The very best *guslari* found themselves invited to the households of the nobility, even of kings. The famed Huso Husović was fetched from Serbia to the Viennese court of Franz Joseph, where he sang to his *gusle* for a month and received 100 sheep and 100 napoleons for his trouble. He returned home, gave the sheep to his family, pocketed the coins, and went off to sing some more, traveling "from kingdom to kingdom."[68] Husović was certainly a professional, but there were many among the singers studied by Parry and Lord who might be counted butchers and other nonmusical specialists. A singer "is not an oral poet because he is a farmer, a shopkeeper or bey. He can belong to the 'folk,' the merchant class, or the aristocracy."[69] In fact, many *guslari* were quite amateur; it would appear that many unprominent households boasted of a resident singer to the *gusle*.

There are other similarities and differences between oral poets in the epic poems and those in other traditional societies. The explanation a Kirghiz *akin* gives of the source of his song is remarkably similar to what one finds in the *Odyssey*. When Radloff asked one of the better singers whether he could sing this song or that, the singer replied:

> I can sing any song at all, for God has implanted this gift of song in my heart. He gives me the word on my tongue, without my having to seek it. I have learned none of my songs. Everything flows forth from my insides, from out of me.[70]

We recall that Phemius claims, in a single sentence, almost exactly this: "I am self-taught, and god planted in my breast song ways of every kind."[71] While it is not clear from the studies of Radloff, Parry, and Lord that the esteem granted the *akin* and the *guslar* is in any way connected to this appeal to god, the fact that the singer's skill was practiced by all the Kirghiz and by a large percentage of the Serbians with more or less success but with universally equal enthusiasm suggests an agreement among members of the audience that the best of singers or a singer at his best has a special relationship with god or god's emissary. Each is a Caedmon.[72]

We can see from these analogues that if an oral singer of any period had the talent that Husović had, he might choose full-time singing as his occupation, and the source of his livelihood would then of course depend both

---

68. Parry 1971, 438.
69. Lord 1960, 20.
70. Radloff 1885, xvii.
71. 22.347–48.
72. A similar situation obtains among the Tamil bards (Kailasapathy 1968, chap. 2).

on his own ability to perform acceptable material and on his audiences' ability to reward him. Whether he traveled would depend on the leading households' ability to support him. Singers are not by definition travelers; but if opportunity arises, a trip may be taken. Husović's singing at Franz Joseph's court is not very different from Hesiod's trip to Chalcis, and this brings us back to eighth-century Greece and to the important subject of recitational context.

Recitational Contexts and Audiences

For the period around and after 750, we can presume a specific variety of contexts for oral recitation. Most of the evidence is extracted from the monumental poems, the rest deduced with the help of the archaeological record. The broad categories are secular and sacred, with some predictable overlapping.

Strictly secular contexts included the *daites* at which Greeks listened to recitations by *aoidoi*. Repeatedly in the *Odyssey*, Phemius sings for the gastronomic suitors. Demodocus sings at the court of Alcinous. He also sings at the conclusion of the athletic contests on Scheria, which suggests regular recitations in such purely secular contexts.

The received date for the beginning of the great Panhellenic gatherings at Olympia, Delos, and Delphi is approximately 750 B.C. It is a fair general observation that in the latter half of the eight century the Panhellenic centers witnessed an unprecedented influx of metal offerings, a reflection of several phenomena, among them a "redirection of attention towards the communal sanctuary and away from the individual grave."[73] Olympia's "official" starting date of 776 is more or less borne out by the appearance in the archaeological record of many terra-cotta and bronze dedications beginning before 750.[74] Although Alfred Mallwitz has recently argued for a late eighth-century institutionalization of the athletic competition at Olympia,[75] we can only surmise how early there may have been regular recitations, competitive or otherwise. There is no reason not to think recitations had become a routinized component by the time the Olympic Games became truly Panhellenic, shortly after 700, when specialized competitors from as far away as Ionia to the east and Sicily and Italy to the west began to compete.[76]

---

73. Snodgrass 1980a, 54. Anthony Snodgrass notes "the general and sudden rise in activity [at Greek sanctuaries] in the eighth century" (p. 55).

74. Yalouris in PECS, p. 647, col. 1. See further Herrmann 1972, 70–79; Rolley 1983, 111.

75. Mallwitz 1988.

76. Finley and Pleket 1976, 69, 70.

The Ionian *panegyris* at Delos is at least as old as the *Homeric Hymn to Delian Apollo,* which on linguistic grounds may be dated to the lifetime of Hesiod.[77] The *aoidos* of the *Hymn* describes a gathering of significant size:

> But in Delos, Phoebus, you especially delight your heart, where the long-robed Ionians gather with their children and upright wives. They are mindful to delight you with boxing and dancing and song (*aoide*), whenever they put on the competition. Whoever should come encounter them when the Ionians were gathered would say that they were immortal and forever ageless; for he would see the grace of them all, and he would delight in his heart to see the men and the fair-girdled women and their swift ships and many possessions. . . . [The girls of Delos] know how to mimic the tongues and castanet-playing of all men. Each man would say that he himself was singing, for so well is their fine song (*aoide*) put together.[78]

Although the emphasis on Ionians at first indicates that the Delian festival from the start was only of regional interest, the reference to foreign tongues suggests that non-Ionian speakers were also in attendance. By the early seventh century, then, there were recitational competitions at Delos, which was at least in the process of becoming a Panhellenic center.[79]

In the eighth century, the importance of the Delphic oracle appears only regional (Corinth, Chalcis, Thessaly, Sparta), but it grew so that by about 690, communities as distant as Paros and Rhodes consulted it before acting overseas.[80] At the Pythian Games, recitational competitions preceded by many years the athletic events that were introduced by the Amphictyony

---

77. See Janko 1982, 106. A snippet of hexameters attributed to Hesiod may well have been composed in response to the existence at Delos of competitions in both "Homeric" and "Hesiodic" hymns (frag. 357):

In Delos at that time for the first time I and Homer, *aoidoi*, celebrated, weaving a song (*aoide*) in new hymns, Phoebus Apollo of the golden sword, whom Leto bore.

See further Janko, pp. 113–14.

78. *Hymn. Hom. Ap.* 146–55, 162–64.

79. There are cult buildings at Delos before the end of the eighth century (Boardman 1982b, 769), but the importance of the place as a meeting place is indeterminate.

80. Forrest 1957, esp. 173. The Homeric evidence for the rise of Delphi is Achilles' refusal to accept "as much as the marble threshold of the archer contains within it, of Phoebus Apollo, in rocky Pytho" (*Il.* 9. 404–5). Such evidence dates itself rather than Delphi. (That a number of eighth-century artifacts, including several large bronze votive tripods [Themelis 1983a, 248], have been found at Delphi tells us rather little.) Likewise the brief reference to an oracle at *Od.* 8.79–82. Cf. H. T. Wade-Gery's ingenious suggestion that the poet of the *Iliad* and his audience were familiar with the *panegyreis* not only at Delos, but also at Ephesus and at Mt. Mycale in the Samian *peraea* (Wade-Gery 1952, 2–4); C. J. Emlyn-Jones (1980, 17) clearly demonstrates that is unlikely that Mycale was important so early: again, if Wade-Gery's passages date anything, it is probably the text.

only in about 585, about the same time the *Homeric Hymn to Pythian Apollo* was composed.[81]

The earliest panegyrical development of Olympia, Delos, and Delphi is in keeping with our observation in the preceding chapter that in the latter half of the eighth century a portion of the Greek population made a concerted effort to create a kind of Panhellenic elitism. These gatherings, attended for the most part by wealthy persons (like the fair-girdled Ionian women with their Homeric ships and numerous possessions, brought for display purposes), provided opportunities to share common interests, to buttress common goals, and to demonstrate a solidarity of superiority to any peripheral members who might be present. How else can we conclude other than that the same persons who participate in the *xenie* networks participate in the *panegyreis*? The same ideology of separation that drives the *xenie* networks and resides behind the interment of the firedog kits generated these *panegyreis*.

To these Panhellenic contexts may be added other religious milieus for recitation. Funeral games, predictably, provided competitions among *aoidoi*. At the games of Amphidamas, Hesiod won a tripod, perhaps with the *Theogony*, but certainly with a poem like it. Funeral games were held in honor of Ekpropos at Thebes in the early seventh century, although it is uncertain that singing was featured.[82] At hero-cult celebrations, as may be suggested by the presence of the *megaron* at the Eretrian West Gate and the great hall at Lefkandi (albeit much earlier), it is highly plausible that meals were consumed to honor the hero, and it is not unlikely that a song was presented of similar function.

Of course, a very important part of an oral recitation's context is the audience, at least two and perhaps three different types of which can be identified. First, there was the exclusively aristocratic audience, such as the suitors at Ithaca and the *aristoi* at Alcinous's palace. The members of this audience are *aristoi* only, as at a *dais* or a hero meal. Second, we may assume the existence of mixed audiences, such as the mixed local crowd at the funeral games of Amphidamas. Certainly mixed, but predominantly aristocratic (for obvious reasons of availability of leisure time to attend) were the audiences at the great *panegyreis* at Delphi, Delos, Olympia, and elsewhere. Perhaps the crowd that filled the spaces abutting Alcinous's main hall could hear the strains from Demodocus's lyre.[83]

It is no surprise that there is no certain example, either in the archaeological record or in Homer and Hesiod, of the third type of audience, a

---

81. On the dating of the hymn, see Janko 1982, 132.
82. Jeffery 1961a, 94, no. 2; see Roller 1981, 2.
83. 8.57–58.

purely nonaristocratic one that may have been comprised exclusively of peripheral members of a community. The only possibility seems to be a group of local persons sitting around the *lesche* in the winter, who might listen to a song from a singer:

> Pass by the smithy's seat and the warm *lesche* in wintertime, when the cold keeps men from their works; at that time a diligent man would support his *oikos* greatly [by performing household chores].[84]

The Linus song on the Shield is an accompaniment to work:

> In [the vineyard workers'] midst, a boy played delightfully on the lyre (*phorminx*), and he sang (*aeide*) a pretty Linus song with his delicate voice.[85]

REMEMBERING

How does orality function within political contexts, especially as regards change? An oral tradition does not prevent change; rather, it disguises it, and the changes that do occur either are restricted to the elite or extend to the community at large. Writing, on the other hand, encourages change, especially in relations between those out of power and those in it.

There are two categories of knowledge that societies of all sizes and periods need to retain: secular and sacred. Both types of information are needed for the transmission of cultural values and practical advice from generation to generation and for the maintenance of the immediate social organization. Both serve to encourage members of a community to act in accordance with what is collectively perceived as the community's best interests.

When the fifth-century historians of Greece began their inquiries into the past and started to compile their lists of kings, leaders, and victors, their sources were often local lists, some perhaps kept in written form, but most kept in the memories of those assigned the task.[86] These people, who retained this and other information on behalf of their communities, were apparently called *mnemones*,[87] "rememberers," or *istores*,[88] "knowers." The

---

84. Hes. *WD* 493–95. That idlers and the homeless spent time at *leschai* is borne out by *Od.* 18.327–29 (Melantho to the unrevealed Odysseus):

Wretched stranger, you are but someone touched in the head; you are unwilling to go to a smithy's place to sleep, or to some *lesche*. Rather, you chatter away here.

The *lesche* evolved into a serious institution in Sparta (Buxton 1994, 41); see further chapter 8, note 23.

85. *Il.* 18.569–71.

86. See Jeffery 1976, 36. On the genealogy's relationship to history see Fornara 1983, 4–12.

87. *Mnemon* (*mnamon* in certain dialects) is first an adjective, "mindful," then a noun, "rememberer" (Frisk 1973, 2: 239–40).

88. *Istor* is an agent noun from *oida*, "I have seen," "I know" (Frisk 1973, 1: 740–41).

evidence for this office is mostly rather late; but this circumstantial evidence, combined with what we find in the *Iliad* and the *Theogony*, forcefully supports the notion that the position, whatever its title, is very ancient. An inscription from Cretan Arkades (modern Afrati), dated to about 500, names a certain Spensithios to be scribe (*poinikastas*) and rememberer (*mnamon*):

> Gods. The Dataleis resolved, and we the city, five (representatives) from each tribe, pledge to Spensithios subsistence and immunity from all taxes to him and his descendants, so that he be for the city its *poinikastas* and *mnamon*[89] in public affairs both sacred and secular. No one else is to be *poinikastas* and *mnamon* in public affairs.[90]

The inscription goes on to assign to Spensithios rights equal to a *kosmos*, apparently a position that involved juridical duties.[91] The Law Code of Gortyn (about 480) mentions a *mnamon* who reported to the *kosmos*.[92] Although this evidence is from Crete, we need not conclude that the position of *mnamon* was uniquely Cretan, for Aristotle tells us that in certain (unidentified) Greek city-states the magistrate charged with registering private contracts and decisions of the law courts was called a *mnemon*.[93]

We see in the Arkades inscription that "the duties and rights described specifically are those of the *poinikastas*, though the definition of the office is [to serve as *poinikastas* and to serve as *mnamon*]. We may speculate that the ancient office of Remembrancer . . . is now merged in the new technical one."[94] That is, we may surmise that until literacy became sufficiently common to render the writing of public records useful, many Greek communities in the archaic period, if not earlier, had an individual known as a rememberer, whose function, perhaps inherited, was to retain and share as needed the laws of the community. This supposition seems to be borne out by the controversial passage depicting the dispensation of justice in the *Iliad*:

> The people (*laoi*) were gathered in the *agora*. For there had arisen a quarrel (*neikos*), and two men were engaging in a *neikos* over the payment for a man murdered. One claimed that he had paid in full, declaring thus to the people

---

89. The Greek actually has a pair of infinitives: *poinikazen*, i.e., *phoinikazein*, "to make Phoenician marks," "to write," "to serve as *poinikastas*," and *mnamoneuwen*, i.e., *mnemoneuein*, "to serve as *mnemon*." It is not certain exactly what the etymology of *poinik-* may be (Beattie 1975, 25–30; Edwards and Edwards 1977).

90. A.1–7 (text in Jeffery and Morpurgo-Davies 1970, 124). I give the translation from Jeffery and Morpurgo-Davies 1971/72, 26. The text is also edited, translated, and discussed by Henri van Effenterre (1973).

91. B.1–4 (Jeffery and Morpurgo-Davies 1970, 124).

92. IX.32, XI.16, 53 (text in Willetts 1967, 47, 49).

93. *Pol.* 1321B, 39.

94. Jeffery and Morpurgo-Davies 1970, 150.

(*demos*); the other refused to accept anything.[95] Both were eager to receive the verdict before the *istor.* The people (*laoi*) were cheering both, supporting both sides. Heralds restrained the people (*laos*), and there were old men sitting on polished stones within a sacred circle, and they were holding in their hands the staffs of the clear-voiced heralds. With these then they were darting up, and they were giving judgments each in turn. And in their midst there lay two talents of gold, to award to the man among them who might enunciate the straightest judgment (*dike*).[96]

Before we consider the *istor* in this passage, let us note that the only other named *istor* in early Greek literature is Agamemnon, proposed (though he is never needed) to arbitrate a wager between Idomeneus and the Lesser Ajax on the leadership in a chariot race.[97] Compare the adjectival use (without helpful context) in Hesiod: "On the great twentieth (of the month), at midday, is born an *istor* man."[98] And in a (probably late) *Homeric Hymn* the Muses, the daughters of Mnemosyne ("Memory"), are "*istores* of song,"[99] which shows us how close an *istor* is to a *mnemon.*

To return to the litigation passage in the *Iliad,* the least controversial aspect of it seems to be the *istor.* Either the *istor* will decide on and make binding the opinion of the old man who gives the straightest judgment or the old man who gives the straightest judgment will be acclaimed *istor* (by the onlookers). The *istor* will receive the two talents put up, one each, by the two litigants.[100]

This is not the place to join the on-going debate on the strict meaning of this thorny passage, but I might cite what may be a strong, useful parallel in the Old Icelandic system of justice, where the *lögsögumaðr,* "law speaker," elected to a three-year term and expected annually to recite one-third of the law, was regularly called upon to decide fine points of law and was able himself to consult five *lögmenn,* "law men."[101] Thus Icelandic law was retained

95. Some would render this as "the other denied that he had received anything." But see Leaf and Bayfield 1898, ad loc.: the verb just does not have this force in Homer.

96. *Il.* 18.497–508. Controversy seems to exist over whether these two talents are meant as a prize for the better litigator or for the best of the old men delivering their opinions. Robert Bonner (1911, 24–25; Bonner and Smith 1930, 39) thinks the former; the Greek words indicate fairly clearly the latter. A detailed analysis of this controversial passage is beyond the scope of this study; see Gagarin 1986, 26–33, and bibliography, p. 26 n. 26; esp. Hommel 1969 and-MacDowell 1978; add Andersen 1976.

97. *Il.* 23.486.

98. *WD* 792.

99. *Hymn. Hom.* 32.3.

100. Thus we are wise to keep in mind the possibility that Hesiod's "gift-eating" *basilees* may in fact be *istores* who consistently give "straight judgments," and so often receive the stakes put up by the litigants. See Gagarin 1986, 85 n. 15. Hans Julius Wolff (1946, 39) believes that the old man who gives the straightest judgment will receive the stakes.

101. See *Kulturhistorisk Leksikon,* s.v. *lögsögumaðr;* Byock 1982, 216.

and transmitted orally for a long time after the introduction of writing, until the office of *lögsögumaðr* was abolished with the appearance of the first Norwegian laws in 1271, a situation perhaps similar to the subsumption of the *mnemon* by the new office of "writer" at Arkades. Compare also the role of the *mazkir,* "testifier," "recorder," in the Old Testament,[102] translated by the Septuagint as *anamimneiskon,* "rememberer." Of one such *mazkir* we read: "Eliezer, the son of Hyrcanus, is a cemented cistern, which loses not a drop."[103] *Zakar,* the verb related to the agent noun *mazkir,* is used in the meaning "to bear witness," "testify," and is translated by the Septuagint as *marturein;* thus we see a likely (additional?) juridical role for the *mazkir.* Each time a *mazkir* is named a scribe is also present, which suggests a situation similar to that at Arkades, where a single man holds both positions. To the Icelandic and Hebrew analogues may be compared the Maori *tohungas,* who could be called upon to testify on land claims by reciting genealogies. Tamarau, of the Ngati-Koura clan, took the "stand in the Native Land Court for three days, and gave from memory lines of descent that contained over fourteen hundred names of persons."[104]

The rememberer in early Greece (by whatever title) was probably often a local *basileus,* his follower, or one of his kin. In Homer, disputes are handled by *basilees* or by their proxies. Achilles calls the holders of the staff of kingship *dikaspoloi,* "dispensers of judgments";[105] they guard the laws (*themistes*), which come from Zeus.[106] In the underworld, Anticlea tells her son Odysseus that Telemachus is running the royal Ithacan household well, in spite of his youth, as a good *dikaspolos* should.[107] A good *basileus* maintains *eudikie,* "good justice,"[108] and there are at least two cases where non-"kings" decide law cases (*themistes*)[109] and disputes (*neikea*), the latter being contained in an odd simile in the *Odyssey,* where we are told that Charybdis appeared at the same hour as "when a man stands up from the *agora* for his dinner, a man who sorts out many *neikea* of men seeking *dike.*"[110] In Hesiod,

102. 2 Sam. 8:16, 20:24; 1 Kings 4:3; 1 Chron. 18:15 (Jehoshaphat); 2 Kings 18:18, 37; 2 Chron. 34:8; Isa. 36:3, 22 (Joah).

103. Pirke Avot II.11 (Hertz 1945, 37).

104. Best 1924, 1: 344–45. Even in nongenealogical, non-"legal" contexts, the "Maori are cunning mythologists, who are able to select from the supple body of traditions those most appropriate *to the satisfaction of their current interests, as they conceive them* (Sahlins 1985, 55; italics added).

105. *Il.* 1.238. The staff itself is described genealogically later (2.102–8). On the use of the staff in the epic world see Combellack 1947/48.

106. Hence *basilees* are *themistopoloi* at Hes. frag. 10.26; *Hymn. Hom. Dem.* 103, 215, 473.

107. *Od.* 11.186.

108. *Od.* 19.109–11.

109. *Il.* 16.386.

110. *Od.* 12.439–40.

juridical disputes are handled by *basilees,* who themselves may be the rememberers or are able to consult them. Although it is rather unlikely that there is in place a system for the retention of something like a common law, perhaps based on precedental cases, there is clearly in place a procedural system and adjudicators in it to provide binding (i.e., acceptable) pronouncements in the adjudicating, as the need arose, of disputes over rules.[111] The "explanation" of successful adjudicating includes acknowledgment of the knowledge or experience of the adjudicators: that is why they are called *istores.* Homer seems to speak with admiration of the *istor* and the old men on the Shield; Hesiod uses similar language to describe the juridical activities of *basilees* in the *Theogony:*

> Whomsoever of the Zeus-nourished *basilees* the daughters of great Zeus honor and gaze upon at birth, they shed sweet dew upon his tongue, and words flow sweet from his mouth. And all the people (*laoi*) watch him as he decides law cases with straight judgments (*dikai*); and he, speaking surely, would wisely put a stop to even a great quarrel (*neikos*). For therefore there are *basilees* with wise hearts, because when the people (*laoi*) are being misled in the *agora,* they easily settle cases that might bring harm, moving them with soothing words. When he goes through the assembly, they greet him as a god, and he is conspicuous among those gathered.[112]

In *Works and Days,* however, we see that Hesiod has changed his opinion, no doubt (in part) because he has lost a judgment to his brother. Though we can concede that the *basilees* may be characteristically *dorophagoi,* "gift eaters," in the oral tradition, either because they accept gifts that are then eaten—recall the yams in chapter 4 and the suitors in the *Odyssey*—or because they discharge their duties as *istores* successfully (see above), Hesiod's use of the epithet in *Works and Days*[113] is clearly intended as pejorative: now the *basilees* are *dorophagoi,* because they are easily swayed in their judgments by receipts of unjust gains. We will return to Hesiod's change of heart.

One activity (if not the specific office) of the rememberer, well documented in many preindustrial societies, is the retention of community or even "national" genealogies. Among the best known and most impressive of these is the genealogy of the Hebrew people in Genesis 10. Its original and simpler form, which would have had Abraham descended from Noah through the eponymous Eber, was expanded to include other eponyms accounting for many of the rival peoples of Anatolia (e.g., Javan, eponym

---

111. See Gagarin 1986, chap. 1; of the process Michael Gagarin observes: "Its purpose was not so much to punish violations of rules as to settle disputes and thus eliminate or at least lessen strife in society" (p. 23).

112. *Th.* 81–92.

113. *WD* 39, 221, 264.

for the Ionians) and the Near East (e.g., Elam and Assur). Not surprisingly, the accretions (to the greater glory of Noah) carefully assert the special interests of the Hebrews by making sure that the eldest son of Noah was Shem, in whose line was Abraham's descent via Peleg, the elder son of Eber. It is difficult to find an ancient culture that has left a substantial legacy that does not include fairly elaborate (if often predictable) genealogies.[114] In this regard, early Greece is no different, as Martin West demonstrates in his detailed analysis of the Hesiodic *Catalog*.[115] But *any* similarity between the elaborate genealogies of the Greeks and those of other ancient peoples is particularly useful here. In virtually every case, we have inherited *written* genealogies at or near the conclusion of literally hundreds of years of local accretions, deletions, and other alterations, as West makes clear for the Greek material.[116]

The impressive early Greek genealogies that emerged in written form in the sixth century were plausibly taking on their initial forms in the eighth; thus more instructive for our purposes would be examples of genealogies documented by anthropologists and colonial civil servants that illustrate the fluidity of genealogical stemmata in traditional societies.[117] Among the Maoris of New Zealand, for example, the *tohungas* were charged with retaining in their memories the genealogies of the people, especially those of the currently ascendant family or clan. These genealogies were even used as evidence in settling disputes before the English colonial authorities; ownership of land "was predicated on traditional genealogies and could only be resolved through them. The extensive documentation available amply charts the course of this genealogical warfare."[118] These genealogies, assumed by the observers and, presumably, the Maori community as binding and frozen (or binding *because* they were frozen), in fact did undergo alteration as change occurred in social and political hierarchies.

Another example of such fluidity is found within the British administration of the Ntem tribe:

> The Ntem of western Cameroon fell under British control when the Germans were expelled from the area in 1914. In its subsequent administrative arrangements the colonial government in Nigeria placed the Ntem chief under the neighboring Wiya ruler. At first, this suited the expressed wishes of the Ntem chief since his main desire was to escape the onus of Banyo Fulani domination. In 1924 a list of Ntem chiefs was drawn up, showing a genealogy of six

114. Cf. the Tamil evidence also, in Kailasapathy 1968, 126–29.
115. West 1985, 125–64, 174–82.
116. West 1985, 164–71.
117. On these earliest genealogies in the literary tradition see Broadbent 1968, chaps. 2 and 5.
118. Henige 1974, 104.

chiefs in three generations. The fact that the ancestor of the Wiya line was shown as the younger brother of the ancestor of the Ntem line probably reflected the beginnings of Ntem disenchantment with Wiya administrative control. To support his application to the British authorities to this effect he submitted a new history of the Ntem chiefdom. The number of Ntem chiefs now rose to 23 in an unspecified number of generations. The new genealogy was submitted specifically to prove that Wiya should be subordinate to Ntem rather than the reverse. Not surprisingly, the administration of British Cameroons did not see fit to disturb the existing administrative structure in the light of the new Ntem genealogy.[119]

While this ploy proved unsuccessful, it is clear that the Ntem tribe felt that the revised genealogies were as "true" as their predecessors. "An oral—unlike a written—account can easily be bent to fit current political realities, and (failing an outside written record) there is no documentary evidence by which it could be proved to have changed."[120]

This fluidity can be attributed to an eagerness to maintain one's immediate special interests, whether these interests belong to the community (or "nation") at large or to a narrowly bounded group to whom the genealogizer may be beholden. It is precisely the same motive, mutatis mutandis, that I would assign to the rememberers of early Greece. We may see the special interests of the Greek communities served when a local hero is found otherwise inexplicably among the descendants of a prominent, but foreign, genealogy. The Euboean Abas, for example, appears among the descendants of Io. This may reflect the special interest of the Euboeans,[121] but it seems much more feasible that it reflects the special interest of the Abantes in Euboea. It is important to note whether the Abantes are eager to become associated with nobility from Thebes and/or Argos or wish to enhance their status at home; but it is perhaps more important that the presence of Abas in the genealogy is the result of the genealogy's flexibility as a form and as a tool. What is of paramount importance is that the Io genealogy is capable of alteration to serve local interests, although we must not lose sight of the genealogy as a Panhellenizing institution that served to reconcile conflicting epichorisms.[122]

119. Henige 1974, 104–5.

120. Ruth Finnegan's (1988, 20) remark on the tale of the Gonja people of Ghana. Early in the twentieth century a story was recorded by an outsider that the founder of the Gonja kingdom left the rule to his seven sons at his death. There happened at the time of this recounting to be seven administrative divisions. Many years later, the administrative divisions were reduced in number to five, and when the myth was recorded again, the founder had only five sons. See more fully Goody and Watt 1968, 33.

121. So West 1985, 149–52.

122. Charles Fornara (1983, 4) speaks of Hesiod's "impulse to bring order to the genealogical confusion that must have confounded poets and audience alike."

Let us leave the secular and turn to the sacred. There appears to have been no priestly class in the Geometric period.[123] Other societies in antiquity have regularly featured this priestly group, whose purpose within the community was to act as repositor and articulator of religious history, beliefs, and procedures. But it is clear from the epics and from the earliest records of the archaic period that in Greece there were no such persons.[124] Maron, the priest (*hiereus*) of Apollo who gave Odysseus the wine that undid Polyphemus the Cyclops, was protected with his family by Odysseus during the looting of Ismarus;[125] it is not stated whether the reverence that motivated the protection was for Apollo or the priest (or even for the wine). To judge from Agamemnon's treatment of Chryses at the opening of the *Iliad*, priests seem to have had little or no temporal power. In Chryses' case, Apollo listened to his prayer and sent an avenging plague. But in neither example do we see either any special knowledge attributed to priests or (more important) any exceptionally respectful treatment accorded them. It is perhaps pertinent that any head of a collective (a family or army, for example) may lead a sacrifice; in fact, anyone with sufficient means, including women and slaves, may do so. Never is a priest required.[126]

Seers appear at first different, for Calchas is able with impunity to name Agamemnon's action as the cause of the plague. But it may be Achilles' public assurance of safety, more than the respect Calchas commanded from either the shepherd of the people himself or the people, that prevented Agamemnon from having the seer's head. Calchas interprets signs and, thanks to his special skill, pronounces the meaning of them. But like other prominent seers in the epics, such as Teiresias,[127] the renowned Theban seer in the underworld, and Theoclymenus,[128] who foresees doom for the suitors, Calchas does not enjoy special status because he is perceived by the community as having any special information pertaining to the gods' wills, be it stored up or available on request. Respect for seers is based on their

---

123. "There is no priestly caste with a fixed tradition, no Veda and no Pyramid texts; nor is there any authoritative revelation in the form a sacred book" (Burkert 1985, 119). Apart (necessarily) from the matter of writing, Walter Burkert states that "Greek religion might almost be called a religion without priests: there is no priestly caste as a closed group with fixed tradition, education, initiation and hierarchy" (p. 95). In the archaic and classical Periods, a priest's duties were administrative and liturgical (Garland 1984, 76).

124. The *hieromnemones* in Aristotle's *Politics* (1321B, 39) have no parallel in the epics.

125. *Od.* 9.197–201.

126. Burkert 1985, 95.

127. *Od.* 11.90–151. He drinks blood (96–98), not to inspire himself, but to acquire the strength to speak at length.

128. The Argive Theoclymenus makes his first appearance at *Od.* 15.256ff. He gives his prophecy at 20.350–57.

ability to interpret signals universally available to the human senses better than most (if not all) other witnesses.

A survey of the other priests and seers in the *Iliad* and *Odyssey* makes it rather clear that they enjoyed no special status. The only named priests in the *Iliad* apart from Chryses are Dares, devoted to Hephaestus, whose sons are killed by Diomedes,[129] and Laogonus, a priest of Zeus, who is slain by Meriones with impunity.[130] Otherwise priests are merely mentioned together with seers and/or dream interpreters (*oneiropoloi*).[131] A number of seers are named in the epics, such as Merops,[132] Polyidus,[133] Melampus,[134] Telemus,[135] and Polypheides, grandson of Amphiaraus and father of Theoclymenus.[136] Seers are associated with bird interpreters.[137]

Who then was the repositor and articulator of sacred wisdom? It was the *aoidos,* who had not only special methods available to him, but also (like the Old Testament prophets) a direct hookup to the gods themselves. It was the *aoidos* who fulfilled not only the expected role within traditional society of the local historian (in the modern sense), but also that of distributor of the latest information from on high. The blind Demodocus, for instance, is praised by Odysseus for narrating events of the Trojan War as if he had been an eyewitness to them:

> Demodocus, indeed I praise you beyond all men. Either a Muse, daughter of Zeus, taught you or Apollo did. For you sing (*aeideis*) of the calamity of the Achaeans with uncanny accuracy, all the things they did and suffered, and all they endured, as if somehow you yourself had been there or had heard it from another.[138]

Of course, the implication is that a Muse or Apollo dictated this information to Demodocus. Does Calchas or Teiresias have such a direct line? No, emphatically. The *aoidoi* do.

Hesiod's credentials, we have already seen, are based on his meeting with the Muses on Helicon: "And they breathed into me a divine voice in order that I might celebrate the things that will be and the things that were."[139]

129. 5.10.
130. 10.604.
131. 1.62–63, 24.221.
132. *Il.* 2.832, 11.330.
133. *Il.* 13.663.
134. *Od.* 11.99, 15.225.
135. *Od.* 9.508.
136. *Od.* 15.243–55.
137. *Od.* 1.202.
138. *Od.* 8.487–91.
139. *Th.* 31–32.

Thus they gave him the same ability that seers have, to know the past and future,[140] the fundamental difference being that Hesiod does not need to read and interpret signs. Like Demodocus, he just sings what he knows. It is not for nothing that the Muses are the daughters of Mnemosyne, "Memory."

As should be clear from the controls articulated above, the *basileus* (big man in the schema) ultimately is the controller of what the rememberer "remembers." The rememberer recalls from his memory what is convenient, and thus the rememberer in a traditional society is in fact a powerful agent of continuity. By continuity I mean maintenance of a status quo, regardless of how recently or precariously it has been established. By definition, then, this continuity is not necessarily a conservative activity in the long term; the status quo that is being continued is immediate in chronological terms, regardless of how long this immediate status quo has been in place.

It seems likely that the rememberers were behind the development of many charter myths in early Greece. For example, the earliest explanation of why the Eupatrids controlled the best parcels of land was no doubt conveniently discovered in a corner of a rememberer's memory. And this secular rememberer could always call on an agreeable (and perhaps hungry) *aoidos* to verify his juridical decision by bringing forth a tale involving "long-forgotten" divine interventional circumstances. Heracles certainly visited many communities.

Clearly, the rememberer in a traditional society "remembers" what is convenient. So too, clearly, an oral poet in a traditional society sings what is convenient. This is as true of the Kirghiz and Serbian poets as it is of Phemius and Demodocus. These repositors of knowledge, these referees, these promulgators of the big man's interest, are agents of continuity, for their ability and power to create ersatz "traditions" enabled the current *agathoi*, or "good men," to suppress those for the time being out of power, the *kakoi*, or "bad men." But, more important, the singers contributed to the suppression of the eternal *kakoi*, the dispossessed periphery.

What the *Iliad*, *Odyssey*, and *Theogony* especially have in common is that they respond to the controls that we expect to find in an oral recitational context. They respond both generally and specifically, for each generally

---

140. So Calchas (*Il.* 1.70).

supports the powerful centers and each specifically abets the attempt to disguise the recent radical change in the economic infrastructure. We have seen that Homeric economy and society match up quite well with primitive formations articulated by anthropologists, and in the epics, where the focus is almost always on the center, goods move within a redistributive system, the center being regularly portrayed as good. We have seen that on Ithaca, Eumaeus serves the center, both in better times (before Odysseus left for the war) and in current times (when the suitors, for all their meanness, provide protection for Eumaeus in exchange for swine).[141] Although Odysseus is gone, the center is still functioning, because the system operates without concern for who occupies its center. Not only Eumaeus but also Melanthius, Philoetius, Melantho, and the other nonelite figures in the *Odyssey* reap the benefits of the redistributive formation that Odysseus has left behind. Workers in the *Iliad*, on Achilles' shield and in the similes, work gleefully on community plots, bringing in the harvests of fields and vineyards:

> And on [the shield] he set soft fallow land, a rich field, broad and thrice-plowed. Many plowmen wheeling their yokes on it drove back and forth. And whenever after turning they reached the edge of the field, then a man would come forward and give into their hands a cup of honey-sweet wine. The plowmen turned along the furrows, hurrying to reach the edge of the deep fallow land.
>
> On it he placed a *temenos* of a *basileus*, where workers were harvesting, holding sharp sickles in their hands. . . . Among them in silence at the furrow stood a *basileus*, scepter in hand, delighting in his heart.
>
> On it he placed a vineyard. . . . Maidens and youngsters were lightheartedly carrying honey-sweet fruit in their woven baskets. In their midst a boy played a pleasant song on the shrill lyre and sang the Linus song with his clear voice. And the workers striking the earth in unison did follow with shout and dance, keeping time with their feet.[142]

What fun it is to work! We see in these passages perhaps how the community used to work common lands, including the *temenos* of a *basileus;* how eagerly they work—men, women, and children alike—with a spirit of solidarity.

As we saw in the preceding chapter, the system of justice, to the extent that we get a glimpse of it, is of course fair. The *basilees* of the epics and in the *Theogony* are good at settling disputes. The absence in the epics of non-one-time markets may be explained as an example of "epic distancing,"[143]

141. *Od.* 14.80–83, 107–8.
142. *Il.* 18.541–47, 550–51, 556–57, 561–72.
143. See chapter 1.

but it seems that this specific case of "distancing" is especially easy to choose, for the absence of regular markets diverts attention from a primary cause of the social upheaval that has spread throughout Greece.

In fact, just about every aspect of epic society not only resembles the way things actually used to be done but also is shown as good. This is very important, for in the world of the Homeric epics and of the *Theogony*, big men were good and, as we saw from Sarpedon's remarks to Glaucus,[144] they derived the support of the people from that goodness and depended on the people for their wealth. The heroes of the "distant past" (though recognizable and so in fact not actually distant) and contemporary rulers are clearly linked by their behavior. Amphidamas enjoys funeral games just as Patroclus did; leaders in Argos, Crete, Eretria, and Cyprus are interred in a manner similar to one another and similar to the way Patroclus was; monumental *amphorae* and kraters from the eighth century[145] simultaneously illustrate not only the public laying-out of deceased leaders but also the interest of those leaders in keeping large animal herds, just as Odysseus and others kept them in the epics.[146] Good men keep herds, and those who would rather use bottomlands for agricultural production are reminded of this reality.

The heroes of the epics are good men who deserve their wealth; the big men of the present and the heroes of the epics exchange gifts, receive warrior burials, and have meetings; the big men of today have much wealth: therefore they are good men and deserve to have it and probably even more. Heroes are good at *boule*, as are contemporary leaders:

> All the people watch [the *basileus*] as he decides law cases with straight *dikai;* and he, speaking surely, would put a stop to even a great *neikos*. For therefore there are *basilees* with wise hearts, for when the people are being misled in the *agora*, they easily settle cases that might bring harm, moving them with soothing words. When he goes through the assembly, they greet him as a god, and he is conspicuous among those gathered.[147]

---

144. *Il.* 12.310–14, discussed above in chapter 4.

145. For the layings-out, see Ahlberg 1971b, figures in vol. 2; also Coldstream 1968, pls. 6–8. For herds of horses see Coldstream 1968, pls. 4, 5, 7–10, 14, 35.

146. See, for example, Eumaeus's litany of his master's wealth, delivered to the disguised Odysseus at *Od.* 14.98–103: "Twenty men do not have so much wealth as he. I will list it for you: twelve herds of cows on the mainland; as many flocks of sheep; as many of swine; as many broad flocks of goats. . . . Here there are all told eleven broad flocks of goats." Walter Donlan (1981, 104) calculates fifty-nine flocks and herds belonging to Odysseus's *oikos;* Eumaeus kept 960 swine for his master.

147. *Th.* 84–92.

The "distant" and contemporary especially converge generally in the recitations at Panhellenic gatherings and specifically in the context of Amphidamas's heroic funeral games, regardless of whether it was the *Theogony* that won Hesiod his tripod there. Since an oral recitation is perceived by the audience to be the "same" on each and every occasion, it is easy to see how such recitations, beholden as they are to the new elite, are the most powerful tool of exclusion.[148]

148. In support of my broad thesis is Gregory Nagy's (1981, 1995) reading of the epics as a Panhellenizing institution.

EIGHT

Response from the Periphery

*Si le temps d'Homère est un temps heureux, le temps d'Hésiode
est un temps malheureux.*

MARCEL DETIENNE,
CRISE AGRAIRE ET ATTITUDE RELIGIEUSE CHEZ HÉSIODE

Epic was not the only response to a new world. We also have Hesiod's *Works
and Days.* There are two reasons that it is important to look at this poem
closely. First, the poem was composed from an entirely different perspective
and under radically different circumstances than the *Iliad, Odyssey,* and the
Theogony, for *Works and Days* does not appear to have been subject to the
controls we expect to find in place in oral recitational contexts. (It is far less
pertinent that *Works and Days* was composed later than the other three
poems.)[1] Thus *Works and Days* appears to have been composed with a purpose precisely opposite to the other poems: it is a response not from the
center but from the periphery. Second, *Works and Days* offers us a good
glimpse of Hesiod's quotidian economic activities, which along with his
advice to his brother and neighbors can provide us with a fuller understanding of the change in economic formations to which the poem is
responding.

AN ANTIARISTOCRATIC TRADITION?

It has been argued that there is a strain of antiaristocratic sentiment in the
epics.[2] Walter Donlan adduces two passages to support this observation. In

---

1. Janko 1982, 228–31. See above, chapter 1.

2. See Donlan 1973, esp. 150–52. S. G. Farron argues that the *Odyssey* in its entirety is
antiaristocratic (Farron 1979/80; see also previous discussions of this position, which Farron
cites on p. 59 n. 1, esp. Rose 1975).

a simile, Homer compares the speed of retreating Trojan horses to the flood that Zeus sends

> when in irritation he grows angry at men who by violence render crooked judgments in the *agora* and drive out *dike,* not paying heed to the vengeance of the gods.[3]

This warning against injustice is certainly (*Works and Days*) Hesiodic in tone and diction but, it seems to me, unnecessarily termed "antiaristocratic." The passage is more generally cautionary than antiaristocratic, not dissimilar to the cautionary tone of Sarpedon's statement to Glaucus.[4] There are proper and improper ways to do things in the epics, so we may expect an occasional cautionary message next to the many examples of correct action. An important example in the epics of such misbehavior by the elite is the general behavior of the suitors at Ithaca, whose punishment at the hands of both man and god (Athena) is well deserved. A different matter altogether is the explicit example (Donlan's second) in Homer of antiaristocratic sentiment: the Thersites incident in the second book of the *Iliad.* Upset by the bickering between Achilles and Agamemnon, Thersites delivers his well-known speech:

> Son of Atreus, what are you complaining about this time? What do you need now? Your tents are filled with bronze; many choice women are in your tents, whom the Achaeans give to you because you are in the first position, whenever we take a citadel. Or do you still need gold, which some one of the horse-taming Trojans will bring out of Troy as ransom for his son? Or is it a new woman you want, in order to lie with her in lovemaking, whom you yourself will keep apart from others? It is not seemly for a man who is their leader to bring evils upon the sons of the Achaeans. O softies, base reproaches, Achaean women not Achaean men, let us go home with our ships and leave this fellow here in Troy to gobble up his prizes, so that he may see whether we too are of use to him, or not. For just now he dishonored Achilles, a much better man than himself, for he has snatched and keeps the prize, taking it away himself. But certainly there is no anger in Achilles' heart, but he ignores it. Otherwise, son of Atreus, you would play the insolent one now for the last time.[5]

---

3. *Il.* 16.386–88.

4. *Il.* 12.310–21, discussed above in chapter 4.

5. *Il.* 2.225–42. Heinz Munding (1959, 110–40) in fact argues that the Thersites episode is a post-Hesiodic addition to the *Iliad,* a "Hesiodreaktion."

Note, however, that apart from the matter of scale, what happens to Thersites is precisely what happened to Agamemnon's bard. Odysseus

> struck him on the back and shoulders. [Thersites] cowered, and a great tear fell from him; a bloody welt rose from his back from the golden scepter. He sat himself down, and fear took him; stung by pain and with a look of helplessness, he wiped away the tear.[6]

The onlooking host, "though irked (*achnumenoi*), did break into sweet laughter at him."[7] "Never again," they murmured in Homeric unison, "will his proud spirit drive him to bring a quarrel (*neikos*) against *basilees* with reviling words."[8]

I am convinced that the oral tradition contained this antiaristocratic strain (where it may have thrived I will discuss below); this strain of the oral tradition enjoyed its most elevated articulation in *Works and Days* and then in Archilochus, Tyrtaeus, Solon, Xenophanes, and others;[9] but in the hands of Homer and within the oral recitational context of the *Iliad*, the public expression of such sentiment is demonstrably ill-advised. To underline Thersites' unworthiness to speak out against the *basilees*, Homer describes him as the ugliest of the Achaeans,

> the basest[10] man who came to Troy. He was bandy-legged,[11] and lame in one foot. His two shoulders were hunched over, bent in over the chest, and above them was a pointed head, and a thin patch of fuzz grew on it.[12]

Thersites' appearance matches his judgment, and his punishment is an object lesson for those who would emulate him.

Both of these passages are reminiscent of *Works and Days*. The rendering of crooked judgments and the destruction that attends those who pay no heed to the vengeance of the gods are both notions that appear in Hesiod's

---

6. 2.265–69.

7. 2.270.

8. 2.276–77. Recall that *neikos* is the term in Homer and Hesiod for incidents that appear litigious in nature. These are perused in chapter 7 and also below.

9. See Donlan 1973, esp. 146–48.

10. "Basest" is *aischistos*, translated often also as "ugliest." It more likely means "most shame-causing" (Lowry 1980); within the framework of praise poets and blame poets (Nagy 1979, chaps. 12–14; on Thersites, pp. 259–62) Hesiod's position is clear, and it may be an ability to write that lets him avoid the stick.

11. This word, *pholkos*, is of uncertain meaning and along with many others in this brief passage is extremely rare, and so highly marked.

12. *Il.* 2.216–19.

poem. Thersites' criticism of the unfair acquisition of wealth resonates there. But look what happens to Thersites when he articulates these ideas *publicly*. Although they laugh at Thersites' punishment, the onlooking Achaeans are explicitly upset (*achnumenoi*). The witnesses cheer for the same reason that Thersites should not have spoken out.

The Achaean laughter-cum-discomfort is certainly problematic. There is at least one other reasonable explanation for it. Peter Rose proposes in a very clear argument that the Achaeans feel genuine discomfort at the sight of one of their own being thrashed but laugh at Thersites "because of his incomprehensibly stupid failure to foresee the consequences of his outburst in a society where he is utterly powerless."[13] Geoffrey Kirk explains the laughter by pointing out that elsewhere in the *Iliad* the host sends forth the same "sweet laughter" when Ajax slips in the footrace[14] and fills his mouth and nose with dung and when Zeus first sees Artemis when she has been wounded by Hera.[15] This leads Kirk to conclude: "Misfortune and undignified appearance are the two things that normally seem to cause heroic— and divine—amusement in the *Iliad;* in the *Odyssey* laughter usually comes from the suitors, and is of the derisive kind."[16] Add Paris's sweet laughter when he wounds Diomedes;[17] and be aware that the only two sweet laughters in the *Odyssey* are dismissive laughter in response to idle threats from Theoclymenus[18] and Telemachus.[19] This may be sufficient distribution to warrant the sort of generalization Kirk would like to make. The soldiers are not happy to see Thersites being beaten. The soldiers are in public/oral space. Hesiod isn't.

Hesiod's *Works and Days* clearly differs from Thersites' outburst because it enjoys immunity from the big man's stick. It follows then that *Works and Days* must have a very different genesis and context from the other poems, for its singer is not dependent, in the way the *mnemon* or the successful *aoidos* is, on the big man, and the only way to talk around the head of the big man is by avoiding a recitation in his presence.

First, we should dispose of the scenario that Hesiod is a singer in an oral recitational context who has the support of one big man in competition

---

13. Rose 1988, 21. If Peter Rose is right, his analysis may find a parallel in Thomas Hubbard's explanation of the hawk-nightingale *ainos*, discussed below.

14. 23.784.

15. 21.508.

16. Kirk 1985, ad 2.270.

17. *Il.* 11.378.

18. 20.358.

19. 21.376.

with another. One may perceive this possibility in Calchas's confident denunciation of Agamemnon, apparently feasible only after Achilles' assurance of protection. When Achilles indirectly asks Calchas to articulate the cause of the pestilence in the Achaean camp, the seer responds with a plea for protection:

> I will speak, but you consider and swear to me that you will willingly defend me with words and hands, for I think that I will make irate a man who rules mightily over many Achaeans and whom the Achaeans obey. For a *basileus* is stronger whenever he is irate at an inferior man. . . . Consider if you will keep me safe.[20]

But in the specific context of late eighth- and early seventh-century Greece, one should note generally that demagogic populist tyrannies will not arise for quite some time and specifically that Hesiod is not seeking support for an alternate leadership, but a better-behaved leadership. With predictable peasant spirit (see further below), he is simultaneously criticizing the center and pleading with his fellows to try to survive with the inevitable fact of the center as currently constituted.

We are left, it appears, with only two ploys to avoid the wrath of the center. First, there is the situation where the poet is able to be independent, in terms of livelihood, of the economic and political center controlled by the leaders of the community. But we saw in chapter 7 that such contexts were not demonstrably available, and furthermore, if, as G. P. Edwards, Richard Janko, and Berkley Peabody have separately demonstrated,[21] *Works and Days* is the culmination of the same or a similar tradition as the epics, an additional problem arises: how long can the passages that are so critical of the status quo have been in existence if recitational contexts were as restricted (hence restrictive) as I have suggested? How can the poem's virulent criticism have evolved within the oral tradition if there were so few opportunities for its exercise? Since antiaristocratic sentiment could not be publicly employed, it must have been practiced in private space, which had always existed. The most likely private-space contexts for the recitation of antiaristocratic sentiment would probably be informal gatherings of peripheral members of the community during leisure time at such places as the local *lesche*, where the epics and Hesiod suggest that such leisure time, which all small-scale cultures cherish, was spent. Melantho the maid

---

20. *Il.* 1.76–80. Only after Achilles assures Calchas of his safety, even if he names Agamemnon (85–91), does Calchas boldly pronounce Agamemnon's dishonoring of Apollo's priest the cause of the plague (93–100).

21. G. P. Edwards 1971; Peabody 1975; Janko 1982, esp. 188–99.

implies that this was the very value of a *lesche,* when she says to the unre-vealed Odysseus:

> Wretched stranger, you are but someone touched in the head; you are unwill-ing to go to a smithy's place to sleep, or to some *lesche.* Rather, you chatter away here.[22]

And Hesiod specifically admonishes Perses for spending too much time at such places:

> Pass by the smithy's seat and the warm *lesche* in the wintertime, when the cold keeps men from their works.[23]

Hesiod's vitriolic comments may then be compared with the Kirghiz *akin's* acerbic song when the big man is away:

> If only poor persons are his listeners, he does not hesitate to insert venomous remarks about the presumptions of the nobles and the rich.[24]

The Kirghiz analogue, however, serves only to support the notion that we can expect antiaristocratic sentiment to exist in *any* oral tradition.

A fundamental and instructive difference between the Kirghiz situation and the arrangement in early Greece is that the Kirghiz singer may be easi-ly observed in such private or semiprivate space by an anthropologist or a Radloff. We have no such vantage point on antiquity, and so must rely on analogues, for the only verses available to us for study are those that are frozen in and by *public* space. The portion of the oral tradition that comes down to us is what was practiced in public space; since public space is clear-ly controlled by the center, what survives will be that deemed appropriate by those in control and will be predictably proaristocratic. Public space does not seem a possible avenue of survival for the antiaristocratic strain within the oral tradition, if I am right in my interpretations of the incident concerning Agamemnon's bard (see chapter 7) and the predicament of Thersites.

---

22. *Od.* 18.327–29.

23. *WD* 493–95. Thus in Homer and Hesiod the *lesche* appears to be a place where leisure time was passed, and thus its visitors might be open to accusations of idling, but it is the case that later the *lesche* developed into a place where very serious talk also occurred: in Sparta, the *lesche* is where Spartan men decided which babies would be allowed to grow up and which would be exposed (Plut. *Lyc.* 16). See further Buxton 1994, 41–44.

24. Radloff 1885, xv iii-xix.

It would appear that the only other way for a specific example from this antiaristocratic strain to survive is in written form, which obviates the big man and also transcends private space, becoming something special, just as the epics (eventually) became. The epics were frozen at an early date; they probably remained an important tool for a brief time. *Works and Days,* on the other hand, appears to have been written down from the start, both in order to survive and in order to retain the specificity of its complaint (including Hesiod's name). Under the reasonable ground rules here laid down, in order for the social criticism of *Works and Days* to become frozen it must have been able to obviate public space, and this seems plausible only if the poem was written down. Furthermore, in addition to the poem's content, the structure and the nature of the transitions between sections of the poem support the notion that Hesiod composed his poem in writing.[25]

Turning to the problem of recitational contexts and controls, as they concern writing poets, there is little question that when a poet and a portion of his audience have the ability to write and read, the rules can change. For criticism to be effective, the poet must enjoy independence from the big man. Only then can a poet produce what the audience wants to hear. To return to our schema, we have

The big man is no longer the player he once was, for literacy allows the poet to "talk around" the head of that big man; hence the poet is able to criticize without facing the consequences. Agamemnon's singer illustrates very well the limitations of criticism within a context of exclusively oral performance, just as Phemius shows how necessary (and, to Odysseus, forgivable) it is to "play the game" within the same context. What can a written text accomplish that an oral performance cannot? The Muse becomes the singer's tool, no longer that of the big man. If the singer supports the big man's opposition, writing becomes the tool of these opposing interests.

In conclusion, effective criticism must avoid the big man and be good. Only writing meets both demands, for oral poetry is at its best only when in

---

25. West 1977, esp. 64–66. Compare Peter Walcot's (1961) broad argument that Hesiod used writing in composing *Works and Days;* Walcot concludes generally: "Allowance must be made for the influence of writing on the oral poet and the effect it had on the composition of Hesiod's verse" (p. 19). Add Havelock (1963, 296): "[Hesiod] is operating with the help of the written word."

the presence of immediate reward. Written poetry may be good without this consideration.

THE INTRODUCTION OF WRITING

Because of the perishability of many of the materials on which alphabetic (and nonalphabetic) signs may be applied, we can be certain neither when Linear B actually ceased being used (or for that matter what uses Linear B may have been put to apart from record keeping, which survives on the clay tablets) nor when the later Greek system of writing first came into use and for what it was used.[26] Limited as we are to writing samples that survive on durable materials, such as clay and metal, it is difficult to decide how early the Homeric poems may have been written down, since surely a medium different than clay or metal must have been employed, such as animal skins, wood, or perhaps even papyrus.[27]

It is reasonable, however, to conclude that writing became available to the Greek-speaking world through Greek exposure to the northern Semit-ic alphabet at Al Mina in northern Syria, where we now have an eighth-century example of Greek writing.[28] It may be that Homer and his bardic colleagues found support for their craft primarily on the trade routes; if so, we may conclude, for different reasons than usually put forth, that the *aoidoi* were somehow responsible for the introduction of the alphabet into Greece.[29] But those ultimately responsible for the introduction of the

26. In what follows, I will not address (except in this note) the arguments, based on let-ter shapes, put forth recently for a ninth-century (Sass 1991, 94–98) or eleventh-century trans-mission (Naveh 1987, chap. 6; Fergus Millar [1983, 93–94] is not unsympathetic) and even a transmission before 1400 (Bernal 1987, 1990). Edward Lipiński points out clear similarities between ninth-century Aramaic letter shapes and seventh-century Greek letter shapes (Lipiński 1988, 244–45, 258, fig. 13). There is certainly no question that we have no certain examples of writing before 800, and while this may change, it is unlikely that we will find enough to change the fact that writing begins to get used quite a bit more after 800.

27. F. Dornseiff (1939) does not rule out papyrus as available for writing down Greek in the eighth century.

28. Boardman 1982a. There has been for a long time the alternative position that the Greek alphabet developed on Crete. The Phoenician inscription found near Knossos, dated to about 900 or perhaps earlier (Sznycer 1979, 91), offers the possibility that the Greek alphabet may have been generated on Crete. But, as we will see below, there are Phoenicians every-where, and the alphabet could have developed almost anywhere.

29. H. T. Wade-Gery (1952, 13–14), Eric Havelock (1963, 51), Kevin Robb (1978), and Barry Powell (1989), for example, assume or argue that the earliest metrical inscriptions were the work of singers. Powell argues "that the epigraphic evidence is consonant with Wade-Gery's thesis that the Greek alphabet was designed specifically in order to record hexametric poetry" (1989, 350), the thesis of his later book (Powell 1991). Havelock (1982, 187 and n. 5) recant-ed his support of this position, one difficult to defend indeed (see Morris 1993b).

alphabet were almost certainly the movers of goods on the trade routes, that is, the Euboean traders.

One of the earliest examples of writing in Greek is the enigmatic and anomalous hexameter scratched on a Dipylon *oenochoe* about 740. It is enigmatic in its meaning, "the one who of all the dancers performs most nimbly (, his is the prize),"[30] and anomalous because it is the only example of writing in Athens that is certainly pre-seventh century. Probably close to the truth is L. H. Jeffery's suggestion that it is the work of an outsider,[31] perhaps from Al Mina,[32] visiting a nonliterate Athens. Until recently, most of the earliest cases of writing, such as "Nestor's Cup" at Pithekoussai and graffiti at Rhodes,[33] have been found on the Euboean frontier and the trade route. "Nestor's Cup" may betray acquaintance with a portion of the oral tradition that appears also in Homer (the portion in quotation marks is two hexameters):

> I am the well-drunk cup of Nestor. "Whoever drinks from this cup, straight-away will desire of fair-crowned Aphrodite seize that one."

At Lefkandi on Euboea, we have a clear, early use of the Greek alphabet for an owner's mark at least as early as 760[34] and two others dated between 750 and 700.[35] There are some eighth-century graffiti from Eretria now, including one that is remarkably similar to "Nestor's Cup."[36] Recently excavated on the island of Naxos is a potsherd from a krater dated to about 770 with some Euboean lettering on it (although the lettering was excised after the krater was broken and so is of uncertain date).[37] No other example of writing in the Aegean is certainly earlier than the example from Lefkandi. Pending the discovery of other "texts," it would be difficult to overstate the

---

30. L. H. Jeffery's (1982, 828) translation. Merle Langdon reads the end of the inscription with greater certainty: "let him accept this" (Langdon 1975, 140).

31. Jeffery 1961a, 76.

32. Jeffery 1961a, 16, 68.

33. For Pithekoussai: Jeffery 1961a, 235–36 (and pl. 47), where there are also early shards (Jeffery 1982, 828); older than "Nestor's Cup" is the amphora with both Greek and Phoenician writing on it in Grave 575 of Pithekoussai (Buchner 1978, 1982; Johnston 1990, 453, A and pl. 76). For Rhodes: Jeffery 1961a, 347 (and pl. 67).

34. It reads either left to right *AM-* or right to left *-SA*. Jeffery (in Popham, Sackett, and Themelis 1980, 89; no. 102 on p. 90; see pl. 69) dates it coincident with Attic MG II (800–760); also reproduced in Popham and Sackett 1968, 34, fig. 79.

35. Jeffery in Popham, Sackett, and Themelis 1980, 89; nos. 100 and 101 on pp. 89–90; see pl. 69; also reproduced in Popham and Sackett 1968, 33, fig. 78.

36. Johnston 1990, 434, nos. A and B, pl. 73; Johnston and Andriomenou 1989.

37. Touchais 1982, 604, fig. 132, 605. Powell (1987, 12) notes that the writing was on the inside of the shard and dates the krater to 775.

importance of the Euboeans in the dissemination of this newly acquired skill.[38]

The earliest Greek writing is now (1995) from the Euboean west, found at Gabii, about 25 kilometers east of Rome in central Italy. The example from Gabii appears to be an owner's mark on a pot. It belongs to the period 830–770, presumably (for the moment) to the latter end of the period.[39] This swings the focus back to the frontier. At Pithekoussai, of course, there was an important Phoenician presence, emphatically betrayed, in fact, by samples of Phoenician writing;[40] this is explanation enough for the adaptation of the alphabet first in the west. There are Phoenicians not only there, but also at Al Mina; we have thus far found ninth-century Phoenician writing on Crete,[41] on Cyprus and Sardinia,[42] and at Eretria and on Samos.[43] The ubiquity of the Phoenicians makes it nearly impossible even to address the actual locus of the alphabetic transmission or adaptation, and while we can be certain that there will soon appear new evidence that will push the date back even farther and refocus our geographical sights, it is difficult to imagine that the context will not include Euboeans.

If Al Mina and the Euboeans are to be credited, respectively, as source and agent of the introduction of writing into Greece, we are left with the curious scenario of writing sharing the same genesis as the economic/social upheaval that rocked the Greek communities and generated the kind of *written* social criticism of which *Works and Days* may be a leading example. Such a scenario is curious—perhaps even paradoxical—because the presence of writing qua tool of criticism would be highly disadvantageous to those in power, for, as we saw in chapter 7, it is clearly to the advantage of those in power to keep rules in an oral, and so a flexible and conserving, form.

HESIOD'S WORLD

It is about the time that we can date the broader proliferation of Greek alphabetic writing that Hesiod's father arrived in central Boeotia, which was

38. Alan Johnston's distribution map (1983, 65, fig. 5) shows this clearly; see also Powell's (1989, esp. 321–25) more recent survey.

39. Bietti Sestieri, De Santis, and La Regina 1990, 83–88; Ridgway 1994, 42–43. J. N. Coldstream (1994a, 49) dates the shard "not later than the early eighth century." One can only gasp at the statement by Dionysius of Halicarnassus that Faustulus sent the youthful Romulus and Remus to Gabii, where they learned their Greek letters (1.84.5), especially with a date for the shard of about 770!

40. Giorgio Buchner 1978. Buchner (1978, 139) dates the writing to the last quarter of the eighth century; David Ridgway (1992b, 117) to the last decade.

41. Sznycer 1979, 91; see above, note 28.

42. Albright 1941, 15–20.

43. A ninth-century inscribed horse bit was found in two parts in seventh-century contexts in sanctuaries at Eretria and on Samos (Kyrieleis and Röllig 1988).

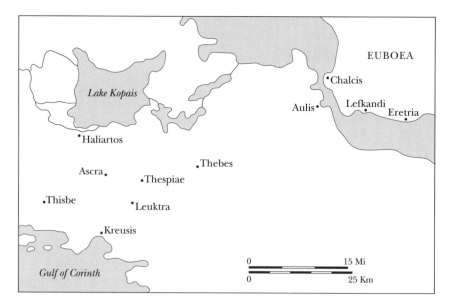

Map 4. Boeotia

probably only recently resettled after virtual depopulation and subsequent desolation during the Dark Age.[44] We may surmise, then, that the effects of this rather sudden resettlement would be similar to the effects of the population pressures building elsewhere in Greece shortly before this time. Hesiod's father was able to get the use of unwanted land, which by the end of his life appears to have become more valuable than before, partly because of the subsequent arrival of other immigrants from the east.[45] He, and his sons after him, worked land that was not the best in Boeotia; that had been taken by earlier settlers.[46] This is how Hesiod tells it:

> Just so my father and yours, Perses, you utter fool, used to sail in ships, because he was in need of a good livelihood (*bios*). Once he came here in his black

44. In much of what follows I follow Paul Millett's analysis of Hesiod and his world (Millett 1984).
   According to the Boeotia survey, in Boeotia between about 1000 and 800 B.C. there are "virtually no sites on the landscape" (Bintliff 1985, 215). Ascra itself shows signs of occupation only in the ninth century (Bintliff and Snodgrass 1988, 61).
   45. Albert Schachter (1985, 146–48) argues reasonably for "a considerable—but not necessarily massive—immigration into central Boeotia during the Geometric and early Archaic period, of people from Asia Minor and the Aegean" (p. 148).
   46. "Hesiod's father's farm was an upland farm, on poor soil, as Hesiod explicitly states, and not a farm on the 'deep-soiled' plain, the sort of land that the original (and less numerous) settlers will have occupied" (Lacey 1968, 334).

ship, after making it across much open sea, having left behind Aeolian Kyme. He was not fleeing riches, wealth, and prosperity, but the evil poverty that Zeus gives to men. He settled near Helicon in a pitiful village, Ascra, bad in winter, painful in summer, never any good.[47]

To judge from the weather of Boeotia today, it is not the climate about which Hesiod is complaining.[48]

According to Strabo,[49] Ascra was 40 stadia northwest of Thespiae. John Bintliff and Anthony Snodgrass locate Ascra at the same spot (about 7 or 8 kilometers from Thespiae), and their 1982 survey indicates a surface area of about 25 hectares (just over 60 acres), "comparable with that of the city-area of Thisbe and actually larger than the combined area of citadel and lower town at Haliartos, a neighboring polis";[50] in Hesiod's time Ascra was "no mere hamlet, but the main settlement of its district."[51] Later Greeks (as Hesiod himself) would call Ascra a *kome*, or "village," in Ascra's case a large settlement, but in political terms dependent on the dominant polis of the area, Thespiae, which was exceptional for having as many as three *komai* in its territory.[52]

Hesiod: Who Was He?

Hesiod tells us a lot about himself. Paul Millett[53] successfully argues that Hesiod fits clearly into the mold of the peasant, thus silencing recent and not-so-recent efforts to make him something else. Benedetto Bravo argued that Perses and Hesiod were, like their father before them, impoverished *aristoi*;[54] Alfonso Mele saw Hesiod as a spokesperson of the aristocracy, advocating among other things the propriety of nonprofessional "trade" by the *aristoi*.[55] We can dismiss as modernizing Chester Starr's portrait of Hesiod

---

47. *WD* 633–40.

48. On the climate see West 1978, 317, and further references there; add Rackham 1983, 295–96. N. J. Richardson suggests that Hesiod is merely "echoing what his father, with an exile's typical nostalgia, used to say. He is, in fact, talking about his father here" (Richardson 1979, 171).

49. Strabo 9.2.25.

50. Bintliff and Snodgrass 1985, 137; they have since reduced Ascra to a "15-acre [6-hectare] site" (Snodgrass and Bintliff 1991, 88). Paul Wallace (1974, 10–11) effectively argues against placing Ascra farther south near Xeronomi (so Wilamowitz and Kirsten: see Wallace 1974, 10 n. 12); for other placements see the bibliography in Wallace 1974, 7 n. 2.

51. Snodgrass 1985b, 90.

52. See Snodgrass 1990, 132.

53. Millett 1984.

54. Bravo 1977.

55. Mele 1979.

(and of his father) as a "semi-aristocrat,"[56] and we can dismiss as pure speculation Wilamowitz's suggestion that Hesiod's father was a non-*aristos* who when he came to Ascra fooled the local population into thinking that he was a descendant of Boeotian *aristoi* who had once emigrated to Aeolis.[57] There is really no evidence to support these other positions.[58]

On the other hand, much can be said for the arguments that Hesiod is more persona than person. Richard Martin noticed the similarities between Hesiod's narrative of his family's immigration to Ascra and the narrative of Phoenix's own immigration to Phthia just preceding his advice to Achilles to relent in his wrath (*Iliad* 9.475–85) and concluded "that even in its smallest details, especially those of his father's career, the *persona* of Hesiod is a *traditional* way of framing the type of 'exhortation to wisdom' poetry embodied in [*Works and Days*]."[59] That is, there would appear to have been a tradition in early Greece of posing as an immigrant when giving advice. Utilizing a similar approach, Ralph Rosen has ingeniously proposed that Hesiod's discussion of sailing at *Works and Days* 618–94 should not be taken literally but is intended as a metaphor for poetry and as an argument explaining that he writes Hesiodic poetry, not Homeric (epic) poetry.[60]

Even if Martin and Rosen are essentially right that Hesiod takes on a particular persona or poetic character, this does not mean, for example in Martin's case, that the details of Hesiod's outsiderness are not in fact true (or true enough); or, in Rosen's, that Hesiod did not actually go to Chalcis and win a tripod at the funeral games of Amphidamas. And so, while these clear and legitimate readings of the poet of *Works and Days* may seem at first to threaten or compromise the verisimilitude of Hesiod's arrangements in Ascra, nevertheless at the end of the day Hesiod's world is as intact as a literal reading would suggest. I do not think my approach to Hesiod's world is incompatible with Martin's or Rosen's, but it is important to acknowledge that the situations that Hesiod describes in his world and the conditions that are being imposed on the fields by the town are real, reflecting the world as Hesiod or "Hesiod" perceives it. As Millett has put it, "It is difficult to imagine any reason why the poet should want to confuse his audience by deliberately archaizing or otherwise misrepresenting social institutions." I agree that *Works and Days* is a "faithful formulation of Hesiod's world."[61]

56. Starr 1977, 125–27; 1982, 432–33, 434; 1986, 93–94.

57. Wilamowitz 1928, 76.

58. I am not sure what to do with R. M. Cook's admitted speculation that "Hesiod's father married an heiress, the only child of a fairly prosperous farmer" (1989, 170). Recently Anthony Edwards (forthcoming) has lucidly argued against Hesiod as peasant; we disagree.

59. Martin 1992, 19.

60. Rosen 1990.

61. Millett 1984, 86.

As Millett shows, Hesiod's position vis-à-vis the powerful *basilees* in Thespiae is quite characteristically a peasant one. Before land became less easy to come by, Ascra depended to some extent on Thespiae but was for all intents and purposes an independent community, able to look after its own affairs. Hesiod's father would have produced enough food for his family, perhaps occasionally taking extra production to Thespiae, probably less often (given his pre-Boeotian history) taking goods to sea, as Hesiod would later. According to my model, Hesiod's father found physical and economic support in Thespiae. Hesiod's quotidian activities no doubt resembled his father's. At the time of the *Theogony*, this is almost certainly the case. But something changed before *Works and Days,* and Hesiod's attitude toward the *basilees* has become antagonistic. Hesiod found himself, for reasons articulated in chapter 5 and explored below, at odds with the *basilees* and alienated from polis life in Thespiae. Hesiod makes this clear with a fable:

> Now I will tell a fable to *basilees,* although they themselves perceive it. Thus the hawk addressed the speckle-necked nightingale, as he carried her very high in the clouds, keeping her snatched in his talons. She was weeping piteously, pierced by his curved talons; he addressed her haughtily: "Strange one, why do you scream? Now one who is much superior holds you. You will go wherever I myself carry you, even though you may be a singer (*aoidos*). A meal I will make of you, if I see fit, or I shall let you go. Foolish is he who sees fit to set himself up against those who are better; he both loses the victory and suffers pain in addition to disgrace." So spoke the swift-winged hawk, the long-winged bird.[62]

That Hesiod fails to put the behavior of the hawk (= *basilees*) against the nightingale (appropriately an *aoidos* [208] = Hesiod) in a negative light has been noted often.[63] A partial explanation is offered later:

> Forget about force completely. For this usage the son of Cronus granted to men: fishes and land animals and winged birds eat each other because *dike* is not in them. But to men he gave *dike*, which is by much the best thing.[64]

Thus we are to understand that these animals behave that way because they are animals (without *dike*), not people, who know better. But this explanation is rather distant (some seventy lines) from the fable, which, as a fable, is supposed to represent animals as distinctly human in behavior and motivation. It is absurd to have an animal fable whose lesson is that animals are different from people! Thomas Hubbard has suggested in a learned

---

62. *WD* 202–12.
63. West 1978, ad loc., with bibliography.
64. 275–80.

paper[65] that the eagle represents the *basilees* and the singer Hesiod's brother Perses, who has attempted to put himself on the same level as the *basilees* and is learning the consequences of such inappropriate behavior. Thus we see another "stay-in-your-place" admonition quite similar to the Thersites incident as interpreted by Rose and as discussed earlier in this chapter.

This antagonism between Hesiod and the *basilees* matches up well with Eric Wolf's observation that "it is only when a cultivator is integrated into a society with a state—that is, when the cultivators become subject to the demands and sanctions of power-holders outside his social culture—that we can appropriately speak of peasantry."[66] In response to Wolf, Frank Ellis usefully emphasizes the "idea of transition" in an accurate definition of the peasantry: peasants are "often thrust out of where they were by powerful world forces outside their previous experience (e.g. colonialism) and they are undergoing a continuous process of adaptation to the changing world around them."[67] The phenomenon of economic exclusivity, the arrival of limited markets characterized by the introduction of private property (see chapter 5)—these are the new challenges that face Hesiod and his fellows on the periphery.[68]

Life in Ascra

Hesiod grows grains and vines on his land and tends livestock, the same trio of productive categories that Homer describes for Tydeus's farm in the

---

65. Hubbard 1995.

66. Wolf 1966, 11, quoted also in Starr 1982, 424 n. 7 and Millett 1984, 92, but to different ends. Wolf's sharp definition is a focusing of the traditional view; for example, "the peasant is a rural native whose long established order of life takes important account of the city" (Redfield 1953, 31; see further pp. 31–40). Cf. Rosen 1975, chaps. 1–2. Daniel Thorner's (1965, 288–90) five criteria for identifying a "peasant economy" are designed explicitly for modern, large-scale economies, but with the exception of the first one, they are also clearly present in *Works and Days:* (1) roughly half of the total production is agricultural; (2) more than half of the population is engaged in agriculture; (3) there exists a state power that has weakened the traditional kinship order; (4) towns are present; (5) the standard unit of production is the family household. G. E. M. de Ste. Croix (1981, 210–11) offers a seven-part definition of the ancient Greek peasant. In fact, there have been many attempts to define "peasant," none of them achieving universal acceptance; for some good reasons why consensus is difficult to achieve, see Landsberger 1974, esp. 6–10. I think important progress is reflected in Victor Magagna's emphasis on the peasants as a community rather than a class (Magagna 1991, chap. 1)

67. Ellis 1988, 5.

68. Wolf's definition of the start-up of the peasantry and the importance within this definition of the clash between (newly) centralized power and social expectations on the periphery are reminiscent of African examples of renewed interest in culture in response to colonial pressures, to which I will return.

Iliad.[69] Also in the *Iliad,* Phoenix tells us that Meleager was offered a large tract that was half arable and half suitable for viticulture.[70] In the *Odyssey,* Eumaeus specializes in raising swine *ep' eschatien,*[71] in the forested edges of unusable wilderness, probably unclaimed, "public" land, the sort that Hesiod and his neighbors also occasionally use, to judge from Hesiod's reference to eating the meat of a bovid *hylophagos,* "fed in the woods."[72]

But Hesiod's advice about production is mostly about grain production. His careful advice about this kind of production, especially perhaps his detailed dissertation on how to construct a plow, may imply that grains are new, a response in Boeotia and elsewhere to the population increase and its effect on production. Hesiod uses either a two- or a three-field bare-fallow[73] system: "Sow a fallow plowland when the ground is still light. A fallow field is a protector against ruin and a soother of children."[74] To plow he uses a pair of oxen and also asses.[75] He also gives advice on the proper tending of vines[76] and appears to have a flock of sheep and some goats.[77] Note, however, that in contrast to the aristocratic interest in keeping herds (reflected in both art and epic) Hesiod focuses consistently on agricultural use of the land. His sheep and goats do not compete with crops. This instructs us perhaps more clearly than any other fact or argument: in the tension of bottomland use, Hesiod clearly comes out on the grain side.

Hesiod's farm was part of his *oikos* and was worked on by members of his *oikos,* the unit of economic organization that operated essentially independently of the polis and its authority. The people who lived in and around Ascra, that is, on the geographical and economic periphery, formed a community of such households. Schematically, they resided on the "rim" of a wheel that had new spokes. Either on the basis of explicit statement or by

69. *Il.* 14.122–24.

70. *Il.* 9.579–80.

71. *Od.* 24.150.

72. *WD* 591.

73. As opposed to annual manuring or cereal/pulse rotation, on whose relative merits see Halstead 1987, 81–85; on early manuring techniques in northern Europe see Fenton 1981. Hesiod does not mention manuring, but he does mention sheep over and over, and a single sheep can produce 500 kilograms of manure *per annum:* "In some contexts [manure production] has been regarded as the sheep's main asset" (Garnsey 1988b, 207).

74. *WD* 463–64.

75. Oxen esp. at *WD* 436; asses at 46, 607.

76. *WD* 570, 571–73. He seems to refer to making his own wine at 674. Curiously, Hesiod makes no mention of olive production; this is perhaps to be explained by local conditions in Boeotia (Boardman 1977, 190).

77. Sheep are everywhere in *Works and Days* (234, 308, 516, 775); there are also goats (511, 543, 585, 590). A boar (790) and horses (816) make appearances in the last part of the poem, *Days,* but I suspect that *Days* is a set piece that does not reflect Hesiod's actual holding.

inference from his advice to Perses, we can say the following about the constitution of Hesiod's *oikos*. There is a slave woman who follows his plow (probably to break up clods); she also keeps the house in order.[78] There is also a woman (the same one?), called an *erithos,* who does chores in the house.[79] He has a laborer to help with the plowing; he is a forty-year-old man.[80] Hesiod hires an occasional *thes* (pl. *thetes*), whose employment is seasonal;[81] he also hires a friend.[82] Hesiod has slaves of indeterminate number. They build granaries,[83] help with the sowing,[84] the reaping,[85] and the processing,[86] and plow the field for fallow after the harvest.[87] They are given some amount of independent responsibility.[88] Hesiod presumably has a wife, for he appears to have at least one son;[89] nevertheless, he is always careful to avoid the approach of a "fancy-assed" woman: she may be after his granary.[90]

Most all of these people belonged to the *oikos* and shared its prosperity and shortages. The friend whom Hesiod occasionally hires presumably belongs to another *oikos;* the hired workers who are *thetes* do not belong anywhere, which makes them the lowest caste of person in early Greece: slaves at least belong to an *oikos.* In Hesiod's *oikos, thetes* are thrown out when their seasonal labor is no longer needed.[91] Achilles' words in Hades are moving because the *thes* was lowest of the low: "I would rather work the land for another man as a *thes,* even for a man who had no *kleros,* for a man who had hardly any livelihood, than be ruler over all the corpses that are dead."[92]

---

78. *WD* 405–6. If 406 is spurious, this may be an indirect reference to Hesiod's wife, who then does not work in the field.

79. *WD* 603–4. *Erithos* is used by Homer to refer to reapers who are twisting sheaves together (*Il.* 18.550, 560); later the word is associated with *erion,* "wool," and comes to mean "weaver" (first in Sophocles; see LSJ, s.v. *erithos*). Hesiod's *erithos* may be a weaver. In the *Days* section (779), a female worker weaves. Mark Edwards declares the *erithoi* in the *Iliad* to be "hired farm-hands" (Edwards 1991, 223), apparently because 450 years later in Demosthenes this is the term given to hired harvesters. Edwards makes the good point that there is no clear distinction between the Homeric *erithoi* and *thetes.*

80. *WD* 441–46.

81. *WD* 602.

82. *WD* 370.

83. *WD* 502–3.

84. *WD* 469–71.

85. *WD* 573.

86. *WD* 597.

87. This is how I take *WD* 607–8; others might see this as a reference to threshing.

88. *WD* 765–66.

89. *WD* 271, 376–77.

90. *WD* 373–74.

91. *WD* 600–3. The Greek in 602 says either "Put your *thes* out of the *oikos*" or "Engage a *thes* who has no *oikos*." Either way, the *thes* depends on seasonal work.

92. *Od.* 11.489–91.

How many persons, then, populate Hesiod's *oikos?* Hesiod, his wife, one or two sons, a daughter or daughters, one or two female slaves, perhaps three male slaves, including the forty-year-old man, one *thes* (seasonally): this gives eight to twelve persons. To support this number, Hesiod would need between 15 and 20 acres (6 to 8 hectares) of arable, perhaps as few as 9 (4).[93] If we add a small amount of space for vines and assume that his sheep and goats are grazing on "common" land, a plot not enormously exceeding the standard 15 acres (6 hectares) of the seventh-century and later zeugite farms[94] would meet the needs of his *oikos* well. Hesiod does not feel that his *oikos* is overpopulated: "Easily would Zeus give unquenchable prosperity to more persons. The care of more hands is more, and the increase is greater."[95]

One goal of an *oikos* was self-sufficiency. It was supported by and gave support and protection to its membership, which was made up of both family and slaves: only the hired *thes* was excluded. An *oikos* typically existed as a result of inheritance and would survive to the next generation by the same mechanism: therefore a man's *oikos* was by definition incomplete without a wife and an heir.[96] Hesiod recommended one son, two if one intended to live long enough to accumulate wealth enough for both to inherit.[97] Apparently it was better to run the risk of losing an only son than to jeopardize the integrity of the *oikos* by dividing it between two (or more) sons, which

93. If each of the eight to ten persons consumes on average about 475 pounds of wheat per year (2.6 hectoliters: Roebuck 1945, 161; this figure may be on the high side: see Garnsey 1985, 67 n. 19; more recently Garnsey has offered 506 pounds [230 kilograms]: Garnsey 1988a, 90) and Hesiod's land generates between 9 and 12 bushels per acre (the modern yield in Boeotia: Bintliff 1985, 210; Carl Roebuck [1945, 160, following Jardé] estimated 10 hectoliters per hectare = 11.5 bushels per acre), a bushel weighing 64 pounds, the following may be determined: total production needed, 3,800–5,700 pounds; yield per acre, 576–768 pounds; land needed, between 5,700/576 and 3,800/768 = 5 to 10 acres. One-sixth of the production is used for seed, which increases necessary land to 6 to 12 acres. Of course, the bovines needed to be fed, and people did occasionally eat meat (*WD* 591) and vegetables, but this should not skew the result too much (although dependence on a large number of work animals might have increased production demand [Halstead 1987, 84]). If a three-field system is assumed, Hesiod needs no more than 18 acres (7.3 hectares), no less than 9 (4); if a two-field, 30 (12) and 12 (5). (There are other average yields that might be applied [e.g., Wagstaff, Augustson, and Gamble 1982, 174–77]; the results are not very different.) A bit more generous calculation (25–30 acres [10–12 hectares]) may be found in Tandy and Neale 1996.

94. Pecírka 1973, 142; Andreyev 1974, 14–16; Cooper 1977/78, 169; Burford 1993, 39, 67.

95. *WD* 379–80.

96. See further Lacey 1968, 15–16.

97. The necessary meaning of *WD* 376–77: "May there be an only son to feed his father's *oikos,* for thus wealth increases in the halls; may you die an old man, if you leave behind a second son." M. L. West (1978) suggests that the second son is a grandson. Karl Polanyi observed

appears to be what happened to Hesiod's father. Whatever the father's thinking may have been, he had (at least) two sons, and Hesiod and Perses inherited, half (or less) each, the *oikos* of their father, which may have been quite sizable. Perses appears to have lost his share and has brought or is bringing an action of some sort against Hesiod and his *oikos*.

We can surmise that there had been a time when *basilees* at Thespiae oversaw an apparently acceptable process by which goods moved to the general benefit of the general population. Now things are different. The *basilees* have changed the rules to the specific benefit of themselves, and Hesiod is forced to look for support elsewhere—from neighboring *oikoi*. Hard work, of course, will help maintain autarky, but neighbors are necessary, too, more necessary even than kin: "For if a problem arises at your place, neighbors come ungirt, while in-laws gird themselves."[98] Hesiod is also required to find his own outlet for his surplus production, now recognized and named a surplus because it no longer travels "naturally" to the center.

Interannual variability of rainfall must have translated into high frequency of crop failure.[99] One may surmise that a reasonably employed storage system would allow fairly easy survival in a given single year. But consecutive bad years would have required long-distance transportation of grains and their change of hands by gift or market exchange. Perhaps under these very conditions, Hesiod's surplus production could be fairly "profitably" taken to other places, probably the Gulf of Corinth and certainly to a peripheral market; his advice to Perses about moving surplus production is very clear on this:

> Praise a little ship, but put your cargo in a big one; the greater the cargo, the greater will be the *kerdos* on top of *kerdos*, if the winds hold back the evil blasts.[100]

The statement that the only risk is in the transportation ("if the winds hold back the heavy blasts") indicates a peripheral market, either controlled or one-time, where prices are fixed or where the *kerdos* is assured because costs are so low. The implication is that this cargo would be comprised typically of surplus grains, the outcome of Hesiod's *erga*, the movement of which is thus one *ergon* of many *erga*.[101] But such statements as "Do not put your

---

that "the advantages of division of labor may outweigh the burden of fragmentation of the land through inheritance" (Polanyi 1977, 152).

98. *WD* 344-45.

99. See Garnsey 1988a, 8–16; Garnsey and Morris 1989; Halstead 1989, esp. 72–75; Halstead and O'Shea 1989b, esp. 3–6.

100. *WD* 643-45.

101. It has always been assumed that Hesiod's freight was surplus grains (see, for example, Knorringa 1926, 13, and Mele 1979, 42); on "*ergon* commerce" see chapter 3.

entire substance (*bios*) in hollow ships, but leave most behind and load less,"[102] and "What lies stored up in his *oikos* does not wear down a man: it is better in the *oikos*, since what is outside is at risk"[103] suggest an ambiguity: perhaps Hesiod would occasionally move nonperishables of uncertain nature. (Interannual rain variability could rather suddenly shift grains into near-luxury status!)

Hesiod almost certainly would have brought his goods—both his *oikos* production and luxury items—to the port of Kreusis, called the *epineion*, "seaport," "shipping place," of Thespiae by both Pausanias and Strabo.[104] As the crow flies, Ascra is about 16 kilometers or so from Kreusis. Traveling to Thespiae and then south via Leuktra to Kreusis would have been a trip of under about 30 kilometers; a very old stone road, perhaps but not certainly Mycenaean, has been traced between Thespiae and Kreusis.[105] Hesiod's reference to the heavy blasts at sea fits to a tee the Krisaean Gulf, on which Kreusis is located.[106] It may be that Hesiod would have gained access to the sea on the Dombraina Gulf, just south of Thisbe, northwest of Kreusis; that road is a bit longer (perhaps 40 kilometers) but easier (almost all river valley). At a speed of 3 kilometers per hour (ox limit) an Ascran could make either port by either route in a day. Hesiod appears to have made regular trips there, although he did not himself take his goods onto the sea any more than he went fishing, another *ergon*.[107]

Why are how and where Hesiod brought his surplus production important? If Hesiod is moving surplus agricultural production by sea, we may infer that there is no central point at Thespiae to which he might bring it, that there is no longer a structure within which goods move in and out from the periphery to a center and back again. If Hesiod is moving luxury goods to a port of trade on the Gulf of Corinth, we may infer the (relatively) nearby presence of long-distance trade of precisely the sort that can make a redistributive formation precarious by introducing unobligated goods. In

---

102. *WD* 689–90. Hesiod may be advising that one should "leave the more valuable things behind and lade the less valuable," which would be a more difficult rendering of *pleo/meiona* than the usual one.

103. *WD* 364–65.

104. Paus. 9.32.1; Strabo 9.2.25.

105. Pritchett 1965, 54; it is drawn clearly in Buck 1979, iv, map 2.

106. Pausanias speaks of the violent winds (*anemoi biaioi*) that blow down from the headlands on the marine approach to Kreusis (9.32.1).

107. Tom Gallant (1985, 40–42) argues that fishing would be an appropriate long-term preventive option against temporary food shortages; one might catch and then smoke or dry fish in anticipation of times (probably summer) when grain in storage might be low. This may have been the case with some *oikoi*, but Hesiod makes no mention of fishing, and it would appear that he usually has a surplus of grain and thus—no doubt to his immense relief—does not need to go to sea to fish.

either case, we can see that the very fact that Hesiod is moving goods as he is implies that the redistributive structure that was presumably in place rather recently is now absent. Regardless of how we decide the details of Hesiod's seafaring activity, it is clear that such activity is a result of involuntary independence, caused, according to my argument, by the collapse of a redistributive formation and the introduction of limited markets. There is an interrelatedness between Hesiod's seafaring, on the one hand, and land alienations and debt, on the other.

THE ADVICE THAT IS NOT ABOUT PRODUCTION, BRINGING TO MARKET, OR THE AGORA

The critical sections of *Works and Days* are in fact ad rem, composed to address a specific set of problems that lies before the poet and his audience, problems that may not be addressed in the presence of the *basilees* who stand accused of creating the problems. While it would be circular to argue that *Works and Days* is not oral because it is critical, it is certainly legitimate to suggest that one of the reasons that the criticism was able to sustain itself was because it was disseminated by new means. Not only does the poet of *Works and Days* clearly concern himself with different subject matter than the epics; he also addresses an entirely different audience, for the beneficiaries of *Works and Days* are not the elite whom the epic serves, but the peripheral members of the community, those faced with *kleros* alienation, the dispossessed of the present and of the future. Hesiod restricts his argument to survival under new or newly perceived rules. The text, because of Hesiod's obsession with autarky, is therefore focused on general advice that may encourage industry among his fellow rim-dwellers.

These critical portions of *Works and Days* are internally consistent in tone and content; they are probably the product of a single poet, perhaps named Hesiod, and probably from Ascra in Boeotia.[108] As we saw above, it really does not matter whether Hesiod actually existed; it is unlikely that his world did *not* exist. The so-called Panhellenic aspects of the poem, such as the attempt to normalize the days of the month,[109] belong to the oral tradition and are unlikely original with Hesiod.[110] The Panhellenic spirit of the latter

108. G. P. Edwards (1971, 192 n. 13) considers it "very likely" that Hesiod's name entered the *Theogony* (22) when it was finally put down into writing, the result of the poet's notoriety. I believe that this is perfectly plausible. The critical portions of *Works and Days,* on the other hand, I have to conclude must have been composed and distributed in writing, for I cannot convince myself of any other explanation.

109. *WD* 765–828; see West ad loc.; Nagy 1989.

110. Although West and Nagy (see note 108) believe to the contrary, many scholars argue that the *Days* section (765–828) is a later accretion to the text. I agree but believe that there is no need for the section to be in essence any younger than the rest of the poem. It appears near-

part of *Works and Days* dovetails well with the Panhellenic opening of the *Theogony*. We are concerned with the socially "practical" portions of the poem, which may be called Panhellenic perversely and only in their universal applicability and utility for the dispossessed periphery, those portions of the poem that give advice that may protect.

Works and Days appears designed to inform the audience of the perils of the polis and its institutions, especially the law courts, which, on the one hand, can fascinate and thus undermine one's responsibility to one's land and, on the other hand, can, because they are by nature pernicious, take away one's land.[111] Perses clearly suffered on both counts:

> Do not let the evil-rejoicing Strife hold your spirit back from work while you closely watch wranglings (*neikea*) and play the listener in the *agora*. There is little interest in *neikea* and *agora* activities for the man whose seasonal sustenance does not lie stored up in abundance indoors, what the earth bears, Demeter's grain. When you have collected your fill of sustenance, then you might support *neikea* and contention over the possessions of others.[112]

Perses continued to neglect the *kleros* that he had inherited, with the result that he lost it.

The public space of the polis, which once belonged to all persons in the community, now appears to be controlled by a few *basilees*. What used to provide security has become a threat to the livelihoods of individuals; what was appropriative has become exploitative. Private space, a recent innovation apart from the traditional place for leisure activities, is the only source of refuge and of honor. Since there is nothing good happening at the center, one should stay out, retreat to one's *oikos,* and operate it as independently of the polis as possible. Handouts will no longer be forthcoming. The only community that remains is the one the individual creates within the *oikos* and with his neighbors, which means an emphasis on or a return to the way things used to be done, through "sharing" and "generosity," two aspects of the old life completely absent from the current set of rules governing relations between polis and periphery. It may be the case that "status follows wealth" on the periphery now also, but there are older rules that may bring a self-respect no longer obtainable by the present set of rules.

Hence the traditional guidelines for cropping, husbandry, and the rest,

---

ly to be a set piece, and Hesiod's mention of horses (816) conflicts with his position in the rest of the poem. Hesiod and his neighbors had no horses.

111. Perses appears to have lost his land (*WD* 403–7), but the language of Hesiod's description of the fraternal dispute does not suggest that Perses has deprived Hesiod of any land yet (see below, note 123).

112. *WD* 28–34.

no doubt part of the oral tradition, become a defense against dependence on the center. Most all of Hesiod's practical advice is geared toward independence, toward successful autarkic survival: one must know both how to build a plow and how many to build;[113] one must become aware of and then remember the importance of the two- or three-field system—"A fallow field is a protector against ruin and a soother of children"[114] because it is part of a calculated system of production that thinks ahead. This traditional wisdom becomes an important weapon of the dispossessed periphery against the new center, because such agricultural commitment both encourages aloof autarky and actually reifies the principles of the peasant fringe.

The general criticism and advice in *Works and Days* may be perceived as growing out of two specific situations, each created by the general economic and social changes that have occurred. First, Hesiod is irritated specifically by a verdict (or a potential verdict), generally by the system. Second, his brother Perses has a big problem that is specific but typical, and so emblematic, of the general problem. Hesiod's specific complaint to Perses is that Perses has colluded with the *basilees* in an attempt to cheat Hesiod, or perhaps even without collusion has tried through litigation to obtain some of Hesiod's inheritance that Hesiod does not agree should go to Perses.[115] Perses' specific problem is that someone has deprived him of his *kleros* and *oikos*. Perses seems to have been briefly in cahoots with the *basilees* and then fell from favor; now he needs instruction on survival. Therefore he is warned about the agora, where both brothers have been harmed, and he is encouraged to better himself *outside* the public space of the agora, in the narrowly public space of the neighborly periphery and in the private space of the *oikos*. A *neikos* is a bad thing that should never arise, for a *neikos* unresolved through self-help finds resolution in the public space of the agora,

---

113. *WD* 414–35.

114. *WD* 464. The fallow field soothes children because it provides for the future. To the contrary, see Marquardt 1984 (an elaborate explanation); West (1978, 274–75) reviews the varying interpretations over the years and then emends the text.

115. Michael Gagarin puts the options before us well. The traditional view holds that Perses "not content with his share of their father's estate . . . has bribed the judges in order to acquire some of Hesiod's share and is still trying to get more of this share through legal wrangling" (Gagarin 1974, 104); so, for example, Rose (1975, 134): the *basilees* "yielded to the blandishments of [Hesiod's] brother and settled the inheritance dispute in Perses' favor." Gagarin suggests that something closer to the truth may be found in van Groningen's argument that "Perses lost his earlier suit against Hesiod and that he thus never obtained any of his brother's possessions and is now nearly destitute" (Gagarin 1974, 104). Perses is destitute because he was forced to put up a substantial fee in exchange for the judges' ruling, which when he gained nothing left him destitute.

where justice is for sale and one can hear the "clamor when Justice (Dike) is dragged wherever gift-eating men carry her as they sort out decisions with crooked judgments (*dikai*)."[116] Better to deal with one's neighbors away from that crooked public space. Hesiod appeals to his brother: "Right here [both temporally and locatively, i.e., away from the polis] let us settle our *neikos*."[117] It would appear that Hesiod is responding to early efforts of the nascent polis to establish its authority juridically and, in Michael Gagarin's words (in reference to the first written laws in the seventh century), "to reduce the scope of and bring under control the traditional means of self-help, which had long been the province of the family."[118]

In order for self-help to be effective, there must be good sense, and there must be cooperation among neighbors and neighboring *oikoi*, the kind of cooperation that characterizes *xenie*. Private-space *xenie*, practiced by peripheral persons, appears precisely analogous to the display *xenie* practiced by the elite. But ever since the redistributive formation collapsed, and the spokes have ceased to act as reciprocal conduits for goods and other obligations, *xenie* is no longer practiced across the barrier that has been set up in the spokes by the new rule makers.[119] The center has established itself as a class, apart from nonparticipants; Hesiod's response to this *fait* is to appeal for solidarity on the outside by encouraging the formation of a new community. Hence he speaks of the importance of neighborly reciprocity and of the peripheral *dais*, that is, *xenie* on the defensive cultural plane, *xenie* on the rim:

> Do not be stormy at a well-attended *dais;* pleasure is greatest and cost the smallest when the *dais* is shared by the community.[120]

Hesiod's Assessment of the Polis: The Dangers of the Agora

Let us look at Hesiod's specific complaint, the point of departure of *Works and Days:*

> Right here let us settle our *neikos* with straight *dikai*, which are from Zeus and best. For we had already distributed the *kleros*, but you snatched and carried off many other things, energetically feeding the pride of gift-eating *basilees*,

---

116. *WD* 220–21.
117. *WD* 35.
118. Gagarin 1986, 136.
119. The *xenie* shown by Eumaeus to Odysseus upon the latter's return to Ithaca is not across-line *xenie*, nor is the post-recognition relationship between Odysseus and his hands, since they all belong together to Odysseus's *oikos*.
120. *WD* 722–23.

who are willing to propose a *dike* in this case.[121] Fools, they do not know by how much half is more than the whole, nor how great a blessing there is in mallow and asphodel.[122]

The precise nature of Perses' action cannot be determined beyond the fact that "carried off" strongly implies movable goods, whatever they may have been.[123] Hesiod is eager to settle his *neikos* with Perses away ("right here") from the agora, where Perses has been spending far too much time, as we saw above. The agora is a place where property is lost and people's (including Perses'?) possessions are taken by others. How Hesiod's attitude toward public space has changed since the *Theogony*! An important passage from the *Theogony* bears repeating:

> All the people watch [the *basileus*] as he decides law cases with straight *dikai;* and he, speaking surely, would put a stop to even a great *neikos*. For therefore there are *basilees* with wise hearts, for when the people are being misled in the agora, they easily settle cases that might bring harm, moving them with soothing words. When he goes through the assembly, they greet him as a god, and he is conspicuous among those gathered.[124]

We also read in the *Theogony* that "in the agora [the *basileus*] whom Hecate favors is conspicuous among the people."[125] Is Hesiod suffering from sour grapes? Perhaps, but now he seems to have some recourse. In the *Theogony*, Hesiod is a Phemius, singing under the necessity of the big man's control. Now he can sing the song of Agamemnon's bard without facing the same consequences.

We see then that in Hesiod's current opinion the agora has become a bad place to go, for no useful activity takes place there. Perses suffered by participating in the agora, and the baseness of the men in Hesiod's Iron Race,

---

121. So Gagarin (1974, 108), who also gives a review of the various interpretations of this thorny phrase (p. 108 n. 13). Compare Evelyn-White: "who love to judge such a case as this"; West: "who see fit to make this their judgment"; Verdenius (1985, ad loc.): "who are used to pronouncing the kind of verdict as is known here."

122. *WD* 35–41.

123. Perhaps more accurately rendered (after Gagarin 1974, 109) "tried to carry off," the conative force of the imperfect *ephoreis* being more logical than the iterative ("continued to carry off").

124. *Th.* 84–92.

125. *Th.* 429–434–430 (Schoemann's ordering of the verses, followed by Rzach [1913], Solmsen [1970], and West [1966]). Cf. 431–33: "And whenever men arm themselves for man-destroying war, then the goddess is at hand, to offer victory and grant glory to whomever she favors." It is worth noting here that there is no significant reference to warfare in *Works and Days*. The periphery would, it seems, be concerned about ravagings of their countryside, were there any warfare, but Hesiod expresses no such apprehension, which perhaps suggests that he is aware that the military trappings of the elite are mere specious posturings.

while perhaps remediable, is centered on activity in the agora (in the following passages, *dike* is "justice"; Dike is the goddess personification of it):

> There will be no goodwill for him who keeps his oath, nor for the just, nor for the good man, but men will sooner honor for his violence the man who is a doer of evils. *Dike* will be in [strength of] hands, and shame will not exist. The evil man will hurt the superior man by speaking with crooked words and will swear an oath on them.[126]

But there is hope:

> O Perses, listen to Dike and do not support violence. For violence is evil for a wretched mortal; not even a good man can bear it easily, but he is weighed down by it when he has met with calamities. By the other way is the better road [to travel on and] to reach just things. *Dike* holds violence in check when it comes to the reckoning, as a fool realizes after suffering. For Oath straightway chases down crooked *dikai,* and there is a clamor when Dike is dragged wherever gift-eating men carry her as they sort out decisions with crooked *dikai.* Wailing and wrapped in mist, Dike pursues the polis and the haunts of the people, bringing with her evil for men who would drive her out and who have dealt out *dike* that was not straight.[127]

And the hope Hesiod describes is a hope that the polis will succeed, though clearly a different kind of leadership is required. (He is *not,* as I pointed out above, supporting a specific change in leadership; he is not taking sides.) He indirectly calls for the leadership of just men, who can help a polis flourish, just as bad men can bring it to ruin (we recognize the language and tone of Homer's cautionary remarks about bad dispensers of *dike*):[128]

> But those who give straight *dikai* to outsiders and insiders and do not diverge at all from what is just, for them the polis thrives, and the people in it bloom. And Peace, who nurtures children, is throughout the land; Zeus the Wide-Viewer never assigns painful war to them. And never do Hunger or Calamity attend upon men of straight *dikai,* but they enjoy the fruits at festivities, the fruits of the works they have tended. For them the earth bears much sustenance, and in the mountains the oak bears acorns on top and bees in the middle. Their woolly sheep become heavy all over from their fleeces; women bear children that resemble their parents. They thrive with good things continually. And therefore they do not go onto ships, but the grain-bearing plowland bears [enough] produce [every year].
>
> To those whose care is evil violence and cruel works Zeus the Wide-Viewer, the son of Cronus, assigns *dike.* Many times even the entire polis fares ill for an evil man who commits offenses and plots actions of outrage. On them the son

---

126. *WD* 190–94.
127. *WD* 213–24.
128. *Il.* 16.386–88; see above, at the beginning of this chapter.

of Cronus brings a great disaster from heaven: hunger and plague together. The people die; women do not give birth; *oikoi* become diminished by the ploys of Olympian Zeus. At different times in turn the son of Cronus destroys their wide army or their wall or exacts atonement from their ships upon the open sea.[129]

Hesiod continues, returning to the personified Dike, but addressing now the *basilees* themselves and sharpening his focus on the line that has been drawn between those in control and those who participate only peripherally:

> O *basilees*, you too observe well this *dike*, for the deathless ones, who are near among men, observe all those who wear each other out with crooked *dikai*, paying no attention to the vengeance of the gods. For there are over the much-nourishing earth thirty thousand deathless guardians of mortal men, sent from Zeus; they watch for *dikai* and cruel works, wrapped in mist, wandering everywhere over the earth. And there is the virgin Dike, born from Zeus, majestic and revered among the gods who hold Olympus. And whenever somebody hurts her by scorning her crookedly, she straightway seats herself at the side of father Zeus, the son of Cronus, and tells him about the unjust[130] thinking of men, until the *demos* atones for the outrages of the *basilees*, who, by thinking pernicious thoughts, veer off the right track by pronouncing *dikai* crookedly. Watching for these things, O *basilees*, straighten your words, gift eaters, and forget entirely crooked *dikai*.[131]

Here the *demos* is differentiated from the center:[132] it is they who suffer as a result of the leaders' misdeeds. Note also that Hesiod here invokes aid from a divine source, which is in keeping with the poet's prerogative and power.[133] Of course, this has an Old Testament-prophet effect; it may be no coincidence that in *Works and Days* Hesiod seems to sound so much like Amos, whose situation and date may be parallel to Hesiod's own.[134]

Less Explicit Criticism

In addition to this explicit criticism of the leadership in Thespiae, there may also be implicit criticism of the aristocratic strategy of identifying heroes of the past with the leaders of the present. In his narrative of the Races of Man, borrowed from the East, Hesiod inserts between the Bronze (the third) and

---

129. *WD* 225–47.

130. Reading *adikon* with omicron; see Verdenius 1985, ad loc., p. 140.

131. *WD* 248–64.

132. Such tension between *basilees* and *demos* is absent in Homer; see Donlan 1970, 383–85.

133. See chapter 7.

134. Amos's prophetic career had begun by the time of Jeroboam's death in 742. A number of the parallels are collected in Andrews 1943.

Iron (the fifth and last) races, in rather clear reference to the actors in the epics, a race of heroes. This is what he says about them:

> When also this [bronze] race the earth covered over, in turn Zeus, the son of Cronus, made another one, the fourth, on the much-nourishing ground, more just and so superior, a godly race of hero men, who are called demigods, the race before ours over the immense earth. Evil war and the dreadful battle cry destroyed some of these below seven-gated Thebe, the land of Cadmus, as they fought for the sheep of Oedipus. Others [perished] in their ships after war carried them over the great maw of the sea to Troy for fair-haired Helen's sake. There indeed the end of death covered some of them; to the rest father Zeus, the son of Cronus, offered sustenance and haunts apart from men and settled them at the boundaries of the earth. And these reside with woe-free spirit on the Islands of the Blessed Ones on the shore of deep-eddying Ocean.[135]

The individual members of this race either died in battle or were whisked off to eternal bliss. Implicit in Hesiod's description of their demise is that there is no continuity with the race that followed. Thus Hesiod severs any possible genealogical tie between past and present, in an effort (I am suggesting) to contradict those who actually claimed descent from the epic heroes.[136] This is Hesiod's refraction of his world.

New (?) Directions

What Hesiod is urging as a solution—this appears to be his broadest and most optimistic goal—is also articulated in these passages: a polis with full participation is possible. By full participation, of course, Hesiod means a return to a (recent) system in which there is not yet a separation of leadership and periphery, a time when by *demos* one meant the entire community, when public space was still good. Of course, this is almost precisely parallel to the response of Bulu villagers to the intrusion of Western markets described in chapter 5: the changes wrought by outside forces "reinforced the concept of Bulu society."[137] Hesiod specifically calls for the maintenance of traditional values, such as generosity and *xenie* (although there has

135. *WD* 156–71.
136. The most notorious example of this phenomenon is the ingenious explanation for the appearance, on a Dipylon workshop krater dating to about 750 and nine more times in the subsequent fifty years, of battle scenes featuring a pair of Siamese twins. Nestor of Pylos fought the two Aktorione or Molione in his youth (*Il.* 11.709–10), and Hesiod reports that they shared a body (frag. 17a.14–17). *If* it is true that there was a family in Athens that claimed descent from Nestor, these illustrations would reflect the assertion of that descent. See Coldstream 1991, 51, who believes that there was a prominent Neleid *genos* in Athens in the eighth century.
137. Horner 1962, 186. See above, chapter 5, on dominant markets.

perhaps been a shift in emphasis from kin to neighbor), and generally hopes for a return to the old ways, when the community was of one spirit, and participation in its workings was available to all.

Perses has lost his land because he accumulated too many *chrea* (see chapter 5). Without any visible means of support, that is, without belonging to an *oikos* (much less running one), Perses seems on the verge of becoming a beggar, and although beggars used to be in some way protected by Zeus,[138] there is little success to be gained by such a tactic any longer:

> Perses, you fool, work the works that the gods have assigned to men, lest at some time with your children and wife and with an ache in your spirit you may seek sustenance among your neighbors, and they do not care. For twice, perhaps three times, you will get results; but if you vex them further, you will not achieve a thing.[139]

Because the redistributive formation has collapsed, there is no social constitution to fall back on. As has been pointed out often, we are witness to the "rise of the individual," but this does not mean that these individuals have undertaken their rise voluntarily.[140]

Hesiod's Wisdom in the Fields

Now that we have heard Hesiod's advice on production and his critique of the agora in the polis, let us return to the fields.

Hesiod tells his brother to go out and get an *oikos*. Just how Perses is supposed to acquire a *kleros* when already in debt is difficult to imagine, but *if* Perses is to be successful in starting over, Hesiod has plenty of advice, which falls into two categories, what to do and what not to do. The former sort of advice is actually more than just practical advice for the small holder, for it is also advice on how to survive *away* from public space. Hence it is fairly inseparable from the latter type of advice, which is simply to stay out of the polis. Perhaps what locks these two types of advice together is the spirit of community, or rather the appeal to older, traditional values and behaviors, which pervades all of Hesiod's thought. Let us look at some samples of Hesiodic wisdom. We see the expression of traditional values in the following:

> Stay friendly to your friend; spend time with him who calls on you; give to him who gives, and do not give to him who does not give. One gives to a giver, but one does not give to a nongiver. Give is a good, but Snatch is evil, a giver of

---

138. "From Zeus are all strangers and beggars" (*Od.* 6.208); cf. *Od.* 17.475.

139. *WD* 397–402.

140. On the rise of the individual see the markedly different Polanyi 1977, 147–57, and Starr 1986.

death. For he who gives willingly, even when he gives something great, rejoices in the giving and delights in his own spirit. But he who himself seizes, after trusting in shamelessness, even if it be something little, freezes his victim's poor heart.[141]

There is a striking parallel between this response to new rules and what we saw among the Bulu (see chapter 5 and above): the eager embracing of traditional cultural values in the face of an outside force that threatens them. In the passage that immediately precedes this one we see some of the same sentiments, but also a curious dependence on neighbors instead of kin.

> Call your friend to a *dais*, but leave your enemy alone. Call especially him who resides near you. For if a problem arises at your place, neighbors come ungirt, while in-laws gird themselves. A bad neighbor is a disaster as much as a good neighbor is a great blessing. He has his share of honor who has a good neighbor. And an ox would not become lost unless your neighbor should be bad. Take good measure from a neighbor, and pay it back well, with the same measure, or more if you can, so that you may later find him reliable should you need him.[142]

This shift from kin to neighbor may be satisfactorily explained as a reflex of two related phenomena. First, the shift from ranking to stratified organization has rendered kin relations less important than legal ones. Kin cannot be counted on to hold greater allegiance to an individual than to the center. (This is of course an old observation, going back to Henry Maine's status and contract and to Ferdinand Toennies's *Gemeinschaft* and *Gesellschaft*.)[143] Second, not only has the lockout of Hesiod and his neighbors from the economic mainstream forced self-sufficiency upon each *oikos;* it has also forced the individual *oikoi* along the rim to band together, at least informally, against the center, the enemy on whom they are forced to rely, in keeping with the standard peasantry-city model.[144]

No longer can an individual or an *oikos* turn to the center for relief. One must work out a new system to avoid debt and hunger:

> For if you should put away a little on top of a little, and you should do this often, quickly even that little would become big. He who adds to what is there wards off blazing hunger. What lies stored up in his *oikos* does not wear down a man: it is better in the *oikos*, since what is outside is at risk. It is good to take

---

141. *WD* 353–60.
142. *WD* 342–51.
143. Maine 1963, 164–65; Toennies 1935, 37–39. See Polanyi 1957a, 69.
144. See above, note 66.

hold of what is at hand; it is a disaster to the spirit to need what is absent. I command you to consider these things.[145]

This passage may be another reference to occasional trade, treated here with disparagement. "At risk" refers, presumably, to the risk in the transfer of goods and not to any risk in getting the price one is seeking for them. Prices in the controlled market that Hesiod and his colleagues would be participating in were almost certainly fixed; if one-time markets, costs were fully absorbed in the *oikos* and thus negligible. Hence, risk is restricted to transportation only.

Kerdea and the Reification of Culture

As I have pointed out (in chapter 5 and again just above), fixed prices or negligible costs are indicated by Hesiod's reference to gaining a large *kerdos:* the greater the cargo, the greater will be the *kerdos* upon *kerdos*, "provided the winds hold back the heavy blasts."[146] Elsewhere, Hesiod mentions *kerdos* as a desirable thing: "And then drag the swift ship seaward, and put a fitting cargo in it, in order that you may bring a *kerdos* home";[147] though there is a bad kind (that corresponds no doubt to the bad Eris): "Do not pursue base *kerdea*. Base *kerdea* are like ruins";[148] *Kerdos* can lure the unwary man into violent or dishonest behavior.[149] (He also uses *kerdos* metaphorically: "If a man should sow evils, he would reap evil *kerdea*.")[150]

For Hesiod, properly acquired *kerdos* is a good thing, perhaps even a necessary thing, for survival. In Homer, *kerdos* appears to mean "advantage (for oneself)," in contradistinction to *ophelos*, "advantage (for another)."[151] Hesiod clearly uses *kerdos* in this way also: it is a gain or advantage to oneself as opposed to one that is intended for or obligated to others. Hesiod's choice of diction reflects the need to look after oneself in the absence of the support once provided by the redistributive formation, now collapsed; the very use of this term underlines the reluctant "rise of the individual." We may conclude that social and "economic" *kerdos* is the

145. *WD* 361–67.
146. *WD* 644–45.
147. *WD* 631–32.
148. *WD* 352.
149. *WD* 321–24.
150. Frag. 286.1, from the *Megala Erga,* attributed to Hesiod. It should come as no surprise that Hesiod uses neither *kerdos* nor *chreos* in the *Theogony,* for these are subjects the *basilees* do not want mentioned.
151. For a discussion of Homeric *kerdos* and *ophelos,* see de Jong 1987.

obverse of *chreos*. Amassing *kerdea* is a defense against the *chrea* that can lead to *oikos*-lessness.

We must presume that if Hesiod is able to speak against base *kerdea,* there must be someone acquiring them. Some of these base *kerdea* may be advantages (thefts) gained from the community by the new center that controls the movements of goods and land. Other ill-gotten *kerdea* might just be unnecessary external acquisitions of goods for their own sake, in which case we are reminded of the Trobriander saying when reciprocal relations are strained in an exchange: "He did it like a *gimwali* " (see above, chapter 5). Not only do ill-gotten *kerdea* attract no approval from Hesiod; ill-gotten *kerdea* are equated with major social and familial "crimes" and are punishable by the gods:

> For if someone seizes great prosperity even by force of hands or carries it off with his tongue, as many times happens whenever *kerdos* deceives the intellect of men and Shamelessness chases away Shame, then easily the gods make him obscure, and they diminish that man's *oikos,* and prosperity attends him for a short time. Likewise with him who mistreats a suppliant or with him who mistreats a *xeinos* and with him who might climb into his brother's bed for the secret bed pleasures of his wife, acting against what is proper, and with him who offends on account of his follies against somebody's fatherless children, and with him who raises a *neikos* with his old father at the evil threshold of old age, assailing him with hard words. With that man Zeus himself indeed is indignant.[152]

And so there is good wealth and bad wealth. Although both types can attract good standing in the community at large, "*Arete* and *kudos* attend upon wealth."[153] But for Hesiod the wealth must be properly acquired to deserve the admiration among his neighbors, and in this regard the people on the periphery differ from those in the center. The proper kind of wealth, of course, derives only from hard work, from one's *erga*: "If you work, the idler will quickly envy you as you become wealthy."[154] "If the spirit in your breast desires wealth, do these things, and pile work upon work (*kai ergon ep' ergoi ergazesthai*)."[155] Attention to proper effort will lead to "*kerdos* upon *kerdos,*"[156] the same syntactical idiom as "work upon work": repetitive actions lead to cumulative results. Ill-gotten gains are those goods acquired without hard effort or great risk, the increase enjoyed by the "gift-eating" *basilees* in

152. *WD* 321–33.
153. *WD* 313.
154. *WD* 312–13.
155. *WD* 381–82.
156. *WD* 644.

the new public space that they control. Perses is urged to stop sitting on the fence between the center and the periphery. He ought to stop dallying about the agora, where only those who neglect their holdings go, a neglect that can lead to *kleros* alienation. By joining the solidarity of the periphery and by subscribing to the necessary activities of giving and sharing and helping one's neighbors, a similar but new kind of security can be achieved, a security no longer founded in community solidarity in support of all, but one based on a defensive solidarity in the face of the new rule makers.

To repeat, community solidarity and cultural retreat are reflected also in the agricultural advice. Many times Hesiod's advice has been cited in arguments that Hesiod could not be a peasant because peasants already know how to do all these things; therefore, Hesiod and his audience must be down-and-out aristocrats, quondam *agathoi* now *kakoi*. But the archaeological record suggests that grain production was not necessarily a long-practiced activity at this point in time, so that perhaps there was need for this practical advice. More to the point, however, is that the agricultural advice dovetails with much of the comparative evidence, including that of the Bulu: it is part of the broader polemic against the changes that have occurred. Repeatedly Hesiod calls on his brother and his neighbors to practice the productive activities that are traditionally associated with themselves as a group. He evokes with his advice the image of the ideal small-scale agriculturalist, whom all should emulate.

To do X at this time of year and Y at another is a reification of culture. As the Bulu invented themselves, so here the Ascran peasantry asserts itself through its spokesperson, Hesiod. On a couple of occasions Hesiod makes some unspecific, formulaic statements about wealth and speaks of animal wealth in terms of goats and sheep. For the most part, Hesiod ignores bovine herds and horses, both of which are fundamental symbols of aristocratic status in the Homeric epics and contemporary elite art. This observed, we know on which side of the fence to find Hesiod. In the eighth-century crisis over how to utilize bottomlands—for symbolic herds or for edible grains?—Hesiod is on the agricultural side. If Hesiod were a dispossessed aristocrat, his values would remain aristocratic.

Success in Ascra was inhibited by external economic and political structural factors. New rules coming out of Thespiae prevented Hesiod from participating in the mainstream of the regional economy; when an outsider did participate, as his brother Perses did, disaster always seemed to follow. These new rules—market rules—especially affected land use. What Hesiod especially speaks to is a new solidarity of community that can function broadly as a replacement for the protective mechanisms once provided by the now-defunct redistributive formation. Thus autarky through continuous work is his theme. It has been said, correctly, that the Greek polis embraced rural peasants in its citizenry; but in the beginning, the new, reconstituted urban settlements that emerged from the static poverty of the Dark Age excluded the rural small landowner such as Hesiod. And this exclusion from the economic and political mainstream was a big reason why Ascra was in Hesiod's opinion "bad in winter, painful in summer, never any good."[157]

157. *WD* 640.

NINE

Conclusions

Now to tie together what has been simultaneously a series of individual studies and a continuous argument. If my attempts here prove open to charges of theoretical or evidentiary aggressiveness, let me respond by asserting that only in this way can studies such as this one have some impact on the economic and social crises of our own time. I am not pleading for the primitivism-modernism argument redivivus and stood on its head; this is a matter of how human experiences of the past can help us today and tomorrow. This is history. In these last few pages I want to recapitulate the survey that has taken us around the Mediterranean and into Hesiod's *oikos,* and then try briefly to realign our focus, away from Hesiod's peripheral world in the fields to the town, where one of the first citizen-states is newly forming.

As I argued in chapter 2, we are able to discern an increase in population density in many communities in Greece as the ninth century draws to a close, this after several centuries of reduced population. By the mid- to late eighth century, there has been a significant increase in density in many communities, especially, apparently, in Athens and Attica, but also in the Argolid. New settlements in the Aegean also reflect this increase. There are social and biological explanations for this increase, but more important are its consequences, among which were new human behaviors, especially in the handling and treatment of the deceased (specifically, who received burial, how, and where) and in shrine activity (both volume and offering type), also at midcentury. These new behaviors, we saw, are best explained as responses to population pressure, although, seeing that new behaviors are found in communities that show no other signs of population increase (Corinth, for example), other explanations may be possible.

One other explanation for these new behaviors is that they are responses to new activities abroad, the focus of chapter 3. These new activities were trading and processing under the leadership of the Euboean Greeks and in partnership with the Phoenicians, who had been plying the Mediterranean end to end for several hundred years when the Euboeans joined them at Al Mina shortly before 800 and within the same human generation set up a cooperative venture with them on the island of Pithekoussai near Naples. Goods began to come into Greek communities from abroad just as populations were growing. In the last third of the eighth century, the "colonizing" movement produced new Greek settlements throughout Sicily and southern Italy, a response, by my argument, to opportunities abroad rather than overpopulation at home. (Both opportunities and population pressure—itself partly explicable in terms of opportunities—played important roles in shaping activities abroad.) The ordering and timing of the Euboean, Corinthian, Spartan, and Achaean settlements in the west appear to be a reflection of a contrived development there, part and parcel of a trade network that ran from Al Mina to Pithekoussai (and even farther west with the Phoenicians) and back again. The movement of goods in the network is reflected in an increase in goods at settlements throughout the Aegean and also the eastern Mediterranean (Cyprus). The new wealth that was generated abroad came under the control of the elite still at home in Old Greece.

The picture is not completely clear, and no explanation is universally accepted. But one way to get comfortable with the evidence is to apply theory to it, to sift the evidence through some theoretical sieves. The discussion in chapters 4 and 5 is not scintillating per se, but it is by far (in my opinion) the most important component of this study. Without it, I don't think it is possible to connect these ancient materials to comprehensible human experience. The political-anthropological and economic models included in chapters 4 and 5 are offered to help us envision the eighth-century Mediterranean world. Also included is some compelling comparative ethnographical evidence from small-scale societies. With such models and comparative evidence I have tried to articulate *theoretically* through contextualization and generalization what I believe can be seen happening in the latter half of the eighth century—the fundamental change in economic organization at home that developed, again as a response, as a result of the double-barreled pressure of increase in population and increase in wealth. There was, furthermore, a change in the *nature* of this wealth and the role the new kind of wealth played in society. In short, there was a shift in how wealth and status interacted. Before the change, wealth followed status; after the change, status followed wealth. This fundamental change leads us to consider a new form of economic integration, what I have named the limited market system, which proved to be the machine that generated the eventual consequences of the economic and social shift: the beginning of private property, land alienations, debt, and the polis.

This shift in how people lived their lives was so profound that an entire second set of human behaviors appeared in its wake, this time not in isolation but spread across an enormous landscape, even more dramatic in their execution than the earlier ones. These are the tools of exclusion identified and discussed in chapter 6, inseparable from the birth of the polis, the citizen-state of equal participants. These tools—hero cults and warrior burials, feasts and councils, gift exchange in public space—were designed to create a solidarity of the leaders of the separate Greek communities with one another, simultaneously separating them as a class from the rest of the members of their communities. The blurring of the distinction between the heroic past (when wealth followed status) and the elite present (when the obverse obtained) served to disguise the dramatic shift in economic institutions that had in fact happened between the past and the present. As we saw in chapter 8, Hesiod criticized this specific strategy by denying any connection between the Race of Heroes and the Iron Race in his Myth of the Five Races.

Of course (as argued in chapter 7), the greatest of these tools, in part because they integrate, implement, and complement the others, were the epics. The *Iliad* and *Odyssey*, and the *Theogony*, too, were produced under these conditions of social stress. It is clear to me also that social stress was the driving force behind their monumental construction. Just as hero cults and warrior burials were essentially indistinguishable phenomena, so also the epics attempted to equate heroes of the past and the leaders of the present. The manipulative power of orality in public space is illustrated well by the rememberers of the early Greek poleis, who are paralleled by figures in many other cultures, perhaps especially by the *mazkir* of the contemporary Hebrew tradition. These manipulations of reality and orality drove a historically unprecedented wedge between the leadership and the less fortunate.

As demonstrated in chapter 8, Hesiod's *Works and Days* was a critical and negative response to all of this. It was a response from the periphery, literal and figurative. Hesiod, spokesperson for the dominated peasantry, was willing (and, significantly, able) to fight back.

He fought back in a variety of ways. While providing us not only with valuable information about how he produced his agrarian goods and how he (sometimes) took them to market, but also with his own opinions about how (poorly) the nearby polis was functioning, Hesiod seems to be defending peasant values, urging his neighbors to continue their commitment to fairness, generosity and sharing, and, in general, community. When community is celebrated through the sharing of values and activities, the routinized actions of individuals in society become a reification of culture. Production is ideology.

Hesiod's criticism of the leadership in the town was an overt rejection of polis hegemony, but Hesiod also offered more subtle resistance when he took his goods to market. He did not take them to his local village (Ascra), nor to the nearest polis (probably Thespiae); rather, he took them to the sea. Hesiod can't or doesn't want to participate in an exchange of goods with the town—an effect or reaction to the arrival of certain kinds of market forces. The wholesale shift in values has created a very bad situation for the agrarian producers in Boeotia and presumably in any number of places in Greece. This bad situation has been replicated any number of times and in any number of places subsequently even to this day. One of the main purposes of this study was to identify how the opposition between town and fields developed. I have to conclude that this was very probably among the very first times this opposition developed in this particular way, and, needless to say, not the last.

But let's leave Hesiod and his fellow peasants in the fields now and see how the polis might have been viewing things from the town, in Thespiae perhaps. A tried-and-true theory will support some final words on the economic miracle of the eighth-century Aegean. We will see that it is remarkable that development was able to be sustained.

Since at least the time of Adam Smith, political economists have observed the fundamental relation between town and field. In his *Wealth of Nations* Smith himself observed:

> The great commerce of every civilized society, is that carried on between the inhabitants of the town and those of the country. . . . The country supplies the town with the means of subsistence, and the materials of manufacture. The town repays this supply by sending back a part of the manufactured produce to the inhabitants of the country.[1]

One of the outstanding characteristics of this back-and-forth is the easily observed built-in advantage enjoyed by the town:

> Whatever regulations, therefore, tend to increase those wages and profits beyond what they otherwise would be, tend to enable the town to purchase, with a smaller quantity of its labour, the produce of a greater quantity of labour of the country. . . . By means of those regulations a greater share of [the annual produce] is given to the inhabitants of the town than would otherwise fall to them; and a less to those of the country.[2]

---

1.   Smith 1776, 3.1. Elsewhere: "Every town draws its whole subsistence, and all the materials of its industry from the country. . . . The whole annual produce of the labour of the society is annually between these two different sets of people" (1776, 1.10.c.19). Marx elaborates on the division (1845/46, 38).

2.   Smith 1776, 1.10.c.19. On the incremental advantage see further Sombart 1916, 1.142.

I argued in chapter 8 that in Hesiod's world this net movement into the town is comprised at least partly of *chrea* (debts). These *chrea*—together with hunger the great fear of the periphery—are the solitary means by which landholdings were alienated, as happened to Hesiod's brother Perses. Within the context of consumer-city theory, the facility of the accumulation of these *chrea* was part of the advantage enjoyed by the town. The process of dispute settlement that we see on Achilles' Shield (probably) and the dispute-solving *basileus* in the opening of the *Theogony* (certainly) are mechanisms that work to capture this incremental advantage. Town markets, with their special rules, worked with the same result.³ The tools of exclusion, including epic, work to complete this picture, offering a refracted vision of the world to those who are watching and listening. Collectively, these mechanisms serve to create a centripetal force that draws peripheral persons into a dependent arrangement with the city, much like what we saw in chapter 8 in our examination of peasant theory.⁴

But if central Boeotia is typical, we are able to contemplate how contingent economic development in the early Greek polis must have been, for the market that would normally provide incremental income for the town was not being served by the fields, in some cases not at all, in others only partially. If we can observe that Hesiod is bringing his surplus to a different market than Thespiae's regular one, then we can conclude that Thespiae is at some disadvantage, compared to other poleis (or even not so compared). Some amount of the (elsewhere) observable centripetal increment is not coming in. It is possible that field producers of a different polis are bringing their surplus to Thespiae, for which they have no antagonism. We do not know this, however, but in any case we can see, in the case of Thespiae, just how contingent a proposition successful economic development must have been.

In good years, Thespiae would not need Hesiod's extra grains, for it had all it needed, presumably. In bad years, Hesiod would have nothing extra to offer. At critical junctures of development, however, Thespiae needs to

---

3. Here I am following Weber: "If we were to attempt a definition [of 'city'] in purely economic terms, the city would be a settlement whose inhabitants live primarily from commerce and the trades rather than from agriculture. . . . Economic diversity can be called forth in two ways: by the presence of a court, or by that of a market. . . . A city is always a market center. It has a local market which forms the economic center of the settlement and on which both the non-urban population and the townsmen satisfy their wants for crafts products or trade articles by means of exchange on the basis of an existing specialization in production. It was originally quite normal for a city, wherever it was structurally differentiated from the countryside, to be both a seignorial or princely residence *and* a market place and thus to possess economic centers of both types, *oikos* and market" (Weber 1921, 1213–14).

4. I am pursuing this more fully (Tandy forthcoming).

store, and it needs to make regular, incremental centripetal gains from market activity. Not all centripetal gains come through the market, but the city's economic and political development would face a formidable obstacle when it was not possible to accomplish such market gains.

This possible dependence on distant producers and this certain failure to hegemonize its own hinterland must have been together an enormous drag on more than one early polis. Those poleis that eventually succeeded did so in conjunction with the successful transition from domination to hegemony. A closer look at this economic and political phenomenon would be a promising undertaking. Just as scrutiny of Hesiod's world can help us appreciate the plight of individuals and communities that are oppressed by the force of the market in a late capitalist world, so also might a closer study of the precariousness of this earliest economic development in the west teach us how, in a world that appears hellbent on allowing the market to drive communities, cultures, societies, and nations without restraint, to orchestrate resources today within national and international political economies.

The struggle will continue. This study is about one of its first and most amazing arenas. From our perspective in the late capitalist world, the world of the Dipylon master and Homer—as well as the peripheral world of Hesiod—is nothing other than the beginning of a historical trajectory that may finally now be coming to an end.

BIBLIOGRAPHY

Abramson, Herbert. 1979. A hero shrine for Phrontis at Sounion? *California Studies in Classical Antiquity* 12: 1–19.

Acker, Cheryl L., and Patricia K. Townsend. 1975. Demographic models and female infanticide. *Man* 10: 469–70.

Acsádi, Gy., and J. Nemeskéri. 1970. *History of human life span and mortality.* Translated by K. Balás. Budapest: Akadémiaí Kiadó.

Adams, John, and Nancy Hancock. 1970. Land and economy in traditional Vietnam. *Journal of Southeast Asian Studies* 1.2: 90–98.

Adams, Robert McC. 1966. *The evolution of urban society.* Chicago: Aldine.

———. 1974. Anthropological perspectives on ancient trade. *Current Anthropology* 15: 239–49.

Adkins, Arthur W. H. 1960a. "Honour" and "punishment" in the Homeric poems. *Bulletin of the Institute of Classical Studies* 7: 23–32.

———. 1960b. *Merit and responsibility: A study in Greek values.* Oxford: Clarendon Press.

———. 1963. "Friendship" and "self-sufficiency" in Homer and Aristotle. *Classical Quarterly* 13: 30–45.

———. 1970. *From the many to the one.* Ithaca, N.Y.: Cornell University Press.

———. 1971. Homeric values and Homeric society. *Journal of Hellenic Studies* 91: 1–14.

———. 1972a. Homeric gods and the values of Homeric society. *Journal of Hellenic Studies* 92: 1–19.

———. 1972b. *Moral values and political behaviour in ancient Greece.* London: Chatto and Windus.

Agnew, Jean-Cristophe. 1979. The threshold of exchange: Speculations on the market. *Radical History Review* 21: 99–118.

Ahlberg, Gudrun. 1971a. *Fighting on land and sea in Greek Geometric art.* Skrifter utgivna av Svenska institutet i Athen, 4°, XVI. Stockholm: Paul Åströms Förlag.

———. 1971b. *Prothesis and ekphora in Greek Geometric art.* 2 vols. Studies in Mediterranean Archaeology, vol. 32. Göteborg: Paul Åströms Förlag.

Ahlström, Gösta W. 1993. *The history of ancient Palestine from the palaeolithic period to Alexander's conquest.* Edited by Diana Edelman. Journal for the Study of the Old Testament Supplement Series, no. 146. Sheffield: JSOT Press.

Akurgal, Ekrem. 1983. *Alt-Smyrna.* Vol. 1, *Wohnschichten und Athenatempel.* Ankara: Türk Tarih Kurumu Basimevi.

Albright, W. F. 1941. New light on the early history of Phoenician colonization. *Bulletin of the American Schools of Oriental Research* 83: 14–22.

Allee, W. C., Alfred E. Emerson, Orlando Park, Thomas Park, and Karl P. Schmidt. 1949. *Principles of animal ecology.* Philadelphia: W. B. Saunders.

Amandry, Pierre. 1956. Chaudrons à protomés de taureau en Orient et en Grèce. In Weinberg 1956, 239–61.

Ammerman, A. J., and L. L. Cavalli-Sforza. 1973. A population model for the diffusion of early farming in Europe. In *The explanation of culture change: Models in prehistory,* edited by Colin Renfrew, 343–57. London: Duckworth.

Amouretti, Marie-Claire. 1986. *Le pain et l'huile dans la Grèce antique.* Paris: Les Belles Lettres.

Andersen, Øivind. 1976. Some thoughts on the Shield of Achilles. *Symbolae Osloenses* 51: 5–18.

Andreev, Juri V. 1979. Könige und Königsherrschaft in den Epen Homers. *Klio* 61: 361–84.

——— (as Andreyev, Yu. V.). 1991. Greece of the eleventh to the ninth centuries B.C. in the Homeric epics. In Diakonoff 1991, 328–46.

Andrewes, Antony. 1961. Phratries in Homer. *Hermes* 89: 129–40.

———. 1967. *The Greeks.* New York: Knopf.

Andrews, Mary E. 1943. Hesiod and Amos. *Journal of Religion* 23: 194–205.

Andreyev, V. N. 1974. Some aspects of agrarian conditions in Attica in the fifth to third centuries B.C. *Eirene* 12: 5–46.

Angel, J. Lawrence. 1972/73. Ecology and population in the eastern Mediterranean. *World Archaeology* 4: 88–105.

Antonaccio, Carla. 1993. The archaeology of ancestors. In Dougherty and Kurke 1993, 46–70.

———. 1995. *An archaeology of ancestors: Tomb cult and hero cult in early Greece.* Lanham, Md.: Rowman and Littlefield.

Arnheim, M. T. W. 1977. *Aristocracy in Greek society.* London: Thames and Hudson.

Arnold, Robin. 1957. A port of trade: Whydah on the Guinea coast. In Polanyi, Arensberg, and Pearson 1957, 154–76.

Asheri, David. 1963. Laws of inheritance, distribution of land, and political constitutions in ancient Greece. *Historia* 12: 1–21.

———. 1966. *Distribuzioni di terre nell' antica Grecia.* Classe Morali, 4th ser., vol. 10. Turin: Accademia delle Scienze dei Torino.

Aubet, Maria Eugenia. 1993. *The Phoenicians and the west: Politics, colonies, and trade.* Translated by Mary Turton. Cambridge: Cambridge University Press.

Austin, M. M., and P. Vidal-Naquet. 1977. *Economic and social history of ancient Greece: An introduction.* Translated by M. M. Austin. Berkeley: University of California Press.

Bailey, F. G. 1957. *Caste and the economic frontier: A village in highland Orissa.* Manchester: Manchester University Press.

Bairoch, Paul. 1975. *The economic development of the Third World since 1900.* Translated by Cynthia Poston. Berkeley: University of California Press.

Bakhuizen, S. C. 1976. *Chalcis-in-Euboea, iron, and Chalcidians abroad.* Leiden: E. J. Brill.

———. 1977/78. Greek steel. *World Archaeology* 9: 220–34.

———. 1985. *Studies in the topography of Chalcis on Euboea: A discussion of the sources.* Leiden: E. J. Brill.

Balikci, Asen. 1970. *The Netsilik Eskimo.* Garden City, N.Y.: Natural History Press.

Barceló, Pedro. 1993. *Basileia, monarchia, tyrannis.* Historia Einzelschriften 79. Stuttgart: Franz Steiner.

Baslez, Marie-Françoise. 1984. *L'étranger dans la Grèce antique.* Paris: Les Belles Lettres.

Baumbach, L. 1988. Mycenaean and Greek lexicon. In Morpurgo-Davies and Duhoux 1988, 127–42.

Beattie, A. J. 1975. Some notes on the Spensitheos decree. *Kadmos* 14: 8–47.

Beidelman, T. O. 1989. Agonistic exchange: Homeric reciprocity and the heritage of Simmel and Mauss. *Cultural Anthropology* 4: 227–59.

Belshaw, Cyril S. 1965. *Traditional exchange and modern markets.* Englewood Cliffs, N.J.: Prentice-Hall.

Bender, Barbara. 1978/79. Gatherer-hunter to farmer: A social perspective. *World Archaeology* 10: 204–22.

Benedict, Burton. 1970. Population regulation in primitive societies. In *Population control,* edited by Anthony Allison, 165–80. London: Penguin.

Bengtson, Hermann. 1988. *History of Greece, from the beginnings to the Byzantine era.* Translated and updated by Edmund F. Bloedow. Based on the 4th ed. (Munich: C. H. Beck). Ottawa: University of Ottawa Press.

Benton, Sylvia. 1934/35. Excavations in Ithaca, III. *Annual of the British School at Athens* 35: 45–73.

Bérard, Claude. 1970. *Eretria.* Vol. 3, *L'hérôon à la porte de l'ouest.* Bern: A. Francke.

———. 1972. Le sceptre du prince. *Museum Helveticum* 29: 219–27.

———. 1982. Récupérer la mort du prince: Héroisation et formation de la cité. In Gnoli and Vernant 1982, 89–105.

———. 1983. L'héroisation et la formation de la cité: Un conflit idéologique. *Architecture et Societé* 1983: 43–62.

Beringer, Walter. 1982. "Servile status" in the sources for early Greek history. *Historia* 31: 13–32.

Bernabò-Brea, Luigi, and Madeleine Cavalier. 1959. *Mylai.* Novara: Istituto Geografico de Agostini.

Bernal, Martin G. 1987. On the transmission of the alphabet to the Aegean before 1400 B.C. *Bulletin of the American Schools of Oriental Research* 267: 1–19.

———. 1990. *Cadmean letters: The transmission of the alphabet to the Aegean and further west before 1400 B.C.* Winona Lake, Ind.: Eisenbrauns.

———. 1993. Phoenician politics and Egyptian justice in ancient Greece. In *Anfänge politischen Denkens in der Antike: Die nah-östlichen Kulturen und die Griechen,* edited by K. Raaflaub, 241–61. Munich: Historisches Kolleg.

Best, Elsdon. 1924. *The Maori.* 2 vols. Memoirs of the Polynesian Society, vol. 5. Wellington, New Zealand: H. H. Tombs.

Bietti Sestieri, A. M., A. De Santis, and A. La Regina. 1990. Elementi di tipo cultuale e doni personali nella necropoli laziale di Osteria dell' Osa. *Scienze dell' Antichità* 3–4: 65–88.

Bintliff, John L. 1985. The Boeotia survey. In *Archaeological field survey in Britain and abroad*, edited by Sarah Macready and F. H. Thompson, 196–216. London: The Society of Antiquaries of London.

Bintliff, J. L., and A. M. Snodgrass. 1985. The Cambridge/Bradford Boeotian expedition: The first four years. *Journal of Field Archaeology* 12: 123–61.

———. 1988. Mediterranean survey and the city. *Antiquity* 62: 57–71.

Birdsell, Joseph B. 1957. Some population problems involving Pleistocene man. In *Population studies: Animal ecology and demography*, edited by M. Demerec, 47–69. Cold Spring Harbor Symposium on Quantitative Biology, vol. 22. Cold Spring Harbor, N.Y.: Cold Spring Harbor Biological Laboratory.

———. 1972. *Human evolution*. Chicago: Rand McNally.

Blainey, Geoffrey. 1976. *Triumph of the nomads: A history of aboriginal Australia*. Woodstock, N.Y.: Overlook Press.

Blakeway, Alan. 1933. Prolegomena to the study of Greek commerce with Italy, Sicily, and France in the eighth and seventh centuries B.C. *Annual of the British School at Athens* 33: 170–208.

———. 1935. Demaratus: A study in some aspects of the earliest Hellenisation of Latium and Etruria. *Journal of Roman Studies* 25: 129–49.

Bloch, Marc. 1961. *Feudal society*. Translated by L. A. Manyon. Chicago: University of Chicago Press.

———. 1966. The rise of dependent cultivation and seignorial institutions. In *The Cambridge economic history of Europe*, 1: 235–90. 2d ed. Cambridge: Cambridge University Press.

Blome, Peter. 1984. Lefkandi und Homer. *Würzburger Jahrbücher für die Altertumswissenschaft* 10: 9–22.

Boardman, John. 1957. Early Euboean pottery and history. *Annual of the British School at Athens* 52: 1–29.

———. 1965. Tarsus, Al Mina, and Greek chronology. *Journal of Hellenic Studies* 85: 5–15.

———. 1967. *Excavations in Chios, 1952–1955: Greek Emporio*. London: Thames and Hudson.

———. 1971. Ship firedogs and other metalwork from Kavousi. *Kretika Chronika* 23: 5–8.

———. 1977. The olive in the Mediterranean: Its culture and use. In *The early history of agriculture*, 187–96. Philosophical Transactions of the Royal Society of London, B., vol. 275, no. 936. London: Royal Society.

———. 1980. *The Greeks overseas*, 3d ed. London: Thames and Hudson.

———. 1982a. An inscribed sherd from Al Mina. *Oxford Journal of Archaeology* 1: 365–67.

———. 1982b. The islands. In *The Cambridge ancient history*, vol. 3, pt. 1, 754–78. 2d ed. Cambridge: Cambridge University Press.

———. 1988a. The trade figures. *Oxford Journal of Archaeology* 7: 371–73.

———. 1988b. Trade in Greek decorated pottery. *Oxford Journal of Archaeology* 7: 27–33.

———. 1990. Al Mina and history. *Oxford Journal of Archaeology* 9: 169–90.

Boardman, John, M. A. Brown, and T. G. E. Powell, eds. 1971. *The European community in later prehistory: Studies in honour of C. F. C. Hawkes.* London: Routledge and Kegan Paul.

Bohannan, Paul, and Laura Bohannan. 1968. *Tiv economy.* Evanston, Ill.: Northwestern University Press.

Bohannan, Paul, and George Dalton, eds. 1962a. *Markets in Africa.* Evanston, Ill.: Northwestern University Press.

———. 1962b. Introduction. In Bohannan and Dalton 1962a, 1–26.

Bohringer, François (= de Polignac, q.v.). 1980. Megare: Traditions mythiques, espace sacré et naissance de la cité. *L'Antiquité Classique* 49: 5–22.

Bolkestein, H. 1922. The exposure of children at Athens and the *egkytristriai. Classical Philology* 17: 222–39.

Bonfante, Larissa, ed. 1986a. *Etruscan life and afterlife: A handbook of Etruscan studies.* Detroit: Wayne State University Press.

———. 1986b. Introduction: Etruscan studies today. In Bonfante 1986a, 1–17.

Bongaarts, John, and Robert G. Potter. 1983. *Fertility, biology, and behavior: An analysis of the proximate determinants.* New York: Academic Press.

Bonner, Robert J. 1911. Administration of justice in the age of Homer. *Classical Philology* 6: 12–36.

Bonner, Robert J., and Gertrude Smith. 1930. *The administration of justice from Homer to Aristotle.* Vol. 1. Chicago: University of Chicago Press.

Boserup, Ester. 1965. *The conditions of agricultural growth: The economics of agrarian change under population pressure.* Chicago: Aldine.

———. 1970. *Woman's role in economic development.* London: Allen and Unwin.

Bourriot, Felix. 1976. *Recherches sur la nature du génos: Étude d'histoire sociale Athénienne, Périodes archaïque et classique.* Paris: H. Champion.

Bowra, C. M. 1934. Homeric words in Cyprus. *Journal of Hellenic Studies* 54: 54–74.

Bradley, Edward M. 1975. On King Amphidamas' funeral and Hesiod's Muses. *La Parola del Passato* 30: 285–88.

Braudel, Fernand. 1972. *The Mediterranean and the Mediterranean world in the age of Philip II.* Translated by Siân Reynolds. New York: Harper and Row.

Braun, T. F. R. G. 1982. The Greeks in the Near East. In *The Cambridge ancient history,* vol. 3, pt. 3, 1–31. 2d ed. Cambridge: Cambridge University Press.

Bravo, Benedetto. 1974. Une lettre sur plombe de Berezan: Colonisation et modes de contact dans le Pont. *Dialogues d'Histoire Ancienne* 1: 110–87.

———. 1977. Remarques sur les assises sociales, les formes d'organisation et la terminologie du commerce maritime grec à l'époque archaïque. *Dialogues d'Histoire Ancienne* 3: 1–59.

———. 1984. Commerce et noblesse en Grèce archaïque: A propos d'un livre d'Alfonso Mele. *Dialogues d'Histoire Ancienne* 10: 99–160.

Bredow, Iris von. 1989. Der *qasireu* in der Gesellschaftsstruktur des pylischen Staates. *Klio* 71: 28–35.

Broadbent, Molly. 1968. *Studies in Greek genealogy.* Leiden: E. J. Brill.

Brock, J. K. 1957. *Fortetsa: Early Greek tombs near Knossos.* Cambridge: Cambridge University Press.

Brown, W. Edward. 1956. Land tenure in Mycenaean Pylos. *Historia* 5: 385–400.

Buchner, Giorgio. 1966. Pithekoussai: Oldest Greek colony in the West. *Expedition* 8.4: 4–12.

———. 1969. Mostra degli scavi di Pithecusa. *Dialoghi di Archeologia* 3: 85–101.

———. 1978. Testamonianze epigrafiche semitiche dell'VIII secolo a.C. a Pithekoussai. *La Parola del Passato* 33: 130–42.

———. 1979. Early Orientalizing: Aspects of the Euboean connection. In Ridgway and Ridgway 1979, 129–44.

———. 1982. Die Beziehungen zwischen der euböischen Kolonie Pithekoussai auf der Insel Ischia und dem nordwestsemitischen Mittelmeerraum in der zweiten Hälfte des 8. Jhs. v. Chr. In Niemeyer 1982, 277–98.

Buchner, Giorgio, and John Boardman. 1966. Seals from Ischia and the lyre-player group. *Jahrbuch des Deutschen Archäologischen Instituts* 81: 1–62.

Buchner, Giorgio, and David Ridgway. 1993. *Pithekoussai I*. Rome: Giorgio Bretschneider Editore.

Buck, Robert J. 1979. *A history of Boeotia*. Alberta: University of Alberta Press.

Burford, Alison. 1993. *Land and labor in the Greek world*. Baltimore: Johns Hopkins University Press.

Burke, Edmund M. 1992. The economy of Athens in the classical era: Some adjustments to the primitivist model. *Transactions of the American Philological Association* 122: 199–226.

Burkert, Walter. 1985. *Greek religion: Archaic and classical*. Translated by John Raffan. Oxford: Basil Blackwell.

Burling, Robbins. 1962. Maximization theories and the study of economic history. *American Anthropologist* 64: 802–21.

Burn, Andrew Robert. 1960. *The lyric age of Greece*. London: Edward Arnold.

Burstein, Stanley M. 1976. Fragment 53 of Callisthenes and the test of *Iliad* 2. 853–55. *Classical Philology* 71: 339–41.

Buxton, R. G. A. 1994. *Imaginary Greece: The contexts of mythology*. Cambridge: Cambridge University Press.

Byock, Jesse L. 1982. *Feud in the Icelandic saga*. Berkeley: University of California Press.

Calder, William M., III. 1984. Gold for bronze: *Iliad* 6.232–236. In *Studies presented to Sterling Dow on the occasion of his eightieth birthday*, edited by K. J. Rigsby, 31–35. Durham, N.C.: Duke University Press.

Calligas, Peter G. 1982. Corcyra, colonization, and epos (in Greek). *Annuario della Scuola Archeologica di Atene* 60: 57–68.

———. 1988. Hero-cult in early Iron Age Greece. In Hägg, Marinatos, and Nordquist 1988, 229–34.

———. 1992. From the Amyklaion. In Sanders 1992, 31–48.

Cambitoglou, Alexander. 1970. Zagora, Andros: A settlement of the Geometric period. *Archaeology* 23: 302–9.

———. 1972. Anaskaphi Zagoras Androu (1971). *Praktika* 1972, 251–73.

Cambitoglou, Alexander, Ann Birchall, J. J. Coulton, and J. R. Green. 1988. *Zagora*. Vol. 2, *Excavation of a Geometric town on the island of Andros*. Athens: Athens Archaeological Society.

Cambitoglou, Alexander, J. J. Coulton, Judy Birmingham, and J. R. Green. 1971. *Zagora*. Vol. 1. Sydney: Sydney University Press.

Cameron, A. 1932. The exposure of children and Greek ethics. *Classical Review* 46: 105–14.

Camp, John McK., II. 1979. A drought in the late eighth century B.C. *Hesperia* 48: 397–411.

Carlier, Pierre. 1984. *La royauté en Grèce avant Alexandre*. Strasbourg: AECR.

———. 1991. La procédure de décision politique du monde mycénien à l'époque archaïque. In Musti et al. 1991, 85–95.

Carney, T. F. 1973. *The economies of antiquity: Controls, gifts, and trade*. Lawrence, Kans.: Coronado.

Carpenter, Rhys. 1948. The Greek penetration of the Black Sea. *American Journal of Archaeology* 52: 1–10.

Carr-Saunders, A. M. 1922. *The population problem: A study in human evolution*. Oxford: Clarendon Press.

Carter, Jane. 1995. Ancestor cult and the occasion of Homeric performance. In Carter and Morris 1995, 285–312.

Carter, Jane B., and Sarah P. Morris, eds. 1995. *The ages of Homer: A tribute to Emily C. Vermeule*. Austin: University of Texas Press.

Cartledge, Paul. 1979. *Sparta and Lakonia: A regional history, 1330–362 b.c.* London: Routledge and Kegan Paul.

———. 1983. "Trade and politics" revisited: Archaic Greece. In Garnsey, Hopkins, and Whittaker 1983, 1–15.

———. 1988. Yes, Spartan kings were heroized. *Liverpool Classical Monthly* 13: 43–44.

———. 1992. Early Lacedaimon: The making of a conquest-state. In Sanders 1992, 49–55.

Casson, Lionel. 1971. *Ships and seamanship in the ancient world*. Princeton: Princeton University Press.

Catling, Hector W. 1978/79. Knossos, 1978. *Archaeological Reports* 25: 43–58.

———. 1980/81. Archaeology in Greece, 1980–81. *Archaeological Reports* 27: 3–48.

———. 1981/82. Archaeology in Greece, 1981–82. *Archaeological Reports* 28: 3–62.

———. 1983. New light on Knossos in the 8th and 7th centuries B.C. *Annuario della Scuola Archeologica di Atene* 61: 31–43.

———. 1986/87. Archaeology in Greece, 1986–87. *Archaeological Reports* 33: 3–61.

———. 1993. The bronze amphora and burial urn. In Popham, Calligas, and Sackett 1993, 81–96.

———. 1995. Heroes returned? Subminoan burials from Crete. In Carter and Morris 1995, 123–36.

Cépède, Michel, Françoise Houtart, and Linus Grond. 1964. *Population and food*. New York: Sheed and Ward.

Chadwick, H. Munro, and N. Kershaw Chadwick. 1940. *The growth of literature*. Vol. 3. Cambridge: Cambridge University Press.

Chantraine, Pierre. 1968. *Dictionnaire étymologique de la langue grecque: Histoire des mots*. Vol. 1. Paris: Éditions Klincksieck.

Charbonnet, André. 1986. Le dieu aux lions d'Érétrie. *Annali dell' Istituto Universitario Orientale di Napoli (archeol.)* 8: 117–73.

Cherry, John F. 1984. The emergence of the state in the prehistoric Aegean. *Proceedings of the Cambridge Philological Society* 210: 18–48.

————. 1988. Pastoralism and the role of animals in the pre- and protohistorical economies of the Aegean. In Whittaker 1988, 6–34.

Cipolla, Carlo M., ed. 1972. *Fontana economic history of Europe*. Vol. 1. Hassocks, England: Harvester Press.

————. 1978. *The economic history of world population*. 7th ed. London: Penguin.

Cleary, John J., and Daniel C. Shartin, eds. 1989. *Proceedings of the Boston area colloquium in ancient philosophy*. Vol. 4. Lanham, Md.: University Press of America.

Codere, Helen. 1950. *Fighting with property: A study of Kwakiutl potlatching and warfare, 1792–1930*. New York: J. J. Augustin.

————. 1968. Exchange and display. In *International Encyclopedia of the Social Sciences*, 5: 239–45. New York: Macmillan.

Coldstream, J. N. 1968. *Greek Geometric pottery*. London: Methuen.

————. 1969. The Phoenicians of Ialysos. *Bulletin of the Institute of Classical Studies* 16: 1–8.

————. 1976. Hero-cults in the age of Homer. *Journal of Hellenic Studies* 96:8–17.

————. 1977. *Geometric Greece*. New York: St. Martin's.

————. 1982. Greeks and Phoenicians in the Aegean. In Niemeyer 1982, 261–72.

————. 1983. Gift exchange in the eighth century B.C. In Hägg 1983c, 201–7.

————. 1989. Early Greek visitors to Cyprus and the eastern Mediterranean. In *Cyprus and the East Mediterranean in the Iron Age*, edited by Veronica Tatton-Brown, 90–96. London: British Museum.

————. 1991. The Geometric style: Birth of the picture. In *Looking at Greek vases*, edited by Tom Rasmussen and Nigel Spivey, 37–56. Cambridge: Cambridge University Press.

————. 1993. Mixed marriages at the frontiers of the early Greek world. *Oxford Journal of Archaeology* 12: 89–107.

————. 1994a. Prospectors and pioneers: Pithekoussai, Kyme, and central Italy. In Tsetskhladze and De Angelis 1994, 47–59.

————. 1994b. Warriors, chariots, dogs, and lions: A new Attic Geometric amphora. *Bulletin of the Institute of Classical Studies* 39: 85–94.

Collis, John. 1984. *The European Iron Age*. London: B. T. Batsford.

Combellack, Frederick M. 1947/48. Speakers and scepters in Homer. *Classical Journal* 43: 209–17.

Compernolle, René van. 1960. *Étude de chronologie et d'historiographie siciliotes*. Brussels: L'Institut Historique Belge de Rome.

Connor, W. R. 1987. Tribes, festivals, and processions: Civic, ceremonial, and political manipulation in archaic Greece. *Journal of Hellenic Studies* 107: 40–50.

Cook, J. M. 1953. The Agamemnoneion. *Annual of the British School at Athens* 48: 30–68.

————. 1962. Reasons for the foundation of Ischia and Cumae. *Historia* 11: 113–14.

————. 1975. Greek settlement in the eastern Aegean and Asia Minor. In *The Cambridge ancient history*, vol. 2, pt. 2, 773–804. 2d ed. Cambridge: Cambridge University Press.

Cook, R. M. 1958. Speculations on the origins of coinage. *Historia* 7:257–62.

————. 1989. Hesiod's father. *Journal of Hellenic Studies* 109: 170–71.

Cook, Scott. 1966. The obsolete "anti-market" mentality: A critique of the substantive approach to economic anthropology. *American Anthropologist* 68: 323–45. Reprinted in and cited from Fried 1968, 239–61.

———. 1969. The "anti-market" mentality reexamined: A further critique of the substantive approach to economic anthropology. *Southwestern Journal of Anthropology* 25: 378–406.

Cooper, Alison Burford (= Alison Burford, q.v.). 1977/78. The family farm in Greece. *Classical Journal* 73: 162–75.

Copans, Jean, and David Seddon. 1978. Marxism and anthropology: A preliminary survey. In Seddon 1978, 1–46.

Coulton, J. 1993. The Toumba building: Description and analysis of its architecture. In Popham, Calligas, and Sackett 1993, 33–70.

Courbin, Paul. 1957. Une tombe géométrique d'Argos. *Bulletin de Correspondance Hellénique* 81: 322–86.

———. 1959a. Response to Deonna 1959. *Bulletin de Correspondance Hellénique* 83: 252–53.

———. 1959b. Valeur comparée du fer et de l'argent lors de l'introduction du monnayage. *Annales: Économies, Sociétés, Civilisations* 14: 209–33.

———. 1966. *La céramique géométrique de l'Argolide*. Paris: Éditions E. de Boccard.

———. 1977. Une pyxis géométrique Argienne(?) au Liban. *Berytus* 25: 147–57.

———. 1983. Obéloi d'Argolide et d'ailleurs. In Hägg 1983c, 149–56.

Cozzo, Andrea. 1988. *Kerdos: Semantica, ideologie e società nella Grecia antica*. Rome: Edizioni dell' Ateneo.

Crawford. H. E. W. 1973/74. Mesopotamia's invisible exports in the third millennium B.C. *World Archaeology* 5: 232–41.

Cristofani, Mauro. 1979. *The Etruscans: A new investigation*. London: Orbis.

———, ed. 1985. *Civiltà degli Etruschi*. Milan: Electa.

Cristofani, Mauro, and Paola Pelagatti, eds. 1985. *Il commercio etrusco arcaico*. Rome: Consiglio nazionale delle ricerche.

Curtin, Philip D. 1984. *Cross-cultural trade in world history*. Cambridge: Cambridge University Press.

d'Agostino, Bruno. 1977. Grecs et "indigènes" sur la côte tyrrhénienne au VIIᵉ siècle: La transmission des idéologies entre élites sociales. *Annales: Économies, Sociétés, Civilisations* 32.1: 3–20.

———. 1990. Relations between Campania, Southern Etruria, and the Aegean in the eighth century B.C. In Descoeudres 1990, 73–85.

Dalton, George. 1960. A note of clarification on economic surplus. *American Anthropologist* 62: 483–90.

———. 1961. Economic theory and primitive society. *American Anthropologist* 63: 1–25.

———. 1962. Traditional production in primitive African economies. *Quarterly Journal of Economics* 76: 360–78. Reprinted in and cited from Dalton 1967, 61–80.

———. 1963. Economic surplus, once again. *American Anthropologist* 65: 389–94.

———. 1965a. History, politics, and economic development in Liberia. *Journal of Economic History* 25: 569–91.

———. 1965b. Review of Firth and Yamey 1964. *American Anthropologist* 67: 121–22.

———, ed. 1967. *Tribal and peasant economies: Readings in economic anthropology*. Garden City, N.Y.: Natural History Press.

————, ed. 1968a. *Primitive, archaic, and modern economies: Essays of Karl Polanyi*. Garden City, N.Y.: Anchor Books.

————. 1968b. Introduction. In Dalton 1968a, ix–liv (an expansion of his essay in Helm 1965, 1–24).

————. 1969. Theoretical issues in economic anthropology. *Current Anthropology* 10: 63–80.

————. 1975. Karl Polanyi's analysis of long-distance trade and his wider paradigm. In Sabloff and Lamberg-Karlovsky 1975, 63–132.

————. 1977. Aboriginal economies and stateless societies. In Earle and Ericson 1977, 191–212.

————. 1981. Comment. *Research in Economic Anthropology* 4: 69–93.

Darnton, Robert. 1984. *The great cat massacre and other episodes in French cultural history*. New York: Basic Books.

Davies, John K. 1977/78. Athenian citizenship: The descent group and the alternatives. *Classical Journal* 73: 105–21

De Angelis, Franco. 1994. The foundation of Selinous: Overpopulation or opportunities? In Tsetskhladze and De Angelis 1994, 87–110.

Demand, Nancy. 1995. The origins of the polis: The view from Cyprus. Forthcoming in the proceedings of the conference "Res Maritimae 94."

Deonna, Waldemar. 1959. Haches, broches et chenets dans une tombe géométrique d'Argos. *Bulletin de Correspondance Hellénique* 83: 247–52.

Desborough, V. R. d'A. 1952. *Protogeometric Pottery*. Oxford: Clarendon Press.

————. 1972. *The Greek Dark Ages*. London: E. Benn.

————. 1979. A postscript to an appendix. In Karageorghis et al. 1979, 119–22.

Descoeudres, Jean-Paul. 1973. Zagora auf der Insel Andros: Eine eretrische Kolonie? *Antike Kunst* 16: 87–88.

————, ed. 1990. *Greek colonists and native populations*. Oxford: Clarendon Press.

Descoeudres, Jean-Paul, and Rosalinde Kearsley. 1983. Greek pottery at Veii: Another look. *Annual of the British School at Athens* 78: 9–53.

Detienne, Marcel. 1963. *Crise agraire et attitude religieuse chez Hésiode*. Brussels: Latomus.

————. 1967. *Les maîtres de vérité dans la Grèce archaïque*. Paris: François Maspero.

Detienne, Marcel, and Jean-Pierre Vernant, eds. 1989 [1979]. *The cuisine of sacrifice among the Greeks*. Translated by Paula Wissing. Chicago: University of Chicago Press. (French original is Paris: Éditions Gallimard, 1979.)

Diakonoff, I. M., ed. 1991. *Early Antiquity*. Translated by Alexander Kirjanov. Chicago: University of Chicago Press.

Diamant, Steven. 1982. Theseus and the unification of Attica. In *Studies in Attic epigraphy, history, and topography presented to Eugene Vanderpool*, 38–47. Hesperia Suppl. 16. Princeton: American School of Classical Studies at Athens.

Dickinson, O. T. P. 1986. Homer, the poet of the Dark Age. *Greece and Rome* 33: 20–37.

Dikaios, Porphyrios. 1963. A "royal" tomb at Salamis, Cyprus. *Archäologischer Anzeiger* 1963, 126–208.

Di Vita, A. 1990. Town planning in the Greek colonies of Sicily from the time of their foundations to the Punic War. In Descoeudres 1990, 343–63.

Dodgshon, Robert A. 1988. The ecological basis of Highland peasant farming,

1500–1800 A.D. In *The cultural landscape—Past, present and future,* edited by Hilary H. Birks, H. J. B. Burks, Peter Emil Kaland, and Dagfinn Moe, 139–51. Cambridge: Cambridge University Press.

Donlan, Walter. 1970. Changes and shifts in the meaning of *demos* in the literature of the archaic period. *La Parola del Passato* 25: 381–95.

——. 1973. The tradition of anti-aristocratic thought in early Greek poetry. *Historia* 22: 145–54.

——. 1979. The structure of authority in the *Iliad. Arethusa* 12: 51–70.

——. 1981. Scale, value, and function in the Homeric economy. *American Journal of Ancient History* 6: 101–17.

——. 1982a. The politics of generosity in Homer. *Helios* 9.2: 1–15.

——. 1982b. Reciprocities in Homer. *Classical World* 75.3: 137–75.

——. 1985. The social groups of Dark Age Greece. *Classical Philology* 80: 293–308.

——. 1986. Economy and society in the Greek Dark Age. Paper read at the University of Tennessee, Knoxville, October 1986.

——. 1989a. Homeric *temenos* and the land economy of the Dark Age. *Museum Helveticum* 46: 129–45.

——. 1989b. The pre-state community in Greece. *Symbolae Osloenses* 64: 5–29.

——. 1989c. The unequal exchange between Glaucus and Diomedes in light of the Homeric gift-economy. *Phoenix* 43: 1–15.

——. 1993. Duelling with gifts in the *Iliad:* As the audience saw it. *Colby Quarterly* 29: 155–72.

——. 1994. Chief and followers in pre-state Greece. In Duncan and Tandy 1994, 34–51.

Donlan, Walter, and Carol G. Thomas. 1993. The village community of ancient Greece: Neolithic, Bronze, and Dark Ages. *Studi Micenei ed Egeo-anatolici* 31: 61–71.

Doorninck, Frederick H. van, Jr. 1982. Protogeometric longships and the introduction of the ram. *International Journal of Nautical Archaeology and Underwater Exploration* 11: 277–86.

Dornseiff, F. 1939. Homer und das Papier. *Hermes* 74: 209–10.

Dougherty, Carol. 1993. *The poetics of colonization: From city to text in archaic Greece.* New York and Oxford: Oxford University Press.

Dougherty, Carol, and Leslie Kurke, eds. 1993. *Cultural poetics in archaic Greece: Cult, performance, politics.* Cambridge: Cambridge University Press.

Drews, Robert. 1976. The earliest Greek settlements on the Black Sea. *Journal of Hellenic Studies* 96: 18–31.

——. 1983. *Basileus: The evidence for kingship in Geometric Greece.* New Haven: Yale University Press.

——. 1993. *The end of the Bronze Age: Changes in warfare and the catastrophe ca. 1200.* Princeton: Princeton University Press.

Droop, J. P. 1905/6. Dipylon vases from the Kynosarges site. *Annual of the British School at Athens* 12: 80–92.

Drucker, Philip. 1965. *Cultures of the North Pacific coast.* San Francisco: Chandler.

Duban, Jeffrey M. 1980. Poets and kings in the *Theogony* invocation. *Quaderni Urbinati di Cultura Classica* 33: 7–21.

Duby, Georges. 1974. *The early growth of the European economy.* Translated by H. B. Clarke. Ithaca, N. Y.: Cornell University Press.

Dumond, Don E. 1965. Population growth and culture change. *Southwestern Journal of Anthropology* 21: 302–24.

———. 1972. Population growth and political centralization. In Spooner 1972, 286–310.

Dumont, Louis. 1980. *Homo hierarchicus: The caste system and its implications.* Translated by Mark Sainsbury, Louis Dumont, and Basia Gulati. 2d rev. English ed. Chicago: University of Chicago Press.

Dunbabin, T. J. 1948. *The western Greeks.* Oxford: Clarendon Press.

Duncan, Colin A. M. 1996. *The centrality of agriculture: Between humankind and the rest of nature.* Montreal and Kingston: McGill-Queen's University Press.

Duncan, Colin A. M., and David W. Tandy, eds. 1994. *From political economy to anthropology: Situating economic life in past societies.* Montreal: Black Rose Books.

Earle, Timothy K. 1977. A reappraisal of redistribution: Complex Hawaiian chiefdoms. In Earle and Ericson 1977, 213–32.

———, ed. 1991a. *Chiefdoms: Power, economy, and ideology.* Cambridge: Cambridge University Press.

———. 1991b. The evolution of chiefdoms. In Earle 1991a, 1–15.

Earle, Timothy K., and Jonathon E. Ericson, eds. 1977. *Exchange systems in prehistory.* New York: Academic Press.

Easterling, P. E. 1989. Agamemnon's *skeptron* in the *Iliad.* In *Images of authority: Papers presented to Joyce Reynolds,* edited by Mary Margaret Mackenzie and Charlotte Roueché, 104–21. Cambridge Philological Society Suppl. vol. 16. Cambridge: Cambridge Philological Society.

Edel, Matthew. 1970. Discussion of Rotstein 1970. *Journal of Economic History* 30: 127–30.

Edmunds, Lowell. 1989. Commentary on Raaflaub. In Cleary and Shartin 1989, 26–33.

Edwards, Anthony. Forthcoming. Hesiod the peasant? Paper read at the annual meeting of the American Philological Association, San Diego, Calif., December 29, 1995.

Edwards, G. P. 1971. *The language of Hesiod in its traditional context.* Oxford: Basil Blackwell.

Edwards, G. Patrick, and Ruth B. Edwards. 1977. The meaning and etymology of *poinikastas. Kadmos* 16: 131–40.

Edwards, Mark W., ed. 1991. *The Iliad: A commentary.* Vol. 5, *Books 17–20.* Cambridge: Cambridge University Press.

Effenterre, Henri van. 1967. Téménos. *Revue des Études Grecques* 80: 17–26.

———. 1973. Le contrat de travail du scribe Spensithios. *Bulletin de Correspondance Hellénique* 97: 31–46.

Eisenstadt, S. N. 1954. *The absorption of immigrants: A comparative study based mainly on the Jewish community in Palestine and the state of Israel.* London: Routledge and Kegan Paul.

———. 1963. *The political systems of empires.* Glencoe, Ill.: Free Press.

Ellis, Frank. 1988. *Peasant economics: Farm households and agrarian development.* Cambridge: Cambridge University Press.

Emlyn-Jones, C. J. 1980. *The Ionians and Hellenism: A study of the cultural achievements of early Greek inhabitants of Asia Minor.* London: Routledge and Kegan Paul.

Engels, Donald. 1980. The problem of female infanticide in the Greco-Roman world. *Classical Philology* 75: 112–20.

———. 1984. The use of historical demography in ancient history. *Classical Quarterly* 34: 386–93.

Farnell, L. R. 1921. *Greek hero cults and ideas of immortality.* Oxford: Clarendon Press.

Farrar, Cynthia. 1988. *The origins of democratic thinking: The invention of politics in classical Athens.* Cambridge: Cambridge University Press.

Farron, S. G. 1979/80. The *Odyssey* as an anti-aristocratic statement. *Studies in Antiquity* 1: 59–101.

Feil, D. K. 1987. *The evolution of highland Papua New Guinea societies.* Cambridge: Cambridge University Press.

Fenton, Alexander J. 1981. Early manuring techniques. In *Farming practice in British prehistory,* edited by Roger Mercer, 210–17. Edinburgh: Edinburgh University Press.

Ferguson, Yale. 1991. Chiefdoms to city-states: The Greek experience. In Earle 1991a, 169–92.

Figueira, T. J. 1984. Karl Polanyi and ancient Greek trade: The port of trade. *The Ancient World* 10: 15–30.

Fine, John V. A. 1983. *The ancient Greeks: A critical study.* Cambridge, Mass.: Harvard University Press.

Finkelberg, Margalit. 1990. A creative oral poet and the Muse. *American Journal of Philology* 111: 293–303.

———. 1991. Royal succession in heroic Greece. *Classical Quarterly* 41: 303–16.

Finkelstein (Finley), Moses I. 1935. *Emporos, naukleros,* and *kapelos:* A prolegomena to the study of Athenian trade. *Classical Philology* 30: 320–36.

Finley, Moses I. 1954. Marriage, sale, and gift in the Homeric world. *Seminar* 12: 7–33. (This appeared with the same title and in almost the same form in *Revue Internationale des Droits de l'Antiquité,* ser. 3, 2 (1955): 167–94, which was reprinted in Finley 1983, 233–45.)

———. 1957a. Homer and Mycenae: Property and tenure. *Historia* 6: 133–59. Reprinted in Finley 1983, 213–32.

———. 1957b. Mycenaean palace archives and economic history. *Economic History Review,* ser. 2, 10: 128–41. Reprinted in Finley 1983, 199–212.

———. 1962a. Classical Greece. In Finley 1962b, 11–35.

———, ed. 1962b. *Trade and politics in the ancient world.* Deuxième Conférence Internationale d'Histoire Économique, Aix-en-Provence, 1962, vol. 1. Paris: Mouton, 1965.

———. 1963/64. Between slavery and freedom. *Comparative Studies in Society and History* 6: 233–49.

———. 1965. La servitude pour dettes. *Revue Historique de Droit Français et Étranger* 43: 159–84. Reprinted as "Debt-bondage and the problem of slavery" and cited from Finley 1983, 150–66.

———. 1968a. The alienability of land in ancient Greece: A point of view. *Eirene* 7: 25–32. Reprinted in Finley 1975, 153–60.

————. 1968b. Comments. In *La città e il suo territorio*, 186–88, 326–27. Naples: Centre Jean Bérard.

————, ed. 1973. *Problèmes de la terre en Grèce ancienne*. Paris: Mouton.

————. 1975. *The use and abuse of history*. New York: Viking.

————. 1976. Colonies—An attempt at a typology. *Transactions of the Royal Historical Society*, 5th ser., 26: 167–88.

————. 1976/77. The ancient city: From Fustel de Coulanges to Max Weber and beyond. *Comparative Studies in Society and History* 19: 305–27. Reprinted in Finley 1983, 1–23.

————. 1978. *The world of Odysseus*. 2d rev. ed. London: Penguin.

————. 1979a. *Ancient Sicily*. Rev. ed. London: Chatto and Windus.

————, ed. 1979b. *The Bücher-Meyer controversy*. New York: Arno.

————. 1980. *Ancient slavery and modern ideology*. London: Chatto and Windus. Cited from Penguin edition (New York, 1983).

————. 1983. *Economy and society in ancient Greece*. Edited by Brent D. Shaw and Richard P. Saller. London: Penguin.

Finley, M. I., and H. W. Pleket. 1976. *The Olympic games: The first thousand years*. New York: Viking.

Finnegan, Ruth. 1977. *Oral poetry: Its nature, significance, and social context*. Cambridge: Cambridge University Press.

————. 1988. *Literacy and orality: Studies in the technology of communication*. Oxford: Basil Blackwell.

Firth, Raymond. 1936. *We, the Tikopia*. London: Allen and Unwin.

Firth, Raymond, and B. S. Yamey, eds. 1964. *Capital, saving, and credit in peasant societies*. Chicago: Aldine.

Fischer, David Hackett. 1970. *Historians' fallacies: Toward a logic of historical thought*. New York: Harper and Row.

Fischer, Franz. 1973. *Keimelia:* Bemerkungen zur kulturgeschichtlichen Interpretation des sogenannten Südimports in der späten Hallstatt- und frühen Latène-Kultur des westliches Mitteleuropa. *Germania* 51: 436–59.

Fisher, N. R. E. 1986. Review of Carlier 1984 and Drews 1983. *Journal of Hellenic Studies* 106: 236–37.

Foley, Anne. 1988. *The Argolid, 800–600 b.c.: An archaeological survey*. Göteborg: Paul Åströms Förlag.

Foley, John Miles. 1992. The problem of aesthetics in oral and oral-derived texts. In Pinsent and Hurt 1992, 51–63.

Fontenrose, Joseph. 1968. The hero as athlete. *California Studies in Classical Antiquity* 1: 73–104.

Forbes, Hamish. 1976. The "thrice-ploughed field": Cultivation techniques in ancient and modern Greece. *Expedition* 19.1: 5–11.

Fornara, Charles William. 1983. *The nature of history in ancient Greece and Rome*. Berkeley: University of California Press.

Forrest, W. G. 1957. Colonisation and the rise of Delphi. *Historia* 6: 160–75.

————. 1969. *A history of Sparta, 950–192 b.c.* New York: Norton.

————. 1986. Greece: The history of the archaic period. In *The Oxford history of the classical world*, edited by John Boardman, Jasper Griffin, and Oswyn Murray, 19–49. Oxford: Oxford University Press.

Förster, Hugo. 1891. *Die Sieger in den olympischen Spielen*. Zwickau: R. Zückler.

Francis, E. D., and Michael Vickers. 1985. Greek Geometric pottery at Hama and its implications for Near Eastern chronology. *Levant* 17: 131–38.

Frankfort, Henri. 1956. *The birth of civilization in the Near East*. Garden City, N.Y.: Doubleday.

Fratta, A. 1994. Nuovi scavi a Ischia. *Il Mattino* (Naples), 31 January 1994, p. 10.

Frederiksen, Martin. 1984. *Campania*. Edited with additions by Nicholas Purcell. London: British School at Rome.

French, E. B. 1990/91. Archaeology in Greece, 1990–91. *Archaeological Reports* 37: 3–78.

———. 1991/92. Archaeology in Greece, 1991–92. *Archaeological Reports* 38: 3–70.

———. 1992/93. Archaeology in Greece, 1992–93. *Archaeological Reports* 39: 3–81.

———. 1993/94. Archaeology in Greece, 1993–94. *Archaeological Reports* 40: 3–84

Fried, Morton H. 1966. On the concepts of "tribe" and "tribal society." *Transactions of the New York Academy of Science* 28: 527–40.

———. 1967. *The evolution of political society: An essay in political anthropology*. New York: Random House.

———, ed. 1968. *Readings in anthropology*. Vol. 2. 2d ed. New York: Crowell.

———. 1978. The state, the chicken, and the egg; or, What came first? In *Origins of the state: The anthropology of political evolution*, edited by Ronald Cohen and Elman R. Service, 35–47. Philadelphia: Institute for the Study of Human Issues.

Frisk, Hjalmar. 1973. *Griechisches etymologisches Wörterbuch*. 3 vols. Heidelberg: Carl Winter, Universitätsverlag.

Frontisi-Ducroux, Françoise. 1986. *La cithare d'Achille: Essai sur la poétique de l'Iliade*. Rome: Edizioni dell' Ateneo.

Furtwängler, Andreas E. 1980. Zur Deutung der Obeloi in Lichte samischer Neufinde. In *Tainia: Festschrift Roland Hampe*, edited by Herbert A. Cahn and Erika Simon, 81–98. Mainz am Rhein: von Zabern.

Gagarin, Michael. 1974. Hesiod's dispute with Perses. *Transactions of the American Philological Association* 104: 103–11.

———. 1986. *Early Greek law*. Berkeley: University of California Press.

———. 1992. The poetry of justice: Hesiod and the origins of Greek law. *Ramus* 21.1: 61–78.

Gallant, T. W. 1982. Agricultural systems, land tenure, and the reforms of Solon. *Annual of the British School at Athens* 77: 111–24.

———. 1985. *A fisherman's tale: An analysis of the potential productivity of fishing in the ancient world*. Miscellanea Graeca, fasc. 7. Gent: Belgian Archaeological Mission in Greece.

Garlan, Yvon. 1973. L'oeuvre de Polanyi: La place de l'économie dans les sociétés. *La Pensée* 171: 118–27.

Garland, Robert S. J. 1984. Religious authority in archaic and classical Athens. *Annual of the British School at Athens* 79: 75–123.

———. 1985. *The Greek way of death*. Ithaca, N.Y.: Cornell University Press.

Garnsey, Peter. 1985. Grain for Athens. In *Crux*, edited by P. A. Cartledge and F. D. Harvey, 62–75. Exeter: Imprint Academic.

———. 1988a. *Famine and food supply in the Greco-Roman world: Responses to risk and crisis*. Cambridge: Cambridge University Press.

————. 1988b. Mountain economies in southern Europe: Thoughts on the early history, continuity, and individuality of Mediterranean upland pastoralism. In Whittaker 1988, 196–209.

————. 1992. Yield of the land. In Wells 1992, 147–53.

Garnsey, Peter, Keith Hopkins, and C. R. Whittaker, eds. 1983. *Trade in the ancient economy.* Berkeley: University of California Press.

Garnsey, Peter, and Ian Morris. 1989. Risk and the *polis:* The evolution of institutionalised responses to food supply problems in the ancient Greek state. In Halstead and O'Shea 1989a, 98–105.

Gathercole, P., and David Lowenthal, eds. 1990. *The politics of the past.* London: Unwin Hyman.

Gebhard, Elizabeth R. 1993. The evolution of a pan-Hellenic sanctuary: From archaeology towards history at Isthmia. In Marinatos and Hägg 1993, 154–77.

Geddes, A. G. 1984. Who's who in "Homeric" society? *Classical Quarterly* 34: 17–36.

Geertz, Clifford. 1960. *The religion of Java.* Glencoe, Ill.: Free Press.

————. 1963. *Peddlers and princes: Social change and economic modernization in two Indonesian towns.* Chicago: University of Chicago Press.

————. 1973. *The interpretation of cultures: Selected essays.* New York: Basic Books.

————. 1980a. *Negara: The theatre state in nineteenth-century Bali.* Princeton: Princeton University Press.

————. 1980b. Ports of trade in nineteenth-century Bali. *Research in Economic Anthropology* 3: 109–22.

Georgiev, Vladimir I. 1984. Griech. *anax* "Herrscher, Herr, Fürst" und *basileus* "König." *Indogermanische Forschungen* 89: 125–28.

Gernet, Louis. 1948. La notion mythique de la valeur en Grèce. *Journal de Psychologie* 41: 415–62. Translated in Gernet 1968, 73–111.

————. 1981. *The anthropology of ancient Greece.* Translated by John Hamilton and Blaise Nagy. Baltimore: Johns Hopkins University Press.

Gerriets, Marilyn. 1987. Kingship and exchange in pre-Viking Ireland. *Cambridge Medieval Celtic Studies* 13: 39–72.

Gesell, Geraldine C., Leslie Preston Day, and William D. E. Coulson. 1995. Excavations at Kavousi, Crete, 1989 and 1990. *Hesperia* 64: 67–120.

Gill, David W. J. 1988a. Expression of wealth: Greek art and society. *Antiquity* 62: 735–43.

————. 1988b. "Trade in Greek decorated pottery": Some corrections. *Oxford Journal of Archaeology* 7: 669–70.

Gill, David W. J., and Michael Vickers. 1987. Pots and kettles. *Revue Archéologique* 55: 297–303.

Giovannini, Adalberto. 1989. Homer und seine Welt. In *Vom frühen Griechentum bis zur römischen Kaiserzeit: Gedenk- und Jubiläumsvorträge am Heidelberger Seminar für Alte Geschichte,* 25–39. Stuttgart: F. Steiner.

Gjerstad, Einar. 1979. A Cypro-Greek royal marriage in the 8th cent. B.C.? In Karageorghis et al. 1979, 89–93.

Gledhill, John, and Mogens Larsen. 1982. The Polanyi paradigm and a dynamic analysis of archaic states. In *Theory and explanation in archaeology,* edited by Colin Renfrew, Michael J. Rowlands, and Barbara Abbott Segraves, 197–229. New York: Academic Press.

Gnoli, Gherardo, and Jean-Pierre Vernant, eds. 1982. *La mort, les morts dans les sociétés anciennes.* Cambridge: Cambridge University Press.

Golden, Mark. 1981. Demography and the exposure of girls at Athens. *Phoenix* 35: 316–31.

———. 1990. *Children and childhood in classical Athens.* Baltimore: Johns Hopkins University Press.

Gomme, A. W. 1937. Traders and manufacturers in Greece. In *Essays in Greek history and literature,* chap. 3. Oxford: Basil Blackwell.

Gomme, A. W., A. Andrewes, and K. J. Dover. 1970. *A historical commentary on Thucydides, books V.25-VII.* Oxford: Clarendon Press.

Goody, Jack, and Ian Watt. 1968. The consequences of literacy. In *Literacy in traditional societies,* edited by Jack Goody, 27–68. Cambridge: Cambridge University Press.

Goold, G. P. 1960. Homer and the alphabet. *Transactions of the American Philological Association* 91: 272–91.

Gosden, Chris. 1985. Gifts and kin in early Iron Age Europe. *Man* 20: 475–93.

———. 1986. Comment on Rowlands 1986. *Man* 21: 756–57.

Gow, A. S. F. 1914. The ancient plough. *Journal of Hellenic Studies* 34: 249–75.

Graham, A. J. 1958. The date of the Greek penetration of the Black Sea. *Bulletin of the Institute of Classical Studies* 5: 25–42.

———. 1960. The authenticity of the *horkion ton oikisteron* of Cyrene. *Journal of Hellenic Studies* 80: 94–111.

———. 1971. Patterns in early Greek colonization. *Journal of Hellenic Studies* 91: 35–47.

———. 1982. The colonial expansion of Greece. In *The Cambridge ancient history,* vol. 3, pt. 3., 83–162. 2d ed. Cambridge: Cambridge University Press.

———. 1983. *Colony and mother city in ancient Greece.* 2d ed. Chicago: Ares.

———. 1986. The historical interpretations of Al Mina. *Dialogues d'Histoire Ancienne* 12: 51–65.

———. 1990. Pre-colonial contacts: Questions and problems. In Descoeudres 1990, 45–65.

Gramsci, Antonio. 1971. *Selections from the prison notebooks.* Edited and translated by Quintin Hoare and Geoffrey Nowell Smith. New York: International Publishers.

Grant, Michael. 1980. *The Etruscans.* London: Weidenfield and Nicolson.

Gray, Dorothea. 1974. *Seewesen.* Archaeologia Homerica, vol. 1G. Göttingen: Vandenhöck and Ruprecht.

Gray, G. H. F. 1954. Metal-working in Homer. *Journal of Hellenic Studies* 74: 1–15.

Green, Peter. 1984. *Works and days* 1–285: Hesiod's invisible audience. In *Mnemai: Classical studies in memory of Karl K. Hulley,* edited by Harold D. Evjen, 21–39. Chico, Calif.: Scholars Press.

Grierson, P. J. Hamilton. 1903. *The silent trade.* Edinburgh: W. Green and Son. Reprinted and cited from *Research in Economic Anthropology* 3 (1980): 1–74.

Grigg, David. 1982. *The dynamics of agricultural change: The historical experience.* New York: St. Martin's.

Gschnitzer, Fritz. 1965. *Basileus:* Ein terminologischer Beitrag zur Frühgeschichte des Königstums bei den Griechen. *Innsbrucher Beiträge zur Kulturwissenschaft* 11: 99–112.

Gwynn, Aubrey. 1918. The character of Greek colonisation. *Journal of Hellenic Studies* 38: 88–123.

Hackens, T., Nancy D. Holloway, and R. Ross Holloway, eds. 1984. *Crossroads of the Mediterranean*. Providence/Louvain-la-Neuve: Brown University/Université Catholique de Louvain.

Hadzisteliou Price, Theodora. 1973. Hero-cult and Homer. *Historia* 22: 129–44.

———. 1979. Hero cult in the "age of Homer" and earlier. In *Arktouros: Hellenic studies presented to Bernard M. W. Knox on the occasion of his 65th birthday,* edited by Glen W. Bowersock, Walter Burkert, and Michael C. J. Putnam, 219–28. Berlin: Walter de Gruyter.

Hägg, Robin. 1974. *Die Graber der Argolis in submykenischer, protogeometrischer und geometrischer Zeit.* Stockholm: Almquist and Wiksell.

———. 1982. Zur Stadtwerdung des dorischen Argos. In *Palast und Hütte: Beiträge zum Bauen und Wohnen im Altertum von Archäologen, Vor- und Frühgeschichtlern,* edited by Dietrich Papenfuss and Volker Michael Strocka, 297–307. Mainz am Rhein: von Zabern.

———. 1983a. Burial customs and social differentiation in 8th-century Argos. In Hägg 1983c, 27–31.

———. 1983b. Funerary meals in the Geometric necropolis at Asine? In Hägg 1983c, 189–93.

———, ed. 1983c. *The Greek renaissance of the eighth century b.c.: Tradition and innovation.* Stockholm: Paul Åströms Förlag.

———. 1987. Gifts to the heroes in Geometric and archaic Greece. In *Gifts to the gods,* edited by Tullia Linders and Gullög Nordquist, 93–99. Stockholm: Almqvist and Wiksell.

Hägg, Robin, Nanno Marinatos, and Gullög C. Nordquist, eds. 1988. *Early Greek cult practice.* Stockholm: Paul Åströms Förlag.

Hahn, István. 1977. Temenos and service land in the Homeric epics. *Acta Antiqua Academiae Scientiarum Hungaricae* 25: 299–316.

———. 1983. Foreign trade and foreign policy in Archaic Greece. In *Trade and famine in classical antiquity,* edited by Peter Garnsey and C. R. Whittaker, 30–36. Cambridge: Cambridge University Press.

Hainsworth, Bryan. 1993. *The Iliad: A Commentary.* Vol. 3, *Books 9–12.* Cambridge: Cambridge University Press.

Halperin, Rhoda H. 1984. Polanyi, Marx, and the institutional paradigm in economic anthropology. *Research in Economic Anthropology* 6: 245–72.

Halstead, Paul. 1987. Traditional and ancient rural economy in Mediterranean Europe: Plus ça change? *Journal of Hellenic Studies* 107: 77–87.

———. 1988. On redistribution and the origin of Minoan-Mycenaean palatial economies. In *Problems in Greek prehistory,* edited by Elizabeth B. French and K. A. Wardle, 519–30. Bristol: Bristol Classical Press.

———. 1989. The economy has a normal surplus: Economic stability and social change among early farming communities of Thessaly, Greece. In Halstead and O'Shea 1989a, 68–80.

———. 1992. The Mycenaean palatial economy: Making the most of the gaps in the evidence. *Proceedings of the Cambridge Philological Society* 218: 57–86.

Halstead, Paul, and Glynis Jones. 1989. Agrarian ecology in the Greek islands: Time stress, scale, and risk. *Journal of Hellenic Studies* 109: 41–55.

Halstead, Paul, and John O'Shea. 1982. A friend in need is a friend indeed: Social storage and the origins of social ranking. In *Ranking, resource, and exchange: Aspects of the archaeology of early European society,* edited by Colin Renfrew and Stephen Shennan, 92–99. Cambridge: Cambridge University Press.

————, eds. 1989a. *Bad year economics: Cultural responses to risk and uncertainty.* Cambridge: Cambridge University Press.

————. 1989b. Introduction: Cultural responses to risk and uncertainty. In Halstead and O'Shea 1989a, 1–7.

Halverson, John. 1985. Social order in the *Odyssey. Hermes* 113: 129–45.

————. 1986. The succession issue in the *Odyssey. Greece and Rome* 33: 119–28.

Hanfmann, George M. A. 1956. On some Eastern Greek wares found at Tarsus. In Weinberg 1956, 165–84.

Hansen, Mogens Herman, ed. 1993a. *The ancient Greek city-state.* Historisk-filosofiske Meddelelser, vol. 67. Copenhagen: Munksgaard.

————. 1993b. Introduction. The *polis* as a citizen-state. In Hansen 1993a, 7–29.

Harris, Marvin. 1959. The economy has no surplus? *American Anthropologist* 61: 185–99.

————. 1977. *Cannibals and kings: The origins of cultures.* New York: Random House.

————. 1985. *Good to eat: Riddles of food and culture.* New York: Simon and Schuster.

Harris, William V. 1982. The theoretical possibility of extensive infanticide in the Graeco-Roman world. *Classical Quarterly* 32: 114–16.

Harrison, E. L. 1971. Odysseus and Demodocus: Homer, *Odyssey* 8.492f. *Hermes* 99: 378–79.

Hasebroek, Johannes. 1933. *Trade and politics in ancient Greece.* Translated by L. M. Fraser and D. C. MacGregor. London: G. Bell and Sons. Reprint. Chicago: Ares, 1976.

Havelock, Eric A. 1963. *Preface to Plato.* Cambridge, Mass.: Harvard University Press.

————. 1982. *The literate revolution in Greece and its cultural consequences.* Princeton: Princeton University Press.

Heichelheim, Fritz M. 1960. Review of Polanyi, Arensberg, and Pearson 1957. *Journal of Economic and Social History of the Orient* 3: 108–10.

Helm, June, ed. 1965. *Essays in economic anthropology: Dedicated to the memory of Karl Polanyi.* Seattle: University of Washington Press.

Henige, David P. 1974. *The chronology of oral tradition.* Oxford: Oxford University Press.

Herrmann, Hans-Volkmar. 1966. *Die Kessel der orientalisierenden Zeit.* Berlin: de Gruyter.

————. 1972. *Olympia: Heiligtum und Wettkampfstätte.* Munich: Hirmer.

Herskovits, Melville J. 1940. *The economic life of primitive peoples.* New York: Knopf.

Hertz, Joseph H. 1945. *Sayings of the Fathers.* New York: Behrman House.

Heubeck, Alfred, and Arie Hoekstra, eds. 1989. *A commentary on Homer's Odyssey.* Vol. 2, *Books IX-XVI.* Oxford: Clarendon Press.

Heubeck, Alfred, Stephanie West, and J. B. Hainsworth, eds. 1988. *A commentary on Homer's Odyssey.* Vol. 1, *Introduction and books I-VIII.* Oxford. Clarendon Press.

Hiller, Stefan. 1988. Dependent personnel in Mycenaean texts. In *Society and economy in the eastern Mediterranean (c. 1500–1000 b.c.)*, edited by Michael Heltzer and E. Lipiński, 53–68. Leuven: Uitgeverij Peeters.

———. 1991. The Greek Dark Ages: Helladic traditions, Mycenaean traditions in culture and art. In Musti et al. 1991, 117–32.

Hodder, B. W. 1965. Some comments on the origins of traditional markets in Africa south of the Sahara. *Transactions of the Institute of British Geographers* 36: 97–105.

Hodges, Robert. 1978. Ports of trade in medieval Europe. *Norwegian Archaeological Review* 2: 97–101.

Hodkinson, Stephen. 1986. Land tenure and inheritance in classical Sparta. *Classical Quarterly* 36: 378–406.

———. 1988. Animal husbandry in the Greek polis. In Whittaker 1988, 35–74.

———. 1989. Inheritance, marriage, and demography: Perspectives upon the success and decline of classical Sparta. In A. Powell 1989, 79–121.

———. 1992. Sharecropping and Sparta's economic exploitation of the Helots. In Sanders 1992, 123–34.

Hoekstra, A. 1986. Review of Janko 1982. *Mnemosyne* 39: 158–63.

Hollingsworth, T. H. 1969. *Historical demography.* Ithaca, N.Y.: Cornell University Press.

Holloway, R. Ross. 1984. Recent research in Greek and Punic Sicily. In Hackens, Holloway, and Holloway 1984, 267–76.

———. 1991. *The archaeology of ancient Sicily.* London: Routledge.

Holton, R. J. *Cities, capitalism, and civilization.* London: Allen and Unwin.

Hommel, Hildebrecht. 1969. Die Gerichtsszene auf dem Schild des Achilleus: Zur Pflege des Rechts in homerischer Zeit. In *Politeia und res publica,* edited by Peter Steinmetz, 11–38. Wiesbaden: Franz Steiner Verlag.

Hooker, James T. 1976. *Mycenaean Greece.* London: Routledge and Kegan Paul.

———. 1979. The *wanax* in Linear B texts. *Kadmos* 18: 100–11.

———. 1989. Gifts in Homer. *Bulletin of the Institute of Classical Studies* 36: 79–90.

Hope Simpson, R. 1957. Identifying a Mycenaean state. *Annual of the British School at Athens* 52: 231–59.

———. 1966. The seven cities offered by Agamemnon to Achilles. *Annual of the British School at Athens* 61: 113–31.

Hopper, R. J. 1979. *Trade and industry in classical Greece.* London: Thames and Hudson.

Horner, George W. 1962. The Bulu response to European economy. In Bohannan and Dalton 1962a, 170–89.

Howe, Thalia Phillies. 1958. Linear B and Hesiod's breadwinners. *Transactions of the American Philological Association* 89: 44–65.

Howell, Nancy. 1979. *Demography of the Dobe !Kung.* New York: Academic Press.

Hubbard, Thomas K. 1995. Hesiod's fable of the hawk and the nightingale reconsidered. *Greek, Roman and Byzantine Studies* 36: 161–71.

Hughes, J. Donald. 1993. *Pan's travail: Environmental problems of the ancient Greeks and Romans.* Baltimore: Johns Hopkins University Press.

Humphreys, S. C. 1969. History, economics, and anthropology: The work of Karl Polanyi. *History and Theory* 8: 165–212. Reprinted with addendum in Humphreys 1978, 31–75.

————. 1977. Review of Gray 1974. *Classical Philology* 72: 347–55.

————. 1977/78. Public and private interests in classical Athens. *Classical Journal* 73: 97–104.

————. 1978. *Anthropology and the Greeks*. London: Routledge and Kegan Paul.

————. 1990. Review of Morris 1987. *Helios* 17: 263–68.

Hurwit, Jeffrey M. 1984. Review of Hägg 1983c. *American Journal of Archaeology* 88: 602–4.

————. 1985. *The art and culture of early Greece, 1100–480 b.c.* Ithaca, N.Y.: Cornell University Press.

Huxley, G. L. 1962. *Early Sparta*. London: Faber and Faber.

Hymer, Stephen H. 1970. Economic forms in pre-colonial Ghana. *Journal of Economic History* 30: 33–50.

James, Peter, I. J. Thorpe, Nikos Kokkinos, Robert Morkot, and John Frankish. 1991. *Centuries of darkness: A challenge to the conventional chronology of Old World archaeology*. London: Jonathan Cape.

Jameson, Michael H. 1977/78. Agriculture and slavery in classical Athens. *Classical Journal* 73: 122–45.

————. 1988. Sacrifice and animal husbandry in classical Greece. In Whittaker 1988, 87–119.

————. 1992. Agricultural labor in ancient Greece. In Wells 1992, 135–46.

Jameson, Michael H., Curtis N. Runnels, and Tjeerd H. van Andel. 1994. *A Greek countryside: The southern Argolid from prehistory to the present day*. Stanford: Stanford University Press.

Janko, Richard. 1982. *Homer, Hesiod, and the hymns: Diachronic development in epic diction*. Cambridge: Cambridge University Press.

Jeffery, L. H. 1961a. *The local scripts of archaic Greece*. Oxford: Clarendon Press.

————. 1961b. The pact of the first settlers at Cyrene. *Historia* 10: 139–47.

————. 1976. *Archaic Greece: The city-states c. 700–500 b.c.* London: Methuen.

————. 1982. Greek alphabetic writing. In *The Cambridge ancient history*, vol. 3., pt. 1, 819–33. 2d ed. Cambridge: Cambridge University Press.

Jeffery, Lillian H., and Anna Morpurgo-Davies. 1970. *Poinikastas* and *poinikazein:* BM 1969.4–2.1, a new archaic inscription from Crete. *Kadmos* 9: 118–54.

————. 1971/72. An archaic Greek inscription from Crete. *British Museum Quarterly* 36: 24–29.

Johnston, Alan. 1983. The extent and use of literacy: The archaeological evidence. In Hägg 1983c, 63–68.

————. 1990. Supplement. In *The local scripts of archaic Greece*, by L.H. Jeffery, rev. ed., 423–81. Oxford: Clarendon Press.

Johnston, Alan W., and Angeliki K. Andriomenou. 1989. A Geometric graffito from Eretria. *Annual of the British School at Athens* 84: 217–20.

Jones, A. H. M. 1967. *Sparta*. Cambridge, Mass.: Harvard University Press.

Jones, Donald W. 1993. Phoenician unguent factories in Dark Age Greece: Social approaches to evaluating the archaeological evidence. *Oxford Journal of Archaeology* 12: 293–303.

Jong, Irene de. 1987. Homeric *kerdos* and *ophelos*. *Museum Helveticum* 44: 79–81.

Jongman, Willem. 1988. Adding it up. In Whittaker 1988, 210–12.

Jowitt, Ken. 1992. *New world disorder: The Leninist extinction.* Berkeley: University of California Press.

Kailasapathy, K. 1968. *Tamil heroic poetry.* Oxford: Clarendon Press.

Kanelopoulos, Charles. 1991. L' agriculture d'Hésiode. *Techniques et Culture* 15: 131–58.

Kaplan, David. 1968. The formal-substantive controversy in economic anthropology: Reflections on its wider implications. *Southwestern Journal of Anthropology* 24: 228–51.

Karageorghis, Vassos. 1963. Une tombe de guerrier à Palaepaphos. *Bulletin de Correspondance Hellénique* 87: 265–300.

———. 1967. Chronique des fouilles et découvertes archéologique à Chypre en 1966. *Bulletin de Correspondance Hellénique* 91: 275–370.

———. 1969. *Salamis in Cyprus: Homeric, Hellenistic, and Roman.* London: Thames and Hudson.

———. 1970. Note on sigynnae and obeloi. *Bulletin de Correspondance Hellénique* 94: 35–44.

———. 1971. Chronique des fouilles à Chypre en 1970. *Bulletin de Correspondance Hellénique* 95: 335–432.

———. 1972. Two built tombs at Patriki, Cyprus. *Report of the Department of Antiquities, Cyprus* 1972, 161–80.

———. 1974. Pikes or obeloi from Cyprus and Crete. In *Antichità Cretesi: Studi in onore di Doro Levi,* 2: 168–72. Catania: Università di Catania.

———. 1982a. Cyprus. In *The Cambridge ancient history,* vol. 3, pt. 1, 511–33. 2d ed. Cambridge: Cambridge University Press.

———. 1982b. Cyprus. In *The Cambridge ancient history,* vol. 3, pt. 3, 57–70. 2d ed. Cambridge: Cambridge University Press.

———. 1995. Cyprus and the western Mediterranean: Some new evidence for interrelations. In Carter and Morris 1995, 93–97.

Karageorghis, V., H. W. Catling, K. Nicolaou, A. Papageorghiou, M. Loulloupis, D. Christou, and I. Nicolaou, eds. 1979. *Studies presented in memory of Porphyrios Dikaios.* Nicosia: Zavallis.

Katz, Solomon H. 1972. Biological factors in population control. In Spooner 1972, 351–69.

Kearsley, Rosalinde. 1989. *The pendent semi-circle skyphos: A study of its development and chronology and an examination of it as evidence for Euboean activity at Al Mina.* Bulletin supplement 44. London: Institute of Classical Studies.

Keller, Werner. 1974. *The Etruscans.* New York: Knopf.

Kelly, Thomas. 1976. *A history of Argos to 500 b.c.* Minneapolis: University of Minnesota.

al-Khalifa, Shaikha Haya Ali, and Michael Rice, eds. 1986. *Bahrain through the ages: The archaeology.* London: KPI.

Killen, J. T. 1988. The Linear B tablets and the Mycenaean economy. In Morpurgo-Davies and Duhoux 1988, 241–305.

———. 1994. Thebes sealings, Knossos tablets, and Mycenaean state banquets. *Bulletin of the Institute of Classical Studies* 39: 67–84.

Kirk, G. S. 1949. Ships on Geometric vases. *Annual of the British School at Athens* 44: 93–153.

————, ed. 1985. *The Iliad: A commentary.* Vol. 1, *Books 1–4.* Cambridge: Cambridge University Press.

Kleiner, Gerhard. 1968. *Die Ruinen von Milet.* Berlin: de Gruyter.

Knorringa, Heiman. 1926. *Emporos: Data on trade and trader in Greek literature from Homer to Aristotle.* Amsterdam: H. J. Paris.

Konner, Melvyn, and Carol W. Worthman. 1980. Nursing frequency, gonadal function, and birth spacing among the !Kung hunter-gatherers. *Science* 207: 788–91.

Kopcke, Günter. 1992. What role for Phoenicians? In Kopcke and Tokumara 1992, 103–13.

Kopcke, Günter, and Isabelle Tokumara, eds. 1992. *Greece between east and west: 10th-8th centuries b.c.* Mainz am Rhein: von Zabern.

Kosmetatou, Elizabeth. 1993. Horse sacrifices in Greece and Cyprus. *Journal of Prehistoric Religion* 7: 31–41.

Kraay, Colin M. 1964. Hoards, small change, and the origin of coinage. *Journal of Hellenic Studies* 84: 76–91.

Kulturhistorisk Leksikon for Nordisk Middelalder fra Vikingetid til Reformationstid. Vol. 11. Copenhagen: Rosenkilde og Bagger, 1966.

Kurimoto, Shinichiro. 1980. Silent trade in Japan. *Research in Economic Anthropology* 3: 97–108.

Kurke, Leslie. 1991. *The traffic in praise: Pindar and the poetics of social economy.* Ithaca, N.Y.: Cornell University Press.

————. 1995. Herodotus and the language of metals. *Helios* 22: 36–64.

Kurtz, Donna C., and John Boardman. 1971. *Greek burial customs.* Ithaca, N.Y.: Cornell University Press.

Kyrieleis, Helmut, and Wolfgang Röllig. 1988. Ein altorientalischer Pferdeschmuck aus dem Heraion von Samos. *Mitteilungen des Deutschen Archäologischen Instituts* 103: 37–75.

Labaree, Benjamin W. 1957. How the Greeks sailed into the Black Sea. *American Journal of Archaeology* 61: 29–33.

Lacey, W. K. 1968. *The family in classical Greece.* Ithaca, N.Y.: Cornell University Press.

Lambert, S. D. 1993. *The phratries of Attica.* Ann Arbor: University of Michigan Press.

Lambrinoudakis, V. 1988. Veneration of ancestors in Geometric Naxos. In Hägg, Marinatos, and Nordquist 1988, 235–45.

Landsberger, Henry A. 1974. Peasant unrest: Themes and variations. In *Rural protest: Peasant movements and social change,* edited by Henry A. Landsberger, 1–64. London: Macmillan.

Langdon, Merle K. 1975. The Dipylon oenochoe again. *American Journal of Archaeology* 79: 139–40.

————. 1976. *A sanctuary of Zeus on Mt. Hymettos.* Hesperia Suppl. 16. Princeton: American School of Classical Studies at Athens.

Latacz, Joachim. 1977. *Kampfparänese, Kampfdarstellung und Kampfwirklichkeit in der Ilias, bei Kallinos und Tyrtaios.* Munich: Beck.

————. 1979. *Homer, Tradition und Neuerung.* Darmstadt: Wissenschaftliche Buchgesellschaft.

————. 1989. *Homer: Der erste Dichter des Abendland.* 2d ed. Munich: Artemis.

————, ed. 1991. *Zweihundert Jahre Homer Forschung: Rückblick und Ausblick.* Stuttgart: B. G. Teubner.

Leaf, Walter, and M. A. Bayfield, eds. 1898. *The Iliad of Homer.* London: Macmillan.

LeClair, Edward E., Jr. 1962. Economic theory and economic anthropology. *American Anthropologist* 64: 1179–1203.

LeClair, Edward E., Jr., and Harold K. Schneider, eds. 1968. *Economic anthropology: Readings in theory and analysis.* New York: Holt, Rinehart and Winston.

Lee, Richard B. 1972. Population growth and the beginnings of sedentary life among the !Kung Bushmen. In Spooner 1972, 329–42.

Le Goff, Jacques. 1972. The town as an agent of civilisation, 1200–1500. In Cipolla 1972, 71–106.

Legon, Ronald P. 1981. *Megara: The political history of a Greek city-state to 336 b.c.* Ithaca, N.Y.: Cornell University Press.

Lejeune, Michel. 1971. *Mémoires de philologie mycénienne.* Vol. 1. Rome: Edizioni dell' Ateneo.

Lemos, Irene S., and Helen Hatcher. 1991. Early Greek vases in Cyprus: Euboean and Attic. *Oxford Journal of Archaeology* 10: 197–208.

Lenz, John. 1993a. Kings and the ideology of kingship in early Greece (c. 1200–700 b.c.): Epic, archaeology, and history. Ph.D. diss., Columbia University.

———. 1993b. Was Homer Euboian? A reply [to Powell 1993]. *Electronic Antiquity* 1.3.

Lepore, Ettore. 1968. Per una fenomenologia storica del rapporto città-territorio in Magna Grecia. In *La città e il suo territorio,* 29–66. Naples: Centre Jean Bérard.

Lessing, Gotthold Ephraim. 1766. *Laokoon.* In *Gesammelte Werke,* 5: 7–346. Berlin: Aufbau-Verlag, 1955.

LeVine, Robert. 1962. Wealth and power in Gusiiland. In Bohannan and Dalton 1962a, 520–36.

Lévy, Jean-Philippe. 1967. *The economic life of the ancient world.* Translated by John G. Biram. Chicago: University of Chicago Press.

Lindgren, Margareta. 1973. *The people of Pylos.* Vol. 2. Stockholm: Almqvist and Wiksell.

Lipiński, Edward. 1988. Les Phéniciens et l'alphabet. *Oriens Antiquus* 27: 231–60.

Lis, Catharina, and Hugo Soly. 1979. *Poverty and capitalism in pre-industrial Europe.* Hassocks, England: Harvester Press.

Liverani, Mario. 1990. *Prestige and interest: International relations in the Near East ca. 1600–1100 b.c.* Padua: Sargon.

Long, A. A. 1970. Morals and values in Homer. *Journal of Hellenic Studies* 90: 121–39.

Lord, Albert B. 1960. *The singer of tales.* Cambridge, Mass.: Harvard University Press.

Lowry, Eddie R., Jr. 1980. Thersites: A study in comic-shame. Ph.D. diss., Harvard University.

LSJ = Liddell, Henry G., Robert Scott, and Henry Stuart Jones, eds. 1940. *A Greek-English lexicon.* 9th ed. Oxford: Clarendon Press.

Lukermann, Fred E., and Jennifer Moody. 1978. Nichoria and vicinity: Settlements and circulation. In Rapp and Aschenbrenner 1978, 78–112.

MacDowell, Douglas M. 1978. *The law in classical Athens.* Ithaca, N.Y.: Cornell University Press.

Magagna, Victor V. 1991. *Communities of grain: Rural rebellion in comparative perspective.* Ithaca, N.Y.: Cornell University Press.

Maine, Henry Sumner. 1963. *Ancient law: Its connection with the early history of society and its relation to modern ideas.* Boston: Beacon.

Malinowski, B. 1920. *Kula:* The circulating exchange of valuables in the archipelagoes of eastern New Guinea. *Man* 51: 97–105. Reprinted in and cited from Dalton 1967, 171–84.

———. 1921. The primitive economics of the Trobriand islanders. *Economic Journal* 31: 1–16.

———. 1922. *Argonauts of the western Pacific.* London: Routledge and Kegan Paul. Pp. 156–94 reprinted in and cited from "Tribal Economics in the Trobriands," in Dalton 1967, 185–223.

Malkin, Irad. 1987. *Religion and colonization in ancient Greece.* Leiden: E. J. Brill.

Mallon, Florencia E. 1983. *The defense of community in Peru's central highlands: Peasant struggle and capitalist transition, 1860–1940.* Princeton: Princeton University Press.

Mallwitz, Alfred. 1988. Cult and competition locations at Olympia. In *The archaeology of the Olympics: The Olympics and other festivals in antiquity,* edited by Wendy J. Raschke, 79–109. Madison: University of Wisconsin Press.

Malthus, Thomas Robert. 1798. *An essay on population.* New York: Dutton, 1914.

Manville, Philip Brook. 1990. *The origins of citizenship in ancient Athens.* Princeton: Princeton University Press.

Marinatos, Nanno, and Robin Hägg, eds. 1993. *Greek sanctuaries: New approaches.* London: Routledge.

Markoe, Glenn E. 1992. In pursuit of metal: Phoenicians and Greeks in Italy. In Kopcke and Tohumara 1992, 60–84.

Marquardt, Patricia. 1984. Hesiod's *Op.* 464: Gaia as "soother of children." *Classical World* 77.5: 297–99.

Marshall, Lorna. 1976. *The !Kung of Nyae Nyae.* Cambridge, Mass.: Harvard University Press.

Martin, Richard P. 1984. Hesiod, Odysseus, and the instruction of princes. *Transactions of the American Philological Association* 114: 29–48.

———. 1992. Hesiod's metanastic poetics. *Ramus* 21.1: 11–33.

Martin, Roland. 1974. *L'urbanisme dans la Grèce antique.* 2d ed. Paris: Picard.

Marx, Karl. 1845/46. *The German ideology.* Moscow: Progress Publishers, 1964.

———. 1973. *Grundrisse.* Translated by Martin Nicolaus. New York: Vintage Books.

Maunier, René. 1949. *The sociology of colonies: An introduction to the study of race contact.* Translated by E. O. Lorimer. London: Routledge and Kegan Paul.

Mauss, Marcel. 1921. Une forme ancienne de contrat chez les Thraces. *Revue des Études Grecques* 34: 388–97.

———. 1925. *The gift.* Translated by Ian Cunnison. New York: Norton, 1967.

———. 1950. *Seasonal variations of the Eskimo: A study of social morphology.* Translated by James J. Fox. London: Routledge and Kegan Paul, 1979.

Mayhew, Anne. 1980. Atomistic and cultural analyses in economic anthropology: An old argument repeated. In *Institutional economics: Contributions to the development of holistic economics—Essays in honor of Allan G. Gruchy,* edited by John Adams, 72–81. The Hague: Martinus Nijhoff.

———. 1989. *The double movement in the United States, 1870–1914.* Occasional paper of the Karl Polanyi Institute of Political Economy. Montreal: Karl Polanyi Institute of Political Economy.

Mayhew, Anne, Walter C. Neale, and David W. Tandy. 1985. Markets in the ancient Near East: A challenge to Silver's argument and use of evidence. *Journal of Economic History* 45: 127–34.

Maynard Smith, John. 1974. *Models in ecology*. Cambridge: Cambridge University Press.

Mazarakis Ainian, Alexander. 1987. Geometric Eretria. *Antike Kunst* 30: 3–24.

Mazzarino, Santo. 1966. *The end of the ancient world*. Translated by George Holmes. London: Faber and Faber.

McDonald, William A., and William D. E. Coulson. 1983. The Dark Age at Nichoria: A perspective. In *Excavations at Nichoria in southwest Greece*, Vol. 2, *Dark age and Byzantine occupation*, edited by William A. McDonald, William D. E. Coulson, and John Rosser, 316–29. Minneapolis: University of Minnesota Press.

McDonald, William A., and Richard Hope Simpson. 1972. Archaeological exploration. In *The Minnesota Messenia expedition: Reconstructing a Bronze Age regional environment*, edited by William A. McDonald and George R. Rapp, Jr., 117–47. Minneapolis: University of Minnesota Press.

McEvedy, Colin, and Richard Jones. 1978. *Atlas of world population history*. Harmondsworth: Penguin.

McGlew, James F. 1989. Royal power and the Achaean assembly at *Iliad* 2.84–393. *Classical Antiquity* 8: 283–95.

McGuire, Randall H. 1983. Breaking down cultural complexity: Inequality and heterogeneity. *Advances in Archaeological Method and Theory* 6: 91–142.

Meiggs, Russell, and David Lewis. 1988. *A selection of Greek historical inscriptions to the end of the fifth century b.c.*. Rev. ed. Oxford: Clarendon Press.

Meikle, Scott. 1979. Aristotle and the political economy of the polis. *Journal of Hellenic Studies* 99: 57–73.

———. 1991. Aristotle on equality and market exchange. *Journal of Hellenic Studies* 111: 193–96.

Meillassoux, Claude. 1962. Social and economic factors affecting markets in Guro Land. In Bohannan and Dalton 1962a, 279–98.

———. 1972. From reproduction to production: A Marxist approach to economic anthropology. *Economy and Society* 1: 93–105.

Mele, Alfonso. 1979. *Il commercio greco arcaico: Prexis ed emporie*. Cahiers du Centre Jean Bérard, no. 4. Naples: Institut Français de Naples.

———. 1986. Pirateria, commercio e aristocrazia: Replica a Benedetto Bravo. *Dialogues d'Histoire Ancienne* 12: 67–109.

Meyer, Eduard. 1895. *Die wirtschaftliche Entwicklung des Altertums*. Cited from his *Kleine Schriften*, 1: 79–168. Halle: M. Niemeyer, 1924. Reprinted also in Finley 1979b.

Michell, John, and Robert Michell, eds. and trans. 1865. *The Russians in central Asia*. London: E. Stanford.

Millar, Fergus. 1983. Epigraphy. In *Sources for ancient history*, edited by Michael Crawford, 80–136. Cambridge: Cambridge University Press.

Miller, Molly. 1970. *The Sicilian colony dates*. Albany: State University of New York Press.

Millett, Paul. 1984. Hesiod and his world. *Proceedings of the Cambridge Philological Society* 210: 84–115.

Mitchell, Stephen. 1989/90. Archaeology in Asia Minor, 1985–1989. *Archaeological Reports* 36: 83–131.

Mommsen, Wolfgang J. 1974. *The age of bureaucracy: Perspectives on the political sociology of Max Weber.* Oxford: Basil Blackwell.

Montet, Pierre. 1958. *Everyday life in Egypt in the days of Ramesses the Great.* Translated by A. R. Maxwell-Hyslop and Margaret S. Drower. New York: St. Martin's Press. Reprint. Philadelphia: University of Pennsylvania Press, 1981.

Morel, Jean-Paul. 1984. Greek colonization in Italy and in the west: Problems of evidence and interpretation. In Hackens, Holloway, and Holloway 1984, 123–61.

Morgan, Catherine. 1988. Corinth, the Corinthian Gulf, and western Greece during the eighth century B.C. *Annual of the British School at Athens* 83: 313–38.

———. 1990. *Athletes and oracles: The transformation of Olympia and Delphi in the eighth century b.c.* Cambridge: Cambridge University Press.

———. 1991. Ethnicity and early Greek states: Historical and material perspectives. *Proceedings of the Cambridge Philological Society* 217: 131–63.

———. 1993. The origins of pan-Hellenism. In Marinatos and Hägg 1993, 18–44.

Morpurgo-Davies, Anna, and Yves Duhoux, eds. 1988. *Linear B: A 1984 survey.* Louvain-la-Neuve: Peeters.

Morris, Ian. 1986a. Gift and commodity in archaic Greece. *Man* 21: 1–17.

———. 1986b. The use and abuse of Homer. *Classical Antiquity* 5: 81–138.

———. 1987. *Burial and society: The rise of the Greek city-state.* Cambridge: Cambridge University Press.

———. 1988. Tomb cult and the "Greek renaissance": The past and the present in the 8th century B.C. *Antiquity* 62: 750–61.

———. 1989. Attitudes toward death in archaic Greece. *Classical Antiquity* 8: 296–320.

———. 1991. The early polis as city and state. In Rich and Wallace-Hadrill 1991, 25–57.

———. 1993a. Poetics of power: The interpretation of ritual action in archaic Greece. In Dougherty and Kurke 1993, 15–45.

———. 1993b. Review of Powell 1991. *Classical Philology* 88: 71–77.

———. 1994a. Archaeologies of Greece. In Morris 1994c, 8–47.

———. 1994b. The Athenian economy twenty years after *The Ancient Economy. Classical Philology* 89: 351–66.

———, ed. 1994c. *Classical Greece: Ancient histories and modern archaeologies.* Cambridge: Cambridge University Press.

———. 1994d. The community against the market in classical Athens. In Duncan and Tandy 1994, 52–79.

Morrison, J. S. 1994. Review of Wallinga 1993. *Journal of Hellenic Studies* 114: 206–8.

Morrison, J. S., and R. T. Williams. 1968. *Greek oared ships, 900–322 b.c.* Cambridge: Cambridge University Press.

Muhly, John D. 1970. Homer and the Phoenicians. *Berytus* 19: 19–64.

Mumford, Lewis. 1970 [1938]. *The culture of cities.* Rev. ed. New York: Harcourt Brace Jovanovich.

Munding, Heinz. 1959. *Hesiods Erga in ihrem Verhältnis zur Ilias: Ein Vergleich und seine Folgerungen für die Entstehung der Gedichte.* Frankfurt am Main: V. Klostermann.

Murakawa, Kenturô. 1957. Demiourgos. *Historia* 6: 348–415.

Murray, Oswyn. 1980. *Early Greece.* Brighton, England: Harvester Press. Cited from 1983 ed. Palo Alto, Calif.: Stanford University Press.

———. 1983a. The Greek symposion in history. In *Tria corda: Scritti in onore di Arnaldo Momigliano,* edited by Emilio Gabba, 257–72. Como: Edizioni New Press.

———. 1983b. Symposion and Männerbund. In *Concilium Eirene XVI: Proceedings of the 16th International Eirene Conference, Prague, 31.8–4.9.1982,* 47–52. Prague: Kabinet pro Studia Recka, Rimska a Latinska.

———. 1983c. The symposion as social organisation. In Hägg 1983c, 195–99.

———, ed. 1990. *Sympotica: A symposium on the symposium.* Oxford: Clarendon Press.

Murray, Oswyn, and Simon Price, eds. 1990. *The Greek city: From Homer to Alexander.* Oxford: Clarendon Press.

Murray, Penelope. 1981. Poetic inspiration in early Greece. *Journal of Hellenic Studies* 101: 87–100.

Musti, D., A. Sacconi, L. Rocchetti, M. Rocchi, E. Scafa, L. Sportiello, and M. E. Giannotta, eds. 1991. *La transizione dal Miceneo all'alto arcaismo: Dal palazzo all città.* Rome: Istituto per gli Studi Micenei ed Egeo-Anatolici.

Nagy, Gregory. 1979. *The best of the Achaeans: Concepts of the hero in archaic Greek poetry.* Baltimore: Johns Hopkins University Press.

———. 1981. An evolutionary model for the text fixation of the Homeric epos. In *Oral traditional literature: A Festschrift for Albert Bates Lord,* edited by John Miles Foley, 390–93. Columbus: Slavica.

———. 1982. Hesiod. In *Ancient writers: Greece and Rome,* edited by T. James Luce, 1: 43–73. New York: Charles Scribner's Sons.

———. 1989. The pan-hellenization of the "days" in the *Works and days.* In *Daidalikon: Studies in honor of Raymond V. Schoder, S.J.,* edited by Robert F. Sutton, 273–77. Chicago: Bolchazy-Carducci.

———. 1992. Oral poetry and ancient Greek poetry, broadenings and narrowings of terms. In Pinsent and Hurt 1992, 15–37.

———. 1995. An evolutionary model for the making of Homeric poetry: Comparative perspectives. In Carter and Morris 1995, 163–79.

Nash, Manning. 1958/59. Some social and cultural characteristics of economic development. *Economic Development and Cultural Change* 7: 137–50.

———. 1964. The organization of economic life. In *Horizons of anthropology,* edited by Sol Tax, 171–80. Chicago: Aldine. Reprinted in and cited from Dalton 1967, 3–12.

———. 1966. *Primitive and peasant economic systems.* San Francisco: Chandler.

———. 1967. Reply to reviews of Nash 1966. *Current Anthropology* 8: 249–50.

———. 1969. Comment following Dalton 1969. *Current Anthropology* 10: 87–88.

Naveh, Joseph. 1987. *Early history of the alphabet: An introduction to West Semitic epigraphy and palaeography.* Leiden: E. J. Brill.

Neale, Walter C. 1957a. The market in theory and history. In Polanyi, Arensberg, and Pearson 1957, 357–72.

———.1957b. Reciprocity and redistribution in the Indian village: Sequel to some notable discussions. In Polanyi, Arensberg, and Pearson 1957, 218–36.

———. 1962. *Economic change in rural India: Land tenure and reform in Uttar Pradesh, 1800–1955.* New Haven: Yale University Press.

———. 1969. Land is to rule. In *Land control and social structure in Indian history,* edited by Robert Eric Frykenberg, 3–15. Madison: University of Wisconsin Press.

———. 1989. *Exposure and protection: The double movement in the economic history of rural India.* Occasional paper of the Karl Polanyi Institute of Political Economy. Montreal: Karl Polanyi Institute of Political Economy.

———. 1990. Karl Polanyi and American institutionalism: A strange case of convergence. In *The life and work of Karl Polanyi,* edited by Kari Polanyi-Levitt, 145–51. Montreal: Black Rose Books.

———. Forthcoming. Economic systems: Rules as roles and verse as folkview.

Neale, Walter C., and David W. Tandy. 1988. Review of Silver 1986. *Journal of Economic History* 48.2: 442–43.

Negbi, Ora. 1992. Early Phoenician presence in the Mediterranean islands: A reappraisal. *American Journal of Archaeology* 96: 599–615.

Niemeyer, Hans Georg, ed. 1982. *Phönizier im Westen.* Mainz am Rhein: von Zabern.

———. 1984. Die Phönizier und die Mittelmeerwelt im Zeitalter Homers. *Jahrbuch des Römisch-Germanische Zentralmuseums Mainz* 31: 3–94.

———. 1990. The Phoenicians in the Mediterranean: A non-Greek model for expansion and settlement in antiquity. In Descoeudres 1990, 469–89.

Nock, A. D. 1944. The cult of heroes. *Harvard Theological Review* 37: 141–74.

Nye, P. H., and D. J. Greenland. 1960. *The soil under shifting cultivation.* Technical Communication, no. 51. Farnham Royal, England: Commonwealth Bureau of Soils.

Ober, Josiah. 1989. *Mass and elite in democratic Athens: Rhetoric, ideology, and the power of the people.* Princeton: Princeton University Press.

O'Connor, David. 1972. A regional population in Egypt to circa 600 B.C. In Spooner 1972, 78–100.

Onians, R. B. 1951. *The origins of European thought about the body, the mind, the soul, the world, time, and fate.* Cambridge: Cambridge University Press.

Oppenheim, A. Leo. 1954. The seafaring merchants of Ur. *Journal of the American Oriental Society* 74: 6–17.

———. 1977. *Ancient Mesopotamia.* Rev. ed., completed by Erica Reiner. Chicago: University of Chicago Press.

Osborne, Robin. 1992. "Is it a farm?" The definition of agricultural sites and settlements in ancient Greece. In Wells 1992, 21–25.

O'Sullivan, James N. 1990. Nature and culture in *Odyssey* 9? *Symbolae Osloenses* 65: 7–17.

Ottenberg, Simon, and Phoebe Ottenberg. 1962. Afikpo markets: 1900–1960. In Bohannan and Dalton 1962a, 118–69.

Oudenrijn, Cornelius Marcus Antonius van den. 1951. *Demiourgos.* Assen: van Gorcum.

Owens, E. J. 1991. *The city in the Greek and Roman world.* London and New York: Routledge.

Pallottino, Massimo. 1991. *A history of earliest Italy.* Translated by Martin Ryle and Kate Soper. London: Routledge.

Palmer, L. R. 1954. Mycenaean Greek texts from Pylos. *Transactions of the Philological Society* 1954, 18–53b.

Panizo, Alfredo. 1965. Infanticide and population. *Unitas: Revista de cultura y vida* 38: 599–610.

Parry, Jonathan. 1986. *The gift,* the Indian gift and the "Indian gift." *Man* 21: 453–73.

Parry, Milman. 1971. *The making of Homeric verse: The collected papers of Milman Parry,* edited by Adam Parry. Oxford: Clarendon Press.

Parsons, Talcott, and Neil J. Smelser. 1956. *Economy and society: A study in the integration of economic and social theory.* Glencoe, Ill.: Free Press.

Patterson, Cynthia. 1985. "Not worth the rearing": The causes of infant exposure in ancient Greece. *Transactions of the American Philological Association* 115: 103–23.

Peabody, Berkley. 1975. *The winged word.* Albany: State University of New York Press.

Pearson, Harry W. 1957a. The economy has no surplus: Critique of a theory of development. In Polanyi, Arensberg, and Pearson 1957, 320–41.

———. 1957b. The secular debate on economic primitivism. In Polanyi, Arensberg, and Pearson 1957, 3–11.

Pease, Franklin. 1982. The formation of the Tawantinsuyu: Mechanisms of colonization and relationship with ethnic groups. In *The Inca and Aztec states: Anthropology and history,* edited by George A. Collier, Renato I. Rosaldo, and John D. Wirth, 173–98. New York: Academic Press.

Pecírka, Jan. 1973. Homestead farms in classical and Hellenistic Hellas. In Finley 1973, 113–47.

PECS = *The Princeton encyclopedia of classical sites,* edited by Richard Stillwell. Princeton: Princeton University Press, 1976.

Pellegrini, Giuseppe. 1903. Tombe greche archaiche di Cuma. *Monumenti Antichi* 13: 210–94.

Persson, Karl Gunnar. 1988. *Pre-industrial economic growth: Social organization and technological progress in Europe.* Oxford: Basil Blackwell.

Perysinakis, I. N. 1991. Penelope's *eedna* again. *Classical Quarterly* 41: 297–302.

Peters, M. 1983. Review of Janko 1982. *Die Sprache* 29: 109.

Piggott, Stuart. 1965. *Ancient Europe from the beginnings of agriculture to classical antiquity: A survey.* Chicago: Aldine.

———. 1971. Firedogs in Iron Age Britain and beyond. In Boardman, Brown, and Powell 1971, 243–70.

Pinsent, J. 1992. The Odyssised *Iliad.* In Pinsent and Hurt 1992, 75–84.

Pinsent, J., and H. V. Hurt, eds. 1992. *Homer 1987: Papers of the Third Greenbank Colloquium.* Liverpool: Liverpool Classical Monthly.

Pirenne, Henri. 1933. *Economic and social history of medieval Europe.* Translated by I. E. Clegg. New York: Harcourt Brace, 1937.

Piteros, Christos, Jean-Pierre Olivier, and José L. Melena. 1990. Les inscriptions de linéaire B des nodules de Thèbes (1982): La fouille, les documents, les possibilités d'interprétation. *Bulletin de Correspondance Hellénique* 114: 103–84.

Polanyi, Karl. 1944. *The great transformation.* New York: Holt, Rinehart and Winston.

————. 1947. Our obsolete market mentality. *Commentary* 13: 109–17. Reprinted in and cited from Dalton 1968a, 59–77.

————. 1953. Anthropology and economic theory. In Fried 1968, 216–38. Reprint of *Semantics of general economic history*. New York: Columbia University Research Project on "Origins of Economic Institutions."

————. 1957a. Aristotle discovers the economy. In Polanyi, Arensberg, and Pearson 1957, 64–94.

————. 1957b. The economy as instituted process. In Polanyi, Arensberg, and Pearson 1957, 243–70.

————. 1957c. Marketless trading in Hammurabi's time. In Polanyi, Arensberg, and Pearson 1957, 12–26.

————. 1960. On the comparative treatment of economic institutions in antiquity, with illustrations from Athens, Mycenae, and Alalakh. In *City invincible,* edited by Carl H. Kraeling and Robert M. Adams, 329–50. Chicago: University of Chicago Press. Reprinted in Dalton 1968a, 306–34.

————. 1963. Ports of trade in early societies. *Journal of Economic History* 23: 30–45. Reprinted in and cited from Dalton 1968a, 238–60.

————. 1966. *Dahomey and the slave trade: An analysis of an archaic economy.* Seattle: University of Washington Press.

————. 1975. Traders and trade. In Sabloff and Lamberg-Karlovsky 1975, 133–54. Also in Polanyi 1977, 81–96.

————. 1977. *The livelihood of man.* Edited by Harry W. Pearson. New York: Academic Press.

Polanyi, Karl, Conrad Arensberg, and Harry W. Pearson, eds. 1957. *Trade and market in the early empires.* Glencoe, Ill.: Free Press.

Polignac, François de (= Bohringer, q.v.). 1984. *La naissance de la cité grecque: Culte, espace et société, VIIIe-VIIe siècles avant J.-C.* Paris: Éditions la Découverte.

————. 1992. Influence extérieure ou évolution interne? L'innovation cultuelle en Grèce géométrique et archaïque. In Kopcke and Tokumara 1992, 114–27.

————. 1995. *Cults, territory, and the origins of the Greek city-state.* Revision of de Polignac 1984, translated by Janet Lloyd. Chicago: University of Chicago Press.

Popham, Mervyn. 1987. An early Euboean ship. *Oxford Journal of Archaeology* 6.3: 353–59.

————. 1993. The sequence of events, interpretation, and date. In Popham, Calligas, and Sackett 1993, 97–101.

————. 1994. Precolonisation: Early Greek contact with the east. In Tsetskhladze and De Angelis 1994, 11–34.

————. 1995. An engraved Near Eastern bronze bowl from Lefkandi. *Oxford Journal of Archaeology* 14: 103–7.

Popham, Mervyn, H. Hatcher, and A. M. Pollard. 1980. Al Mina and Euboea. *Annual of the British School at Athens* 75: 151–61.

Popham, Mervyn, and Irene Lemos. 1992. Review of Kearsley 1989. *Gnomon* 64: 152–55.

————. 1995. A Euboean warrior trader. *Oxford Journal of Archaeology* 14: 151–57.

Popham, M. R., P. G. Calligas, and L. H. Sackett, eds. 1993. *Lefkandi.* Vol. 2, *The protogeometric building at Toumba.* Pt. 2, *The excavation, architecture, and finds.* Athens: British School of Archaeology at Athens.

Popham, M. R., and L. H. Sackett. 1968. *Excavations at Lefkandi, Euboea, 1964–1966: A preliminary report*. London: Thames and Hudson.

Popham, M. R., L. H. Sackett, and P. G. Themelis, eds. 1980. *Lefkandi*. Vol. 1, *The iron age*. London: Thames and Hudson.

Popham, M. R., E. Touloupa, and L. H. Sackett. 1982. The hero of Lefkandi. *Antiquity* 56: 169–74.

Postlethwaite, Norman. 1988. Thersites in the *Iliad*. *Greece and Rome* 35: 123–36.

Potter, J. 1965. The growth of population in America, 1700–1860. In *Population in history: Essays in historical demography*, edited by D. V. Glass and D. E. C. Eversley, 631–88. London: Edward Arnold.

Powell, Anton, ed. 1989. *Classical Sparta: Techniques behind her success*. Norman: University of Oklahoma Press.

Powell, Barry B. 1987. The origin of the puzzling supplementals φ Χ Ψ. *Transactions of the American Philological Association* 117: 1–20.

———. 1989. Why was the Greek alphabet invented? The epigraphical evidence. *Classical Antiquity* 8: 321–50.

———. 1991. *Homer and the origin of the Greek alphabet*. Cambridge: Cambridge University Press.

———. 1993a. Did Homer sing at Lefkandi? *Electronic Antiquity* 1.2.

———. 1993b. Did Homer sing at Lefkandi? A reply to J. Lenz. *Electronic Antiquity* 1.3.

Price, John A. 1980. On silent trade. *Research in Economic Anthropology* 3: 75–96.

Pritchett, W. Kendrick. 1965. *Studies in ancient Greek topography*. Part 1. Berkeley: University of California Press.

Pucci, Pietro. 1987. *Odysseus polutropos*. Ithaca, N.Y.: Cornell University Press.

Purcell, Nicholas. 1990. Mobility and the *polis*. In Murray and Price 1990, 29–58.

Qviller, Bjørn. 1980. Prolegomena to a study of the Homeric *demiourgoi* (Murakawa's theory re-examined). *Symbolae Osloenses* 55: 5–21.

———. 1981. The dynamics of the Homeric society. *Symbolae Osloenses* 56: 109–55.

Raaflaub, Kurt A. 1989. Homer and the beginnings of political thought in Greece. In Cleary and Shartin 1989, 1–25.

———. 1991. Homer und die Geschichte des 8. Jh.s v. Chr. In Latacz 1991, 205–56.

———. 1993. Homer to Solon: The rise of the *polis*—The written sources. In Hansen 1993a, 41–105.

Rackham, Oliver. 1983. Observations on the historical ecology of Boeotia. *Annual of the British School at Athens* 78: 291–351.

Radcliffe, William. 1921. *Fishing from the earliest times*. London: John Murray. Reprint. Chicago: Ares, 1974.

Radloff, W. 1885. *Proben der Volkslitteratur der nördlichen türkischen Stämme*. Vol. 5, pt. 2. St. Petersburg: Eggers.

Rakoff, Abraham E. 1963. Discussion of chapter 14 in *Advances in neuroendocrinology*, edited by Andrew V. Nalbandov. Urbana: University of Illinois Press.

Rapp, George T., and S. E. Aschenbrenner, eds. 1978. *Excavations at Nichoria in southwest Greece*. Vol. 1, *Site, environs, and techniques*. Minneapolis: University of Minnesota Press.

Rapp, George, Jr., S. E. Aschenbrenner, and John Kraft, 1978. The Holocene environmental history of the Nichoria region. In Rapp and Aschenbrenner 1978, 13–25.

Rathje, Annette. 1979. Oriental imports in Etruria in the eighth and seventh centuries B.C.: Their origins and implications. In Ridgway and Ridgway 1979, 145–83.

Rathje, William L. 1969/70. Socio-political implications of lowland Maya burials: Methodology and tentative hypotheses. *World Archaeology* 1: 359–74.

Reden, Sitta Von. 1994. *Exchange in ancient Greece.* London: Duckworth.

Redfield, James M. 1975. *Nature and culture in the Iliad: The tragedy of Hector.* Chicago: University of Chicago Press.

———. 1977/78. The women of Sparta. *Classical Journal* 73: 146–61.

———. 1983a. The economic man. In *Approaches to Homer,* edited by Carl W. Rubino and Cynthia W. Shelmerdine, 218–47. Austin: University of Texas Press.

———. 1983b. Review article of Gernet 1968. *American Journal of Philology* 104: 398–403.

———. 1986. The development of the market in archaic Greece. In *The market in history,* edited by B. L. Anderson and A. J. H. Latham, 29–58. London: Croon Helm.

Redfield, Robert. 1947. The folk society. *American Journal of Sociology* 52: 293–308.

———. 1953. *The primitive world and its transformations.* Ithaca, N.Y.: Cornell University Press.

———. 1956. *Peasant society and culture.* Chicago: University of Chicago Press.

Reed, C. M. 1984. Maritime traders in the archaic Greek world: A typology of those engaged in the long-distance transfer of goods by sea. *Ancient World* 10: 31–44.

Reinhold, M. 1946. Historian of the classical world: Critique of Rostovtzeff. *Science and Society* 10: 361–91.

Renfrew, Colin. 1969. Trade and culture process in European prehistory. *Current Anthropology* 10: 151–60.

———. 1972. *The emergence of civilisation: The Cyclades and the Aegean in the third millennium b.c.* London: Methuen.

———. 1975. Trade as action at a distance. In Sabloff and Lamberg-Karlovsky 1975, 3–59.

———. 1979a. *Before civilization: The radiocarbon revolution and prehistoric Europe.* 2d ed. Berkeley: University of California Press.

———. 1979b. Systems collapse as social transformation: Catastrophe and anastrophe in early state societies. In *Transformations: Mathematical approaches to culture change,* edited by Colin Renfrew and Kenneth L. Cooke, 481–506. New York: Academic Press.

———. 1987. *Archaeology and language: The puzzle of Indo-european origins.* Cambridge: Cambridge University Press.

Renfrew, Colin, and Malcolm Wagstaff, eds. 1982. *An island polity: The archaeology of exploitation in Melos.* Cambridge: Cambridge University Press.

Revere, Robert B. 1957. "No man's coast": Ports of trade in the eastern Mediterranean. In Polanyi, Arensberg, and Pearson 1957, 38–63.

Reyes, A. T. 1994. *Archaic Cyprus: A study of the textual and archaeological evidence.* Oxford: Clarendon Press.

Rhodes, Peter J. 1984. Review of Drews 1983. *Phoenix* 38: 179–83.

———. 1993. The Greek *poleis:* Demes, cities, and leagues. In Hansen 1993a, 161–82.

Rich, John, and Andrew Wallace-Hadrill, eds. 1991. *City and country in the ancient world.* London: Routledge.

Richardson, Emeline. 1964. *The Etruscans: Their art and civilization.* Chicago: University of Chicago Press.

———. 1986. An archaeological introduction to the Etruscan language. In Bonfante 1986a, 215–31.

Richardson, N. J. 1979. Review of West 1978. *Journal of Hellenic Studies* 99: 169–71.

Richardson, N. J., and Stuart Piggott. 1982. Hesiod's wagon: Text and technology. *Journal of Hellenic Studies* 102: 225–29.

Ridgway, David. 1973. The first western Greeks: Campanian coasts and southern Etruria. In *Greeks, Celts, and Romans: Studies in venture and resistance,* edited by Christopher Hawkes and Sonia Hawkes, 5–38. London: J. M. Dent and Sons.

———. 1990. The first western Greeks and their neighbours, 1935–1985. In Descoeudres 1990, 61–72.

———. 1992a. Demaratus and his predecessors. In Kopcke and Tokumara 1992, 85–92.

———. 1992b. *The first western Greeks.* Cambridge: Cambridge University Press. (2d ed. of *L'alba della Magna Grecia.* Archeologia 7. Milan: Longanesi, 1984.)

———. 1994. Phoenicians and Greeks in the west: A view from Pithekoussai. In Tsetskhladze and De Angelis 1994, 35–46.

Ridgway, David, and Francesca R. Ridgway, eds. 1979. *Italy before the Romans: The iron age, orientalizing and Etruscan periods.* London: Academic Press.

Rihll, Tracey. 1986. "Kings" and "commoners" in Homeric society. *Liverpool Classical Monthly* 11: 86–91.

———. 1992. The power of the Homeric *basileis.* In Pinsent and Hurt 1992, 39–50.

Rizza, Giovanni. 1979. Tombes de chevaux. In *The relations between Cyprus and Crete, ca. 2000–500 b.c.,* 294–97. Nicosia: Department of Antiquities.

Robb, Kevin. 1978. Poetic sources of the Greek alphabet: Rhythm and abecedarium from Phoenician to Greek. In *Communication arts in the ancient world,* edited by Eric A. Havelock and Jackson P. Hershbell, 23–36. New York: Hastings House.

Robertson, Martin. 1940. The excavations at al Mina, Sueidia, IV: The early Greek vases. *Journal of Hellenic Studies* 60: 2–21.

Rodinson, Maxime. 1973. *Islam and capitalism.* Translated by Brian Pearce. New York: Pantheon.

Roebuck, Carl. 1945. A note on Messenian economy and population. *Classical Philology* 40: 149–65.

———. 1959. *Ionian trade and civilization.* New York: Archaeological Institute of America.

———. 1962. Comment on Will 1962 in Finley 1962b, 97–106.

———. 1972. Some aspects of urbanization in Corinth. *Hesperia* 41: 96–127.

Roesch, P., and G. Argoud, eds. 1985. *La Béotie antique.* Paris: Éditions du CNRS.

Roisman, Hanna S. 1994. Like father like son: Telemachus' *kerdea. Rheinisches Museum* 137: 1–22.

Roller, Lynn E. 1981. Funeral games for historical persons. *Stadion* 7: 1–18.

Rolley, Claude. 1983. Les grands sanctuaires panhélleniques. In Hägg 1983c, 109–14.

Rose, Peter W. 1975. Class ambivalence in the *Odyssey*. *Historia* 24: 129–49.

———. 1988. Thersites and the plural voices of Homer. *Arethusa* 21: 5–25.

Rosen, George. 1975. *Peasant society in a changing economy: Comparative development in southeast Asia and India*. Urbana: University of Illinois Press.

Rosen, Ralph M. 1990. Poetry and sailing in Hesiod's *Works and Days*. *Classical Antiquity* 9: 99–113.

Rotstein, Abraham. 1961. A note on the surplus discussion. *American Anthropologist* 63: 561–63.

———. 1970. Karl Polanyi's concept of non-market trade. *Journal of Economic History* 30: 117–26.

Rottenberg, Simon. 1958. Review of Polanyi, Arensberg, and Pearson 1957. *American Economic Review* 48: 675–78.

Rounds, J. 1982. Dynastic succession and the centralization of power in Tenochtitlan. In *The Inca and Aztec states, 1400–1800: Anthropology and history*, edited by George A. Collier, Renato I. Rosaldo, and John D. Wirth, 63–89. New York: Academic Press.

Roussel, Denis. 1976. *Tribu et cité: Études sur les groupes sociaux dans les cités grecques aux époques archaïque et classique*. Paris: Les Belles Lettres.

Rowlands, Michael J. 1986. Modernist fantasies in prehistory? *Man* 21: 745–46.

———. 1987a. Centre and periphery: A review of a concept. In Rowlands, Larsen, and Kristiansen 1987, 1–11.

———. 1987b. The concept of Europe in prehistory. *Man* 22: 558–59.

———. 1987c. "Europe in prehistory": A unique form of primitive capitalism? *Culture and History* 1: 63–78.

Rowlands, Michael J., Mogens Larsen, and Kristian Kristiansen, eds. 1987. *Centre and periphery in the ancient world*. Cambridge: Cambridge University Press.

Ruiz, Ramón Eduardo. 1988. *The people of Sonora and Yankee capitalists*. Tucson: University of Arizona Press.

Runciman. W. G. 1986. Review of Sagan 1985. *New York Review*, 18 December, 64–65.

———. 1987. Response to Sagan 1987. *New York Review*, 23 April, 49.

———. 1990. Doomed to extinction: The *polis* as a evolutionary dead-end. In Murray and Price 1990, 347–67.

Runnels, Curtis N., and Tjeerd H. van Andel. 1987. The evolution of settlement in the southern Argolid, Greece: An economic explanation. *Hesperia* 56: 303–34.

Rupp, David W. 1988. The "royal tombs" at Salamis (Cyprus): Ideological message of power and authority. *Journal of Mediterranean Archaeology* 1: 111–39.

———. 1989. Puttin' on the Ritz: Manifestations of high status in Iron Age Cyprus. In *Early society in Cyprus*, edited by Edgar Peltenburg, 336–62. Edinburgh: Edinburgh University Press.

Russell, J. C. 1958. *Late ancient and medieval population*. Transactions of the American Philosophical Society, vol. 48, pt. 3. Philadelphia: American Philosophical Society.

——— 1972. Population in Europe 500–1500. In Cipolla 1972, 25–70.

Russo, Joseph, Manuel Fernández-Galiano, and Alfred Heubeck, eds. 1992. *A commentary on Homer's Odyssey.* Vol. 3, *Books XVII-XXIV.* Oxford: Clarendon Press.

Rutter, Jeremy. 1992. Cultural novelties in the post-palatial Aegean world: Indices of vitality or decline? In Ward and Joukowsky 1992, 61–78.

Sabloff, Jeremy A., and C. C. Lamberg-Karlovsky, eds. 1975. *Ancient civilization and trade.* Albuquerque: University of New Mexico Press.

Sackett, L. H. 1986. The burial building at Lefkandi: Evidence for Euboean leadership and overseas enterprise during the "Dark Age." Paper read at the Archaeological Institute of America annual meeting, 27 December 1986; abstract in *American Journal of Archaeology* 91 (1987): 269.

Sackett, L. H., V. Hankey, R. J. Howell, T. W. Jacobsen, and M. R. Popham. 1966. Prehistoric Euboea: Contributions toward a survey. *Annual of the British School at Athens* 61: 33–112.

Sackett, L. H., and M. R. Popham. 1972. Lefkandi: A Euboean town of the Bronze Age and the early Iron Age (2100–700 B.C.). *Archaeology* 25: 8–19.

Sagan, Eli. 1985. *At the dawn of tyranny: The origins of individualism, political oppression, and the state.* New York: Knopf.

———. 1987. Response to Runciman 1986. *New York Review,* 23 April, 48–49.

Sahlins, Marshall D. 1960a. Political power and the economy in primitive society. In *Essays in the science of culture in honor of Leslie A. White,* edited by Gertrude E. Dole and Robert L. Carneiro, 390–415. New York: Crowell.

———. 1960b. Production, distribution, and power in a primitive society. In *Men and cultures: Selected papers of the Fifth International Congress of Anthropological and Ethnological Sciences,* edited by A. F. C. Wallace, 495–500. Philadelphia: University of Pennsylvania Press.

———. 1962/63. Poor man, rich man, big man, chief: Political types in Melanesia and Polynesia. *Comparative Studies in Society and History* 5: 285–303.

———. 1965a. Exchange-value and the diplomacy of primitive trade. In Helm 1965, 95–129.

———. 1965b. On the sociology of primitive exchange. In *The relevance of models for social anthropology,* edited by Max Gluckman and Fred Eggan, 139–236. London: Tavistock.

———. 1968. *Tribesmen.* Englewood Cliffs, N.J.: Prentice-Hall.

———. 1972. *Stone age economics.* Chicago: Aldine.

———. 1985. *Islands of history.* Chicago: University of Chicago Press.

Ste. Croix, G. E. M. de. 1981. *The class struggle in the ancient Greek world from the archaic age to the Arab conquest.* Ithaca, N.Y.: Cornell University Press.

Sakellariou, M. B. 1989. *The polis-state: Definition and origin.* Athens: Research Center for Greek and Roman Antiquity.

Sale, W. M. 1994. The government of Troy: Politics in the *Iliad. Greek, Roman and Byzantine Studies* 35: 5–102.

Sallares, Robert. 1991. *The ecology of the ancient Greek world.* Ithaca, N.Y.: Cornell University Press.

Salmon, John. 1972. The Heraeum at Perachora, and the early history of Corinth and Megara. *Annual of the British School at Athens* 67: 159–204.

———. 1984. *Wealthy Corinth: A history of the city to 338 b.c.* Oxford: Clarendon Press.

Saltz, D. L. 1978. Greek Geometric pottery in the east. Ph.D. diss., Harvard University.

Sanders, Jan Motyka, ed. 1992. *Philolakon: Lakonian studies in honour of Hector Catling.* London: British School at Athens.

Sarkady, János. 1975. Outlines of the development of Greek society in the period between the 12th and 8th centuries B.C. *Acta Antiqua Academiae Scientiarum Hungaricae* 23: 107–25.

Sass, Benjamin. 1991. *Studia alphabetica: On the origin and early history of the northwest Semitic, south Semitic, and Greek alphabets.* Göttingen: Vandenhöck and Ruprecht.

Schachter, Albert. 1985. Kadmos and the implications of the tradition for Boiotian history. In Roesch and Argoud 1985, 143–53.

Schiering, Wolfgang. 1968. Landwirtschaftliche Geräte. In *Die Landwirtschaft im homerischen Zeitalter,* edited by Will Richter, 147–58. Archaeologia Homerica, vol. 2H. Göttingen: Vandenhöck and Ruprecht.

Schilardi, Demetrius U. 1975. Paros, report II: The 1973 campaign. *Journal of Field Archaeology* 2: 83–96.

———. 1983. The decline of the Geometric settlement at Koukounaries at Paros. In Hägg 1983c, 173–83.

Schmidt, Jens-Uwe. 1986. *Adressat und Paraineseform: Zur Intention von Hesiods "Werken und Tagen."* Göttingen: Vandenhöck and Ruprecht.

Schmitt Pantel, Pauline. 1992. *La cité au banquet: Histoire des repas publics dans les cités grecques.* Rome: École Française de Rome.

Schofield, Malcolm. 1986. *Euboulia* in the *Iliad. Classical Quarterly* 36.1: 6–31.

Scott, James C. 1968. *Political ideology in Malaysia: Reality and the beliefs of an elite.* New Haven: Yale University Press.

———. 1976. *The moral economy of the peasant: Rebellion and subsistence in southeast Asia.* New Haven: Yale University Press.

———. 1990. *Domination and the arts of resistance: Hidden transcripts.* New Haven: Yale University Press.

Scully, Stephen P. 1981. The bard as the custodian of Homeric society: *Odyssey* 3.263–72. *Quaderni Urbinati di Cultura Classica* 37: 67–83.

Seaford, Richard. 1994. *Reciprocity and ritual: Homer and tragedy in the developing city-state.* Oxford: Clarendon Press.

Seddon, David, ed. 1978. *Relations of production: Marxist approaches to economic anthropology.* London: Frank Cass.

Segal, Charles P. 1994. *Singers, heroes, and gods in the Odyssey.* Ithaca, N.Y.: Cornell University Press.

Seltman, C. T. 1924. *Athens: Its history and coinage before the Persian invasion.* Cambridge: Cambridge University Press. Reprint. Chicago: Ares, 1974.

Service, Elman R. 1966. *The hunters.* Englewood Cliffs, N.J.: Prentice-Hall.

———. 1971. *Primitive social organization: An evolutionary perspective.* 2d ed. New York: Random House

———. 1975. *Origins of the state and civilization: The process of cultural evolution.* New York: Norton.

———. 1979. *The hunters.* 2d ed. Englewood Cliffs, N.J.: Prentice-Hall.

Shapiro, Warren. 1988. Ritual kinship, ritual incorporation, and the denial of death. *Man* 23: 275–97.

Shaw, Joseph W. 1980. Excavations at Kommos (Crete) during 1979. *Hesperia* 49: 207–50.

———. 1981. Excavations at Kommos (Crete) during 1980. *Hesperia* 50: 211–51.

———. 1982. Excavations at Kommos (Crete) during 1981. *Hesperia* 51: 164–95.

Shefton, Brian Benjamin. 1982. Greeks and Greek imports in the south of the Iberian peninsula: The archaeological evidence. In Niemeyer 1982, 337–68.

Sherratt, Susan, and Andrew Sherratt. 1992/93. The growth of the Mediterranean economy in the early first millennium. *World Archaeology* 24: 361–78.

Shipley, Graham. 1987. *A history of Samos, 800–188 b.c.* Oxford: Clarendon Press.

Silver, Morris. 1983. Karl Polanyi and markets in the ancient Near East: The challenge of the evidence. *Journal of Economic History* 43: 795–829.

———. 1985. Reply to Mayhew, Neale, and Tandy 1985. *Journal of Economic History* 45: 135–37.

———. 1986. *Economic structures of the ancient Near East.* Totowa, N.J.: Barnes and Noble.

———. 1995. *Economic structures of antiquity.* Westport, Conn.: Greenwood Press.

Singor, H. W. 1991. Nine against Troy: On epic *phalanges, promakhoi,* and an old structure in the story of the *Iliad. Mnemosyne* 44: 17–62.

Skinner, Elliott P. 1962. Trade and markets among the Mossi people. In Bohannan and Dalton 1962a, 237–78.

Skydsgaard, J. E. 1988. Transhumance in ancient Greece. In Whittaker 1988, 75–86.

Slicher van Bath, B. H. 1963. *The agrarian history of western Europe, a.d. 500–1850.* Translated by Olive Ordish. New York: St. Martin's.

Sloan, Robert E., and Mary Ann Duncan. 1978. Zooarchaeology of Nichoria. In Rapp and Aschenbrenner 1978, 60–77.

Smelser, Neil J. 1958/59. A comparative view of exchange systems. Review of Polanyi, Arensberg, and Pearson 1957. *Economic Development and Cultural Change* 7: 173–82.

Smith, Adam. 1776. *An inquiry into the nature and causes of the wealth of nations,* edited by R. H. Campbell and A. S. Skinner, and by W. B. Todd. Oxford: Clarendon Press, 1976.

Smith, Philip E. L., and T. Cuyler Young, Jr. 1972. The evolution of early agriculture and culture in greater Mesopotamia: A trial model. In Spooner 1972, 1–59.

Smithson, Evelyn Lord. 1968. The tomb of a rich Athenian lady, ca. 850 b.c. *Hesperia* 37: 77–116.

Snodgrass, A. M. 1971a. *The Dark Age of Greece.* Edinburgh: Edinburgh University Press.

———. 1971b. The first European body-armour. In Boardman, Brown, and Powell 1971, 33–50.

———. 1974. An historical Homeric society? *Journal of Hellenic Studies* 94: 114–25.

———. 1977. *Archaeology and the rise of the Greek state.* Cambridge: Cambridge University Press.

———. 1980a. *Archaic Greece: The age of experiment.* Berkeley: University of California Press.

————. 1980b. Iron and early metallurgy in the Mediterranean. In Wertime and Muhly 1980, 335–74.

————. 1982. Les origines du culte des héros dans la Grèce antique. In Gnoli and Vernant 1982, 107–19.

————. 1983a. The Greek early iron age: A reappraisal. *Dialogues d'Histoire Ancienne* 9: 73–86.

————. 1983b. Heavy freight in archaic Greece. In Garnsey, Hopkins, and Whittaker 1983, 16–26.

————. 1983c. Two demographic notes: The size of Lefkandi; Population in late eighth-century Attica. In Hägg 1983c, 167–71.

————. 1985a. Greek archaeology and Greek history. *Classical Antiquity* 4: 193–207.

————. 1985b. The site of Askra. In Roesch and Argoud 1985, 87–95.

————. 1986. The historical significance of fortification in archaic Greece. In *La fortification dans l'histoire du mond grec,* edited by P. Leriche and H. Tréeziny, 125–31. Paris: Éditions du CNRS.

————. 1987. *An archaeology of Greece: The present state and future scope of a discipline.* Berkeley: University of California Press.

————. 1989. The coming of the Iron Age in Greece: Europe's earliest bronze/iron transition. In Sørensen and Thomas 1989, 22–35.

————. 1990. Survey archaeology and the rural landscape of the Greek city. In Murray and Price 1990, 113–36.

————. 1991. Archaeology and the study of the Greek city. In Rich and Wallace-Hadrill 1991, 1–23.

————. 1993. The rise of the *polis:* The archaeological evidence. In Hansen 1993a, 30–40.

————. 1994a. The Euboeans in Macedonia: A new precedent for westward expansion. *Annali dell' Istituto Universitario Orientale di Napoli (archeol.)* 16: 88–93.

————. 1994b. The growth and standing of the early western colonies. In Tsetskhladze and De Angelis 1994, 1–10.

Snodgrass, A. M., and J. L. Bintliff. 1991. Surveying ancient cities. *Scientific American,* March 1991, 88–93.

Sokolowski, Franciszek. 1962. *Lois sacrées des cités grecques.* Supplement. Paris: Éditions E. de Boccard.

————. 1969. *Lois sacrées des cités grecques.* Paris: Éditions E. de Boccard.

Sombart, Werner. 1916. *Der Moderne Kapitalismus.* 2d ed. 3 vols. Munich and Leipzig: von Duncker und Hombolt.

Sørensen, Marie Louise Stig, and Roger Thomas, eds. 1989. *The Bronze Age–Iron Age transition in Europe: Aspects of continuity and change in European societies, c. 1200 to 500 b.c.* B.A.R. International Series 483. Oxford: B.A.R.

Sourvinou-Inwood, Christiane. 1983. A trauma in flux: Death in the 8th century and after. In Hägg 1983c, 33–48.

————. 1993. Early sanctuaries, the eighth century, and ritual space: Fragments of a discourse. In Marinatos and Hägg 1993, 1–17.

————. 1995. *"Reading" Greek death: To the end of the classical period.* Oxford: Clarendon Press.

Sparkes, Brian A. 1982. Classical and Roman Melos. In Renfrew and Wagstaff 1982, 45–53.

Spooner, Brian, ed. 1972. *Population growth: Anthropological implications.* Cambridge, Mass.: M.I.T. Press.

Stanley, Philip V. 1986. The function of trade in Homeric society. *Münstersche Beiträge zur antiken Handelsgeschichte* 5.2: 5–15.

Starr, Chester G. 1977. *The economic and social growth of early Greece, 800–500 b.c.* New York: Oxford University Press.

———. 1982. Economic and social conditions in the Greek world. In *The Cambridge ancient history,* vol. 3, pt. 3, 417–41. 2d ed. Cambridge: Cambridge University Press.

———. 1986. *Individual and community: The rise of the polis, 800–500 b.c.* New York: Oxford University Press.

Stevenson, Robert F. 1965. *Population and political systems in tropical Africa.* New York: Columbia University Press.

Stott, D. H. 1962. Cultural and natural checks on population-growth. In *Culture and the evolution of man,* edited by M. F. Ashley Montagu, 355–76. New York: Oxford University Press.

Strøm, Ingrid. 1971. *Problems concerning the origin and early development of the Etruscan orientalizing style.* Odense: Odense Universitetsforlag.

———. 1990. Relations between Etruria and Campania around 700 B.C. In Descoeudres 1990, 87–97.

Sundt, Eilert Lund. 1855. *On marriage in Norway.* Translated by Michael Drake. Cambridge: Cambridge University Press, 1980.

Svenbro, Jesper. 1977. *La parole et le marbre: Aux origines de la poétique grecque.* Lund: Studentlitteratur.

———. 1993. *Phrasykleia: An anthropology of reading in ancient Greece.* Translated by Janet Lloyd. Ithaca, N.Y.: Cornell University Press.

Sznycer, Maurice, 1979. L'inscription phénicienne de Tekke, près de Cnossos. *Kadmos* 18: 89–93.

Tainter, Joseph A. 1988. *The collapse of complex societies.* Cambridge: Cambridge University Press.

Tandy, David W. 1989. *"Never any good": Changing forms of economic integration in Hesiod's world.* Occasional paper of the Karl Polanyi Institute of Political Economy. Montreal: Karl Polanyi Institute of Political Economy.

———. 1992. Review of Ulf 1990. In *American Journal of Philology* 113: 624–27.

———. Forthcoming. *Agroskopia:* Hesiod's oikos and the rise of the consumer-city. Paper read at the annual meeting of the American Philological Association, San Diego, Calif., December 28, 1995.

Tandy, David W., and Walter C. Neale. 1994. Karl Polanyi's distinctive approach to social analysis and the case of ancient Greece: Ideas, criticisms, consequences. In Duncan and Tandy 1994, 9–33.

———. 1996. *Hesiod, Works and days: Translation with introduction and commentary.* Berkeley: University of California Press.

Tausend, Klaus. 1990. Sagenbildung und Heroenkult. *Gymnasium* 97: 145–53.

Taylor, Joan du Plat. 1959. The Cypriot and Syrian pottery from al Mina, Syria. *Iraq* 21: 62–92.

Telebantou, Christina. 1989. Andros (in Greek). *Archaiologikon Deltion* 37 (1982 [published in 1989]): 353–56.

Themelis, Petros G. 1982. Anaskaphai stin Eretria. *Praktika* 1982, 163–80.

————. 1983a. Delphi and its territory in the 8th and 7th centuries B.C.(in Greek). *Annuario della Scuola Archeologica di Atene* 61: 213–55.

————. 1983b. An 8th century goldsmith's workshop at Eretria. In Hägg 1983c, 157–65.

Thomas, Carol G. 1978. From wanax to basileus: Kingship in the Greek Dark Age. *Hispania Antiqua* 6: 187–206.

————. 1981. The Greek polis. In *The city-state in five cultures,* edited by Robert Griffeth and Carol G. Thomas, 31–69. Santa Barbara: ABC-Clio.

————. 1983. Review of Drews 1983. *American Historical Review* 88: 1251.

Thompson, Homer A. 1981. Athens faces adversity. *Hesperia* 50: 343–55.

Thomson, George. 1954. On Greek land-tenure. In *Studies presented to David Moore Robinson,* edited by George E. Mylonas and Doris Raymond, 2: 840–50. St. Louis: Washington University Press.

————. 1961. *Studies in ancient Greek society: The prehistoric Aegean.* 3d ed. London: Lawrence and Wishart.

Thorner, Daniel. 1965. Peasant economy as a category in economic history. In *Deuxième Conférence Internationale d'Histoire Économique, Aix-en-Province, 1962,* 2: 287–300. Paris: Mouton.

Thurnwald, Richard C. 1932. *Economics in primitive communities.* London: Oxford University Press.

————. 1934/35. Pigs and currency in Buin: Observations about primitive standards of value and economics. *Oceania* 5: 119–41. Reprinted in and cited from Dalton 1967, 224–45.

Toennies, Ferdinand. 1935. *Gemeinschaft und Gesellschaft.* Translated by Charles P. Loomis. 8th ed. London: Routledge and Kegan Paul, 1955.

Tomlinson, R. A. 1972. *Argos and the Argolid: From the end of the Bronze Age to the Roman occupation.* Ithaca, N.Y.: Cornell University Press.

————. 1992. *From Mycenae to Constantinople: The evolution of the ancient city.* London: Routledge.

Torelli, Mario. 1986. History: Land and people. In Bonfante 1986a, 47–65.

Touchais, Gilles. 1982. Chronique des fouilles et découvertes archéologiques en Grèce en 1981. *Bulletin de Correspondance Hellénique* 106: 529–635.

————. 1988. Chronique des fouilles et découvertes archéologiques en Grèce en 1987. *Bulletin de Correspondance Hellénique* 112: 611–96.

Traill, David. 1989. Gold armor for bronze and Homer's use of compensatory *timê*. *Classical Philology* 84: 301–5.

Trigger, Bruce G. 1984. Alternative archaeologies: Nationalist, colonialist, imperialist. *Man* 19: 355–70.

Trump, D. H. 1980. *The prehistory of the Mediterranean.* New Haven: Yale University Press.

Tsetskhladze, Gocha R. 1994. Greek penetration of the Black Sea. In Tsetskhladze and De Angelis 1994, 111–35.

Tsetskhladze, Gocha R., and Franco De Angelis, eds. 1994. *The archaeology of Greek colonisation: Essays dedicated to Sir John Boardman.* Oxford University Committee for Archaeology Monograph 40. Oxford: Oxford University Press.

Tsirkin, Yu. B. 1991. Phoenician and Greek colonization. In Diakonoff 1991, 347–65.

Tylecote, R. F. 1992. *A history of metallurgy.* 2d ed. London: Institute of Materials.

Ulf, Christoph. 1990. *Die homerische Gesellschaft: Materialien zur analytischen Beschreibung und historischen Lokalisierung.* Munich: C. H. Beck.

UNDP = United Nations Development Programme. 1993. *Human development report 1993.* New York: Oxford University Press.

Valensi, Lucette. 1974. Anthropologie économique et histoire: L'oeuvre de Karl Polanyi. *Annales: Économies, Sociétés, Civilisations* 29: 1311–19. Translated by Ludgard De Decker and Gregory Blue in *Research in Economic Anthropology* 4 (1981): 3–12.

Vallet, Georges. 1958. *Rhégion et Zancle: Histoire, commerce et civilisation des cités chalcidiennes du détroit de Messine.* Paris: Éditions E. de Boccard.

———. 1968. La cité et son territoire dans les colonies grecques de l'Occident. In *La città e il suo territorio,* 67–142. Naples: Centro Studi sulla Magna Grecia.

———. 1973. Espace privé et espace public dans une cité d'Occident Mégara Hyblaea. In Finley 1973, 83–94.

Vallet, Georges, and François Villard. 1952. Les dates de fondation de Mégara Hyblaea et de Syracuse. *Bulletin de Correspondance Hellénique* 76: 289–346.

Vallet, Georges, François Villard, and Paul Auberson. 1976. *Mégara Hyblaea: Le quartier de l'agora archaïque.* Rome: École Française de Rome.

van Andel, Tjeerd H., and Curtis Runnels. 1987. *Beyond the acropolis: A rural Greek past.* Stanford: Stanford University Press.

Van Hook, La Rue. 1920. The exposure of infants at Athens. *Transactions of the American Philological Association* 51: 134–45.

van Wees, Hans. 1986. Leaders of men? Military organisation in the *Iliad. Classical Quarterly* 36: 285–303.

———. 1988. Kings in combat: Battles and heroes in the *Iliad. Classical Quarterly* 38: 1–24.

———. 1992. *Status warriors: War, violence, and society in Homer and history.* Amsterdam: J. C. Gieben.

Ventris, Michael, and John Chadwick. 1973. *Documents in Mycenaean Greek.* 2d ed. Cambridge: Cambridge University Press.

Verdenius, W. J. 1985. *A commentary on Hesiod, Works and days, vv. 1–382.* Leiden: E. J. Brill.

Vidal-Naquet, Pierre. 1965. Économie et société dans la Grèce ancienne: L'oeuvre de Moses I. Finley. *Archives européennes de sociologie* 6: 111–48.

———. 1970. Valeurs religieuses et mythiques de la terre et du sacrifice dans l'*Odyssée. Annales: Économies, Sociétés, Civilisations* 25: 1278–97. Reprinted in Finley 1973, 270–92. Cited from the translation: Land and sacrifice in the *Odyssey: A study of religious and mythical meanings,* in *Myth, religion, and society,* edited by R. L. Gordon, 80–94 (Cambridge: Cambridge University Press, 1981).

———. 1986. The black hunter revisited. *Proceedings of the Cambridge Philological Society* 212: 126–44.

Wace, A. J. B., M. S. Thompson, and J. P. Droop. 1909. The Menelaion. *Annual of the British School at Athens* 15: 108–57.

Wade-Gery, H. T. 1949. Hesiod. *Phoenix* 3: 81–93.

———. 1952. *The poet of the Iliad.* Cambridge: Cambridge University Press.

Wagstaff, Malcolm, and Siv Augustson. 1982. Traditional land use. In Renfrew and Wagstaff 1982, 106–33.

Wagstaff, Malcolm, Siv Augustson, and Clive Gamble. 1982. Alternative subsistence strategies. In Renfrew and Wagstaff 1982, 172–80.

Wagstaff, Malcolm, and John F. Cherry. 1982. Settlement and population change. In Renfrew and Wagstaff 1982, 136–55.

Wailes, Bernard. 1972. Plow and population in temperate Europe. In Spooner 1972, 154–79.

Walcot, Peter. 1961. The composition of the *Works and days*. *Revue des Études Grecques* 74: 1–19.

Waldstein, Charles. 1902–1905. *The Argive Heraeum*. 2 vols. Boston: Houghton Mifflin.

Wallace, Paul W. 1974. Hesiod and the valley of the Muses. *Greek, Roman and Byzantine Studies* 15: 5–24.

Wallinga, H. T. 1993. *Ships and sea-power before the Persian War: The ancestry of the ancient trireme*. Leiden: E. J. Brill.

Ward, William A., and Martha Sharp Joukowsky, eds. 1992. *The crisis years: The 12th century b.c. from beyond the Danube to the Tigris*. Dubuque, Iowa: Kendall/Hunt.

Weber, Max. 1909. *The agrarian sociology of ancient civilizations*. Translated by R. I. Frank. Atlantic Highlands, N.J.: Humanities Press, 1976.

———. 1921. *Economy and society*. 5th ed. Berkeley: University of California Press, 1978.

Weinberg, Saul S., ed. 1956. *The Aegean and the Near East: Studies presented to Hetty Goldman on the occasion of her seventy-fifth birthday*. Locust Valley, N.Y.: J. J. Augustin.

Weiner, Annette B. 1992. *Inalienable possessions: The paradox of keeping-while-giving*. Berkeley: University of California Press.

Weiss, Johannes. 1986. *Max Weber and the Marxist world*. Translated by Elizabeth King-Utz and Michael J. King. London: Routledge and Kegan Paul.

Wells, Berit, ed. 1992. *Agriculture in ancient Greece*. Stockholm: Paul Åströms Förlag.

Wells, Peter S. 1980. *Culture contact and culture change: Early Iron Age central Europe and the Mediterranean world*. Cambridge: Cambridge University Press.

———. 1984. *Farms, villages, and cities: Commerce and urban origins in late prehistoric Europe*. Ithaca, N.Y.: Cornell University Press.

Wertime, Theodore A. 1980. The pyrotechnologic background. In Wertime and Muhly 1980, 1–24.

Wertime, Theodore A., and James D. Muhly, eds. 1980. *The coming of the age of iron*. New Haven: Yale University Press.

West, M. L., ed. 1966. *Hesiod, Theogony*. Oxford: Clarendon Press.

———, ed. 1978. *Hesiod, Works and days*. Oxford: Clarendon Press.

———. 1981. Is the *Works and days* an oral poem? In *I poemi epice rapsodici non Omerici e la tradizione orale*, edited by C. Brillante, M. Cantilena, and C. O. Pavese, 53–73. Padua: Antenore.

———. 1985. *The Hesiodic Catalogue of women: Its nature, structure, and origins*. Oxford: Clarendon Press.

Wheatley, Paul. 1971. *The pivot of the four quarters: A preliminary enquiry into the origins and character of the ancient Chinese city*. Chicago: Aldine.

———. 1972. The concept of urbanism. In *Man, settlement, and urbanism*, edited by Peter J. Ucko, Ruth Tringham, and G. W. Dimbleby, 601–37. London: Duckworth.

White, Lynn, Jr. 1962. *Medieval technology and social change*. Oxford: Clarendon Press.

———. 1972. The expansion of technology, 500–1500. In Cipolla 1972, 143–74.

Whitehead, David. 1986. *The demes of Attica 508/7-ca. 250 b.c.: A political and social study.* Princeton: Princeton University Press.

Whitehouse, Ruth D., and John B. Wilkins. 1989. Greeks and natives in south-east Italy: Approaches to the archaeological evidence. In *Centre and periphery: Comparative studies in archaeology,* edited by Timothy C. Champion, 102–26. London: Unwin Hyman.

Whitley, James. 1988. Early states and hero cults: A reappraisal. *Journal of Hellenic Studies* 108: 173–82.

———. 1991a. Social diversity in Dark Age Greece. *Annual of the British School at Athens* 86: 341–65.

———. 1991b. *Style and society in Dark Age Greece: The changing face of a pre-literate society, 1100–700 b.c.* Cambridge: Cambridge University Press.

———. 1994. The monuments that stood before Marathon: Tomb cult and hero cult in archaic Attica. *American Journal of Archaeology* 98: 213–30.

Whitman, Cedric H. 1958. *Homer and the heroic tradition.* Cambridge, Mass.: Harvard University Press.

Whittaker, C. R. 1974. The western Phoenicians: Colonisation and assimilation. *Proceedings of the Cambridge Philological Society* 200: 58–79.

———, ed. 1988. *Pastoral economies in classical antiquity.* Cambridge Philological Society Suppl., vol. 14. Cambridge: Cambridge University Press.

Wilamowitz-Moellendorff, Ulrich von, ed. 1928. *Hesiodos Erga.* Berlin: Weidmann.

Will, Edouard. 1954. Trois quarts de siècle de recherches sur l'économie grecque antique. *Annales: Économies, Sociétés, Civilisations* 9: 6–22.

———. 1955. *Korinthiaka.* Paris: Éditions E. de Boccard.

———. 1957. Homère, Hésiode et l'arrière-plan Mycenien. *Revue des Études Anciennes* 59: 5–50.

———. 1962. La Grèce archaïque. In Finley 1962b, 41–96.

Will, Ernest. 1965. Hésiode: Crise agraire? Ou recul de l'aristocratie? *Revue des Études Grecques* 78: 542–56.

Willcock, M. M. 1990. The search for the poet Homer. *Greece and Rome* 37: 1–13.

Willetts, Ronald F., ed. 1967. *The law code of Gortyn.* Kadmos Supplement 1. Berlin: Walter de Gruyter.

———. 1982. Cretan laws and society. In *The Cambridge ancient history,* vol. 3, pt. 3., 234–48. 2d ed. Cambridge: Cambridge University Press.

———. 1991. Aspects of land tenure in Dorian Crete. In Musti et al. 1991, 209–14.

Williams, Charles Kaufman, II. 1982. The early urbanization of Corinth. *Annuario della Scuola Archeologica di Atene* 60: 9–19.

Willigan, J. Dennis, and Katherine A. Lynch. 1982. *Sources and methods of historical demography.* New York: Academic Press.

Winter, Irene J. 1995. Homer's Phoenicians: History, ethnography, or literary trope? [A perspective on early Orientalism]. In Carter and Morris 1995, 247–71.

Wolf, Eric R. 1966. *Peasants.* Englewood Cliffs, N.J.: Prentice-Hall.

Wolff, Hans Julius. 1946. The origin of judicial litigation among the Greeks. *Traditio* 4: 31–87.

Wood, Ellen Meiksins. 1988. *Peasant-citizen and slave: The foundation of Athenian democracy.* London: Verso.

Woodhead, A. G. 1962. *The Greeks in the west.* New York: Praeger.

Woolley, C. L. 1938. Excavations at al Mina, Sueidia, I-II. *Journal of Hellenic Studies* 58: 1–30, 133–70.

———. 1948. The date of al Mina. *Journal of Hellenic Studies* 68: 148.

———. 1953. *A forgotten kingdom.* Baltimore: Penguin.

World Bank. 1986. *World development report 1986.* Oxford: Oxford University Press.

Wright, Erik Olin. 1982. Capitalism's futures. *Socialist Review* 13.2 (no. 68): 77–126.

Wright, H. E., Jr. 1972. Vegetation history. In *The Minnesota Messenia expedition: Reconstructing a Bronze Age regional environment,* edited by William A. McDonald and George R. Rapp, Jr., 188–99. Minneapolis: University of Minnesota Press.

Wrigley, E. A. 1969. *Population and history.* New York: McGraw-Hill.

Young, T. Cuyler, Jr. 1972. Population densities and early Mesopotamian urbanism. In *Man, settlement, and urbanism,* edited by Peter J. Ucko, Ruth Tringham, and G. W. Dimbleby, 827–42. London: Duckworth.

Zaccagnini, Carlo. 1987. Aspects of ceremonial exchange in the Near East during the late second millennium B.C. In Rowlands, Larsen, and Kristiansen 1987, 57–65.

Zipf, George Kingsley. 1949. *Human behavior and the principle of least effort.* Cambridge, Mass.: Addison-Wesley.

Zumthor, Paul. 1990. *Oral poetry: An introduction.* Translated by Kathryn Murphy-Judy. Minneapolis: University of Minnesota Press.

SUBJECT INDEX

Academus, cult of, 150

Achilles, 42, 74, 106, 118n.22, 129, 144, 153–54, 155–56, 161, 163, 168, 179n.80, 184, 188, 191, 195, 198, 206, 210

Agamemnon, 12, 73, 99, 106, 107n.108, 108, 109, 118, 142–44, 153, 155, 156, 161n.105, 163, 165n.136, 174, 183, 188, 195, 198; cult of, 151, 154; singer of, 169, 171–72, 174, 196, 199, 200, 218

agricultural production: Dark Age reduction, 35; Hesiod's, 208–14; as reason for foundation of Cumae, 76

Alcinous, 13, 81, 107, 128, 130n.73, 144–45, 168, 173, 178, 180

Al Mina: Corinthian materials at, 65, 78; east end of trade network, 4, 69, 71, 75, 230; first Greeks at, 62–66; iron into (?), 64, 69; iron out of (?), 63; not colony, 71; Phoenicians at, 62, 64, 68n.35; port of trade, 64, 119; pottery from Pithekoussai at, 71; source of Greek alphabet (?), 201–3.

Amphidamas: funeral games, 14, 154, 173, 180, 192, 193, 206; significance of name, 154–55

Amyklai: founders of Taras from, 80; increased tendance at Amyklaion, 27

antiaristocratic tradition, 174, 194–97, 207

Archias, founder of Syracuse, 82, 131, 155

Argolid: behavior/burials at Argos like those elsewhere, 192; burials, increase in, 2, 19, 23, 30, 46–50, 229; Dark Age reduc-

tion in sites, 21, 21nn.2–3, 49; drought (?), 25n.25, 27n.36; eating places at Asine, 149; firedogs paralleled among Etruscans and La Tène, 161n.121; firedogs as sign of interest in maritime warfare, 161; firedogs and spits, 156–58; goods from at Samos, 71; Heraeum, 159; hero cults at, 149n.33; land given to Tydeus, 128; net movement from Argos to countryside, 27–28; no immigration, 27; pottery from in Lebanon, 62n.3; stratification, increased, 27, 27n.36, 93

Ascra: beneficiary of *Works and Days*, 6, 165; daily life, 208–14; dependence on Thespiae, 207; empty before 900, 21, 204n.44; goods not brought to market there, 232; Hesiod's father settled there, 132–33, 204–5, 206; location and size, 205, 213; no redistribution at, 137; peasantry at, 226

Asine: eating places at: 149, 154n.68

Athens: burial counts, 46–53; burial exclusivity, 24, 26, 51–53; burial increase, 26, 28; burial pattern change, 26, 28, 229; cults of Academus and Erechtheus, 150; Dark Age settlement size, 22; deurbanization, 27–28; earliest writing, 202; eastern goods in ninth century, 70; grain trade in fourth century, 125n.58; growth before 750, 26; Neleid *genos* at (?), 221n.136; Peisistratus, 173–74; possible market economy in fourth century, 124; pottery from in eighth-century Cyprus, 100;

INDEX LOCORUM

ANCIENT AUTHORS

Alcaeus
  70.3: 142n.5
  368.2: 142n.5
Amos
  8:4–6: vii
Appian
  BCiv. 5.1.9: 120n.34
Aristotle
  Pol.
    1257A, 23ff.: 160n.113
    1266B, 20f.: 132
    1266B, 21ff.: 132n.82
    1321B, 39: 182n.93, 188n.124
Athenaeus
  4.167D: 131n.79

1 Chronicles
  18:15: 184n.102
2 Chronicles
  34:8: 184n.102

Demosthenes
  23.39.7: 120n.34
Dionysius of Halicarnassus
  1.84.5: 203n.39

Ezekiel
  27: 119n.31, 160n.113
  27:12–24: 66n.26
  27:13: 120, 121n.40
  27:17: 66n.26

Fragmenta Adespota
  1002: 142n.5
  1009.2: 142n.5

Genesis
  10: 185
  41:34–36: 103n.95
  41:56: 103n.96
  47:25: 104

Herodotus
  1.60: 173n.53
  4.153: 82n.119
  4.196: 117n.17
Hesiod
  Fragments
    10.26: 184n.106
    17a.14–17: 221n.136
    73.5: 40n.100
    206: 143
    211.12: 40n.100
    286.1: 224n.150
    357: 179n.77
  Shield
    29: 40n.100
  Theogony
    22: 214n.108
    22–34: 170
    31–32: 189n.139
    79–93: 173n.51
    80–103: 173n.49
    81–92: 185
    84–92: 192, 218

Maps: Bill Nelson
Composition: Braun-Brumfield
Text: 10/12.5 Baskerville
Display: Baskerville
Printing and binding: Braun-Brumfield